THE BEST OF

Gourmet

THE BEST OF

Gourmet

FROM THE EDITORS OF GOURMET

CONDÉ NAST BOOKS
RANDOM HOUSE, NEW YORK

Random House website address: www.atrandom.com
Gourmet Books website address: www.Gourmetbks.com

All the recipes in this work were published previously in *Gourmet* Magazine.

Printed in the United States of America on acid-free paper.

987654321
First Edition

All informative text in this book was written by Diane Abrams,
Kate Winslow, and Jane Daniels Lear.

The text of this book was set in Trade Gothic. Color reproduction services
were provided by North Market Street Graphics and Quad/Graphics, Inc.
The book was printed and bound at R. R. Donnelley and Sons. Stock is
Sterling Ultra Web Gloss, MeadWestvaco.

FOR RANDOM HOUSE
Lisa Faith Phillips, Vice President/General Manager
Tom Downing, Marketing Director
Deborah Williams, Operations Director
Lyn Barris Hastings, Senior Direct Marketing Manager
Eric Killer, Direct Marketing Associate
Fianna Reznik, Direct Marketing Associate
Elizabeth Walsh, Inventory Manager
Richard Elman, Production Manager

FOR *GOURMET* BOOKS
Diane Abrams, Director
Kate Winslow, Associate Editor

FOR *GOURMET* MAGAZINE
Ruth Reichl, Editor-in-Chief
Richard Ferretti, Creative Director

Zanne Early Stewart, Executive Food Editor
Kemp Miles Minifie, Senior Food Editor
Alexis M. Touchet, Associate Food Editor
Paul Grimes, Food Editor/Stylist
Shelton Wiseman, Food Editor
Ruth Cousineau, Food Editor
Gina Marie Miraglia Eriquez, Food Editor
Melissa Roberts-Matar, Food Editor
Maggie Ruggiero, Food Editor
Lillian Chou, Food Editor
Ian Knauer, Recipe Cross-Tester

Romulo A. Yanes, Photographer

Index illustrations copyright © 2002 by Tobie Giddio

Produced in association with Anne B. Wright and John W. Kern

Front Jacket: Chocolate Layer Cake with Milk Chocolate Frosting
(page 276)
Back Jacket: New Orleans Christmas (page 82)
Frontispiece: Basil Ice Cream (page 192), Hibiscus Tea Sorbet (page 192),
Orange Ice Cream (page 193)

ACKNOWLEDGMENTS

A tremendous amount of work goes into producing the beautiful book in your hands, and, happily, the editors of *Gourmet* Books have a talented team that makes it all happen smoothly.

Thanks to *Gourmet*'s creative director Richard Ferretti, *The Best of Gourmet* has a fresh, updated look that reflects the clean lines and stunning layouts of the magazine. Richard also came up with the magical image that graces our front cover; his vision became reality through the unerring talent of *Gourmet* photographer Romulo Yanes, his assistant Stephanie Foley, cake stylist Karen Tack, prop stylist Bette Blau, and associate art director Nanci Smith.

The interior of this book is equally lovely, thanks to the photography of Sang An, Andrea Fazzari, Matthew Hranek, Richard Gerhard Jung, Alexander Lobrano, John Midgley, Victoria Pearson, Petrina Tinslay, Mikkel Vang, George Whiteside, Anna Williams, and Romulo Yanes.

Once again, Cheryl Brown had the huge task of editing all the book's text, making sure each and every recipe reflects the most up-to-date style of the magazine. We appreciate her meticulous eye.

We also thank Jane Daniels Lear, who provided many of the informative Kitchen Notes that appear throughout this year's Recipe Compendium.

This book simply would not exist without the tireless work of project director Anne Wright and production editor John Kern. They, along with indexer Marilyn Flaig, have long been an indispensable part of our team.

We are also grateful to *Gourmet* production director Stephanie Stehofsky for retrieving electronic files for us, and to Richard Elman, Random House production manager, who handled the production and printing of this book.

Of course, none of this would mean a thing if the recipes weren't exceptional, and for this we tip our hats to *Gourmet*'s creative and hard-working food editors—Alexis Touchet, Paul Grimes, Shelley Wiseman, Ruth Cousineau, Gina Marie Miraglia Eriquez, Melissa Roberts-Matar, Maggie Ruggiero, Lillian Chou, and recipe cross-tester Ian Knauer. Thanks also to executive food editor Zanne Stewart and senior food editor Kemp Minifie, whose guidance helps our annual cookbook reach ever more delicious heights.

TABLE OF CONTENTS

TIPS FOR USING GOURMET'S RECIPES

MEASURE LIQUIDS
in glass or clear plastic liquid-measuring cups.

MEASURE DRY INGREDIENTS
in nesting dry-measuring cups (usually made of metal or plastic) that can be leveled off with a knife.

MEASURE FLOUR
by spooning (not scooping) it into a dry-measuring cup and leveling off with a knife without tapping or shaking cup.

SIFT FLOUR
only when specified in recipe. If sifted flour is called for, sift flour before measuring. (Many brands say "presifted" on the label; disregard this.)

A SHALLOW BAKING PAN
means an old-fashioned jelly-roll or four-sided cookie pan.

MEASURE SKILLETS AND BAKING PANS
across the top, not across the bottom.

A WATER BATH
for baking is prepared by putting your filled pan in a larger pan and adding enough boiling-hot water to reach halfway up the side of the smaller pan.

METAL PANS
used for baking should be light-colored, unless otherwise specified. If using dark metal pans, including nonstick, your baked goods will likely brown more and the cooking times may be shorter.

ALL PRODUCE
must be washed and dried before using.

FRESH HERBS OR GREENS
are prepped by first removing the leaves or fronds from the stems. The exception is cilantro, which has tender stems.

SALTED WATER
for cooking requires 1 tablespoon of salt for every 4 quarts of water.

BLACK PEPPER
in recipes is always freshly ground.

CHILES
require protective gloves when handling.

CHEESES
should be grated just before using. To finely grate Parmigiano-Reggiano and similar cheeses, use the small (1/8-inch) teardrop-shaped holes (not the ragged-edged holes) of a box or similar handheld grater. Other shaped holes, a Microplane rasp, and pregrated cheese yield different volumes.

ZEST CITRUS FRUITS
by removing the colored part of the rind only (avoid the bitter white pith). For strips, use a vegetable peeler. For grated zest, we prefer using a rasplike Microplane zester, which results in fluffier zest, so pack to measure.

TOAST SPICES
in a dry heavy skillet over moderate heat, stirring, until fragrant and a shade or two darker.

TOAST NUTS
in a shallow baking pan in a 350°F oven until golden, 5 to 10 minutes.

TOAST SEEDS
as you would toast spices or nuts.

INTRODUCTION

Twenty years ago *Gourmet* magazine created the first *Best of Gourmet* cookbook, and our then editor-in-chief, Jane Montant, knowingly wrote, "This is the first, but hardly the last. A tradition has begun." That edition, culled from issues that had appeared throughout 1985, offered cocktail parties, intimate New Year's Eve dinners, Easter brunch, a tapas party, Thanksgiving and Christmas feasts, as well as hundreds of individual recipes from the various columns of the day. Though the photography is now somewhat dated, the food remains inviting, delicious, and celebratory. Revisiting those pages, you still want to pull up a seat at every party and join in the fun.

If you had a chance to flip through the entire series, you'd see how *Gourmet*'s kitchen constantly set the pace for food trends while meeting the needs of our readers. As life became more hectic, dishes became less fussy and greater attention was given to meals that could be prepared quickly without sacrificing flavor. When America's chefs started taking a serious interest in organic farming, our own food editors were right there, planning menus around all the good things coming up in the garden.

Shortly thereafter, it seemed that everyone, even those of us who love to indulge now and then, started to pay closer attention to their diets, and *Gourmet* responded with healthier everyday menus. Cheaper foreign travel also gave readers a taste for unusual dishes, and our food editors went on yearly research trips to examine the world's cuisines. The menus those trips inspired became commonplace in the magazine and they encouraged readers to experiment with unfamiliar foods. Beginning in 1992, the Cuisines of the World section made its debut in *The Best of*

Gourmet series: all the wonderful foods of France, Italy, England, Greece, Spain, China, Mexico, India, and Thailand have been explored in depth.

Amidst all the ongoing changes which keep *Gourmet* vital and new, the magazine continues to create enticing entertaining menus. The year 2004 was no exception. Since it's our 20th anniversary we wanted to do something special, so we gathered our celebration menus together in one section. Here you'll find a very special children's birthday party, a colorful and enticing Indian engagement buffet, a Father's Day meal filled with Tuscan flavors, and even a romantic Valentine's Day dinner that your sweetheart will never forget. Of course, the major holidays–Easter, Thanksgiving, Hanukkah, and Christmas–are here, too, and just wait until you see what exciting twists we've given them.

We're as thrilled about this twentieth volume as we were about our first. Pull up a seat and find out why.

THE EDITORS OF GOURMET BOOKS

CELEBRATIONS

As *The Best of Gourmet* neared its twentieth anniversary, we realized that the ideal way to celebrate was to keep the party going as long as possible. And so we decided to collect the year's best holiday and party menus into this special section. These celebrations—some formal and others casual—offer a year of impressive feasts to choose from. • We begin with a *Children's Birthday Party* menu so fun—think hot dog buns made with *pâte à choux*—that adults will be happy to get in on the action. This playful menu includes waffled ham and cheese sandwiches and a chocolate cake adorned with buttercream dots and a jumble of mini cupcakes.

While there are several menus for large parties, our *Valentine's Day* meal requires a table for two. This is a meal for lingering, and you'll savor venison tenderloin and a salad of sweet lobster and avocado. Frozen praline soufflés bring the evening to an end—or is it just beginning?

Invite a crowd over for the magnificent *Russian Easter Feast*. This is a time-consuming meal, but one that will spark conversation about family, traditions, and food. *Pashka* cheese—a creamy mélange of farmer's cheese, sour cream, and golden raisins—celebrates the breaking of the traditional Russian dairy-free fast that precedes Easter. Its slight sweetness provides a counterpoint to the roast leg of lamb, kielbasa, and stuffed veal breast that are at the center of this culinary masterpiece.

Not all of our menus are so complex. Indeed, many, like the Indian-inspired *Engagement Party*, are casual and easy to prepare. Just a few hours in the kitchen will produce tender chicken tikka, cilantro coconut rice, and a tangy spinach salad with crisp pappadam croutons. It's the sort of meal that leaves ample room—and energy—to appreciate dessert, in this case a billowy strawberry and cream cake.

As we wend our way into the winter holiday season, *A Bohemian Thanksgiving* offers fresh spins on seasonal classics, such as roast turkey with pomegranate gravy or a stunning cranberry eggnog tart. You'll also find a delicious *Casual Vegetarian Thanksgiving* menu. Who needs turkey when there is roasted squash tangled with Broccolini, mushrooms, and polenta?

Hanukkah Dinner also gets a shake-up. Start off with savory rugelach filled with hazelnuts and green olives and then move on to celery root latkes and striped bass in *agrodolce* sauce. Ginger-spiced doughnuts round out this lovely, unexpected meal.

There's also a down-home yet elegant *New Orleans Christmas* dinner that skips from oysters Rockefeller to beef tenderloin lapped with espagnole sauce. This lavish spread finishes with a lady-like ambrosia cake, a chic take on big, sassy Southern confections.

Lovers of good food know that the best place to celebrate a momentous occasion is around the table. Inspiration for your next gathering is everywhere in this book, but you'll want to start your year of celebrating right here.

CHILDREN'S BIRTHDAY PARTY

SERVES 12 CHILDREN

ORANGE CRANBERRY JUICE

RANCH DIP WITH VEGETABLES

WAFFLED HAM AND CHEESE SANDWICHES

OVEN-FRIED CHICKEN FINGERS WITH HONEY MUSTARD SAUCE AND HOMEMADE KETCHUP

MINI HOT DOGS IN CHEDDAR BUNS

CHOCOLATE CAKE WITH VANILLA BUTTERCREAM

VANILLA MINI CUPCAKES

ALPHABET COOKIES

ORANGE CRANBERRY JUICE

MAKES 2 QUARTS

Active time: 15 min   Start to finish: 15 min

1 qt chilled fresh orange juice
1 qt chilled cranberry cocktail

▸ Stir together orange and cranberry juices in a large pitcher. Pour into glasses filled with ice.

RANCH DIP WITH VEGETABLES

SERVES 12 CHILDREN

Active time: 30 min   Start to finish: 1½ hr (includes chilling dip)

¾ cup sour cream
½ cup mayonnaise
⅓ cup chopped fresh flat-leaf parsley
¼ cup chopped fresh chives
¼ teaspoon minced garlic
¼ teaspoon salt
¼ teaspoon black pepper
4 carrots, cut into sticks
6 celery ribs, cut into sticks
1 seedless cucumber (usually plastic-wrapped),
    cut into sticks
1 small jicama, peeled, halved lengthwise,
    and cut into sticks
1½ cups grape or cherry tomatoes (9 oz)

▸ Stir together sour cream, mayonnaise, parsley, chives, garlic, salt, and pepper in a bowl until combined well. Chill dip, covered, until slightly thickened, at least 1 hour (for flavors to develop).
▸ Serve dip with vegetables.

Cooks' notes:
• Dip can be chilled up to 2 days.
• Vegetables can be cut 1 day ahead and chilled in sealed plastic bags lined with dampened paper towels.

WAFFLED HAM AND CHEESE SANDWICHES

SERVES 12 CHILDREN (MAKES 32 TRIANGLES)

Active time: 30 min   Start to finish: 40 min

1 stick (½ cup) unsalted butter, softened
16 slices firm white sandwich bread
8 thin slices boiled ham (¼ lb)
8 thin slices Swiss cheese (¼ lb)

Special equipment: a large square or rectangular electric waffle iron (not a Belgian waffle iron)

▸ Preheat waffle iron on high until just beginning to smoke. Reduce heat to moderate and brush generously with some butter.
▸ Spread butter on 1 side of 8 bread slices and turn slices over. Top 4 slices with 1 slice ham and 1 slice cheese, folding in any overhang, then top with remaining 4 buttered bread slices, buttered sides up. Cook sandwiches in batches (number of batches will depend on size of your waffle maker) until bread is golden and crisp, 4 to 6 minutes.
▸ Assemble and cook 4 more sandwiches in same manner.
▸ Just before serving, cut each sandwich into 4 triangles.

Cooks' note:
• Sandwiches can be cooked 4 hours ahead and cooled completely, then kept, wrapped in plastic wrap, at room temperature. Reheat in 1 layer on a baking sheet in a preheated 350°F oven until heated through, about 6 minutes, before cutting into triangles.

CLOCKWISE FROM TOP LEFT: orange cranberry juice; ranch dip with vegetables; waffled ham and cheese sandwiches; oven-fried chicken fingers

OVEN-FRIED CHICKEN FINGERS

SERVES 12 CHILDREN
Active time: 30 min   Start to finish: 45 min

2½ lb skinless boneless chicken breast halves
1½ sticks (¾ cup) unsalted butter, melted
 ¾ teaspoon salt
 ¼ teaspoon black pepper
  7 cups cornflakes (7 oz), coarsely crushed

Accompaniments: honey mustard sauce and homemade
ketchup (recipes follow)

▶ Put oven racks in upper and lower thirds of oven and preheat oven to 425°F. Butter 2 large shallow baking pans.
▶ Gently pound chicken between sheets of plastic wrap with
flat side of a meat pounder or with a rolling pin until ⅓ inch
thick. Cut chicken lengthwise into ½-inch-wide strips.
▶ Stir together butter, salt, and pepper in a shallow dish. Put
cornflakes in another shallow dish. Working with 1 strip at a
time, dip in butter, then dredge in cornflakes, pressing flakes
firmly to help adhere. Transfer as coated to baking pans.

▶ Bake, switching position of pans halfway through baking,
until chicken is golden and cooked through, about 15
minutes total.
▶ Cool chicken in pans on racks to room temperature (crust
will firm up as it cools).

HONEY MUSTARD SAUCE

MAKES ABOUT 1½ CUPS
Active time: 10 min   Start to finish: 10 min

  1 cup mayonnaise
 ⅓ cup Dijon mustard
  2 tablespoons mild honey
 ¼ teaspoon salt

▶ Stir together all ingredients in a bowl until combined well.

Cooks' note:
• Sauce can be made 1 week ahead and chilled, covered.

16

HOMEMADE KETCHUP

MAKES ABOUT 2 CUPS

Active time: 20 min   Start to finish: 3 hr (includes chilling)

- 1 (28-oz) can whole tomatoes in purée
- 1 medium onion, chopped
- 2 tablespoons olive oil
- 1 tablespoon tomato paste
- ⅔ cup packed dark brown sugar
- ½ cup cider vinegar
- ½ teaspoon salt

▶ Purée tomatoes (with purée from can) in a blender until smooth.

▶ Cook onion in oil in a 4-quart heavy saucepan over moderate heat, stirring, until softened, about 8 minutes. Add puréed tomatoes, tomato paste, brown sugar, vinegar, and salt and simmer, uncovered, stirring occasionally, until very thick, about 1 hour (stir more frequently toward end of cooking to prevent scorching).

▶ Purée ketchup in 2 batches in blender until smooth (use caution when blending hot liquids). Chill, covered, at least 2 hours (for flavors to develop).

MINI HOT DOGS IN CHEDDAR BUNS

SERVES 12 CHILDREN (MAKES ABOUT 40)

Active time: 45 min   Start to finish: 1¼ hr

These hot dog buns look very much like éclairs, which is no coincidence—they're made from pâte à choux *instead of yeast dough.*

- 1¼ cups water
- 1½ sticks (¾ cup) unsalted butter, cut into ½-inch cubes
- ½ teaspoon salt
- 1½ cups all-purpose flour
- 5 large eggs
- ¼ lb extra-sharp Cheddar, coarsely grated (2 cups)
- 1 (12-oz) package cocktail frankfurters

Special equipment: **a large sealable plastic bag (not pleated)**
Accompaniments: **yellow mustard and/or homemade ketchup (recipe precedes)**

▶ Bring water, butter, and salt to a boil in a 4-quart heavy saucepan over moderate heat. Reduce heat to low and add flour all at once, then cook, beating with a wooden spoon, until mixture pulls away from side of pan, about 2 minutes.

▶ Transfer mixture to a bowl, then cool slightly. Add eggs 1 at a time, beating well with an electric mixer at medium-high speed (or beating vigorously with wooden spoon) after each addition (batter will be stiff). Add cheese and beat until combined.

▶ Put oven racks in upper and lower thirds of oven and preheat oven to 375°F. Lightly butter 2 large baking sheets.

▶ Snip off 1 corner of plastic bag to create a 1-inch opening and transfer dough to bag, pressing out excess air. Twist bag firmly just above filling, then pipe 18 to 20 (2½- by 1- by ¾-inch) lengths, about 2 inches apart, onto each baking sheet.

▶ Bake, switching position of sheets halfway through baking, until buns are puffed and pale golden, about 30 minutes total. Make 1½-inch lengthwise slits in tops of buns with a sharp paring knife and let dry in turned-off oven 10 minutes.

▶ While buns dry, heat a dry well-seasoned grill pan or heavy skillet over high heat until it smokes. Reduce heat to moderate and cook frankfurters, turning, until heated through and golden brown, about 5 minutes.

▶ Remove buns from oven and nestle a frankfurter in each opening.

Cooks' note:
• Buns can be made (and dried) 1 day ahead and cooled completely, then kept in an airtight container at room temperature. Reheat in a preheated 375°F oven.

CHOCOLATE CAKE WITH VANILLA BUTTERCREAM

SERVES 10 TO 14
Active time: 1 hr Start to finish: 3 hr (includes making buttercream but not cupcakes)

   1 cup boiling-hot water
   ¾ cup unsweetened cocoa powder
   ½ cup whole milk
   1 teaspoon vanilla
   2 cups all-purpose flour
1½ teaspoons baking soda
      Rounded ½ teaspoon salt
   2 sticks (1 cup) unsalted butter, softened
   2 cups packed dark brown sugar
   4 large eggs at room temperature for 30 minutes
   4 cups vanilla buttercream (page 19)
      Various food colorings (see Sources)

Special equipment: a metal offset spatula; several small sealable plastic bags (not pleated)
Garnish: vanilla mini cupcakes (recipe follows)

Make cake layers:

▶ Put oven rack in middle position and preheat oven to 350°F. Butter 2 (9- by 2-inch) round cake pans and line bottom of each with a round of wax paper. Butter paper and dust pans with flour, knocking out excess.
▶ Whisk together hot water and cocoa powder in a bowl until smooth, then whisk in milk and vanilla.
▶ Whisk together flour, baking soda, and salt in another bowl.
▶ Beat together butter and brown sugar in a large bowl with an electric mixer at medium-high speed until pale and fluffy, 3 to 5 minutes. Add eggs 1 at a time, beating well after each addition. Reduce speed to low and add flour and cocoa mixtures alternately in batches, beginning and ending with flour mixture (batter may look curdled).
▶ Divide batter between cake pans, smoothing tops. Bake until a wooden pick or skewer comes out clean and edges of cake begin to pull away from sides of pans, 25 to 35 minutes total. Cool layers in pans on racks 10 minutes, then invert onto racks, removing wax paper, and cool completely.

Assemble cake:

▶ Put 1 cake layer, rounded side up, on a cake stand or platter and, using offset spatula, spread top with about 1 cup buttercream. Top with remaining cake layer, rounded side down, and frost side and top of cake with 2 cups buttercream.

Decorate cake:

▶ For each color (you can make up to 5), transfer 3 tablespoons buttercream to a separate small bowl and tint with food coloring. Snip off 1 corner of each plastic bag to create a ¼-inch opening, then spoon each color of buttercream into a bag, pressing out excess air. Twist each bag firmly just above buttercream, then decoratively pipe colored buttercream onto cake. Chill cake until buttercream is set, about 30 minutes.
▶ Just before serving, arrange 6 to 8 mini cupcakes on top of cake in 1 layer, then stack remaining mini cupcakes on top.

Cooks' notes:
• Cake layers can be made 2 days ahead and kept, wrapped tightly in plastic wrap, at room temperature or frozen 2 weeks.
• Cake can be assembled 4 hours ahead and kept at cool room temperature.

VANILLA MINI CUPCAKES

MAKES 2 DOZEN
Active time: 1 hr   Start to finish: 1¾ hr (includes making buttercream)

  1 cup all-purpose flour
  1 teaspoon baking powder
 ¼ teaspoon salt
 ⅓ cup whole milk
 ½ teaspoon vanilla
 ¾ stick (6 tablespoons) unsalted butter, softened
 ½ cup plus 1 tablespoon sugar
  1 large egg
1¾ cups vanilla buttercream (recipe follows)
    Various food colorings (optional; see Sources)

Special equipment: **2 mini-muffin pans, each with 24 (1¾-inch) muffin cups; 24 foil or paper mini-muffin liners**

▸ Put oven rack in middle position and preheat oven to 350°F. Line muffin cups with liners.
▸ Whisk together flour, baking powder, and salt in a bowl. Stir together milk and vanilla in a small bowl.
▸ Beat together butter and sugar in a large bowl with an electric mixer at medium-high speed until pale and fluffy, about 4 minutes. Add egg and beat until just combined. Reduce speed to low, then add flour and milk mixtures alternately in batches, beginning and ending with flour and mixing until just combined.
▸ Divide batter among muffin cups, filling them two-thirds full, and bake until tops are pale golden and a wooden pick or skewer inserted in centers comes out clean, about 15 minutes. Invert cupcakes onto a rack and cool completely.
▸ For each color, transfer ¼ cup buttercream to a separate small bowl and tint with food coloring (if using), then frost tops of cupcakes.

Cooks' note:
• For best flavor, cupcakes should be eaten the same day they're made.

VANILLA BUTTERCREAM

MAKES ABOUT 6 CUPS
Active time: 30 min   Start to finish: 1 hr

  4 large egg whites at room temperature for 30 minutes
    Rounded ¼ teaspoon salt
 ⅔ cup water
1⅓ cups plus 2 tablespoons sugar
  4 sticks (2 cups) unsalted butter, cut into tablespoon pieces and softened
  2 teaspoons vanilla

Special equipment: **a candy thermometer**

▸ Combine whites and salt in a very large bowl. Stir together water and 1⅓ cups sugar in a 3- to 4-quart heavy saucepan until sugar is dissolved, then bring to a boil over moderate heat, without stirring, brushing any sugar crystals down side of pan with a pastry brush dipped in water.
▸ When syrup reaches a boil, start beating egg whites with an electric mixer at medium-high speed until frothy, then gradually add remaining 2 tablespoons sugar and beat at medium speed until whites just hold soft peaks. (Do not beat again until sugar syrup is ready.)
▸ Meanwhile, put thermometer into sugar syrup and continue boiling until syrup registers 234 to 240°F. Immediately remove from heat and, with mixer at high speed, slowly pour hot syrup in a thin stream down side of bowl into whites, beating constantly. Beat, scraping down side of bowl with a rubber spatula, until meringue is cool to the touch, about 10 minutes in a stand mixer or 15 with a handheld. (It is important to cool meringue before proceeding.)
▸ With mixer at medium speed, gradually add butter 1 piece at a time, beating well after each addition until incorporated. (Buttercream will look soupy after some butter is added if meringue is still warm. If so, briefly chill bottom of bowl in a large bowl filled with ice water for a few seconds before continuing to beat in remaining butter.) Continue beating until buttercream is smooth. (Mixture may look curdled before all of butter is added but will come back together by the time beating is finished.) Add vanilla and beat 1 minute.

Cooks' note:
• The egg whites in this recipe will not be fully cooked. If salmonella is a problem in your area, you can substitute reconstituted egg whites such as Just Whites.

ALPHABET COOKIES

MAKES 3 TO 5 DOZEN COOKIES (DEPENDING ON SIZE OF COOKIE CUTTERS)

Active time: 1½ hr   Start to finish: 4 hr (includes making icing)

2½   cups all-purpose flour
¾   teaspoon salt
1½   sticks (¾ cup) unsalted butter, softened
¾   cup sugar
1   large egg
1   teaspoon vanilla
Decorating icing (recipe follows)
Various food colorings (see Sources)

Special equipment: **2- to 3-inch alphabet cookie cutters (see Sources); several sealable plastic bags (not pleated)**

▸ Whisk together flour and salt in a small bowl.
▸ Beat together butter and sugar in a large bowl with an electric mixer at medium-high speed until pale and fluffy, about 3 minutes in a stand mixer (preferably fitted with paddle attachment) or 6 minutes with a handheld, then beat in egg and vanilla. Reduce speed to low and add flour mixture, mixing until just combined.
▸ Form dough into 2 balls and flatten each into a 6-inch disk. Chill disks, wrapped in plastic wrap, until firm, at least 1 hour.
▸ Put oven rack in middle position and preheat oven to 350°F.
▸ Roll out 1 piece of dough (keep remaining dough chilled) into an 8½-inch round (¼ inch thick) on a well-floured surface with a well-floured rolling pin. (If dough becomes too soft to roll out, rewrap in plastic and chill until firm.) Cut out as many cookies as possible from dough with cutters and transfer to 2 ungreased large baking sheets, arranging about 1 inch apart.
▸ Bake cookies, 1 sheet at a time, until edges are golden, 10 to 12 minutes, then transfer with a metal spatula to racks to cool completely.
▸ Gather scraps and chill until dough is firm enough to reroll, 10 to 15 minutes. Make more cookies with remaining dough and scraps (reroll only once) in same manner on cooled baking sheets.
▸ For each color (you can make up to 7), transfer ¼ cup icing to a separate small bowl and tint with food coloring. Snip off 1 corner of each plastic bag to create a ¼-inch opening, then spoon each color icing into a bag, pressing out excess air. Twist each bag firmly just above icing, then decoratively pipe (or spread) colored icing onto cookies. Let icing dry completely (about 1 hour, depending on humidity) before storing cookies.

Cooks' notes:
• Dough can be chilled up to 3 days.
• Cookies (with or without icing) can be made 1 week ahead and kept in an airtight container, layered between sheets of wax paper or parchment, at room temperature.

DECORATING ICING

MAKES ABOUT 3 CUPS

Active time: 15 min   Start to finish: 15 min

1   (1-lb) box confectioners sugar
4   teaspoons powdered egg whites (not reconstituted) such as Just Whites
⅓   cup water
1   tablespoon fresh lemon juice
1   teaspoon vanilla

▸ Beat together all ingredients in a large bowl with an electric mixer at medium speed until just combined, about 1 minute.
▸ Increase speed to high and continue to beat icing, occasionally scraping down side of bowl with a rubber spatula, until it holds stiff peaks, about 3 minutes in a stand mixer or 10 with a handheld. If not using icing immediately, cover with plastic wrap and a dampened kitchen towel.

Cooks' note:
• If you plan to spread cookies with icing (rather than pipe), stir in more water, 1 teaspoon at a time, to thin to desired consistency.

VALENTINE'S DAY
DINNER

SERVES 2

RASPBERRY SMASH COCKTAILS

HERBED CRÊPES WITH SMOKED SALMON AND RADISHES

LOBSTER, AVOCADO, AND GRAPEFRUIT SALAD

FILLABOA ALBARIÑO '02

VENISON TENDERLOIN WITH MADEIRA GREEN PEPPERCORN SAUCE AND PARSNIP CRISPS

CARROT AND CELERY-ROOT PURÉES

CHÂTEAU CALON-SÉGUR ST.-ESTÈPHE '96

FROZEN PRALINE SOUFFLÉS

DISZNÓKÖ TOKAY 6-PUTTONYOS '97

RASPBERRY SMASH COCKTAILS

MAKES 2 DRINKS
Active time: 5 min   Start to finish: 1 hr (includes macerating)

½   cup raspberries (3 oz)
3   tablespoons Chambord (black raspberry liqueur)
2   teaspoons sugar
1   half bottle (375 ml) demi-sec Champagne or other
     semidry sparkling wine, chilled

▶ Gently stir together raspberries, Chambord, and sugar in
a small bowl, then macerate, covered and chilled, at least
1 hour and up to 2.
▶ Spoon 2 tablespoons raspberries with some juice into each
of 2 Champagne flutes or other glasses and slowly top
off with Champagne.

HERBED CRÊPES WITH SMOKED SALMON AND RADISHES

SERVES 2
Active time: 30 min   Start to finish: 1 hr

*The first crêpe in a batch is often not of the best quality. The
level of heat under the skillet needs to be fine-tuned as you
go. With that in mind, our recipe makes enough batter for 2
crêpes, even though you'll only need 1 for this hors d'oeuvre.*

For crêpes
⅓   cup whole milk
3   tablespoons all-purpose flour
1   large egg
2   teaspoons vegetable oil plus additional for
     cooking crêpes
1   tablespoon finely chopped fresh chives
1   tablespoon finely chopped fresh dill
For filling
1   oz cream cheese (1 tablespoon plus 2 teaspoons),
     softened
1   teaspoon fresh lemon juice
¼   teaspoon finely grated fresh lemon zest
     Rounded ¼ teaspoon coarsely ground black pepper
1   oz thinly sliced smoked salmon
2   medium radishes, cut into ⅛-inch-thick
     matchsticks (¼ cup)

Make crêpes:

▶ Blend milk, flour, egg, and 2 teaspoons oil in a blender until smooth. Add chives and dill and pulse 1 or 2 times to just combine. Chill batter, covered, 30 minutes.

▶ Stir batter to redistribute herbs. Lightly brush a 10-inch nonstick skillet with oil, then heat over moderately high heat until hot but not smoking. Holding skillet off heat, pour in half of batter (¼ cup), immediately tilting and rotating skillet to coat bottom. (If batter sets before skillet is coated, reduce heat slightly for next crêpe.) Return skillet to heat and cook until crêpe is just set and pale golden around edges, 10 to 15 seconds. Loosen edge of crêpe with a heatproof plastic spatula, then flip crêpe over carefully with your fingertips. Cook until underside is set, about 20 seconds more. Transfer crêpe to a plate. Make another crêpe in same manner, brushing skillet again with oil.

Prepare filling and assemble hors d'oeuvre:

▶ Stir together cream cheese, lemon juice, zest, and pepper in a small bowl until smooth.

▶ Put 1 crêpe, browned side up, on a work surface, and spread with all of cheese mixture. Arrange salmon in an even layer over bottom half of crêpe (side nearest you), then scatter radishes over salmon. Beginning at bottom, tightly roll up crêpe, then cut roll crosswise into 4 pieces, trimming ends if desired.

Cooks' notes:

• Crêpes can be made (but not filled) 1 day ahead and chilled, layered between sheets of wax paper and then wrapped in plastic wrap.

• Cheese mixture can be made 1 day ahead and chilled, covered. Bring to room temperature before using.

• Crêpe can be rolled with filling (but not cut) 1 hour ahead and kept, wrapped in plastic wrap, at room temperature. Cut into pieces just before serving.

LOBSTER, AVOCADO, AND GRAPEFRUIT SALAD

SERVES 2 (FIRST COURSE)
Active time: 45 min   Start to finish: 2¾ hr (includes chilling)

1   (1¼- to 1½-lb) live lobster
2   teaspoons finely chopped shallot
1   tablespoon fresh lemon juice
¼   teaspoon table salt
2   tablespoons extra-virgin olive oil
1   pink or ruby-red grapefruit
1   firm-ripe California avocado
1   oz baby arugula (2 cups)
    Coarse sea salt to taste (optional)

▶ Plunge lobster headfirst into an 8-quart pot of boiling salted water (see Tips, page 8). Cook, covered, over high heat 6 minutes (for 1¼-lb lobster) or 7 minutes (for 1½-lb lobster) from time it enters water. Transfer with tongs to sink to drain.

▶ When lobster is cool enough to handle, remove meat from tail and claws, keeping meat intact. Discard tomalley, any roe, and shells. Chill lobster, covered, until cold, at least 1 hour.

▶ While lobster chills, stir together shallot, lemon juice, and table salt in a small bowl and let stand at room temperature 30 minutes. Add oil in a stream, whisking.

▶ Cut peel, including all white pith, from grapefruit with a sharp knife. Cut segments free from membranes and transfer segments to paper towels to drain.

▶ Halve avocado lengthwise, discarding pit. (Save 1 half, wrapped tightly in plastic wrap, for another use.) Halve remaining avocado half lengthwise and peel, then cut crosswise into ⅓-inch-thick slices.

▶ Cut lobster tail meat crosswise into ½-inch-thick slices. Divide avocado and all of lobster meat between 2 salad plates and arrange grapefruit around them. Top with arugula and drizzle with dressing. Sprinkle lightly with sea salt (if using) and serve immediately.

Cooks' notes:

• Lobster can be cooked 1 day ahead and chilled, covered. Slice tail meat just before assembling salad.

• Dressing can be made 1 day ahead and chilled, covered. Whisk well just before drizzling.

VENISON TENDERLOIN WITH MADEIRA GREEN PEPPERCORN SAUCE

SERVES 2
Active time: 15 min   Start to finish: 50 min

 1 (½-lb) piece venison tenderloin (1½ inches in diameter), trimmed, at room temperature for 30 minutes
 ½ teaspoon coarsely ground black pepper
 ½ teaspoon salt
 1½ tablespoons vegetable or olive oil
 ¼ cup finely chopped shallot
 ¼ cup Madeira wine
 ⅓ cup beef or veal demi-glace
 1 teaspoon drained green peppercorns in brine (see Sources), coarsely chopped
 1 teaspoon unsalted butter

Special equipment: **an instant-read thermometer**
Garnish: **parsnip crisps (recipe follows)**

▶ Put oven rack in middle position and preheat oven to 425°F.
▶ Pat venison dry and sprinkle with black pepper and ¼ teaspoon salt. Heat oil in an ovenproof 12-inch heavy skillet over moderately high heat until just smoking, then brown venison on all sides (except ends), about 3 minutes total.
▶ Transfer skillet with venison to oven and roast until thermometer inserted diagonally 2 inches into center registers 115°F, 4 to 5 minutes. Transfer venison with tongs to a plate and let stand, loosely covered with foil, 5 minutes (temperature will rise to 125°F for medium-rare).
▶ While meat stands, add shallot to skillet (handle will be hot) and cook over moderate heat, stirring, until golden, about 2 minutes. Add Madeira and deglaze skillet by boiling, stirring and scraping up brown bits, until liquid is reduced by half, about 1 minute. Add demi-glace and boil, stirring, until sauce is slightly thickened, about 1 minute. Stir in peppercorns, butter, remaining ¼ teaspoon salt, and any meat juices that have accumulated on plate, then remove from heat.
▶ Cut venison into ½-inch-thick slices and serve with sauce.

Cooks' note:
• Beef tenderloin can be substituted for venison. Use 1 (¾-lb) filet mignon (3 inches in diameter). Brown on all sides

(including ends), about 5 minutes total, then roast until thermometer inserted into center registers 120°F, 18 to 20 minutes. Let stand, loosely covered with foil, 10 minutes (temperature will rise to 130°F for medium-rare). Pour off all but 1 tablespoon fat from skillet before making sauce.

PARSNIP CRISPS

SERVES 2 (GARNISH OR SNACK)
Active time: 10 min   Start to finish: 10 min

 About 4 cups vegetable oil
 1 medium or large parsnip

Special equipment: **a deep-fat thermometer; a Y-shaped vegetable peeler**

▶ Heat 1 inch oil in a 2½- to 3-quart heavy saucepan over moderate heat until thermometer registers 360°F.
▶ While oil heats, peel parsnip, then shave as many ribbons as possible from parsnip with vegetable peeler.
▶ Fry ribbons in 3 batches, stirring frequently, until edges are golden but middles are still pale, about 40 seconds to 1 minute per batch. Transfer parsnips as fried with a slotted spoon to paper towels to drain, then season lightly with salt. (Return oil to 360°F between batches.) Parsnips will crisp as they cool.

Cooks' note:
• Parsnip crisps can be made 1 day ahead and kept in an airtight container at room temperature. Recrisp on a baking sheet within 2 hours of serving in a preheated 350°F oven 3 to 5 minutes (be careful not to let them brown). If parsnips are not crisp once cooled, return to oven briefly.

ABOVE: **frozen praline soufflés**

CARROT PURÉE

SERVES 2 (MAKES ABOUT ⅔ CUP)
Active time: 10 min   Start to finish: 25 min

- ½ lb carrots (3 medium), halved lengthwise and cut into
  ½-inch pieces
- 1 small garlic clove
- ⅓ cup reduced-sodium chicken broth
- ¼ teaspoon salt
- 2 tablespoons heavy cream
- 1 teaspoon unsalted butter

▶Simmer carrots, garlic, broth, and salt in a 1- to 2-quart heavy saucepan, covered, until carrots are very tender, 12 to 14 minutes. Purée mixture with cream and butter in a food processor until smooth.

Cooks' note:
• Purée can be made 1 day ahead and cooled, uncovered, then chilled, covered. Reheat in an ovenproof dish, covered with foil, in a preheated 425°F oven 5 to 10 minutes.

CELERY-ROOT PURÉE

SERVES 2 (MAKES ABOUT ¾ CUP)
Active time: 10 min   Start to finish: 25 min

½ lb celery root, peeled with a sharp knife and cut into
    ½-inch cubes (1 cup)
1   small garlic clove
½ cup reduced-sodium chicken broth
¼ teaspoon salt
3   tablespoons heavy cream
1   teaspoon unsalted butter

▶ Simmer celery root, garlic, broth, and salt in a 1- to 2-quart heavy saucepan, covered, until celery root is very tender, 12 to 15 minutes. Purée mixture with cream and butter in a food processor until smooth.

Cooks' note:
• Purée can be made 1 day ahead and cooled, uncovered, then chilled, covered. Reheat in an ovenproof dish, covered with foil, in a preheated 425°F oven 5 to 10 minutes.

FROZEN PRALINE SOUFFLÉS

SERVES 2
Active time: 30 min   Start to finish: 2¾ hr

For praline
½ cup sugar
⅓ cup sliced almonds or whole hazelnuts (1½ oz), toasted
    (see Tips, page 8) and, if using hazelnuts, any loose
    skins rubbed off with a kitchen towel and nuts chopped

For meringue
¼ cup sugar
2   tablespoons water
2   large egg whites at room temperature for 30 minutes
½ cup chilled heavy cream
2   tablespoons Cognac or Armagnac

Special equipment: **2 (4-oz) ramekins; a candy thermometer**

▶ Tear off 2 (3-inch-wide) strips of foil and wrap each tightly around outside of a ramekin, forming a collar that extends at least 1 inch above rim. Tape overlapping ends together.
Make praline:
▶ Line a baking sheet with a sheet of foil, then lightly oil foil.

Cook sugar with a pinch of salt in a dry 8- to 9-inch nonstick skillet over moderate heat, without stirring, until it begins to melt. Continue to cook, stirring occasionally with a fork, until sugar is melted into a deep golden caramel. Immediately remove from heat and stir in nuts with a wooden spoon, then quickly pour onto baking sheet, spreading with back of spoon before praline hardens.
▶ Cool praline on baking sheet 5 minutes, then break into large pieces. Put pieces in a sealable plastic bag, then seal bag, pressing out excess air. Break praline into smaller pieces by lightly pounding and rolling with a rolling pin. Measure out ⅓ cup (serve remainder on the side).
Make meringue and assemble dessert:
▶ Bring sugar and water to a boil in a 1½-quart heavy saucepan over moderate heat, stirring until sugar is dissolved, then wash down crystals from side of pan with a pastry brush dipped in cold water. Boil syrup, without stirring, until thermometer registers 234 to 240°F (soft-ball stage), 3 to 5 minutes.
▶ While syrup boils, beat egg whites with a pinch of salt in a bowl using an electric mixer at medium speed until foamy. Increase speed to high, then add hot syrup in a slow stream (avoid beaters and side of bowl), beating constantly, and continue to beat until meringue holds stiff glossy peaks and is cooled to room temperature, about 5 minutes. Fold praline into meringue.
▶ Whisk cream with Cognac in another bowl until it holds soft peaks, then fold into meringue gently but thoroughly. Spoon mixture into ramekins and freeze, loosely covered with plastic wrap, until firm, 2 to 3 hours. Remove foil collars before serving.

Cooks' notes:
• To take the temperature of a shallow amount of syrup, put bulb of thermometer in skillet and turn thermometer facedown, resting other end against rim of pan. Check temperature frequently.
• Soufflés can be frozen up to 1 day.
• The egg whites in this recipe will not be fully cooked. If salmonella is a problem in your area, you can substitute reconstituted egg whites such as Just Whites.

RUSSIAN EASTER FEAST

PIEROGIES

MAKES 48 PIEROGIES

Active time: 2 hr   Start to finish: 2¾ hr

Though pierogies are a classic Polish dish, they are served in many Russian homes. You'll only need to serve 2 or 3 per person, since they are quite rich.

For dough

- 3 cups all-purpose flour plus additional for kneading
- 1 cup water
- 1 large egg
- 2 teaspoons vegetable oil
- 1 teaspoon salt

For potato filling

- 1½ lb russet (baking) potatoes
- 6 oz coarsely grated extra-sharp white Cheddar (2¼ cups)
- ¼ teaspoon salt
- ¼ teaspoon black pepper
- ⅛ teaspoon ground nutmeg

For onion topping

- 1 medium onion, halved lengthwise and thinly sliced crosswise
- 1 stick (½ cup) unsalted butter

Special equipment: **a 2½-inch round cookie cutter**
Accompaniment: **sour cream**

Make dough:

▶ Put flour in a large shallow bowl and make a well in center. Add water, egg, oil, and salt to well and carefully beat together with a fork without incorporating flour. Continue stirring with a wooden spoon, gradually incorporating flour, until a soft dough forms. Transfer dough to a lightly floured surface and knead, dusting with flour as needed to keep dough from sticking, until smooth and elastic, about 8 minutes (dough will be very soft). Invert a bowl over dough and let stand at room temperature 1 hour.

Make filling while dough stands:

▶ Peel potatoes and cut into 1-inch pieces. Cook potatoes in a large saucepan of boiling salted water (see Tips, page 8) until tender, about 8 minutes. Drain potatoes, then transfer to a bowl along with cheese, salt, pepper, and nutmeg and mash with a potato masher or a handheld electric mixer at low speed until smooth.

▶ When mashed potatoes are cool enough to handle, spoon out a rounded teaspoon and lightly roll into a ball between palms of your hands. Transfer ball to a plate and keep covered with plastic wrap while making 47 more balls in same manner (there will be a little filling left over).

Make onion topping:

▶ Cook onion in butter in a 4- to 5-quart heavy saucepan over moderately low heat, stirring occasionally (stir more frequently toward end of cooking), until golden brown, about 30 minutes. Remove from heat and season with salt and pepper.

Form and cook pierogies:

▶ Halve dough and roll out 1 half (keep remaining half under inverted bowl) on lightly floured surface (do not overflour surface or dough will slide instead of stretch) with a lightly floured rolling pin into a 15-inch round (⅛ inch thick), then cut out 24 rounds with lightly floured cutter. Holding 1 round in palm of your hand, put 1 potato ball in center of round and close your hand to fold round in half, enclosing filling. Pinch edges together to seal completely. (If edges don't adhere, brush them lightly with water, then seal; do not leave any gaps or pierogi may open during cooking.) Transfer pierogi to a lightly floured kitchen towel (not terry cloth) and cover with another towel. Form more pierogies in same manner.

▶ Bring a 6- to 8-quart pot of salted water (see Tips, page 8) to a boil. Add half of pierogies, stirring once or twice to keep them from sticking together, and cook 5 minutes from time pierogies float to surface. Transfer as cooked with a slotted spoon to onion topping and toss gently to coat. Cook remaining pierogies in same manner, transferring to onions. Reheat pierogies in onion topping over low heat, gently tossing to coat.

Cooks' notes:

• Potato filling (before being rolled into balls) can be made 2 days ahead and chilled, covered.
• Onion topping can be made 2 days ahead and chilled, covered.
• Pierogies can be formed (but not cooked) 1 month ahead and frozen. First freeze in 1 layer on a tray until firm, about 2 hours, then transfer to sealable plastic bags.
• Chill leftover cooked pierogies in 1 layer on a tray until surfaces are firm, then chill in an airtight container. Reheat in butter in a skillet over moderately low heat, stirring, until well browned and crisp in spots, about 5 minutes.

RUSSIAN EASTER BREAD
MAKES 2 LOAVES
Active time: 1 hr   Start to finish: 8 hr

A cross between brioche and challah, this bread (called kulich*) is a lightly sweetened, egg-glazed cylinder, often baked in a coffee can to make a tall loaf. The* kulich *would sit proudly in the center of the family Easter basket, surrounded by meats, cheeses, butter, and eggs. It's a central part of the Easter meal, served with sweet* paskha *cheese (page 34) or unsalted butter.*

  1 **cup whole milk**
  ½ **cup sugar plus a pinch**
1½ **sticks (¾ cup) unsalted butter**
     Pinch of saffron threads, crumbled
  2 **teaspoons salt**
2½ **teaspoons active dry yeast (from a ¼-oz package)**
  ¼ **cup lukewarm water (105–115°F)**
  6 **cups all-purpose flour plus additional for dusting**
  4 **large eggs**

Special equipment: **2 (5- to 6-cup) soufflé dishes or 2 (2-lb) cleaned empty coffee cans**

Make dough:
▶ Heat milk, sugar, butter, saffron, and salt in a 1-quart heavy saucepan over moderate heat, stirring occasionally, until butter is melted and sugar is dissolved, about 2 minutes. Remove from heat and cool to lukewarm.
▶ Meanwhile, stir together yeast, warm water, and pinch of sugar and let stand until foamy, about 5 minutes. (If mixture doesn't foam, discard and start over with new yeast.)
▶ Put flour in a large bowl and make a large well in center. Lightly beat 3 eggs and add to well along with milk and yeast mixtures. Carefully stir together with a wooden spoon, gradually incorporating flour, until a soft dough forms. Transfer dough to a lightly floured surface and knead, dusting with just enough flour to keep dough from sticking, until smooth and elastic, about 10 minutes. Put dough in a lightly oiled large bowl, turning to coat with oil, and let rise, covered with a clean kitchen towel, in a draft-free place at warm room temperature until doubled in bulk, about 3 hours.
▶ Punch down dough and let rise again, covered with towel, until doubled in bulk, about 1 hour.

Form loaves:
▶ Generously butter soufflé dishes. Punch down dough and divide in half. Loosely wrap 1 piece in plastic wrap and set aside. Cut away one third of remaining piece of dough and reserve, then roll remaining two thirds into a large ball and transfer to a soufflé dish.
▶ Roll reserved piece of dough into an 18-inch-long rope on work surface with palms of your hands. Cut rope into 3 equal pieces and lay pieces vertically side by side on work surface, about ¼ inch apart. Gather 3 ends farthest from you and press them together, then braid strands, pressing together other ends to secure braid. Lay braid over top of dough in soufflé dish (trim braid if using coffee cans). Form another loaf with remaining dough in same manner.
▶ Cover loaves with clean kitchen towel and let rise in draft-free place at warm room temperature until doubled in bulk, about 1½ hours (loaves will rise about 1 inch above rims of dishes).

Bake loaves:
▶ Put oven rack in middle position and preheat oven to 350°F.
▶ Lightly beat remaining egg with a large pinch of salt, then brush egg over top of each loaf. Bake loaves until golden brown and bread sounds hollow when tapped on bottom, about 1 hour. Turn loaves out onto a rack, then turn right side up and cool completely.

Cooks' note:
• Bread can be made 1 day ahead and kept, wrapped in plastic wrap, at room temperature or frozen 2 weeks.

PASKHA CHEESE

SERVES 10 GENEROUSLY

Active time: 25 min   Start to finish: 25 hr (includes chilling)

The sweetness and creaminess of this cheese celebrate the breaking of the traditional Russian dairy-free fast that precedes Easter and provide a nice contrast to the salty meats and bold flavors of the rest of the holiday menu.

⅓ cup brandy
1 cup loosely packed golden raisins (5 oz)
2 lb farmer cheese (see Sources)
2 hard-boiled large egg yolks (reserve whites for another use if desired)
1 stick (½ cup) unsalted butter, softened
¾ cup sugar
1 cup sour cream
2 teaspoons vanilla
¼ teaspoon salt
1 cup chilled heavy cream

Special equipment: a wooden *paskha* cheese mold (see Sources) or a clean 2-quart terra-cotta flowerpot with a drainage hole and a plate slightly smaller than top of pot; cheesecloth; 2 lb of weights such as large soup or vegetable cans

▶ Heat brandy with raisins in a small saucepan over low heat until warm, then remove from heat and let steep until raisins are softened, about 15 minutes.
▶ Force cheese and yolks through a potato ricer or a medium-mesh sieve into a bowl.
▶ Beat together butter and sugar in a large bowl with an electric mixer at medium speed until pale and fluffy, about 2 minutes. Add cheese mixture, sour cream, vanilla, and salt and beat until just combined. Beat cream in a bowl with cleaned beaters until it holds soft peaks. Fold whipped cream and raisins with any remaining brandy into cheese mixture gently but thoroughly.
▶ Line mold (or flowerpot) with a single layer of cheesecloth, leaving a 2- to 3-inch overhang on all sides. Spoon cheese mixture into mold, then fold ends of cheesecloth over top. Put lid on cheesecloth, then put weights on lid (or on foil and small plate if using flowerpot). Chill mold on a large plate (to catch drips) at least 24 hours.
▶ Remove lid from mold and open cheesecloth. Invert a

serving plate over top of mold and invert mold onto plate. Unlock hinges and open mold, removing cheesecloth. Loosely cover cheese with plastic wrap and let stand at room temperature 30 minutes.

Cooks' note:
• *Paskha* can be chilled in mold up to 3 days.

HERB-STUFFED LEG OF LAMB

SERVES 10 (AS PART OF LARGER MEAL)

Active time: 30 min   Start to finish: 1½ hr

Most Russian Orthodox families roast the meats the day before the feast so that preparation can be kept to a minimum when they come home from church. When you're at the market, the pieces of meat may seem too small to serve ten people, but remember that everyone is served a slice from each of the three meat dishes. The baby lamb is symbolic of Christ as well as an ode to the arrival of spring.

1½ cups coarsely chopped fresh flat-leaf parsley
3 garlic cloves
1 tablespoon finely chopped fresh chives
1 (2½-lb) boneless leg of lamb
1 tablespoon plus ¾ teaspoon kosher salt
¾ teaspoon black pepper
2 tablespoons olive oil

Special equipment: kitchen string; an instant-read thermometer

▶ Put oven rack in middle position and preheat oven to 350°F.
▶ Finely chop parsley and garlic together and transfer to a small bowl, then stir in chives.
▶ Open lamb like a book, fat side down, on a work surface and sprinkle with ¾ teaspoon kosher salt and ½ teaspoon pepper. Spread herb mixture evenly over lamb, then fold lamb back into original shape and tie with string at 1-inch intervals. Pat lamb dry and transfer to a small roasting pan. Rub lamb with oil and sprinkle with remaining tablespoon salt and remaining ¼ teaspoon pepper.
▶ Roast lamb until thermometer inserted diagonally 2 inches into lamb averages 135 to 140°F for medium-rare (test in several places, as different parts of leg cook at different

speeds), 40 to 50 minutes. Transfer to a plate and let stand, loosely covered with foil, 30 minutes before slicing. Cut off and discard string and serve lamb warm or at room temperature.

Cooks' note:
• Lamb can be roasted 1 day ahead and cooled, uncovered, then chilled, wrapped in plastic wrap. Slice while cold, then rewrap and bring to room temperature before serving.

STUFFED VEAL BREAST
SERVES 10 (AS PART OF LARGER MEAL)
Active time: 1 hr   Start to finish: 4½ hr

For this recipe we used what the butcher calls the first cut or brisket cut of the veal breast—it's the thicker, upper portion.

- 2 cups diced (¼ inch) marbled rye bread or a combination of rye and pumpernickel bread
- ½ cup diced (¼ inch) celery
- ½ cup finely chopped onion
- 1 large garlic clove, chopped
- 1½ teaspoons salt
- ¾ teaspoon black pepper
- ½ stick (¼ cup) unsalted butter
- ½ lb chicken livers, trimmed
- 2 large eggs
- ¼ cup whole milk
- 1 tablespoon finely chopped fresh dill
- 1 (3½-lb) piece boneless first- or brisket-cut veal breast (1½ inches thick)
- 2 bacon slices
- 2 tablespoons olive oil
- 1 cup chicken stock or reduced-sodium broth

Special equipment: **an instant-read thermometer**

▶ Put oven rack in middle position and preheat oven to 350°F.
Make stuffing:
▶ Toast bread cubes on baking sheet until dry and beginning to brown on edges, about 15 minutes. (Leave oven on.)
▶ Cook celery, onion, garlic, ¼ teaspoon salt, and ⅛ teaspoon pepper in 2 tablespoons butter in a 12-inch heavy skillet over moderate heat, stirring occasionally, until

vegetables are softened, about 3 minutes. Transfer to a small bowl.
▶ Heat remaining 2 tablespoons butter in cleaned skillet over high heat until foam subsides, then sauté livers with ¼ teaspoon salt and ⅛ teaspoon pepper until edges are browned but livers are still pink inside, about 3 minutes. Transfer to a cutting board and cool completely, then cut livers into ¼-inch dice.
▶ Whisk together eggs and milk in a large bowl, then stir in bread, vegetable mixture, livers, dill, ¼ teaspoon salt, and ⅛ teaspoon pepper. Let stand at room temperature until bread has absorbed liquid, about 10 minutes.
Prepare veal:
▶ Trim as much excess fat as possible from veal, then lay meat on a work surface. Beginning at center of thickest edge of veal breast, insert a large knife horizontally into center of veal and cut a pocket as evenly as possible, leaving a 1-inch border on 3 sides. Open pocket and sprinkle inside with ¼ teaspoon salt and ⅛ teaspoon pepper. Fill pocket with stuffing and cover opening with bacon slices. Rub outside of veal with oil and sprinkle with remaining ½ teaspoon salt and remaining ¼ teaspoon pepper.
▶ Transfer veal to a small roasting pan. Add stock to pan, then cover pan tightly with foil and roast veal 1½ hours.
▶ Remove foil and baste veal with stock, then roast, uncovered, until well browned and thermometer inserted diagonally 2 inches into stuffing registers 190°F, about 1 hour more.
▶ Transfer veal to a platter and let stand, loosely covered with foil, 20 minutes before slicing. Serve warm or at room temperature.

Cooks' note:
• Veal can be roasted 1 day ahead and cooled, uncovered, then chilled, wrapped in plastic wrap. Slice while cold, then rewrap and bring to room temperature before serving.

KIELBASA

SERVES 10 (AS PART OF LARGER MEAL)
Active time: 10 min   Start to finish: 35 min

2   to 2½ lb smoked kielbasa
1   cup water

Accompaniment: horseradish sauces (recipes follow)

▶ Pierce kielbasa 4 or 5 times on each side with tip of a sharp knife. Simmer kielbasa in water in a 12-inch heavy skillet, partially covered with lid, over moderately low heat until heated through, about 30 minutes (check after 15 minutes and add a little more water if skillet is almost dry).
▶ Transfer kielbasa with tongs to a cutting board and cut diagonally into ¾-inch-thick slices. Serve warm or at room temperature.

BEET HORSERADISH SAUCE

MAKES ABOUT 2 CUPS
Active time: 10 min   Start to finish: 2 hr (includes cooking beets)

1   cup finely grated peeled fresh horseradish (½ lb; use small teardrop-shaped holes of a box grater) or drained bottled horseradish
3   cooked medium beets (reserved from pickled quail eggs, page 39), peeled and coarsely chopped (1¾ cups)
½   teaspoon salt
½   teaspoon sugar
¼   cup cider vinegar

▶ Coarsely purée all ingredients in a food processor, scraping down side of bowl as needed, 30 to 40 seconds. Let stand, covered, at room temperature at least 1 hour (for flavors to develop).

Cooks' notes:
• Sauce can be made 2 days ahead and chilled, covered. Bring to room temperature before serving.
• We recommend using the cooked beets left over from the pickled quail egg recipe, but you can substitute canned beets.

WHITE HORSERADISH SAUCE

MAKES ABOUT 1¼ CUPS
Active time: 5 min   Start to finish: 1 hr

1   cup sour cream
3   tablespoons finely grated peeled fresh horseradish (1 oz; use small teardrop-shaped holes of a box grater), or drained bottled horseradish to taste
⅛   teaspoon black pepper

▶ Stir together sour cream, 1½ tablespoons horseradish, and pepper. Taste sauce, then add more horseradish as desired. Let stand, covered, at room temperature at least 1 hour (for flavors to develop).

Cooks' note:
• Sauce can be made 2 days ahead and chilled, covered. Bring to room temperature before serving.

ASPARAGUS WITH LEMON AND BUTTER

SERVES 10
Active time: 15 min   Start to finish: 25 min

4   lb medium to large asparagus, trimmed
2   tablespoons unsalted butter
1   tablespoon fresh lemon juice
¼   teaspoon salt
⅛   teaspoon black pepper

▶ Peel lower half to two thirds of each asparagus stalk with a vegetable peeler. Cook asparagus in a wide 6- to 8-quart pot of boiling salted water (see Tips, page 8), uncovered, until just tender, 5 to 7 minutes. Drain well in a colander, then return to pot and toss with butter, lemon juice, salt, and pepper.

OPPOSITE: herb-stuffed leg of lamb; kielbasa; stuffed veal breast

ABOVE: watercress salad with pickled quail eggs

SAUTÉED MIXED MUSHROOMS

SERVES 10
Active time: 45 min   Start to finish: 45 min

1½ lb whole portabella mushrooms, stems and caps
      separated
½ cup olive oil
1¼ lb small white mushrooms (½ to 1 inch in diameter)
  1 teaspoon fresh lemon juice
  1 teaspoon salt
½ teaspoon black pepper
  1 lb small fresh shiitake mushrooms, stems discarded
  1 lb oyster mushrooms, trimmed and halved lengthwise
      if large
½ cup finely chopped fresh flat-leaf parsley
  1 tablespoon finely chopped garlic

▸Trim portabella stems and thinly slice lengthwise. Scrape
away gills on portabella caps with a spoon, then cut caps into
⅛-inch-thick slices.
▸Heat 2 tablespoons oil in a 12-inch heavy skillet over
moderately high heat until hot but not smoking, then sauté
white mushrooms with lemon juice, ¼ teaspoon salt, and
⅛ teaspoon pepper, stirring occasionally, until liquid
mushrooms give off is evaporated, about 5 minutes. Transfer
cooked mushrooms with a slotted spoon to a large bowl and
keep warm, covered.
▸Sauté shiitakes, oyster mushrooms, and portabellas (caps
and stems) in separate batches in same manner, using 2
tablespoons oil, ¼ teaspoon salt, and ⅛ teaspoon pepper for
each batch, and transferring to bowl with white mushrooms.
▸Return all cooked mushrooms to skillet and sauté with
parsley and garlic over moderately high heat, stirring,
1 minute.

SWEET-AND-SOUR SAUERKRAUT

SERVES 10
Active time: 20 min   Start to finish: 1½ hr

  1 large onion, halved lengthwise and thinly sliced
      crosswise (2 cups)
  2 large garlic cloves, finely chopped
  3 tablespoons vegetable oil
  1 teaspoon cumin seeds, toasted
10 whole allspice, crushed

1 (28-oz) can whole tomatoes in juice
½ cup packed dark brown sugar
1½ teaspoons salt
¼ teaspoon black pepper
3 lb packaged sauerkraut, rinsed well and drained

▶ Cook onion and garlic in oil in a 3½- to 4-quart heavy saucepan over moderately low heat, stirring occasionally (stir more frequently toward end of cooking), until golden brown, about 30 minutes. Increase heat to moderate, then add cumin and allspice and cook, stirring, 30 seconds. Add tomatoes (with juice), brown sugar, salt, and pepper and simmer, stirring occasionally and breaking up tomatoes, 10 minutes. Stir in sauerkraut and bring to a boil, then reduce heat and simmer, partially covered, stirring occasionally, until most of liquid is absorbed, about 30 minutes.

Cooks' note:
• Sauerkraut can be cooked 2 days ahead and cooled, uncovered, then chilled, covered. Reheat with ½ cup water, covered, over low heat.

WATERCRESS SALAD WITH PICKLED QUAIL EGGS

SERVES 10

Active time: 40 min   Start to finish: 2 hr (plus 1 day for pickling eggs)

2 tablespoons pickling liquid from pickled quail eggs (recipe follows)
1 tablespoon Dijon mustard
⅛ teaspoon salt
⅛ teaspoon black pepper
¼ cup vegetable oil
2 tablespoons olive oil
6 oz organic baby watercress (12 cups) or 1½ lb regular watercress (4 large bunches), coarse stems discarded
20 pickled quail eggs (recipe follows) or 5 pickled regular large eggs, halved, quartered, or sliced

▶ Whisk together pickling liquid, mustard, salt, and pepper in a small bowl, then add oils in a slow stream, whisking until emulsified.
▶ Toss watercress with just enough dressing to coat in a large bowl and season with salt and pepper. Serve salad with eggs.

PICKLED QUAIL EGGS

MAKES 24

Active time: 30 min   Start to finish: 26 hr

3 lb beets (8 medium, including greens), scrubbed and stems trimmed to 1½ inches
1 cup cider vinegar
½ cup sugar
1 teaspoon salt
2 Turkish bay leaves or 1 California
5 whole cloves
24 quail eggs (see Sources) or 5 regular large eggs

▶ Cover beets with cold water by 1 inch in a 3-quart heavy saucepan and bring to a boil. Reduce heat and simmer beets, partially covered with lid, until tender, about 40 minutes. Transfer beets to a bowl with a slotted spoon (reserving them for another use), then measure out 2 cups beet cooking liquid, discarding remainder. Bring beet liquid to a boil in a small saucepan along with vinegar, sugar, salt, bay leaves, and cloves, stirring until sugar is dissolved. Remove from heat and cool pickling liquid completely, about 1 hour.
▶ While pickling liquid cools, cover eggs with cold water by 1 inch in a small saucepan and bring to a boil, stirring gently (to help center the yolks in eggs). Reduce heat and gently boil eggs, uncovered and undisturbed, 3 minutes (or 10 minutes for regular eggs). Pour off water and shake pan so eggs hit each other, lightly cracking shells. Cover eggs with cold water and let stand 15 minutes (to stop cooking and facilitate peeling).
▶ Drain and peel eggs, then transfer to a glass jar or deep bowl. Reserve 2 tablespoons pickling liquid (for watercress salad vinaigrette; recipe precedes) and pour remaining liquid over eggs. Let eggs (quail or regular) pickle, covered, 24 hours.

Cooks' notes:
• For best results, pickle eggs no longer than 24 hours—any longer and the whites become too rubbery and the pickling liquid seeps into the yolks.
• When you're ready to slice these eggs, be sure to wipe your knife clean between every cut or you'll get the pink pickling liquid smeared on the yolk.

PRUNE AND CARAWAY ICE CREAM
MAKES ABOUT 3 QUARTS
Active time: 20 min   Start to finish: 13½ hr (includes freezing)

6 cups half-and-half (48 fl oz)
2 tablespoons caraway seeds, toasted (see Tips, page 8)
¾ lb dried pitted prunes (dried plums; 2 cups)
1 cup vodka (8 fl oz)
1½ cups sugar
8 large egg yolks
2 teaspoons vanilla

Special equipment: an instant-read thermometer; an ice cream maker

▶ Bring half-and-half with caraway seeds just to a boil in a 3-quart heavy saucepan, then remove from heat and let steep, uncovered, 30 minutes.
▶ While caraway seeds steep, simmer prunes, vodka, and ½ cup sugar in a 1-quart heavy saucepan, partially covered, until prunes are tender, about 15 minutes. Cool slightly, then purée mixture in a blender, scraping down sides occasionally (use caution when blending hot liquids), until smooth.
▶ Whisk together yolks and remaining cup sugar in a bowl, then add half-and-half (do not strain) in a stream, whisking. Pour custard into 3-quart saucepan and cook over moderately low heat, stirring with a wooden spoon, until it registers 170°F on thermometer, about 8 minutes. Immediately pour custard through a fine-mesh sieve into a metal bowl and whisk in prune purée and vanilla. Chill, stirring occasionally, 30 minutes.
▶ Freeze custard in ice cream maker (in batches if necessary), then transfer to an airtight container and put in freezer to harden, about 12 hours.

Cooks' note:
• Ice cream can be made 3 days ahead.

POPPY SEED SHORTBREADS
MAKES ABOUT 34 COOKIES
Active time 35 min   Start to finish: 1½ hr

Inspired by the poppy seed breads made in many Russian homes, these cookies capture the traditional flavors without the time investment of making a yeast bread.

2 sticks (1 cup) unsalted butter, softened
½ cup sugar
1 teaspoon vanilla
¼ teaspoon salt
2 cups all-purpose flour
⅓ cup poppy seeds

Special equipment: a 1-gallon sealable plastic bag (not stand-up or pleated); a 2½- by 1½-inch fluted oval cookie cutter

▶ Put oven racks in upper and lower thirds of oven and preheat oven to 350°F.
▶ Beat together butter, sugar, vanilla, and salt in a bowl with an electric mixer at medium-high speed until light and fluffy, about 3 minutes. Reduce speed to low, then add flour and poppy seeds and mix until just combined.
▶ Transfer dough to plastic bag and pat out dough to size of bag. Press out excess air and seal bag. Roll out dough with a rolling pin to flatten evenly and to fill bag (dough will be about ¼ inch thick). Freeze dough on a baking sheet until firm, at least 20 minutes.
▶ Open bag and cut apart along seams, reserving bag for rolling scraps. Cut out as many ovals as possible with cookie cutter, reserving scraps, and transfer to 2 ungreased large baking sheets, arranging about ½ inch apart. Bake cookies, switching position of sheets halfway through baking, until edges are golden, 16 to 20 minutes total. Cool cookies on sheets on racks 5 minutes, then transfer with a spatula to racks to cool completely.
▶ Gather and reroll scraps using reserved plastic bag (to keep dough from sticking), then cut out and bake more cookies in same manner.

Cooks' notes:
• Rolled-out dough (in bag) can be frozen up to 5 days. Let stand at room temperature 30 minutes before proceeding.
• Cookies keep in an airtight container at room temperature 1 week.

ENGAGEMENT PARTY

SERVES 10

FRENCH KISS

**CHICKEN TIKKA WITH MANGO AND
RED PEPPER CHUTNEY AND MINT RAITA**

CUMIN AND ORANGE GLAZED CARROTS

CILANTRO COCONUT RICE

**SPINACH SALAD WITH TAMARIND
DRESSING AND PAPPADAM CROUTONS**

DOMAINE ZIND-HUMBRECHT, ZIND '01

**STRAWBERRY AND CREAM CAKE WITH
CARDAMOM SYRUP**

PROSPER MAUFOUX,
MUSCAT DE BEAUMES-DE-VENISE

FRENCH KISS
MAKES 6 DRINKS
Active time: 15 min   Start to finish: 3¼ hr (includes freezing ice cubes)

A lovely prelude to the buffet—you'll need at least two batches of this refreshing drink.

For lemonade ice cubes
- ½ cup fresh lemon juice
- 2 tablespoons sugar
- 1½ cups water

For drinks
- 1½ cups dry vermouth (12 oz)
- 1½ cups sweet vermouth (12 oz)
- 6 strips of fresh lemon peel removed with a vegetable peeler

Special equipment: **6 (6-oz) glasses**

Make ice cubes:
▶ Stir together juice and sugar until sugar is dissolved. Stir in water, then pour into an ice tray and freeze until hard, about 3 hours.

Make drinks:
▶ Stir together vermouths and lemonade ice cubes in a pitcher until vermouth is chilled. Run a lemon strip around rim of each glass and drop into glass. Fill glasses with vermouth mixture, including ice cubes.

CHICKEN TIKKA
SERVES 10
Active time: 1½ hr   Start to finish: 14 hr (includes marinating chicken and preparing accompaniments)

- ¾ teaspoon cumin seeds, toasted (see Tips, page 8)
- ¾ teaspoon coriander seeds, toasted (see Tips, page 8)
- 2 cups whole-milk yogurt
- 4 garlic cloves, chopped
- 1 (1½-inch) piece fresh ginger, peeled and chopped
- 3 tablespoons vegetable oil plus additional for greasing pan
- 2 tablespoons fresh lime juice
- 1½ teaspoons salt
- ¾ teaspoon ground turmeric
- ½ teaspoon garam masala (Indian spice mixture)
- ½ teaspoon black pepper
- ¼ teaspoon cayenne
- 5 lb skinless boneless chicken breasts, cut into 1½-inch cubes

Special equipment: **20 (12-inch) wooden skewers**
Accompaniments: **mango and red pepper chutney and mint raita (recipes follow)**
Garnish: **lime wedges**

▶ Purée all ingredients except chicken in a blender until spices are well ground.
▶ Put chicken in a large bowl, or divide between 2 large sealable plastic bags, and add yogurt mixture, stirring or turning to coat. Marinate chicken, covered and chilled (turning occasionally if using bags), at least 4 hours.
▶ Soak skewers in water 30 minutes. While skewers soak, bring chicken to room temperature.
▶ Preheat broiler and brush a broiler pan lightly with oil.
▶ Divide chicken among skewers (about 5 cubes per skewer), leaving an ⅛-inch space between cubes, and arrange about 5 skewers across pan. Broil chicken about 4 inches from heat, turning over once, until browned in spots and just cooked through, 9 to 12 minutes total.
▶ Transfer cooked skewers to a large platter and, if desired, cover loosely with foil to keep warm. Broil remaining chicken in same manner. Remove chicken from skewers and serve warm or at room temperature.

Cooks' note:
• Chicken can be marinated up to 24 hours.

MANGO AND RED PEPPER CHUTNEY
MAKES ABOUT 4 CUPS
Active time: 35 min   Start to finish: 2 hr (includes cooling)

- 3 firm-ripe mangoes (3 lb total), peeled and cut into ½-inch cubes
- ⅓ cup distilled white vinegar
- ⅓ cup packed dark brown sugar
- ⅓ cup golden raisins
- 1¾ teaspoons salt
- 1 (1-inch) piece fresh ginger, peeled and chopped
- 1 tablespoon chopped fresh jalapeño including seeds

3 garlic cloves, chopped
¾ teaspoon ground cumin
¾ teaspoon ground coriander
½ teaspoon turmeric
2 tablespoons vegetable oil
1 medium onion, chopped
1 red bell pepper, cut into ¼-inch dice
1 (3-inch) cinnamon stick

▶ Toss together mangoes, vinegar, brown sugar, raisins, and 1 teaspoon salt.

▶ Mince and mash ginger, jalapeño, and garlic to a paste with remaining ¾ teaspoon salt using a large heavy knife, then stir in cumin, coriander, and turmeric.

▶ Heat oil in a 4-quart heavy pot over moderately high heat until hot but not smoking, then sauté onion and bell pepper, stirring occasionally, until golden, 8 to 10 minutes. Add garlic paste and cinnamon stick, then reduce heat to moderate and cook, stirring, 1 minute. Stir in mango mixture and simmer, covered, stirring occasionally, until mangoes are tender, about 30 minutes. Discard cinnamon stick and cool chutney, uncovered, about 45 minutes.

Cooks' note:
• Chutney keeps, chilled in an airtight container, 1 month.

MINT RAITA

MAKES ABOUT 2 CUPS
Active time: 15 min   Start to finish: 6¼ hr (includes draining and chilling)

3 cups whole-milk yogurt
1 cup packed fresh mint leaves
¾ teaspoon salt

▶ Drain yogurt in a paper-towel-lined sieve set over a bowl, chilled, 3 hours.

▶ Pulse yogurt, mint, and salt in a blender until mint is finely chopped. Transfer to a bowl and chill, covered, at least 3 hours.

Cooks' note:
• Raita can be chilled in an airtight container up to 1 day (but color will not be as vibrant if made more than 3 hours ahead).

CUMIN AND ORANGE GLAZED CARROTS

SERVES 10
Active time: 50 min   Start to finish: 1½ hr

3 navel oranges
4 lb medium carrots (24)
3½ tablespoons vegetable or olive oil
1½ teaspoons cumin seeds
1¾ cups water
2 tablespoons fresh lemon juice
1 tablespoon sugar
1¼ teaspoons salt
½ teaspoon black pepper

Special equipment: **parchment paper or wax paper**

▶ Cut out a round from parchment paper to fit just inside a 12-inch heavy skillet (3 inches deep), then set round aside.

▶ Cut peel, including all white pith, from oranges with a sharp paring knife. Working over a bowl, cut segments free from membranes, letting segments fall into bowl, then squeeze ½ cup juice from membranes into another bowl (discard membranes). Chop orange segments and reserve.

▶ Cut a 1-inch-thick diagonal slice from a carrot and set aside, then roll carrot away from you 90 degrees and cut another 1-inch-thick diagonal slice. (Shape will resemble a trapezoidal log. If carrots are very thick, cut slices in half lengthwise as well). Cut up rest of carrot in same manner, then repeat with remaining carrots.

▶ Heat oil in skillet over moderate heat until hot but not smoking, then cook cumin seeds, stirring, until fragrant, about 1 minute. Add carrots, water, orange juice, lemon juice, sugar, salt, and pepper. Cover carrots directly with parchment round and simmer, stirring occasionally, 30 minutes. Remove parchment, then continue to simmer, stirring occasionally, until most of liquid is evaporated and carrots are tender and glazed, about 20 minutes more. Serve warm or at room temperature, sprinkled with chopped orange.

Cooks' note:
• Carrots can be cooked 3 hours ahead and chilled, covered. Bring to room temperature before serving.

SPINACH SALAD WITH TAMARIND DRESSING AND PAPPADAM CROUTONS

SERVES 10

Active time: 30 min   Start to finish: 30 min

For pappadam croutons

About 2½ cups vegetable oil for frying

4   (8-inch) plain or black pepper pappadams

For dressing

2½ tablespoons warm water

2   tablespoons fresh lime juice

1   tablespoon mild honey

1¼ teaspoons tamarind concentrate

¾   teaspoon salt

⅓   cup vegetable oil

For salad

24 cups baby spinach (15 oz)

2   seedless cucumbers (usually plastic-wrapped; 1½ lb total), quartered lengthwise, then cut crosswise into ⅓-inch-thick slices

Special equipment: **a deep-fat thermometer**

Fry pappadams:

▶Heat ½ inch oil in a 10-inch heavy skillet (2 inches deep) over moderate heat until thermometer registers 350°F (see cooks' note, below). Fry 1 pappadam, turning over once, until blistered and pale golden, about 1 minute total. Lift pappadam from skillet with tongs, letting excess oil drip back into skillet, and transfer to paper towels to drain (pappadam will crisp as it cools). Return oil to 350°F and fry remaining pappadams, 1 at a time, in same manner.

Make dressing:

▶Whisk together water, lime juice, honey, tamarind concentrate, and salt in a small bowl, then add oil in a slow stream, whisking until combined.

Assemble salad:

▶Toss spinach and cucumbers with dressing in a large bowl. Break pappadams into 1½-inch pieces and add to salad just before serving, tossing gently to combine.

OPPOSITE: cumin and orange glazed carrots; spinach salad with tamarind dressing and pappadam croutons

Cooks' notes:

• To take the temperature of a shallow amount of oil with a metal flat-framed deep-fat thermometer, put bulb of thermometer in skillet and turn thermometer facedown, resting other end (not plastic handle) against rim of skillet. Check temperature frequently.

• Pappadams can be fried and drained 1 day ahead and kept in an airtight container at room temperature.

CILANTRO COCONUT RICE

SERVES 10

Active time: 40 min   Start to finish: 1 hr

3   cups basmati rice (20 oz)

¾   cup sweetened flaked coconut

1   tablespoon finely chopped peeled fresh ginger

1   tablespoon finely chopped fresh jalapeño including seeds

3   tablespoons vegetable oil

4   cups water

1   teaspoon salt

2   cups packed fresh cilantro sprigs

4   scallions, chopped (1 cup)

▶Put oven rack in middle position and preheat oven to 350°F.

▶Wash rice in several changes of cold water in a bowl until water is almost clear. Soak rice in cold water 30 minutes, then drain well in a sieve.

▶Spread coconut in a shallow baking pan and toast in oven, stirring occasionally, until pale golden, 10 to 12 minutes. Cool completely.

▶Cook ginger and jalapeño in 1 tablespoon oil in a 4-quart heavy pot over moderate heat, stirring, until chile is softened, about 2 minutes. Add rice and cook, stirring, until fragrant, about 2 minutes. Stir in water and ½ teaspoon salt and bring to a boil, covered. Reduce heat to low and cook, covered, until rice is tender and water is absorbed, 12 to 15 minutes.

▶Remove from heat and let stand, covered, 5 minutes. Fluff rice with a fork and transfer to a large bowl.

▶While rice cooks, pulse together coconut, cilantro, scallions, remaining 2 tablespoons oil, and remaining ½ teaspoon salt in a food processor until finely chopped.

▶Add cilantro mixture to cooked rice and stir gently until combined well.

STRAWBERRY AND CREAM CAKE WITH CARDAMOM SYRUP

SERVES 10

Active time: 1 hr   Start to finish: 2½ hr

For cake

8	large egg yolks
1½	cups sugar
¼	cup whole milk
1	teaspoon vanilla
½	teaspoon finely grated fresh lemon zest
1	cup all-purpose flour
½	teaspoon salt
4	large egg whites

For syrup

1½	cups Muscat de Beaumes-de-Venise or Essensia (orange-flavored Muscat wine)
¼	cup sugar
¾	teaspoon ground cardamom

For filling

2	cups chilled heavy cream
½	cup sour cream
2	tablespoons sugar
1	teaspoon vanilla
1½	lb strawberries, 5 left whole and remainder trimmed and cut lengthwise into ¼-inch-thick slices

Special equipment: 3 (9- by 2-inch) round cake pans; parchment paper

Make cake layers:

▶ Put oven racks in upper and lower thirds of oven and preheat oven to 350°F. Butter cake pans. Line bottom of each with a round of parchment paper, then butter parchment and dust cake pans with flour, knocking out excess.

▶ Whisk together yolks, 1 cup sugar, milk, vanilla, and zest in a large bowl until smooth. Whisk in flour and salt until combined (batter will be thick).

▶ Beat whites with a pinch of salt in a bowl using an electric mixer at medium-high speed until they just hold soft peaks. Add remaining ½ cup sugar, a little at a time, beating at medium speed, and continue to beat until whites hold stiff glossy peaks, about 2 minutes more.

▶ Fold about one third of whites into batter to lighten, then fold in remaining whites gently but thoroughly.

▶ Divide batter among cake pans and bake, switching position of cake pans halfway through baking, until cakes are springy to the touch and a wooden pick or skewer inserted in center of each comes out clean, 20 to 25 minutes. Cool cakes in pans on racks 10 minutes, then invert onto racks. Carefully peel off parchment, then cool cakes completely.

Make syrup while cakes cool:

▶ Bring wine, sugar, and cardamom to a boil in a 1-quart heavy saucepan, stirring until sugar is dissolved, then boil until reduced to about 1 cup, 6 to 8 minutes. Pour syrup through a fine-mesh sieve and cool completely.

Make filling once cakes and syrup are cool:

▶ Beat together heavy cream, sour cream, sugar, and vanilla in a bowl with cleaned beaters until cream just holds stiff peaks.

Assemble cake:

▶ Prick cake layers all over with wooden pick or skewer, then brush or pour syrup, little by little, evenly over each layer, letting syrup be absorbed before adding more.

▶ Transfer 1 layer (flat side up) to a cake stand or plate, then spread with a rounded cup of cream. Arrange some sliced strawberries in 1 layer over cream. Turn second layer over and spread a thin layer of cream over top, then place it, with the aid of a spatula, cream side down, over layer of strawberries. Continue making layers with cream, strawberries, and cake in same manner. Spread top with remaining cream and decorate with remaining strawberries.

Cooks' notes:

• Layers (without syrup) can be made 2 days ahead and kept, wrapped well in plastic wrap, at room temperature.

• Wine syrup can be made 1 day ahead and chilled, covered. Bring syrup to room temperature before using.

• Cake can be assembled 1 hour ahead and kept at room temperature.

FATHER'S DAY
TUSCAN DINNER

SERVES 8

PEACH AND ARUGULA SALAD

FALCHINI VIGNA A SOLATIO VERNACCIA DI SAN
GIMIGNANO '02

FLORENTINE-STYLE PORTERHOUSE STEAKS

WHITE BEANS WITH ROASTED TOMATOES

SAUTÉED BROCCOLI RABE

PODERE IL PALAZZINO LA PIEVE CHIANTI CLASSICO '01

CHOCOLATE-FILLED HAZELNUT COOKIES

ABOVE: **Florentine-style porterhouse steak; sautéed broccoli rabe; white beans with roasted tomatoes**

PEACH AND ARUGULA SALAD

SERVES 8
Active time: 40 min Start to finish: 40 min

  1 **tablespoon balsamic vinegar**
  2 **teaspoons fresh lemon juice**
¼ **teaspoon salt (preferably sea salt)**
  3 **tablespoons extra-virgin olive oil**
  4 **firm-ripe peaches (1½ lb total)**
24 **thin slices pancetta (Italian unsmoked cured bacon;**
     1¼ lb)
  2 **tablespoons olive oil**
  6 **oz baby arugula (6 cups)**
2½ **oz finely crumbled ricotta salata (½ cup; see Sources)**
     Coarsely ground black pepper to taste

▶ Whisk together vinegar, juice, and salt, then add extra-virgin oil in a stream, whisking until emulsified.

▶ Cut an X in bottom of each peach and immerse in boiling water 15 seconds, then transfer to a bowl of ice water. Peel peaches and cut each into 6 wedges, then wrap one pancetta slice around each wedge, overlapping ends of pancetta. Heat remaining oil in a 12-inch nonstick skillet over moderate heat until hot but not smoking, then cook peaches in 2 batches, turning over occasionally with tongs, until pancetta is browned on all sides and cooked through, about 5 minutes per batch. Transfer to a plate and keep warm, covered loosely with foil.

▶ Divide arugula and warm pancetta-wrapped peaches among 8 salad plates. Drizzle with dressing and sprinkle with ricotta salata and pepper. Serve immediately.

Cooks' notes:
• Dressing can be made 1 hour ahead and kept, covered, at room temperature.
• Peaches can be peeled, tossed with an additional teaspoon lemon juice, and wrapped with pancetta 1 hour ahead. Keep chilled, covered with plastic wrap.

FLORENTINE-STYLE PORTERHOUSE STEAKS

SERVES 8
Active time: 35 min Start to finish: 1 hr

  2 **(2-inch-thick) porterhouse steaks (each about 2½ lb)**
  2 **teaspoons salt (preferably sea salt), plus additional for**
     sprinkling
  2 **tablespoons olive oil for drizzling**

Special equipment: **a large chimney starter (if using charcoal); an instant-read thermometer**
Accompaniment: **lemon wedges**

▶ Pat steaks dry and rub each all over with 1 teaspoon salt.
To cook steaks using a charcoal grill:
▶ Open vents on bottom of grill and on lid. Light a heaping chimneyful of charcoal and pour lit charcoal on 2 opposite sides of bottom of grill, leaving middle clear. Charcoal fire is medium-hot when you can hold your hand 5 inches above rack over coals for 3 to 4 seconds.
▶ Sear steaks on lightly oiled grill rack over coals, uncovered,

until grill marks appear (rotating 90 degrees once on each side for crosshatch marks), about 5 minutes per side. Move steaks to area with no coals underneath and grill, covered, turning over occasionally, until thermometer inserted horizontally 2 inches into meat (do not touch bone) registers about 110°F in larger section of meat and about 125°F in smaller (fillet) section for medium-rare, 12 to 15 minutes.

To cook steaks using a gas grill:

▶ Preheat all burners on high, covered, 10 minutes. Sear steaks on lightly oiled grill rack, covered, until grill marks appear (rotating 90 degrees once on each side for crosshatch marks), about 5 minutes per side. Turn off 1 burner (middle burner if there are 3) and put steaks above shut-off burner. Reduce heat on remaining burner(s) to moderate and grill steaks, covered, turning occasionally, until thermometer inserted horizontally 2 inches into meat (do not touch bone) registers about 110°F in larger section of meat and about 125°F in smaller (fillet) section for medium-rare, 10 to 15 minutes.

To serve steaks:

▶ Transfer steaks to a cutting board and let stand, uncovered, 10 minutes. (Internal temperature will rise to at least 135°F while steaks stand.) Cut each section of meat off bone, then slice each piece crosswise against the grain and arrange slices on a platter. Sprinkle lightly with salt and drizzle with oil.

Cooks' note:

• If you're not able to grill outdoors, steaks can be grilled in a hot lightly oiled well-seasoned large ridged grill pan, uncovered, turning over once, 5 minutes per side. Reduce heat to moderately low and cook steaks, covered with an inverted roasting pan, turning over occasionally, 10 to 15 minutes more.

WHITE BEANS WITH ROASTED TOMATOES

SERVES 8
Active time: 1 hr   Start to finish: 9¼ hr (includes soaking)

For beans

  1   lb dried cannellini beans (2 cups), picked over and rinsed

  1   lb *cipolline* (see Sources) or small boiling onions (left unpeeled)

1½   teaspoons salt (preferably sea salt), or to taste

For tomatoes

  2   lb large tomatoes, cored and halved crosswise

  1   lb cherry tomatoes (preferably mixed colors; 4 cups)

  1   teaspoon salt (preferably sea salt)

  1   teaspoon sugar

 ½   cup extra-virgin olive oil

 ¼   cup torn fresh basil leaves

Cook beans:

▶ Cover beans with cold water by 2 inches in a bowl and soak at room temperature at least 8 hours or quick-soak (see cooks' note, below). Drain well in a colander.

▶ Blanch onions in boiling salted water (see Tips, page 8) 1 minute, then drain and peel.

▶ Cover beans with cold water by about 1 inch in a 5- to 6-quart pot and bring to a boil. Add onions and simmer, partially covered, skimming froth as necessary, until beans and onions are tender, 40 minutes to 1 hour. Stir in salt and let stand (in cooking liquid), uncovered.

Roast tomatoes while beans cook:

▶ Put oven rack in upper third of oven and preheat oven to 500°F.

▶ Toss tomato halves and cherry tomatoes with salt, sugar, and oil in a shallow 3-quart baking dish, then arrange tomato halves cut sides up. Roast tomatoes, uncovered, until large tomatoes are very tender with brown patches and cherry tomatoes are falling apart, 35 to 50 minutes.

Assemble dish:

▶ Transfer warm beans and onions with a slotted spoon to a deep large platter. Arrange tomatoes decoratively on top of beans and pour tomato juices on top. Sprinkle with basil leaves.

Cooks' notes:

• Beans can be cooked 1 day ahead. Cool in liquid, uncovered, then chill, covered. Reheat in liquid over low heat, covered, stirring occasionally, before assembling dish.

• To quick-soak beans, cover dried beans with triple their volume of cold water in a large saucepan. Bring to a boil and cook, uncovered, over moderate heat 2 minutes. Remove from heat and soak beans 1 hour.

• Tomatoes can be roasted 2 hours ahead and kept, uncovered, at room temperature. Reheat, covered with foil, in 350°F oven until heated through, 15 to 20 minutes.

SAUTÉED BROCCOLI RABE
SERVES 8
Active time: 25 min   Start to finish: 30 min

> 2   lb broccoli rabe
> 3   large garlic cloves, thinly sliced lengthwise
> ⅓   cup extra-virgin olive oil
> 1   teaspoon salt (preferably sea salt), or to taste

Accompaniment: **lemon wedges**

► Cut off and discard 1 inch from stem ends of broccoli rabe. Cook broccoli rabe, uncovered, in 2 batches in a 6- to 8-quart pot of boiling salted water (see Tips, page 8) until just tender, about 3 minutes, transferring with a slotted spoon to a large bowl of ice and cold water to stop cooking. Drain well in a colander.
► Cook garlic in oil in a 12-inch nonstick skillet over moderate heat, stirring occasionally, until garlic is golden, about 5 minutes. Add broccoli rabe and cook, tossing to coat with oil, until heated through, 3 to 5 minutes. Toss broccoli rabe with salt.

Cooks' note:
• Broccoli rabe can be boiled and drained 6 hours ahead, then chilled, covered. Bring to room temperature before proceeding.

CHOCOLATE-FILLED HAZELNUT COOKIES
MAKES 50 TO 60 ASSEMBLED COOKIES
Active time: 1¼ hr   Start to finish: 2¼ hr

These classic cookies, known in Italy as baci di dama *("lady's kisses") taste great with espresso. This recipe, by chef Carla Tomasi of the "Tasting Places" cooking course in Tuscany and other regions of Italy, uses hazelnuts instead of the more traditional almonds.*

> ¾   cup hazelnuts, toasted (see Tips, page 8), any loose skins rubbed off in a kitchen towel, and cooled
> 1   cup confectioners sugar
> 1   stick (½ cup) unsalted butter, well softened
> ¼   teaspoon finely grated fresh lemon zest
> ⅛   teaspoon salt

> 1   cup cake flour (not self-rising)
> 3   oz fine-quality bittersweet chocolate (not unsweetened; preferably 70% cacao), chopped

Special equipment: **parchment paper**

► Put oven rack in middle position and preheat oven to 350°F. Line 2 or 3 baking sheets with parchment paper.
► Grind nuts with confectioners sugar in a food processor until powdery (be careful not to process to a paste).
► Mix together butter, zest, salt, and nut mixture in a large bowl with a rubber spatula or wooden spoon until creamy, then add flour, stirring until just incorporated (do not overwork).
► Roll level ½ teaspoons of dough into tiny balls (the size of marbles) and arrange 1 inch apart on baking sheets. Bake, 1 sheet at a time, until very pale golden, 12 to 14 minutes, then slide parchment with cookies onto a rack to cool completely.
► Melt chocolate in a metal bowl set over a saucepan of barely simmering water, stirring occasionally, until smooth. Spoon melted chocolate into a small plastic bag and seal bag, forcing out excess air. Snip off 1 bottom corner of bag with scissors to form a small hole.
► Pipe a small mound (about ⅛ teaspoon) of melted chocolate onto flat sides of 10 cookies, then top with 10 more cookies, pressing flat sides together to help adhere. Repeat with remaining cookies.

Cooks' notes:
• Cookies can be baked and cooled (but not filled) 1 week ahead and kept in an airtight container at room temperature.
• Filled cookies are best eaten the same day, but leftovers keep in an airtight container at room temperature 2 days.

A BOHEMIAN THANKSGIVING

SERVES 8 TO 10

PUMPKIN SOUP WITH RED PEPPER MOUSSE

ONION-RYE FLATBREADS

NINO FRANCO PRIMO PROSECCO
DI VALDOBBIADENE '02

ROASTED CAULIFLOWER, ROMAINE, AND RADICCHIO SALAD

SALVIANO ORVIETO CLASSICO
SUPERIORE '03

ROAST TURKEY WITH POMEGRANATE GRAVY

JEWELED RICE WITH DRIED FRUIT

SWISS CHARD PURSES WITH SAUSAGE STUFFING

YALUMBA HANDPICKED TRICENTENARY
VINES GRENACHE '02

POACHED PEARS WITH QUINCE PASTE IN PARMESAN CLOAKS

CRANBERRY EGGNOG TART WITH CANDIED-ORANGE AND CRANBERRY COMPOTE

FLORIO FINE DOLCE AMBRA MARSALA

PUMPKIN SOUP WITH RED PEPPER MOUSSE

SERVES 8 TO 10 (MAKES ABOUT 14 CUPS)
Active time: 1 hr   Start to finish: 3 hr (includes chilling mousse)

For mousse
- 1 (12-oz) jar roasted red peppers, drained, rinsed, and patted dry
- 1 tablespoon extra-virgin olive oil
- 1 teaspoon Sherry vinegar
- ¼ teaspoon hot smoked paprika
- ¼ teaspoon salt
- ½ teaspoon unflavored gelatin (from a ¼-oz envelope)
- 2 tablespoons water
- ⅓ cup chilled heavy cream

For soup
- 5 carrots, chopped (1½ cups)
- 1 large onion, chopped
- 2 garlic cloves, minced
- 1 Turkish or ½ California bay leaf
- 3 tablespoons extra-virgin olive oil
- 1 (4- to 4½-lb) pumpkin or butternut squash, seeded, peeled, and cut into 1-inch pieces (9 cups)
- 1 teaspoon salt
- ¾ teaspoon ground cumin
- ¼ teaspoon black pepper
- 5 cups reduced-sodium chicken broth (40 fl oz)
- 3½ cups water

Accompaniment: **onion-rye flatbreads (recipe follows)**

Make mousse:
► Purée peppers, oil, vinegar, paprika, and salt in a blender or food processor until very smooth.
► Sprinkle gelatin over water in a 1-quart heavy saucepan and let stand 2 minutes to soften. Heat mixture over low heat, stirring, just until gelatin is dissolved. Remove from heat and whisk in pepper purée 1 tablespoon at a time.
► Beat cream in a bowl with an electric mixer at medium speed until it just holds soft peaks. Fold in pepper mixture gently but thoroughly, then cover surface of mousse with plastic wrap and chill until set, at least 2 hours.
Make soup while mousse chills:
► Cook carrots, onion, garlic, and bay leaf in oil in a 6- to 8-quart heavy pot over moderate heat, stirring occasionally, until vegetables are softened, 5 to 6 minutes. Add pumpkin, salt, cumin, and pepper and cook, stirring occasionally, until

pumpkin begins to soften around edges, about 15 minutes. Stir in broth and water and bring to a boil, then reduce heat and simmer, covered, until vegetables are very tender, 35 to 45 minutes. Discard bay leaf.
► Blend soup in batches in cleaned blender until smooth (use caution when blending hot liquids), transferring to a bowl.
► Just before serving, return soup to pot and reheat over low heat. Ladle soup into bowls and top each serving with 1½ tablespoons mousse.

Cooks' notes:
• Soup can be made 3 days ahead and cooled, uncovered, then chilled, covered. Reheat as directed above.
• Mousse can be chilled up to 2 days.

ONION-RYE FLATBREADS

SERVES 8 TO 10
Active time: 30 min   Start to finish: 3 hr (includes cooling)

- 1 large onion, finely chopped (1¼ cups)
- ¼ cup extra-virgin olive oil
- 1½ teaspoons salt
- 1 (¼-oz) package active dry yeast (2½ teaspoons)
- 1 tablespoon honey
- 1 cup warm milk (105–115°F)
- 2 cups all-purpose flour plus additional for kneading
- 1 cup rye flour
- ¾ teaspoon cracked black pepper
  Cornmeal for sprinkling
- 1 large egg yolk, lightly beaten with 1 tablespoon water
- 2 teaspoons caraway seeds

Make dough:
► Cook onion in oil with ¼ teaspoon salt in an 8- to 9-inch nonstick skillet over moderately low heat, stirring, until softened, about 6 minutes, then cool.
► Stir together yeast, honey, and ¼ cup milk in a small bowl and let stand until foamy, about 5 minutes. (If mixture doesn't foam, discard and start over with new yeast.)
► Stir together flours, pepper, and remaining 1¼ teaspoons salt in a large bowl, then add yeast mixture, onion mixture, and remaining ¾ cup milk, stirring until a soft dough forms. Turn out dough onto a floured surface and knead, adding just enough additional flour to prevent sticking, until smooth and elastic, about 8 minutes.

▶ Form dough into a ball and transfer to an oiled large bowl, turning to coat. Cover bowl with a clean kitchen towel and let dough rise in a draft-free place at warm room temperature until doubled in bulk, at least 1 hour (see cooks' note, below).

Shape and bake bread:

▶ Oil 2 large baking sheets and sprinkle with cornmeal, shaking off excess.

▶ Turn out dough onto a lightly floured surface and knead several times to remove air. Divide dough in half and roll out 1 half with a floured rolling pin into a 12-inch round (½ inch thick). Transfer round to one of baking sheets and prick all over at 1-inch intervals with a fork, then cover loosely with oiled plastic wrap (oiled side down). Make another round in same manner and transfer to other baking sheet. Let rounds rise slightly in a draft-free place at warm room temperature 30 minutes.

▶ While rounds rise, put oven racks in upper and lower thirds of oven and preheat oven to 400°F.

▶ Gently brush rounds with some egg wash, being careful not to deflate dough, then sprinkle with caraway seeds.

▶ Bake, switching position of sheets halfway through baking, until tops are golden and bottoms sound hollow when tapped, 12 to 16 minutes total. Transfer flatbreads to a rack to cool slightly. Serve warm or at room temperature.

Cooks' notes:

• Ball of dough can be allowed to rise in the refrigerator, bowl covered with plastic wrap (instead of kitchen towel), up to 1 day. Bring to room temperature before shaping.

• Flatbreads can be baked 1 week ahead, cooled completely, and frozen, wrapped in foil. Thaw, then reheat, wrapped in foil, in a preheated 350°F oven until warm.

ROASTED CAULIFLOWER, ROMAINE, AND RADICCHIO SALAD

SERVES 8 TO 10

Active time: 45 min   Start to finish: 1¼ hr

  1 large head cauliflower (3 to 3½ lb), cut into 1-inch-wide florets (9 cups)
 ½ cup plus 1 tablespoon extra-virgin olive oil
 ¾ teaspoon salt
 ¼ teaspoon black pepper
 ¼ cup white-wine vinegar
1½ tablespoons finely chopped shallot
  2 heads romaine (2 lb total), cut crosswise into ¼-inch-wide strips
  1 large head radicchio (¾ lb), cut crosswise into ¼-inch-wide strips
  1 cup loosely packed fresh flat-leaf parsley leaves (from 1 bunch)
 ½ cup hazelnuts (2¼ oz), toasted (see Tips, page 8), any loose skins rubbed off in a kitchen towel, and nuts coarsely chopped

▶ Put oven rack in middle position and preheat oven to 450°F.

▶ Toss cauliflower with ¼ cup oil, ½ teaspoon salt, and ⅛ teaspoon pepper in a large bowl. Spread in 1 layer in a shallow baking pan (1 inch deep) and roast, turning over with tongs halfway through roasting, until tender and golden brown, 25 to 30 minutes total. Cool in pan on a rack, then transfer to large bowl.

▶ Whisk together vinegar, shallot, remaining ¼ teaspoon salt, and remaining ⅛ teaspoon pepper in a small bowl, then add remaining 5 tablespoons oil in a slow stream, whisking until emulsified. Add half of dressing to cauliflower and toss to coat. Add romaine, radicchio, parsley, half of nuts, and remaining dressing to cauliflower and toss to coat. Season with salt and pepper and sprinkle with remaining nuts.

Cooks' notes:

• Cauliflower can be roasted and cooled 4 hours ahead, then kept, covered, at room temperature.

• Hazelnuts can be toasted and chopped 1 day ahead and kept in an airtight container at room temperature.

• Romaine, radicchio, and parsley can be washed and dried 1 day ahead and chilled separately in sealed plastic bags lined with paper towels.

ROAST TURKEY WITH POMEGRANATE GRAVY

SERVES 8 TO 10
Active time: 1¼ hr   Start to finish: 4½ hr (includes making turkey giblet stock)

For turkey

- 1 (14- to 16-lb) turkey, any feathers and quills removed with tweezers or needlenose pliers, and neck and giblets (excluding liver) reserved for making stock
- 1¼ sticks unsalted butter, 5 tablespoons softened and 5 tablespoons melted
- 1 tablespoon salt
- 1½ teaspoons black pepper
- 1 onion, quartered
- 4 large fresh thyme sprigs

For gravy

- ½ cup sugar
- ½ cup plus 1 tablespoon fresh pomegranate juice (see cooks' note, below)
  Pan juices (and roasting pan) from turkey
  About 3 cups hot turkey giblet stock (page 63)
- 1 cup water
- 6½ tablespoons all-purpose flour

Special equipment: a small metal skewer; kitchen string; a flat rack or V-rack; an instant-read thermometer
Garnish: quartered pomegranates

Roast turkey:

▶ Put oven rack in lower third of oven and preheat oven to 350°F.

▶ Rinse turkey inside and out and pat dry. Working from neck (small) cavity, run your fingers between skin and meat to loosen skin from breast, legs, and thighs, being careful not to tear skin. Rub softened butter between skin and flesh, then sprinkle turkey cavities and skin with salt and pepper. Fold neck skin under body and secure with metal skewer and fold wing tips under breast. Stuff large cavity with onion and thyme sprigs and tie drumsticks together with kitchen string. Brush skin all over with some melted butter.

▶ Put turkey on rack in a large flameproof roasting pan and roast, basting with some melted butter and/or pan juices every 20 minutes (if turkey is browning too fast, cover loosely with foil), until thermometer inserted into fleshy part of a thigh (do not touch bone) registers 170°F, 2½ to 3½ hours.

▶ Carefully tilt turkey so any juices from inside large cavity run into roasting pan, then transfer turkey to a platter (do not clean roasting pan) and let stand, loosely covered, 30 minutes (temperature of thigh meat will rise to 180°F).

Make gravy while turkey stands:

▶ Cook sugar in a dry 1-quart heavy saucepan over moderate heat, undisturbed, until it begins to melt. Continue to cook, stirring occasionally with a fork, until sugar is melted into a deep golden caramel. Add ½ cup pomegranate juice (use caution; mixture will bubble and steam vigorously) and simmer over low heat, stirring occasionally, until caramel is dissolved. Remove syrup from heat.

▶ Pour pan juices through a fine-mesh sieve into a 1-quart glass measure or bowl, then skim off fat and reserve ¼ cup of it. Add enough turkey stock to pan juices to total 3½ cups liquid. Straddle roasting pan across 2 burners, then add water and deglaze pan by boiling over high heat, stirring and scraping up brown bits, 1 minute. Pour through fine-mesh sieve into glass measure with stock.

▶ Whisk together reserved fat and flour in a 3-quart heavy saucepan and cook roux over moderately low heat, whisking, until pale golden, 7 to 10 minutes. Add hot stock mixture in a stream, whisking constantly to prevent lumps. Bring to a boil, whisking, and add pomegranate syrup, then reduce heat and simmer, whisking occasionally, until thickened, about 5 minutes. Stir in any turkey juices accumulated on platter and simmer gravy 1 minute. Season with salt and pepper and stir in remaining tablespoon pomegranate juice.

▶ Remove string and skewer from turkey and discard onion and thyme from cavity. Serve turkey with gravy on the side.

Cooks' notes:

• We found bottled pomegranate juice too sweet for this recipe. Cut 2 to 3 pomegranates in half crosswise, then juice with a manual or electric juicer; alternatively, remove seeds from pomegranate and pulse seeds in a food processor until juicy, then transfer seeds to a sieve and let drain, pressing on and discarding solids.

• Pomegranate syrup can be made 1 day ahead and kept, covered, at room temperature.

OPPOSITE: **pumpkin soup with red pepper mousse; onion-rye flatbreads**

TURKEY GIBLET STOCK

MAKES ABOUT 3 CUPS

Active time: 15 min   Start to finish: 1½ hr

      Neck and giblets (excluding liver) from turkey
         (page 60), cut into 1-inch pieces
1   tablespoon vegetable oil
1   celery rib, coarsely chopped
1   carrot, coarsely chopped
1   onion, coarsely chopped
1   garlic clove, smashed
2   fresh thyme sprigs
4   whole black peppercorns
5   cups water
3   cups reduced-sodium chicken broth (24 fl oz)

▶ Pat neck and giblets dry. Heat oil in a 6-quart heavy pot over moderately high heat until hot but not smoking, then brown neck and giblets, turning occasionally, 8 to 10 minutes. Add celery, carrot, onion, garlic, thyme, and peppercorns and sauté, stirring occasionally, until vegetables are browned, 7 to 9 minutes. Add water and broth and bring to a boil, then reduce heat and simmer, uncovered, until liquid is reduced to about 3 cups, 45 to 60 minutes.
▶ Pour stock through a fine-mesh sieve into a large bowl, discarding solids. If using stock right away, skim off and discard any fat.

Cooks' note:

• Stock can be made 2 days ahead and cooled completely, uncovered, then chilled, covered. Skim off fat before using (fat will be easier to remove when cool).

CLOCKWISE FROM TOP LEFT: roasted cauliflower, romaine, and radicchio salad; jeweled rice with dried fruit; roast turkey with pomegranate gravy; Swiss chard purses with sausage stuffing

JEWELED RICE WITH DRIED FRUIT

SERVES 8 TO 10

Active time: 25 min   Start to finish: 1½ hr (includes standing time)

3   cups basmati rice (1¼ lb)
4   qt water
3   tablespoons salt
½   cup dried apricots (3½ oz), quartered
½   cup golden raisins (3 oz)
½   cup dried cranberries (2 oz)
1   stick (½ cup) unsalted butter
½   teaspoon ground cardamom
½   teaspoon black pepper
½   cup coarsely chopped shelled unsalted pistachios
         (not dyed red; 2½ oz)

▶ Rinse rice in several changes of cold water in a large bowl until water runs clear. Drain in a large sieve.
▶ Bring water and salt to a boil in a 6-quart heavy pot, then add rice and boil, uncovered, stirring occasionally, 5 minutes from time water returns to boil. Drain rice in sieve.
▶ Toss together dried fruit in a bowl. Melt 6 tablespoons butter with cardamom and pepper in cleaned and dried pot, stirring to combine, then alternately layer rice and dried fruit over it, beginning and ending with rice and mounding loosely. Make 5 or 6 holes in rice to bottom of pot with round handle of a wooden spoon, then cover pot with a kitchen towel and a heavy lid. Fold edges of towel up over lid (to keep towel from burning) and cook rice over moderately low heat, undisturbed, until tender and a crust forms on bottom, 30 to 35 minutes. Remove from heat and let rice stand, tightly covered and undisturbed, at least 30 minutes.
▶ Heat remaining 2 tablespoons butter in a small skillet over moderate heat and cook pistachios, stirring, until lightly browned, 2 to 3 minutes.
▶ Spoon loose rice onto a platter, then break crust into 1-inch pieces and scatter over rice. Sprinkle with pistachios.

Cooks' notes:

• Rice can be parboiled and drained 4 hours ahead and transferred to a bowl. Keep, covered with a dampened kitchen towel, at room temperature.
• Rice can stand off heat up to 1 hour.
• If you're short on time, you can skip letting the rice stand after cooking: Spoon loose rice onto a platter and then dip bottom of pot into a large bowl of cold water for 30 seconds to loosen crust.

SWISS CHARD PURSES WITH SAUSAGE STUFFING

SERVES 8 TO 10

Active time: 1½ hr   Start to finish: 2½ hr

- 5 cups cubed (1-inch) day-old bread (from a baguette or country loaf)
- 2 cups whole milk
- 2 large leeks, outer leaves removed and cut lengthwise into 25 (12- by ¼-inch) strips, then remaining white and pale green parts chopped (2 cups)
- 4½ tablespoons extra-virgin olive oil
- 1 lb bulk sausage (sweet Italian or breakfast sausage)
- 2 lb large green Swiss chard leaves, stems trimmed flush with leaves and then finely chopped and leaves left whole
- ½ teaspoon salt
- ½ teaspoon black pepper
- 2 large eggs, lightly beaten
- ½ cup reduced-sodium chicken broth

Make stuffing:

▶ Soak bread cubes in milk in a large bowl until softened,

20 to 30 minutes. Squeeze out milk, discarding it, then crumble bread into bowl.

▶ Wash chopped leeks well in a bowl of cold water, agitating them, then lift out and transfer to a sieve to drain.

▶ Heat 1 tablespoon oil in a 12-inch heavy skillet over moderately high heat until hot but not smoking. Crumble sausage into skillet and brown, breaking up lumps with a fork, about 3 minutes. Transfer sausage with a slotted spoon to bowl with bread. Add 2 tablespoons oil to skillet, then sauté chopped leek, chard stems, ¼ teaspoon salt, and ¼ teaspoon pepper, stirring frequently, until vegetables are tender and just beginning to brown, 10 to 15 minutes. Stir vegetables into bread mixture, then cool until warm, about 15 minutes. Stir remaining ¼ teaspoon salt and ¼ teaspoon pepper into eggs, then stir eggs into bread mixture.

Prepare leek ribbons and chard leaves:

▶ Wash leek strips, then blanch in a large pot of boiling salted water, uncovered, 2 minutes and transfer with tongs to a bowl of ice and cold water (reserve water in pot). Transfer to a colander and drain well, then transfer to paper towels and pat dry. Blanch chard leaves in water just until wilted, about 30 seconds, and transfer with a slotted spoon to ice water to cool. Drain chard leaves in colander.

Make purses:

▶ Put oven rack in middle position and preheat oven to 350°F.

▶ Spread 1 chard leaf on a work surface, using smaller leaves to patch any holes if necessary. Chard-leaf wrapper should be about 8 by 5 inches (if it's smaller, overlap several small leaves to form a larger wrapper). Mound ¼ cup stuffing in center, then gather chard up over filling to form a purse and tie closed with a leek strip. (You have extra strips in case some break.) Make 19 more purses in same manner.

▶ Oil a 3-quart gratin or other shallow baking dish. Stand purses upright in dish and drizzle with remaining 1½ tablespoons oil. Add broth to dish and cover purses with a sheet of wax paper or parchment, then loosely cover with foil. Bake purses until stuffing is warmed through and egg is set (cut one open on bottom to check), 35 to 40 minutes.

Cooks' notes:

• Stuffing can be made 2 days ahead and cooled completely, uncovered, then chilled, covered.

• Purses can be assembled (but not baked) 1 day ahead and chilled in gratin dish (without broth), covered. Bring to room temperature, then add broth before baking.

POACHED PEARS WITH QUINCE PASTE IN PARMESAN CLOAKS

SERVES 8 TO 10
Active time: 1¾ hr   Start to finish: 5 hr (includes chilling pears and making cloaks)

10 firm-ripe Bosc pears with stems (5 lb total)
¼ cup fresh lemon juice
1 (750-ml) bottle dry white wine
¾ cup sugar
1 vanilla bean
2 (3- by 1-inch) strips fresh lemon zest
1 lb Spanish or Portuguese quince paste (also called *membrillo*; see Sources), cut into 10 equal pieces
10 parmesan cloaks (recipe follows)

Special equipment: a 1-inch melon-ball cutter
Accompaniment: 1 (2-lb) piece Parmigiano-Reggiano

▶ Peel pears, leaving stems intact, then core from bottom with melon-ball cutter to create a 2½-inch-deep cavity. Rub pears all over with lemon juice in a large bowl.
▶ Bring wine, sugar, vanilla bean, and zest to a boil in a wide 6-quart heavy pot (at least 12 inches in diameter) over moderate heat, stirring until sugar is dissolved. Add pears, arranging them on their sides in 1 layer, along with any lemon juice from bowl (pears will not be covered by liquid), then reduce heat to low and poach pears, covered, turning occasionally, until just tender, 15 to 20 minutes. Carefully transfer pears with a slotted spoon to a 13- by 9-inch baking dish, standing pears upright and reserving liquid in pot.
▶ When pears are cool enough to handle, fill cavities with quince paste and stand pears upright in dish again.
▶ Boil liquid in pot over high heat until syrupy and reduced to about ¾ cup, 10 to 15 minutes. Pour syrup over pears and cool, basting occasionally with syrup. Chill, covered, basting occasionally with syrup, until cold, at least 2 hours.
▶ Drizzle each pear lightly with syrup and slip a parmesan cloak over stem. Serve with cheese shavings on the side.

Cooks' note:
• Pears can be chilled up to 2 days.

PARMESAN CLOAKS

MAKES ABOUT 40 WAFERS
Active time: 1 hr   Start to finish: 1 hr

Though you need only 10 cloaks to top the pears, these melt-in-your-mouth wafers are so delicious, your guests will clamor for seconds.

1 oz finely grated Parmigiano-Reggiano (½ cup; see Tips, page 8)
⅓ cup plus 1 tablespoon all-purpose flour
2 tablespoons yellow cornmeal
1½ teaspoons sugar
½ teaspoon baking powder
½ teaspoon salt
2 tablespoons unsalted butter, softened
1 large egg white, at room temperature for 30 minutes
½ cup whole milk, at room temperature

Special equipment: 2 nonstick baking sheets or shallow baking pans; a muffin tin with 6 (½-cup) muffin cups

▶ Put oven rack in middle position and preheat oven to 350°F. Butter baking sheets.
▶ Stir together cheese, flour, cornmeal, sugar, baking powder, and salt. Mix together butter and egg white in a blender at low speed, then add milk and cheese mixture and blend just until smooth.
▶ Working in batches of 6, drop scant teaspoons of batter about 3 inches apart onto a buttered baking sheet. Spread each dollop with the back of a spoon into a 3-inch round (don't worry if batter doesn't spread evenly). Make a ½-inch hole in center of each round with your fingertip.
▶ Bake wafers, 1 sheet at a time, until golden, about 5 minutes. To form cloaks, immediately remove wafers with a very thin metal spatula and drape into muffin cups. (Wafers will crisp as they cool.) If wafers harden before draping, return to oven for a few seconds to soften. Cool baking sheets between batches and rebutter sheets only if wafers begin to stick. Make more wafers in same manner.

Cooks' note:
• Wafers can be made 3 days ahead and kept, layered between sheets of wax paper, in a large airtight container at room temperature. Recrisp on an ungreased baking sheet in a preheated 300°F oven 1 to 2 minutes.

CRANBERRY EGGNOG TART

SERVES 8 TO 10
Active time: 45 min   Start to finish: 5¼ hr (includes making jam and cooling tart)

For cookie crust

1¼ cups all-purpose flour
¼ cup sugar
½ teaspoon salt
7 tablespoons unsalted butter, softened
1 large egg

For filling

1½ (8-oz) packages cream cheese, softened
2 tablespoons crème fraîche or heavy cream
½ cup plus 2 tablespoons sugar
2 whole large eggs
2 large egg yolks
3 tablespoons bourbon
1 teaspoon vanilla
   Scant ½ teaspoon freshly grated nutmeg
   Scant ¼ teaspoon salt

   Cranberry jam (recipe follows)
¼ cup water

Special equipment: a 10-inch fluted metal quiche pan (2 inches deep) with a removable bottom; 3 cups pie weights or raw rice; a pie shield (optional); a small offset spatula
Accompaniment: candied-orange and cranberry compote (page 67)

Make crust:

▶ Pulse together all crust ingredients in a food processor just until a dough forms. Press dough evenly onto bottom and up side of quiche pan with floured fingers. Chill shell until firm, about 30 minutes. Put oven rack in middle position and preheat oven to 350°F.
▶ Line shell with foil and fill with pie weights, then bake until edge is pale golden, 20 to 25 minutes. Carefully remove foil and pie weights and bake shell until edge is golden and bottom is pale golden, 15 to 20 minutes more. Cool completely in pan on a rack.
▶ Reduce oven temperature to 300°F.

Make filling:

▸ Blend cream cheese, crème fraîche, and sugar in cleaned food processor until creamy, about 1 minute. Add whole eggs, yolks, bourbon, vanilla, nutmeg, and salt and process until smooth.

▸ Melt jam with water in a small heavy saucepan over moderately low heat, stirring until smooth. Spread half of jam evenly over bottom of shell (reserving remaining jam in saucepan). Let layer of jam stand until set, about 5 minutes, then gently pour cream cheese mixture over it.

Bake tart:

▸ Cover edge of tart shell with pie shield or foil and bake until filling is set but still trembles slightly in center, 35 to 40 minutes (filling will continue to set as it cools).

▸ Cool tart completely in pan on a rack. Reheat remaining jam over low heat, stirring, until pourable, then pour over filling and spread evenly with offset spatula. Chill tart, uncovered, until cold, at least 2 hours.

▸ Just before serving, remove side of pan.

Cooks' notes:

• Tart shell can be baked 3 days ahead and cooled completely, then kept in pan, wrapped in plastic wrap, at cool room temperature.

• Tart can be chilled up to 2 days (cover after 2 hours).

CRANBERRY JAM
MAKES ABOUT 2 CUPS
Active time: 15 min   Start to finish: 1 hr

  1 **(12-oz) bag fresh or frozen cranberries (not thawed)**
  1 **cup sugar**
  ½ **cup fresh orange juice**
  1 **cup water**

▸ Bring all ingredients to a boil in a 2-quart heavy saucepan over moderate heat, stirring occasionally. Reduce heat and simmer, uncovered, stirring occasionally, until slightly thickened, about 20 minutes (jam will continue to thicken as it cools).

▸ Force jam through a fine-mesh sieve into a bowl, discarding skins and seeds. Cool, stirring occasionally.

Cooks' note:

• Jam can be made 4 days ahead and chilled, covered.

CANDIED-ORANGE AND CRANBERRY COMPOTE
MAKES ABOUT 2 CUPS
Active time: 30 min   Start to finish: 2 hr (includes chilling)

This is a sweet dessert compote—it does not go with the turkey. The oranges are cooked to make sure all the bitterness is released, so it's important that they're sliced very thin—an extremely sharp thin-bladed knife is best for the task.

  ¾ **cup water**
  ¾ **cup sugar**
  1 **large navel orange, quartered lengthwise and sliced crosswise paper thin (including peel)**
  ¼ **cup fresh or frozen cranberries (not thawed), thinly sliced**
  1 **tablespoon Grand Marnier or other orange-flavored liqueur**

▸ Bring water and sugar to a boil in a 2-quart heavy saucepan over moderate heat, stirring until sugar is dissolved. Add orange and gently simmer over moderately low heat, uncovered, stirring occasionally, until peel begins to turn translucent and syrup is reduced to about ⅔ cup, 25 to 35 minutes.

▸ Transfer to a heatproof bowl and cool. Stir in cranberries and Grand Marnier and chill, covered, until cold, about 1 hour.

Cooks' note:

• Compote can be chilled up to 4 days.

CASUAL VEGETARIAN THANKSGIVING

SERVES 6

**BRUSCHETTE WITH CHICKPEA PURÉE
AND CHOPPED ARUGULA SALAD**

BROILED POLENTA STICKS

**ROASTED DELICATA SQUASH AND
MUSHROOMS WITH THYME**

SAUTÉED BROCCOLINI WITH GARLIC

ROASTED VEGETABLE GRAVY

FRIZZLED ONION

CHÂTEAU DES TOURS BROUILLY '03

MERINGUE ROULADE WITH ANISE CREAM

BAKED FIGS IN LEMON SYRUP

BRUSCHETTE WITH CHICKPEA PURÉE AND CHOPPED ARUGULA SALAD

SERVES 6 (FIRST COURSE)
Active time: 50 min   Start to finish: 1½ hr

For toasts
  6 (¾-inch-thick) slices of bread from 1 (7- to 8-inch) round country loaf
  2 tablespoons olive oil

For topping
  1 (19-oz) can chickpeas, rinsed and drained (2 cups)
  ⅓ cup water
  2 tablespoons olive oil
  1½ tablespoons fresh lemon juice
  ½ teaspoon salt
     Chopped arugula salad (recipe follows)

Make toasts:
▶ Put oven rack in middle position and preheat oven to 425°F.
▶ Arrange bread slices in 1 layer on a large baking sheet and brush top of each with 1 teaspoon oil. Bake until golden, about 12 minutes.

Make chickpea purée:
▶ Slip off skins from chickpeas with your fingers (discard skins). Blend chickpeas, water, oil, lemon juice, and salt in a food processor until very smooth (mixture will appear whipped).

Assemble *bruschette*:
▶ Spread toasts with chickpea purée and serve topped with arugula salad.

Cooks' note:
• Chickpea purée can be made 2 days ahead and chilled in an airtight container. Bring to room temperature before serving.

CHOPPED ARUGULA SALAD

SERVES 6 (AS PART OF FIRST COURSE)
Active time: 30 min   Start to finish: 1 hr

  1 garlic clove
  3 tablespoons olive oil
  1½ tablespoons red-wine vinegar
  ¼ teaspoon salt
  ¼ teaspoon black pepper
  ⅛ teaspoon sugar
  2 red bell peppers
  1 small red onion, halved lengthwise, then very thinly sliced crosswise
  ¾ lb arugula, tough stems discarded and leaves cut crosswise into ⅓-inch-wide strips (6 cups)

▶ Mince garlic and mash to a paste with a pinch of salt, then transfer to a large bowl. Whisk in oil, vinegar, salt, pepper, and sugar.
▶ Roast bell peppers on racks of gas burners over high heat, turning with tongs, until skins are blackened, 12 to 15 minutes. (Or broil peppers on a broiler pan about 5 inches from heat, turning occasionally, about 15 minutes.) Transfer to a bowl and cover tightly with plastic wrap, then let stand 20 minutes.
▶ When cool enough to handle, peel peppers, discarding stems and seeds. Cut peppers lengthwise into 1-inch-wide strips, then cut strips crosswise into ¼-inch-wide pieces. Add peppers to dressing along with onion and arugula and toss to coat.

Cooks' notes:
• Dressing can be made 1 day ahead and chilled in an airtight container. Shake before using.
• Bell peppers can be roasted 1 day ahead and chilled, covered with plastic wrap.
• Arugula can be washed and dried (but not chopped) 1 day ahead and chilled in a sealed plastic bag lined with paper towels.

OPPOSITE: roasted delicata squash and mushrooms with thyme; sautéed Broccolini with garlic; broiled polenta sticks; roasted vegetable gravy; frizzled onion

BROILED POLENTA STICKS
SERVES 6 (AS PART OF MAIN COURSE)
Active time: 30 min   Start to finish: 1 hr

The roasted squash and mushrooms and sautéed Broccolini (recipes follow) are meant to be piled onto these creamy polenta sticks, then topped with the roasted vegetable gravy and frizzled onion (page 73).

6½ cups cold water
1½ teaspoons salt
2 cups yellow cornmeal (not stone-ground)
2 teaspoons olive oil plus additional for brushing
½ oz finely grated Parmigiano-Reggiano (⅓ cup; see Tips, page 8)

▸ Brush a 13- by 9-inch baking pan with water.
▸ Combine 6½ cups cold water with salt and cornmeal in a 5-quart heavy pot and bring to a boil over moderate heat, whisking. Reduce heat to moderately low and cook, stirring constantly with a long-handled wooden spoon, until polenta begins to pull away from side of pot, 20 to 25 minutes. Pour polenta into baking pan, spreading evenly with a dampened heatproof rubber spatula. Cool in pan on a rack until polenta is lukewarm and set, about 20 minutes.
▸ Brush a baking sheet with olive oil and invert baking pan with polenta onto sheet to unmold.
▸ Preheat broiler.
▸ Brush polenta with 2 teaspoons oil and sprinkle with cheese. Broil about 4 inches from heat until pale golden, 5 to 7 minutes. Cool 5 minutes, then cut into 3- by 1½-inch sticks.

Cooks' note:
• Polenta can be cooked and unmolded 1 day ahead. Chill on oiled baking sheet, surface covered with lightly oiled parchment (oiled side down), then tightly covered with plastic wrap. Bring to room temperature before brushing with oil, sprinkling with cheese, and broiling.

ROASTED DELICATA SQUASH AND MUSHROOMS WITH THYME
SERVES 6 (AS PART OF MAIN COURSE)
Active time: 25 min   Start to finish: 1 hr

Delicata squash, with its long narrow shape, is easy to work with, and its skin is edible, too.

6 tablespoons olive oil
1 tablespoon chopped fresh thyme
¾ teaspoon salt
½ teaspoon black pepper
2 lb delicata squash (3 medium), halved lengthwise, seeded, and cut crosswise into ½-inch-wide slices
2 lb mixed fresh mushrooms such as cremini, shiitake, and oyster, trimmed (stems discarded if using shiitakes) and halved (quartered if large)

▸ Put oven racks in upper and lower thirds of oven and preheat oven to 425°F.
▸ Stir together oil, thyme, salt, and pepper. Toss squash with 2 tablespoons thyme oil in a shallow baking pan (½ to 1 inch deep) and arrange in 1 layer. Toss mushrooms with remaining ¼ cup thyme oil in another shallow baking pan (½ to 1 inch deep) and arrange in 1 layer. Roast squash and mushrooms, stirring occasionally and switching position of pans halfway through roasting, until vegetables are tender and liquid mushrooms give off is evaporated, 25 to 30 minutes.

SAUTÉED BROCCOLINI WITH GARLIC
SERVES 6 (AS PART OF MAIN COURSE)
Active time: 20 min   Start to finish: 25 min

1½ lb Broccolini (sometimes called baby broccoli; 3 bunches), ends trimmed
¼ cup olive oil
2 garlic cloves, finely chopped
½ teaspoon salt
¼ teaspoon black pepper

▸ Cook Broccolini in a 6- to 8-quart pot of boiling salted water (see Tips, page 8) until stems are crisp-tender, about 5 minutes, then drain in a colander.
▸ Heat 2 tablespoons oil in a 12-inch heavy skillet over moderately high heat until hot but not smoking, then sauté

half of garlic, stirring, until pale golden, about 30 seconds. Add half of Broccolini, ¼ teaspoon salt, and ⅛ teaspoon pepper and cook, stirring, until heated through, about 2 minutes. Transfer to a serving dish and repeat with remaining ingredients.

ROASTED VEGETABLE GRAVY
MAKES ABOUT 3½ CUPS
Active time: 45 min   Start to finish: 2¾ hr (includes making stock)

- 2 tablespoons plus 1 teaspoon unsalted butter
- 3 tablespoons plus 1 teaspoon all-purpose flour
   Roasted vegetable stock (recipe follows), heated
- ¼ teaspoon salt
- ¼ teaspoon black pepper

▶ Melt butter in a 1½- to 2-quart heavy saucepan over moderate heat, then add flour and cook roux, stirring, until pale golden, 2 to 3 minutes. Add stock in a stream, whisking constantly to prevent lumps, and bring to a boil, whisking. Reduce heat and simmer, whisking occasionally, until slightly thickened, about 8 minutes. Stir in salt and pepper.

Cooks' note:
• Gravy can be made 1 day ahead and cooled completely, uncovered, then chilled in an airtight container.

ROASTED VEGETABLE STOCK
MAKES ABOUT 3½ CUPS
Active time: 30 min   Start to finish: 2 hr

- ¾ lb cremini mushrooms, halved
- ½ lb shallots, left unpeeled, then quartered
- ½ lb carrots (3 medium), cut into 1-inch pieces
- 1 red bell pepper, cut into 1-inch pieces
- 2 garlic cloves, coarsely chopped
- 4 fresh flat-leaf parsley sprigs (including long stems)
- 3 fresh thyme sprigs
- 1 tablespoon olive oil
- ½ cup dry white wine
- 1 Turkish or ½ California bay leaf
- ½ cup canned crushed tomatoes
- 1 qt water
- ¾ teaspoon salt

▶ Put oven rack in middle position and preheat oven to 425°F.
▶ Toss together mushrooms, shallots, carrots, bell pepper, garlic, parsley and thyme sprigs, and oil in a flameproof roasting pan. Roast, stirring occasionally, until vegetables are golden, 35 to 40 minutes.
▶ Transfer vegetables with a slotted spoon to a 4-quart saucepan. Straddle roasting pan across 2 burners, then add wine and deglaze pan by boiling over moderate heat, stirring and scraping up brown bits, 1 to 2 minutes. Transfer to saucepan and add bay leaf, tomatoes, water, and salt. Bring to a boil, then reduce heat and simmer, covered, stirring occasionally, 45 minutes. Pour stock through a fine-mesh sieve into a bowl, pressing hard on and then discarding solids.

Cooks' note:
• Stock can be made ahead and cooled completely, uncovered, then chilled, covered, 1 week or frozen in an airtight container up to 1 month.

FRIZZLED ONION
MAKES ABOUT 3 CUPS
Active time: 30 min   Start to finish: 30 min

- 1 large onion (¾ lb), halved lengthwise
   About 3 cups vegetable oil for frying

Special equipment: **a Japanese Benriner (see Sources) or other adjustable-blade slicer; a deep-fat thermometer**

▶ Very thinly slice onion lengthwise with slicer.
▶ Heat 2 inches oil in a 2-quart heavy saucepan over moderate heat until thermometer registers 340°F, then fry onion in 6 batches, stirring occasionally, until golden brown, 1 to 1½ minutes per batch (watch closely; onion can burn easily). Quickly transfer each batch with a slotted spoon to fresh paper towels to drain, then sprinkle lightly with salt. (Onion will crisp as it cools.) Return oil to 340°F between batches.

Cooks' note:
• Onions can be fried 6 hours ahead and kept, uncovered, at room temperature.

MERINGUE ROULADE WITH ANISE CREAM

SERVES 8 TO 10
Active time: 20 min   Start to finish: 1¼ hr

For meringue
Vegetable oil for greasing pan
5   **large egg whites**
⅛   **teaspoon salt**
1¼ **cups superfine granulated sugar**
For anise cream
2   **tablespoons regular granulated sugar**
1½ **teaspoons anise seeds**
1½ **cups chilled heavy cream**

Special equipment: **parchment paper; an electric coffee/spice grinder**
Accompaniment: **baked figs in lemon syrup (recipe follows)**

Make meringue:
▶ Put oven rack in middle position and preheat oven to 350°F. Lightly brush a 15- by 10-inch shallow baking pan (½ inch to 1 inch deep) with vegetable oil and line bottom and sides of pan with parchment paper, then lightly oil parchment.
▶ Beat whites with salt in a bowl with an electric mixer at medium speed until they just hold soft peaks. Add superfine sugar a little at a time, beating, then increase speed to high and continue to beat until whites hold stiff, glossy peaks, about 2 minutes. Spread meringue evenly in baking pan and bake until top is pale golden and crisp, 20 to 25 minutes (interior of meringue will be soft). Put a sheet of parchment over meringue and invert a rack over parchment, then flip meringue onto rack and remove parchment (from baking pan) from top. Cool meringue completely, about 15 minutes.
Make anise cream and assemble roulade:
▶ Finely grind sugar with anise seeds in coffee/spice grinder. Beat cream in a bowl with cleaned beaters until it just holds soft peaks, then add anise sugar, beating until cream just holds stiff peaks.
▶ Slide meringue (still on parchment) off rack and arrange with a long side nearest you, then spread anise cream evenly over bottom two thirds of meringue, leaving a 1-inch border on each short end. Using parchment as an aid and rolling away from you, roll up meringue. Carefully transfer roulade with 2 metal spatulas to a platter and discard paper.

Cooks' note:
• Roulade can be made 1 day ahead and chilled, covered with plastic wrap.

BAKED FIGS IN LEMON SYRUP

SERVES 6
Active time: 30 min   Start to finish: 1¾ hr

½   **cup water**
½   **cup plus 2 teaspoons sugar**
3   **lemons**
1   **tablespoon unsalted butter, softened**
1½ **lb firm-ripe fresh purple figs, trimmed and halved lengthwise**

▶ Put oven rack in middle position and preheat oven to 350°F.
▶ Boil water and ½ cup sugar in a small saucepan, stirring, until sugar is dissolved. Remove syrup from heat. Squeeze enough juice from 2 lemons to measure ⅓ cup and stir into syrup, then discard lemon halves.
▶ Remove zest from remaining lemon in long strips with a vegetable peeler and, if necessary, trim any white pith from zest with a sharp paring knife. Cut zest lengthwise into thin julienne strips. Reserve lemon.
▶ Blanch zest in a 1- to 1½-quart saucepan of boiling water 1 second, then drain in a sieve and add to syrup.
▶ Cut away any remaining pith from lemon. Working over a bowl, cut segments free from membranes.
▶ Spread butter in a 1½-quart flameproof gratin dish or 10-inch heavy ovenproof skillet. Arrange figs, cut sides up, slightly overlapping in 1 layer. Sprinkle with remaining 2 teaspoons sugar and bake until figs are softened and begin to exude juice but still hold their shape, 25 to 30 minutes.
▶ Transfer figs with a slotted spoon to a shallow serving bowl and put gratin dish or skillet over moderately high heat.
▶ Add syrup and deglaze gratin dish or skillet by boiling until syrup is reduced to about ¾ cup, 6 to 8 minutes. Add lemon segments along with any juices in bowl and pour syrup over figs. Cool to warm or room temperature before serving.

Cooks' note:
• Syrup can be made 1 day ahead and cooled completely, uncovered, then chilled, covered. Bring to room temperature before deglazing gratin dish and adding lemon segments.

SERVES 8

HAZELNUT AND OLIVE RUGELACH

STRIPED BASS IN AGRODOLCE SAUCE

**SHAVED FENNEL, RADISH, AND
GRAPEFRUIT SALAD**

CELERY-ROOT AND POTATO LATKES

YARDEN ODEM ORGANIC VINEYARD
GALILEE CHARDONNAY '02

GINGER DOUGHNUTS

BRANDIED HOT CHOCOLATE

HAZELNUT AND OLIVE RUGELACH
MAKES 32 HORS D'OEUVRES
Active time: 45 min   Start to finish: 7½ hr (includes chilling dough)

These savory rugelach are made with a cream-cheese-based dough, which softens quickly. If the dough becomes tricky to work with, chill it until firm, then continue with the recipe.

⅓ cup hazelnuts (1½ oz)
1 cup all-purpose flour plus additional for dusting
¾ teaspoon dried thyme
½ teaspoon coarsely ground black pepper
¼ teaspoon salt
1 stick (½ cup) unsalted butter, softened
4 oz cream cheese, softened
⅓ cup brine-cured green olives (preferably Sicilian), patted dry, pitted, and very finely chopped

Special equipment: **4 (17- by 12-inch) sheets parchment paper**

▶ Put oven rack in middle position and preheat oven to 350°F.
▶ Toast hazelnuts in a shallow (1 inch deep) baking pan in oven until golden, about 10 minutes. (Leave oven on.) Cool slightly, then rub off any loose skins in a kitchen towel while nuts are still warm. When nuts are cool enough to handle, very finely chop.
▶ Whisk together flour, thyme, pepper, and salt in a bowl. Beat together butter and cream cheese in a large bowl with an electric mixer until combined well. Add flour mixture and mix at low speed until a soft dough forms. Gather dough into a ball, then halve dough and wrap each half in plastic wrap. Flatten each half (in plastic wrap) and form into a 4-inch disk. Chill until firm, about 6 hours. Bring dough to cool room temperature (this will take 15 to 20 minutes) before rolling out.
▶ Remove and discard plastic wrap from 1 half of dough, keeping other half wrapped and chilled. Put unwrapped dough in center of 1 sheet of floured parchment paper. Dust dough with flour and cover with another sheet of parchment, then roll out dough into a 9-inch round (⅛ inch thick). Carefully peel off top sheet of parchment and set aside. (If dough is too sticky to remove parchment cleanly, chill until firm, 10 to 20 minutes.) Repeat procedure with remaining half dough. Sprinkle hazelnuts and olives evenly over rounds of dough, then reposition top sheets of parchment on dough and press gently to help nuts and olives adhere.
▶ Remove and discard top sheets of parchment and cut each round into 16 wedges. Roll up 1 wedge of dough as tightly as possible toward pointed end and transfer to an ungreased large baking sheet. Repeat procedure with remaining wedges of dough. (If dough becomes too soft, chill until firmer.)
▶ Bake until golden, 20 to 25 minutes. Cool on baking sheet on a rack. Serve warm or at room temperature.

Cooks' notes:
• Dough (in disks, not rolled out) can be chilled up to 1 day or frozen up to 1 month.
• Rugelach are best eaten the day they are made but can be made 1 day ahead and kept in an airtight container at room temperature. Reheat in a preheated 325°F oven 10 to 12 minutes.

STRIPED BASS IN AGRODOLCE SAUCE
SERVES 8
Active time: 40 min   Start to finish: 2 hr

Agrodolce, an Italian sweet-and-sour sauce, combines vinegar and sugar. For tender sauce results, be sure to peel off any leathery outer layers from the shallots.

½ cup olive oil
1½ lb shallots (10 large or 15 medium), trimmed, leaving root end intact, and quartered lengthwise (halved if small)
1½ cups dry red wine
1 cup white balsamic vinegar
⅔ cup water
⅓ cup sugar
¼ cup golden raisins
1¾ teaspoons salt
½ teaspoon black pepper
1 California bay leaf (or 2 Turkish)
8 (6- to 7-oz) pieces farm-raised striped bass fillet (½ inch thick), skinned

Garnish: **chopped fennel fronds**

▶ Heat ¼ cup oil in a 12- to 13-inch heavy skillet over moderately high heat until hot but not smoking, then sauté shallots, stirring occasionally, until browned and just tender, about 8 minutes. Remove from heat and add wine, vinegar, water, sugar, raisins, 1¼ teaspoons salt, ¼ teaspoon pepper, and bay leaf, then return skillet to heat and briskly simmer, stirring occasionally, until shallots are very tender and liquid is thick and syrupy, 40 to 45 minutes. (If liquid is reduced before shallots are tender, add ½ cup water and continue to simmer.) Remove from heat and keep warm, covered.

▶ Pat fish dry, then sprinkle with remaining ½ teaspoon salt and remaining ¼ teaspoon pepper. Fold fillets in half, skinned side in.

▶ Heat 2 tablespoons oil in a 12-inch nonstick skillet over moderately high heat until hot but not smoking, then sauté 4 folded fillets, turning over once, until deep golden, 4 to 6 minutes total. Put cooked fish (still folded) on top of sauce in heavy skillet. Wipe out nonstick skillet and sauté remaining 4 fillets in remaining 2 tablespoons oil in same manner, transferring to sauce.

▶ Cook, partially covered, over moderate heat until fish is just cooked through, 2 to 3 minutes.

Cooks' note:
• *Agrodolce* sauce can be made 1 day ahead and cooled completely, then chilled, covered. Reheat over moderate heat before cooking fish.

SHAVED FENNEL, RADISH, AND GRAPEFRUIT SALAD
SERVES 8 GENEROUSLY
Active time: 55 min   Start to finish: 2¼ hr (includes steeping)

⅓ cup olive oil
2 tablespoons fennel seeds, lightly crushed
4 medium fennel bulbs (sometimes called anise; about
     3½ lb total), stalks cut off and discarded
1 lb radishes (about 1½ lb total with greens), trimmed
4 pink or red grapefruits
1 medium garlic clove
½ teaspoon salt
¼ teaspoon black pepper

Special equipment: **a Japanese Benriner (see Sources) or other adjustable-blade slicer**

▶ Heat oil with fennel seeds in a small heavy saucepan over

moderate heat until seeds are fragrant and pale golden, 1 to 2 minutes. Remove from heat and let steep 2 hours.

▶ While seeds steep, quarter fennel bulbs lengthwise and cut out and discard most of cores, leaving just enough core to keep quarters of fennel intact. Cut fennel lengthwise into paper-thin slices with slicer. Transfer to a large bowl.

▶ Cut radishes crosswise into very thin slices (slightly thicker than fennel slices) with slicer and add to fennel.

▶ Cut peel, including all white pith, from grapefruits with a small sharp knife. Working over a bowl, cut segments free from membranes and squeeze juice from membranes into bowl. Transfer segments to a cutting board, reserving juice in bowl, and coarsely chop, then add to fennel and radishes.

▶ Pour fennel oil through a fine-mesh sieve into a small bowl. (Discard seeds.)

▶ Mince garlic and mash to a paste with a pinch of salt using a large heavy knife, then transfer to another small bowl. Whisk in salt, pepper, fennel oil, and 5 tablespoons grapefruit juice, then pour over salad, tossing gently to coat.

Cooks' notes:
• Fennel oil can be made 1 day ahead and chilled in an airtight container. Bring to room temperature before using.
• Fennel and radishes can be sliced 6 hours ahead and chilled, covered with dampened paper towels.
• Grapefruit can be chopped 6 hours ahead and chilled, covered. Chill juice separately.
• Dressing can be made 2 hours ahead and kept at room temperature or chilled, covered.

CELERY-ROOT AND POTATO LATKES

MAKES ABOUT 32 LATKES
Active time: 1¼ hr Start to finish: 1¼ hr

  1 **large celery root (sometimes called celeriac; 1½ lb),**
     peeled with a knife
1½ **lb large russet (baking) potatoes (3 large)**
  2 **tablespoons fresh lemon juice**
  1 **lb onions, quartered**
⅔ **cup all-purpose flour**
  4 **large eggs, lightly beaten**
1¼ **teaspoons salt**
½ **teaspoon black pepper**
½ **teaspoon ground celery seeds**
     About 1½ cups vegetable oil

Special equipment: **a kitchen towel (not terry cloth)**

▶ Put oven racks in upper and lower thirds of oven and preheat oven to 250°F.
▶ Coarsely grate celery root into a bowl using ⅓-inch-wide holes of a box grater.

▶ Peel potatoes and coarsely grate into a large bowl. Add lemon juice and toss. Coarsely grate onions into same bowl.
▶ Transfer potatoes and onions to towel, then gather up corners to form a sack and twist tightly to wring out as much liquid as possible.
▶ Return potatoes and onions to cleaned bowl and stir in celery root, flour, eggs, salt, pepper, and celery seeds until combined well.
▶ Heat ⅓ inch vegetable oil in a 12-inch nonstick skillet over moderately high heat until hot but not smoking. Fill a ¼-cup measure (not tightly packed) with latke mixture and carefully spoon it into skillet, then flatten to 3 inches in diameter with a slotted spatula. Form 3 more latkes in skillet, then fry until undersides are deep golden, 1½ to 3 minutes. Turn over using 2 spatulas and fry until deep golden all over, 1½ to 3 minutes more. (If latkes brown too quickly, lower heat to moderate.) Transfer to paper towels to drain briefly. Keep warm in 1 layer on a metal rack set in a shallow baking pan in oven. Make more latkes in same manner. Use a second rack and baking pan to keep last batches warm.

Cooks' note:
• Latkes can be fried 1 hour ahead.

GINGER DOUGHNUTS
MAKES ABOUT 42 SMALL DOUGHNUTS
Active time: 40 min   Start to finish: 40 min

    4 cups all-purpose flour plus additional
          for dusting
    4 teaspoons baking powder
    2 teaspoons baking soda
 1½ teaspoons salt
 1½ teaspoons ground ginger
 1¾ cups sugar
    2 oz crystalized ginger, coarsely chopped (⅓ cup)
 ¾ cup well-shaken buttermilk
 ½ stick (¼ cup) unsalted butter, melted and
          cooled slightly
    2 large eggs
 12 cups vegetable oil

Special equipment: a 1¾-inch round cookie cutter;
a deep-fat thermometer

▶ Whisk together flour, baking powder, baking soda, salt, and
¾ teaspoon ground ginger in a large bowl.
▶ Whisk together 1 cup sugar and remaining ¾ teaspoon
ground ginger in a shallow bowl. Set aside.
▶ Pulse remaining ¾ cup sugar with crystallized ginger in a
food processor until ginger is finely chopped. Transfer to a
bowl and whisk in buttermilk, butter, and eggs until smooth.
▶ Add buttermilk mixture to flour mixture and stir until a
dough forms (dough will be sticky).
▶ Turn out dough onto a well-floured surface and knead
gently just until it comes together, 10 to 12 times, then form
into a ball. Lightly dust work surface and dough with flour,
then roll out dough into a 13-inch round (⅓ inch thick) with
a floured rolling pin. Cut out rounds with floured cutter
and transfer to a lightly floured baking sheet. Gather scraps
and reroll, then cut out additional rounds. (Reroll only once.)
▶ Heat oil in a wide 5-quart heavy pot until thermometer
registers 375°F. Working in batches of 7 or 8, carefully add
rounds, 1 at a time, to oil and fry, turning over once, until
golden brown, 1½ to 2 minutes total per batch. (Return oil to
375°F between batches.) Transfer to paper towels to drain.
Cool slightly, then dredge in ginger sugar.

Cooks' note:
• Doughnuts can be fried (but not dredged in ginger sugar)
4 hours ahead and cooled completely, then kept in an
airtight container at room temperature. Reheat undredged
doughnuts on a baking sheet in a preheated 250°F oven 10 to
15 minutes, then cool slightly and dredge in ginger sugar.

BRANDIED HOT CHOCOLATE
SERVES 8
Active time: 15 min   Start to finish: 15 min

*The thickness and bitterness of your drink will depend on your
chocolate's level of cacao, which varies among brands. We got
great results with Ghirardelli, which produced a full-bodied
cocoa. We also used Lindt to good effect, but needed to add
more cornstarch for extra thickening. Chocolate with more
than 60 percent cacao will be too bitter.*

    2 teaspoons cornstarch
 1½ cups whole milk
 ½ cup water
 10 oz fine-quality bittersweet chocolate (not unsweetened),
          finely chopped
 ½ cup heavy cream
    1 tablespoon unsweetened cocoa powder (optional)
    2 tablespoons brandy (optional), or to taste

▶ Whisk together cornstarch and 2 tablespoons milk.
▶ Bring water to a boil in a 2-quart heavy saucepan, then
reduce heat to moderately low and add chopped chocolate
and a pinch of salt, whisking until smooth.
▶ Add cream and remaining milk (1¼ cups plus
2 tablespoons) and increase heat to moderate, then cook,
whisking occasionally, until mixture is smooth and heated
through. Taste; for a deeper chocolate flavor, whisk in cocoa.
▶ Whisk cornstarch mixture, then add half to chocolate
mixture and simmer, whisking, until slightly thickened,
about 2 minutes. Add brandy (if using) and remaining
cornstarch mixture to thicken if desired, then simmer,
whisking, 1 minute.

OPPOSITE: **striped bass in** *agrodolce* **sauce and celery-root and potato latkes;
brandied hot chocolate and ginger doughnuts**

NEW ORLEANS CHRISTMAS

SERVES 10

**SPANISH OLIVE AND
CREAM CHEESE CANAPÉS**

SPICY TOASTED PECANS

OYSTERS ROCKEFELLER

ROEDERER ESTATE BRUT ROSÉ

SHRIMP COURTBOUILLON WITH RICE

**BEEF TENDERLOIN WITH
MUSHROOMS AND ESPAGNOLE SAUCE**

CREAMED SPINACH

DEVILED ROASTED POTATOES

**MÂCHE SALAD WITH
CREOLE VINAIGRETTE**

MARIMAR TORRES ESTATE DON
MIGUEL VINEYARD PINOT NOIR '01

AMBROSIA LAYER CAKE

PINEAPPLE ANISE SHERBET

SILVAN RIDGE OREGON
EARLY MUSCAT '03

SPANISH OLIVE AND CREAM CHEESE CANAPÉS

MAKES 40 HORS D'OEUVRES
Active time: 40 min   Start to finish: 40 min

 10   slices firm white sandwich bread
 1½   tablespoons unsalted butter, melted
  1   oz Parmigiano-Reggiano
  6   oz cream cheese, softened (¾ cup)
  ⅓   cup pimiento-stuffed green Spanish olives (3 oz),
       rinsed, drained, and finely chopped
  ¼   cup finely chopped scallion
  ¼   cup finely chopped red bell pepper
  ¼   teaspoon sweet paprika
  2   teaspoons medium-dry Sherry

Special equipment: a 1½-inch round cookie cutter; a
Microplane rasp

▶ Put oven rack in middle position and preheat oven to
375°F.

▶ Cut 40 rounds from bread slices with cutter, then brush
1 side of each round with butter and bake on a large baking
sheet until pale golden, about 8 minutes. (Leave toasts on
baking sheet.)
▶ Preheat broiler.
▶ Finely grate Parmigiano-Reggiano using rasp (you will have
about 1 cup). Mash together cream cheese, olives, scallion,
bell pepper, paprika, and Sherry until combined well, then
top each toast with 1 teaspoon cream cheese mixture and
sprinkle with Parmigiano-Reggiano. Broil canapés about
4 inches from heat until Parmigiano-Reggiano begins to turn
golden, about 1 minute.

Cooks' notes:
• Toasts can be made 1 day ahead and cooled completely,
then kept in an airtight container at room temperature.
• Cream cheese mixture can be made 1 day ahead and
chilled, covered. Bring to room temperature before using.

SPICY TOASTED PECANS

MAKES 2½ CUPS

Active time: 10 min   Start to finish: 20 min

3 tablespoons unsalted butter
½ teaspoon Worcestershire sauce
½ teaspoon Tabasco
¼ teaspoon black pepper
¼ teaspoon kosher salt, or to taste
2½ cups pecan halves (10 oz)

▶ Put oven rack in middle position and preheat oven to 375°F.

▶ Melt butter in a 2-quart saucepan over moderate heat, then stir in Worcestershire sauce, Tabasco, pepper, and salt. Remove pan from heat and add pecans, tossing to coat well. Spread in 1 layer in a shallow baking pan and bake until fragrant and a shade darker, 8 to 10 minutes. Serve warm or at room temperature.

Cooks' note:
• Pecans can be baked 1 day ahead and cooled completely, then kept in an airtight container at cool room temperature.

OYSTERS ROCKEFELLER

SERVES 10 (HORS D'OEUVRE)

Active time: 45 min   Start to finish: 1½ hr

Though Louisiana oysters tend to be quite large, it's best to use small ones, such as Kumamoto or Prince Edward Island, for this recipe. The oysters themselves (not the shells) should be no more than 1 to 1½ inches in diameter.

¾ cup firmly packed watercress sprigs (2 oz before discarding coarse stems), finely chopped
1⅓ cups firmly packed baby spinach (1⅓ oz), finely chopped
3 tablespoons finely chopped scallion greens
1 tablespoon finely chopped fresh flat-leaf parsley
2 teaspoons minced celery
3 tablespoons coarse fresh bread crumbs (preferably from a day-old baguette)
3½ tablespoons unsalted butter
1 teaspoon Pernod or other anise-flavored liquor

Pinch of cayenne
3 bacon slices
About 10 cups kosher salt for baking and serving (3 lb)
20 small oysters on the half shell, oysters picked over for shell fragments and shells scrubbed well

▶ Toss together watercress, spinach, scallion greens, parsley, celery, and 1 tablespoon plus 1 teaspoon bread crumbs in a bowl. Melt butter in a 10-inch heavy skillet over moderate heat, then add watercress mixture and cook, stirring, until spinach is wilted, 1 to 2 minutes. Stir in Pernod, cayenne, and salt and pepper to taste, then transfer mixture to a bowl and chill, covered, until cold, about 1 hour.

▶ Put oven rack in middle position and preheat oven to 450°F.

▶ While watercress mixture chills, cook bacon in cleaned skillet over moderate heat, turning, until crisp, then drain on paper towels and finely crumble.

▶ Spread 5 cups kosher salt in a large shallow baking pan (1 inch deep) and nestle oysters (in shells) in it. Spoon watercress mixture evenly over oysters, then top with bacon and sprinkle with remaining tablespoon plus 2 teaspoons bread crumbs. Bake oysters until edges of oysters begin to curl and bread crumbs are golden, about 10 minutes.

▶ Serve warm oysters in shells, nestled in kosher salt (about 5 cups), on a platter.

Cooks' note:
• Watercress mixture can be chilled up to 1 day.

OPPOSITE: Spanish olive and cream cheese canapés; oysters Rockefeller

SHRIMP COURTBOUILLON WITH RICE

SERVES 10 (FIRST COURSE)

Active time: 1¼ hr   Start to finish: 2 hr (includes making fish stock)

1	(15- to 16-oz) can whole tomatoes in juice
5	cups white fish stock (recipe follows)
1¼	lb medium shrimp in shell (31 to 35 per lb), peeled, reserving shells
2¼	teaspoons salt
2½	tablespoons unsalted butter
¼	cup plus 1 tablespoon all-purpose flour
1	cup finely chopped onion (1 medium)
¾	cup finely chopped green bell pepper (½ medium)
2	garlic cloves, minced
2¼	cups water
¼	teaspoon cayenne, or to taste
⅔	cup long-grain white rice
1½	cups thinly sliced scallion greens (from 2 bunches)

▶ Drain tomatoes, reserving juice, and finely chop. Bring stock and shrimp shells to a boil in a 3-quart saucepan, then simmer, partially covered, 15 minutes. Pour stock through a sieve into a bowl, discarding shells. (Stock will appear cloudy.) Devein shrimp, then halve lengthwise and toss with ½ teaspoon salt in a bowl. Chill shrimp, covered, until ready to use.

▶ Melt butter in a 6- to 7-quart heavy pot over moderately low heat, then add flour and cook roux, stirring constantly, until the color of peanut butter, 10 to 15 minutes. Add onion, bell pepper, and garlic and cook, stirring occasionally, until bell pepper is softened, 3 to 5 minutes. Stir in tomatoes (with juice), stock, 1 cup water, 1½ teaspoons salt, and cayenne and bring to a boil, stirring frequently. Reduce heat and simmer courtbouillon, partially covered, 30 minutes.

▶ While courtbouillon simmers, bring remaining 1¼ cups water to a boil in a 1- to 1½-quart heavy saucepan. Add rice and remaining ¼ teaspoon salt and return to a boil. Cover pan, then reduce heat to low and cook until water is absorbed and rice is tender, about 15 minutes. Let stand, covered, 5 minutes, then fluff with a fork.

▶ Add shrimp to courtbouillon and simmer, uncovered, stirring occasionally, until shrimp are just cooked through, about 2 minutes. Stir in scallion greens.

▶ Divide rice among soup plates, then ladle in courtbouillon with shrimp.

Cooks' notes:

• Shrimp can be peeled, deveined, and halved (but not tossed with salt) 1 day ahead and chilled, covered. Chill shrimp shells separately.

• Courtbouillon (without shrimp and scallions) can be made 1 day ahead and cooled completely, uncovered, then chilled, covered. Bring to a simmer before proceeding.

• Rice can be cooked 2 days ahead and cooled completely, then chilled, covered. Reheat in a sieve, covered with a dampened paper towel, set over boiling water or reheat in a microwave.

WHITE FISH STOCK

MAKES ABOUT 12 CUPS

Active time: 15 min   Start to finish: 45 min

  1   tablespoon unsalted butter, softened
  3   lb mixed bones and heads of white-fleshed fish (such as
      cod, grouper, monkfish, porgy, red snapper, striped
      bass, and turbot), gills removed and bones and heads
      rinsed well
  2   large onions, sliced
  1   bunch fresh parsley stems (reserve leaves for
      another use)
  6   tablespoons fresh lemon juice
1½   teaspoons salt
10   cups cold water
1½   cups dry white wine

▶ Spread butter in bottom of a 6- to 8-quart heavy pot. Add fish bones and heads, onions, parsley stems, lemon juice, and salt and cook, covered, over moderately high heat, without stirring, 5 minutes. (Mixture will steam in its own juices.) Add water and wine and bring to a boil, then reduce heat and simmer, uncovered, skimming any froth, 25 minutes.

▶ Pour stock through a fine-mesh sieve into a large bowl, pressing on and then discarding solids.

Cooks' note:
• Stock can be made ahead and cooled completely, uncovered, then chilled, covered, for 2 days or frozen 1 month.

BEEF TENDERLOIN WITH MUSHROOMS AND ESPAGNOLE SAUCE

SERVES 10

Active time: 1½ hr   Start to finish: 9½ hr (includes making sauce)

  2   (2½-lb) pieces trimmed center-cut beef
      tenderloin roast
  1   tablespoon kosher salt
  2   teaspoons black pepper
  3   tablespoons vegetable oil
  3   tablespoons unsalted butter
1½   lb small fresh cremini mushrooms, trimmed
      and cut into ½-inch wedges

½   cup medium-dry Sherry
2⅔   cups espagnole sauce (page 88)

Special equipment: **an instant-read thermometer**

▶ Put oven rack in middle position and preheat oven to 425°F.

▶ Remove any strings from beef if tied, then pat beef dry and sprinkle with kosher salt and pepper. Heat oil in a deep 12-inch heavy skillet over high heat until just smoking, then sear beef 1 piece at a time, turning with tongs, until well browned, about 5 minutes each. (If beef tenderloin pieces are too long to fit into skillet, halve each crosswise, then brown 2 pieces at a time.) Transfer beef to an 18- by 12-inch flameproof roasting pan, reserving skillet.

▶ Roast beef in oven until thermometer inserted diagonally 2 inches into center of each piece registers 120°F, 20 to 25 minutes. Transfer beef to a cutting board, reserving roasting pan, and let stand, loosely covered with foil, 25 minutes. (Beef will continue to cook as it stands, reaching 130°F for medium-rare.)

▶ While beef roasts, heat butter in skillet over moderately high heat until foam subsides, then reduce heat to moderate and cook mushrooms, stirring frequently, until liquid they give off is evaporated and mushrooms are pale golden, 8 to 10 minutes. Remove skillet from heat.

▶ While beef stands, straddle roasting pan across 2 burners, then add Sherry and deglaze pan by boiling over high heat, stirring and scraping up brown bits, 1 minute. Add Sherry mixture and espagnole sauce to mushrooms and cook over moderate heat, stirring, until warm. Cover skillet and remove from heat.

▶ Cut meat crosswise into 10 or 20 slices. Pour any juices on cutting board into sauce and heat over moderate heat, stirring, until hot.

▶ Serve beef with sauce.

OPPOSITE: beef tenderloin with mushrooms and espagnole sauce; creamed spinach; deviled roasted potatoes

ESPAGNOLE SAUCE

MAKES ABOUT 2⅔ CUPS

Active time: 35 min   Start to finish: 8 hr (includes making stock)

Espagnole is a classic brown sauce, typically made from brown stock, mirepoix *(a sautéed mixture of diced vegetables and herbs), and tomatoes, and thickened with roux.*

  1 **small carrot, coarsely chopped**
  1 **medium onion, coarsely chopped**
  ½ **stick (¼ cup) unsalted butter**
  ¼ **cup all-purpose flour**
  4 **cups hot beef stock (recipe follows) or reconstituted
       beef-veal demi-glace concentrate (see Sources)**
  ¼ **cup canned tomato purée**
  2 **large garlic cloves, coarsely chopped**
  1 **celery rib, coarsely chopped**
  ½ **teaspoon whole black peppercorns**
  1 **Turkish or ½ California bay leaf**

▶Cook carrot and onion in butter in a 3-quart heavy saucepan over moderate heat, stirring occasionally, until golden, 7 to 8 minutes. Add flour and cook roux over moderately low heat, stirring constantly, until medium brown, 6 to 10 minutes. Add hot stock in a fast stream, whisking constantly to prevent lumps, then add tomato purée, garlic, celery, peppercorns, and bay leaf and bring to a boil, stirring. Reduce heat and cook at a bare simmer, uncovered, stirring occasionally, until reduced to about 3 cups, about 45 minutes.
▶Pour sauce through a fine-mesh sieve into a bowl, discarding solids.

Cooks' note:
• Sauce can be made 1 day ahead and cooled completely, uncovered, then chilled, covered.

BEEF STOCK

MAKES ABOUT 8 CUPS

Active time: 20 min   Start to finish: 6½ hr

  4 **fresh flat-leaf parsley sprigs**
  1 **fresh thyme sprig**
  1 **Turkish or ½ California bay leaf**
  2 **lb meaty beef shanks, sawed crosswise into
       1-inch slices by butcher**
  2 **lb meaty veal shanks, sawed crosswise into
       1-inch slices by butcher**
  2 **onions (left unpeeled), quartered**
  1 **carrot, quartered**
  4 **qt plus 2½ cups cold water**
  2 **celery ribs, quartered**
1½ **teaspoons salt**

Special equipment: **cheesecloth; kitchen string**

▶Put oven rack in middle position and preheat oven to 450°F.
▶Wrap parsley, thyme, and bay leaf in cheesecloth and tie into a bundle with kitchen string to make a bouquet garni.
▶Spread beef shanks, veal shanks, onions, and carrot in a large flameproof roasting pan, then brown well in oven, turning occasionally, about 1 hour.
▶Transfer meat and vegetables to a 6- to 8-quart stockpot.

Add 2 cups water to roasting pan, then straddle pan across 2 burners and deglaze by boiling over high heat, stirring and scraping up brown bits, 2 minutes. Add deglazing liquid to stockpot along with 4 quarts water, celery, salt, and bouquet garni. Bring to a boil and skim froth. Add remaining ½ cup water, then bring mixture to a simmer and skim any froth.

▶ Simmer gently, uncovered, skimming froth occasionally, until liquid is reduced to about 8 cups, 3 to 5 hours.

▶ Pour stock through a fine-mesh sieve into a bowl, pressing hard on and then discarding solids. If using stock right away, skim off and discard fat. If not, cool stock completely, uncovered, then chill, covered (it will be easier to remove fat when chilled).

Cooks' note:
• Stock keeps, covered and chilled, 1 week or frozen 3 months.

CREAMED SPINACH
SERVES 10
Active time: 30 min   Start to finish: 30 min

    3 lb baby spinach
1¼ cups whole milk
    1 cup heavy cream
    1 small onion, finely chopped
  ½ stick (¼ cup) unsalted butter
  ¼ cup all-purpose flour
  ⅛ teaspoon freshly grated nutmeg

▶ Cook spinach in 2 batches in 1 inch of boiling salted water (see Tips, page 8) in an 8-quart pot, stirring constantly, until wilted, 1 to 2 minutes. Drain in a colander and rinse under cold water until cool. Squeeze small handfuls of spinach to remove as much moisture as possible, then coarsely chop.

▶ Heat milk and cream in a small saucepan over moderate heat, stirring, until warm. Meanwhile, cook onion in butter in a 3-quart heavy saucepan over moderately low heat, stirring occasionally, until softened, about 4 minutes. Whisk in flour and cook roux, whisking, 3 minutes. Add warm milk mixture in a fast stream, whisking constantly to prevent lumps, and simmer, whisking, until thickened, 3 to 4 minutes. Stir in nutmeg, spinach, and salt and pepper to taste and cook, stirring, until heated through.

Cooks' note:
• Creamed spinach can be made 1 day ahead and cooled completely, uncovered, then chilled, covered. Reheat over moderately low heat until hot.

DEVILED ROASTED POTATOES
SERVES 10
Active time: 15 min   Start to finish: 35 min

2¾ lb small red potatoes (about 1½ inches
        in diameter)
    3 tablespoons vegetable oil
    2 teaspoons kosher salt
  ½ stick (¼ cup) unsalted butter
    2 teaspoons cider vinegar
    1 teaspoon Dijon mustard
        Rounded ¼ teaspoon cayenne, or to taste

▶ Put oven racks in upper and lower thirds of oven and preheat oven to 475°F. Put 2 large shallow baking pans (1 inch deep) in oven and preheat 10 minutes.

▶ Quarter potatoes, then toss with oil and 1½ teaspoons kosher salt in a large bowl. Spread potatoes, cut sides down, in hot pans, then roast until undersides are golden, about 12 minutes. Turn potatoes so other cut sides are down, then switch position of pans and roast until potatoes are tender and undersides are golden, 12 to 15 minutes more.

▶ While potatoes roast, melt butter in a small saucepan and whisk in vinegar, mustard, cayenne, and remaining ½ teaspoon kosher salt.

▶ Toss hot potatoes with butter mixture in cleaned large bowl until coated.

Cooks' note:
• If you are preparing this entire menu in a single oven, preheat the pans for these potatoes together on 1 rack while the beef finishes roasting, then roast the potatoes while the beef stands.

Cooks' note:
• *Mâche* is sold in different ways—sometimes it comes in a package with soil plugs attached and sometimes you can find it loose, like mesclun. If you're buying it with plugs attached, you'll need 1½ pounds; if you're buying it loose, you'll need 5 ounces.

MÂCHE SALAD WITH CREOLE VINAIGRETTE

SERVES 10

Active time: 15 min   Start to finish: 30 min (includes hard-boiling egg)

  1 yolk from a large hard-boiled egg
2¾ teaspoons white-wine vinegar
  1 teaspoon Dijon mustard
 ¼ teaspoon salt
 ⅛ teaspoon black pepper
 ¼ cup olive oil
 16 cups loosely packed *mâche* (lamb's lettuce; see cooks' note, below)

▶ Crumble yolk into a blender, then add vinegar, mustard, salt, and pepper and blend until combined well. With motor running, add oil in a slow stream, blending until combined well.
▶ Toss *mâche* with vinaigrette just before serving.

AMBROSIA LAYER CAKE

SERVES 10 TO 12

Active time: 1 hr   Start to finish: 2 hr

For cake
2¾ cups sifted cake flour (not self-rising; sift before measuring)
2½ teaspoons baking powder
 ½ teaspoon salt
1½ sticks (¾ cup) unsalted butter, softened
1½ cups sugar
  4 large whole eggs, at room temperature for 30 minutes
  1 tablespoon finely grated fresh orange zest
1½ teaspoons vanilla
  1 cup whole milk

For orange filling
  2 large whole eggs
 ¾ cup sugar
 ¼ cup cornstarch
 ¾ cup water
 ½ cup fresh orange juice
 ¼ cup fresh lemon juice
  3 tablespoons unsalted butter
  2 teaspoons finely grated fresh orange zest

For seven-minute frosting
  1 (7-oz) bag sweetened flaked coconut (2⅔ cups)
  2 large egg whites
  1 cup sugar
 ¼ cup water
  2 teaspoons light corn syrup
  1 teaspoon vanilla
  1 teaspoon fresh lemon juice

Special equipment: **2 (9- by 2-inch) round cake pans**

Make cake:
▶ Put oven rack in middle position and preheat oven to 350°F. Butter and flour cake pans, knocking out excess flour.
▶ Sift together flour (2¾ cups), baking powder, and salt into a bowl.

▶ Beat together butter and sugar with an electric mixer (fitted with paddle attachment if using a stand mixer) at medium-high speed until pale and fluffy, 3 to 5 minutes. Beat in eggs 1 at a time, then add zest and vanilla and continue beating 5 minutes more. Reduce speed to low, then add flour mixture and milk alternately in 4 batches, beginning with flour mixture and mixing until batter is just smooth. Divide between cake pans, spreading evenly.

▶ Bake cake layers until they begin to pull away from sides of pans and a wooden pick or skewer comes out clean, 20 to 25 minutes. Cool 5 minutes in pans on racks, then invert cake layers onto racks and cool completely. (Leave oven on for toasting coconut.)

Make filling while layers bake:

▶ Whisk eggs in a heatproof bowl until combined well.

▶ With clean dry whisk, stir together sugar, cornstarch, and a pinch of salt in a 1½- to 2-quart heavy saucepan, then whisk in water and juices until smooth. Bring to a boil over moderate heat, whisking, then reduce heat and cook at a bare simmer, whisking constantly, 2 minutes (mixture will be thick).

▶ Add half of hot juice mixture to eggs in a slow stream, whisking, then whisk egg mixture into juices in saucepan and cook over moderately low heat, whisking, just until it reaches a boil. Remove pan from heat, then add butter and zest, whisking until butter is melted. Chill filling, its surface covered with a buttered round of wax paper (buttered side down), until cold, about 30 minutes.

Make frosting:

▶ Spread coconut in a shallow baking pan and toast in oven, stirring occasionally, until golden, 12 to 15 minutes.

▶ Beat together egg whites, sugar, water, corn syrup, and a pinch of salt in a large metal bowl with a handheld electric mixer (clean beaters if necessary) until combined. Set bowl over a saucepan of simmering water and beat mixture at high speed until it holds stiff, glossy peaks, 5 to 7 minutes. (Humid weather may necessitate additional beating time.) Remove bowl from heat, then add vanilla and lemon juice and continue beating until frosting is cooled and very thick, 6 to 10 minutes.

Assemble cake:

▶ Halve each cake horizontally with a long serrated knife. Put 1 layer on a cake stand or large plate and spread with about ¾ cup filling. Stack remaining cake layers using about ¾ cup filling between each layer. Spread top and side of cake with frosting and coat cake with coconut, gently pressing to help it adhere.

Cooks' notes:

• Cake layers (not split horizontally) can be made 3 days ahead and chilled, wrapped individually in plastic wrap.
• Filling can be chilled up to 8 hours. Stir before spreading.
• Frosting can be made 4 hours ahead and chilled, covered.
• Cake can be assembled and frosted 2 hours ahead.

PINEAPPLE ANISE SHERBET

MAKES ABOUT 2 QUARTS
Active time: 30 min   Start to finish: 6 hr (includes chilling and freezing)

 2 cups water
1⅔ cups sugar
 2 teaspoons anise seeds
 1 teaspoon Pernod or other anise-flavored liqueur (optional)
 1 (4-lb) pineapple (labeled "extra sweet"), trimmed, peeled, halved lengthwise, and cored
 1 tablespoon fresh lemon juice

Special equipment: **an ice cream maker**

▶ Bring water, sugar, and anise seeds to a boil in a 2½- to 3-quart heavy saucepan, stirring until sugar is dissolved, then reduce heat and simmer, uncovered, 5 minutes. Remove pan from heat and stir in Pernod (if using). Cool syrup to room temperature, about 1 hour, then pour through a fine-mesh sieve into a bowl.

▶ While syrup cools, cut enough pineapple into 1-inch chunks to measure 5¼ cups (reserve remainder for another use), then purée pineapple in 3 batches in a blender at high speed until very smooth, about 1 minute per batch. Stir purée and lemon juice into cooled syrup until combined well, then chill, covered, until very cold, about 4 hours.

▶ Freeze in ice cream maker, then transfer to an airtight container and put in freezer to harden, at least 1 hour.

Cooks' note:

• Sherbet can be made 3 days ahead. Let soften slightly before serving.

THE MENU COLLECTION

Those of us who enjoy cooking gather family and loved ones around our tables whenever possible, not just for holidays and celebrations. But time is an issue. It can take hours to plan a special menu, and that alone often puts the kibosh on entertaining. Here is a ready-made collection of seventeen delicious seasonal menus from *Gourmet*'s food editors that will encourage you to entertain more often. Most were devised with guests in mind, but there are also a few low-fat weeknight meals.

To add a bit of elegance to a cold, gray winter, consider hosting a *Dinner for a Dozen* in the new year. Don't let the number of guests and the fancy-sounding dishes, like foie gras toasts and braised duck legs, frighten you. The truth is, this menu consists of four easy recipes that can be partially prepared in advance and served either plated or buffet-style. Our little secrets? The foie gras is store-bought; duck legs are much easier to handle than a whole bird; and the shallots and parsnips are braised with the duck (for ease and fabulous flavor). When it comes time for dessert, an impressive Sauternes-soaked genoise offers moist citrusy sweetness.

For a smaller gathering in the spring, turn to a *Toast of the Town* dinner where a few comfort foods from the Emerald Isle have been citified. Ramekins of unctuous potted crab served with thin slices of toasted homemade brown bread are a perfect starter when paired with a bright Chardonnay. Then, potato-stuffed cabbage bundles, thick slices of smoky Irish bacon, and a crisp salad make for a simple yet sophisticated main course. For dessert? A homey rhubarb cake, with a biscuit-like top and bottom crust, reminds us this menu has rustic roots after all.

As the weather turns up the heat, you may want to invite friends out to the country *All Weekend Long*. You'll be ready with four menus that take you from Saturday lunch to Sunday dinner in *Gourmet* style. Imagine unusual dishes, like tahini chicken salad, balsamic zucchini, and honeydew lime Popsicles for lunch; poached halibut with saffron orange aïoli, and a golden beet and sunflower salad for dinner; cornmeal crêpes with ricotta and ham for brunch; and limoncello and mint cocktails and grilled leg of lamb with rosemary salt for a send-off to remember. With the planning complete, all you have to do is shop and cook. Needless to say, this will be a weekend your guests will talk about for quite some time.

When the season turns cool, a *Dinner and a Movie* might be a fun change of pace. Childhood favorites get appealing makeovers in the form of turkey sloppy joes on cheddar buttermilk biscuits and chocolate peanut butter bars with hot fudge sauce. Everyone, including the cook, will feel relaxed, entertained, and indulged.

Why not make a resolution to branch out and entertain more often this year? With fabulous menus like these, there's no reason to wait around for the holidays.

NORDIC NIGHTS

A WINTRY SCANDINAVIAN DINNER

SERVES 8

CURRIED HERRING ON RYE TOASTS

LINIE AQUAVIT

CELERY-ROOT AND BEET SALAD

PORK LOIN WITH APPLES, PRUNES, AND MUSTARD CREAM SAUCE

SAUTÉED GREEN BEANS

HASSELBACK POTATOES

MURPHY-GOODE ROBERT YOUNG VINEYARDS RESERVE MERLOT '00

SABAYON LINGONBERRY MOUSSE

SPICE COOKIES

CURRIED HERRING ON RYE TOASTS

SERVES 8 (MAKES 40 HORS D'OEUVRES)

Active time: 30 min   Start to finish: 35 min

- 4 slices seedless rye bread
- 1½ tablespoons unsalted butter, melted
- ⅛ teaspoon salt
- 1 (7- to 8-oz) jar pickled herring (preferably small), rinsed, drained, and patted dry
- 2½ tablespoons mayonnaise
- 2½ tablespoons sour cream
- 2 tablespoons chopped fresh chives
- 2 teaspoons coarse-grain mustard
- ½ teaspoon curry powder
- ½ teaspoon sugar

Garnish: chopped fresh chives

▶ Put oven rack in middle position and preheat oven to 350°F.

▶ Discard crusts from bread and cut bread into 40 (1½-inch) triangles. Arrange triangles in a shallow baking pan (1 inch deep), then brush tops with butter and sprinkle with salt. Bake until golden, 10 to 12 minutes, then cool.

▶ If using large herring, discard skin and dark flesh. Cut large or small herring into ¼-inch pieces. Whisk together remaining ingredients in a bowl, then stir in herring.

▶ Top each toast with ½ teaspoon curried herring.

Cooks' notes:

• Toasts can be made 1 day ahead and kept in an airtight container at room temperature.

• Curried herring can be made 6 hours ahead and chilled, covered.

CELERY-ROOT AND BEET SALAD

SERVES 8

Active time: 45 min   Start to finish: 2¾ hr

- 6 medium beets (2¼ lb with greens), trimmed, leaving 1 inch of stems attached
- 1 (1-lb) celery root (sometimes called celeriac)
- 2 tablespoons plus 2 teaspoons fresh lemon juice, plus additional to taste
- 2 tablespoons minced shallot
- ¼ cup olive oil
- ¾ teaspoon salt
- ½ cup chopped walnuts (2 oz), toasted (see Tips, page 8) and cooled

▶ Put oven rack in middle position and preheat oven to 425°F.

▶ Wrap beets tightly in foil to make 2 packages (3 beets in each) and roast until tender, about 1¼ hours.

▶ While beets roast, peel celery root with a sharp knife and cut into ⅛-inch-thick matchsticks. Whisk together lemon juice, shallot, oil, salt, and pepper to taste in a large bowl until combined well, then add celery root and toss until coated. Keep at room temperature, covered, until ready to add beets.

▶ Carefully unwrap beets and, when just cool enough to handle, slip off skins and remove stems. Cut beets into ⅛-inch-thick matchsticks and toss with celery root.

▶ Let salad stand, covered, at room temperature 1 hour. Taste salad and season with more lemon juice and salt if necessary, then toss with walnuts.

SAUTÉED GREEN BEANS

SERVES 8

Active time: 25 min   Start to finish: 25 min

- 1½ lb green beans, stem ends trimmed
- 1 tablespoon olive oil

Special equipment: a green-bean frencher (optional)

▶ Force beans, stemmed ends first, through frencher (if using; see cooks' note, below), then diagonally halve crosswise. Blanch beans in a 6-quart pot of boiling salted water (see Tips, page 8), uncovered, until crisp-tender, 1 to 2 minutes. Drain beans in a colander and transfer to a bowl of ice and cold water to stop cooking, then drain well.

▶ Heat oil in a 12-inch heavy skillet over moderately high heat until hot but not smoking, then sauté beans, stirring, until just tender, 2 to 3 minutes. Season with salt and pepper and serve immediately.

Cooks' note:

• If you do not have a frencher, beans can be cut diagonally into 1½-inch pieces instead of frenched.

PORK LOIN WITH APPLES, PRUNES, AND MUSTARD CREAM SAUCE

SERVES 8

Active time: 1 hr   Start to finish: 1½ hr

  1   (4-lb) boneless pork loin roast, tied by butcher
1¾   teaspoons salt
1½   teaspoons black pepper
  1   tablespoon olive oil
  2   Granny Smith apples (¾ lb total)
  1   large onion, chopped
  ½   cup packed dried pitted prunes (sometimes called
       dried plums; 4½ oz), quartered
1½   cups reduced-sodium chicken broth (12 oz)
  ¾   cup water
  ½   cup heavy cream
  2   tablespoons coarse-grain mustard
  ½   cup dry white wine

Special equipment: **an instant-read thermometer**

▶ Put oven rack in lower third of oven and preheat oven to 375°F.

▶ Halve pork loin crosswise, then pat dry and sprinkle with 1 teaspoon salt and ¾ teaspoon pepper (total). Heat oil in a 12-inch heavy skillet over moderately high heat until hot but not smoking, then brown pork, 1 piece at a time, turning occasionally, 6 to 8 minutes per piece. Transfer to a small flameproof roasting pan as browned (do not clean skillet) and roast pork until thermometer inserted diagonally at least 2 inches into meat registers 150°F, 40 to 50 minutes.

▶ While pork roasts, peel, quarter, and core apples, then cut into ¼-inch-thick wedges. Pour off all but 1 tablespoon fat from skillet, then cook onion in skillet over moderate heat, stirring occasionally, until softened, 3 to 5 minutes. Add apples, prunes, broth, and water and simmer, uncovered, stirring occasionally, until apples are tender, 10 to 12 minutes. Stir in cream and mustard and simmer until sauce is slightly thickened, 2 to 3 minutes. Remove from heat and keep sauce warm, partially covered.

▶ Transfer pork to a cutting board and let stand 10 minutes. Straddle roasting pan across 2 burners, then add wine and deglaze pan by boiling over high heat, stirring and scraping up brown bits, until reduced to about ¼ cup, 2 to 3 minutes. Stir pan juices into cream sauce along with remaining ¾ teaspoon

salt and remaining ¾ teaspoon pepper and heat sauce over moderate heat, stirring, until hot.

▶ Discard string from pork and cut each half crosswise into 4 slices. Serve pork with sauce.

HASSELBACK POTATOES

SERVES 8

Active time: 25 min   Start to finish: 1½ hr

  8   russet (baking) potatoes (6 to 8 oz each)
  ¾   stick (6 tablespoons) unsalted butter, melted
  1   teaspoon salt
  3   tablespoons fine dry bread crumbs

Special equipment: **2 wooden chopsticks or wooden spoons with ½-inch-diameter handles; parchment paper**

▶ Put oven rack in middle position and preheat oven to 375°F.

▶ Peel potatoes, transferring to a large bowl of cold water as peeled (to prevent browning). Working with 1 potato at a time, cut a thin sliver lengthwise from 1 side of potato with a sharp paring knife to make it stand flat on a cutting board, if necessary. Lay chopsticks or spoons parallel to each other on cutting board and arrange potato lengthwise between them. Holding chopsticks against potato, make crosswise cuts, ⅛ inch apart, down to chopsticks (do not cut all the way down to chopsticks on narrow ends of potato or slices will fall off). Drop potato back into water after cutting.

▶ Line bottom of a shallow baking pan (1 inch deep) with parchment, then butter parchment. Drain potatoes and pat dry. Brush potatoes all over with 2 tablespoons butter (total), then arrange in baking pan and sprinkle with salt. Cover pan tightly with foil and bake potatoes until just tender, 40 to 45 minutes, then remove foil and bake until tender, 10 to 15 minutes more.

▶ Preheat broiler.

▶ Brush potatoes with 2 tablespoons butter, then sprinkle with bread crumbs and broil about 5 inches from heat until golden, about 2 minutes. Drizzle with remaining 2 tablespoons butter and serve immediately.

Cooks' note:
• If you're making this entire menu in a single oven, bake the potatoes in the middle of the oven while the pork roasts in the lower third.

SABAYON LINGONBERRY MOUSSE

SERVES 8
Active time: 45 min   Start to finish: 2¾ hr

2¼ teaspoons unflavored gelatin (from a ¼-oz envelope)
¼ cup cold water
10 large egg yolks
½ cup plus 2 tablespoons sugar
3 tablespoons brandy
⅛ teaspoon salt
2¼ cups chilled heavy cream
2 cups lingonberry sauce or preserves (from two 14-oz jars; see Sources), stirred

Special equipment: an instant-read thermometer
Garnish: whipped cream and lingonberry sauce or preserves

▸ Sprinkle gelatin over cold water in a small saucepan and let soften 1 minute. Cook over low heat, stirring, until gelatin is dissolved, about 1 minute, then remove from heat.
▸ Beat together yolks, sugar, brandy, salt, and ¼ cup cream in a metal bowl with a handheld electric mixer at medium-high speed until combined well. Set bowl over a saucepan of simmering water and cook mixture, beating constantly at medium-high speed, until very thick and registers 160°F on thermometer, 10 to 12 minutes. Remove bowl from heat, then beat in gelatin mixture until just combined. Cool sabayon 5 minutes.
▸ Beat remaining 2 cups cream with cleaned beaters until it just holds stiff peaks. Stir one fourth of whipped cream into sabayon to lighten, then fold in remaining cream gently but thoroughly.
▸ Spoon layers of mousse and lingonberry sauce alternately into 8 (6- to 8-ounce) stemmed glasses and chill, covered, until set, at least 2 hours.

Cooks' note:
• Mousse can be chilled up to 1 day.

SPICE COOKIES

MAKES ABOUT 42 COOKIES
Active time: 35 min   Start to finish: 1½ hr

1 cup all-purpose flour
½ teaspoon cinnamon
½ teaspoon ground cardamom
¼ teaspoon black pepper
¼ teaspoon salt
½ teaspoon baking soda
1½ teaspoons warm water
1½ teaspoons molasses (not robust or blackstrap)
¾ stick (6 tablespoons) unsalted butter, softened
6 tablespoons superfine granulated sugar

▸ Put oven rack in middle position and preheat oven to 350°F. Butter 2 large baking sheets.
▸ Whisk together flour, spices, and salt in a bowl. Stir baking soda into warm water in a cup until dissolved, then stir in molasses. Beat together butter and sugar in another bowl with an electric mixer at high speed until pale and fluffy, about 3 minutes. Beat in baking soda mixture until combined well, then beat in flour mixture until just combined (dough will be crumbly but will hold together when rolling balls).
▸ Working with half of dough, roll level teaspoons of dough into balls, arranging them about 2 inches apart on 1 baking sheet. Flatten balls into 1¼-inch rounds with tines of a fork, dipping fork in flour to prevent sticking if necessary. Bake cookies until golden brown, 10 to 12 minutes, then transfer to a rack to cool. Make more cookies with remaining dough on remaining baking sheet in same manner.

Cooks' note:
• Cookies, cooled completely, keep in an airtight container at room temperature 1 week.

DINNER FOR
A DOZEN

SERVES 12

PIPERS BROOK VINEYARD PIRIE TASMANIA
SPARKLING WINE '97

**FOIE GRAS TOASTS WITH GREENS AND
VERJUS PORT GLAZE**

PENFOLDS RESERVE BIN EDEN VALLEY
RIESLING '02

**BRAISED DUCK LEGS WITH SHALLOTS
AND PARSNIPS**

WILTED MUSTARD GREENS

EVANS & TATE MARGARET RIVER SHIRAZ '01

**SAUTERNES-SOAKED GÉNOISE WITH
CANDIED KUMQUATS**

JOSEPH LA MAGIA SOUTH AUSTRALIA
BOTRYTIS RIESLING-GEWÜRZTRAMINER '02

FOIE GRAS TOASTS WITH GREENS AND VERJUS PORT GLAZE

SERVES 12
Active time: 1 hr   Start to finish: 1 hr

For Port glaze

2/3 cup white *verjus* (juice of unripe fruits, primarily grapes;
  see Sources) or 3 tablespoons fresh lemon juice
1/2 cup Tawny Port
3 tablespoons sugar

For vinaigrette and salad

1½ tablespoons Sherry vinegar
1/2 teaspoon salt
1/4 teaspoon black pepper
3 tablespoons pure walnut oil (see Sources)
1 lb frisée (pale leafy parts only), torn into small sprigs
  (6 cups)
1 lb Belgian endives (3 or 4), trimmed and cut crosswise
  into 1/4-inch-thick slices (3 cups)
1/2 lb radicchio, halved lengthwise, cores and coarse center
  ribs discarded and leaves torn into bite-size pieces
  (3 cups)

For foie gras toasts

12 (½-inch-thick) slices *pain de mie*, Pullman loaf, or firm
  white sandwich bread, crusts discarded
1 lb chilled foie gras terrine (see Sources), unmolded
  Fleur de sel or kosher salt to taste

Make Port glaze:

▶ Bring *verjus*, Port, and sugar to a boil in a 1-quart heavy saucepan, stirring until sugar is dissolved, then boil until syrupy and reduced to about 1/3 cup, 8 to 12 minutes.

Make vinaigrette and salad:

▶ Whisk together vinegar, salt, and pepper in a bowl, then add walnut oil in a slow stream, whisking.
▶ Just before serving, toss frisée, endives, and radicchio in a bowl with just enough vinaigrette to coat.

Make toasts:

▶ Put oven rack in upper third of oven and preheat oven to 400°F.
▶ Toast bread slices on a baking sheet, turning over once, until pale golden, about 8 minutes. Cut foie gras terrine into 12 slices (about 1/4 inch thick) and put 1 on each toast (trim toasts to size of foie gras if desired). Sprinkle lightly with *fleur de sel*, then halve toasts diagonally. Let toasts stand, loosely covered with plastic wrap, 5 to 10 minutes, to bring foie gras to room temperature.

▶ Put 1 foie gras toast on each of 12 plates and drizzle with Port glaze, then divide salad among plates.

Cooks' notes:
• Glaze and vinaigrette can be made 4 hours ahead and kept separately, covered, at room temperature.
• Foie gras toasts can be prepared 1 hour ahead and kept, covered with plastic wrap, at room temperature.

BRAISED DUCK LEGS WITH SHALLOTS AND PARSNIPS

SERVES 12
Active time: 1¾ hr   Start to finish: 7½ hr (includes making stock)

12 fresh duck legs (7 to 11 lb depending on amount of fat
  on legs; see Sources)
2 lb shallots, peeled and, if very large, halved
4 lb parsnips, peeled and cut diagonally into 1-inch-thick
  slices (halve large slices lengthwise)
2 tablespoons minced garlic
1½ tablespoons chopped fresh thyme or 1 teaspoon dried,
  crumbled
2 Turkish bay leaves or 1 halved California bay leaf
2½ teaspoons salt
1¾ teaspoons black pepper
1/4 teaspoon ground allspice
2 cups dry white wine
6 to 8 cups chicken stock, homemade (page 218) or store-
  bought (preferably not canned broth; 48 to 64 fl oz)

Special equipment: 2 (13- by 9- by 2-inch) baking pans
Garnish: fresh thyme sprigs

Prepare duck and brown vegetables:

▶ Put oven racks in upper and lower thirds of oven and preheat oven to 450°F.
▶ Trim fat and skin from sides of duck legs, leaving a covering of skin on top of legs (there may be fat underneath skin). Reserve 1/2 cup fat (for cooking). Score skin on legs in a ½-inch crosshatch pattern, cutting through fat but not into meat.
▶ Coarsely chop reserved duck fat and heat in a 12-inch heavy skillet over moderate heat, stirring occasionally, until melted. Remove from heat and discard any solids with a slotted spoon.
▶ Divide shallots, parsnips, garlic, thyme, bay leaves,

1 teaspoon salt, and 1 teaspoon pepper between baking pans. Add 2 tablespoons rendered duck fat to each pan, reserving remainder in skillet, and toss to coat vegetables. Roast vegetables, turning occasionally and switching position of pans halfway through roasting, until browned in patches, 20 to 30 minutes total.

Brown duck while vegetables roast:

▶ Pat duck legs dry. Stir together allspice, remaining 1½ teaspoons salt, and remaining ¾ teaspoon pepper in a small bowl and rub all over legs. Heat fat remaining in skillet over moderately high heat until hot but not smoking, then sauté 4 duck legs, skin sides down, until well browned, 3 to 5 minutes. Turn legs over with tongs and sauté until undersides are browned, 2 minutes more. Transfer with tongs to paper towels to drain. Brown remaining duck legs (in batches of 4) in same manner, pouring off all but 2 tablespoons fat from skillet between batches.

Braise duck and vegetables:

▶ Reduce oven temperature to 375°F.

▶ Divide duck legs between baking pans, nestling them, skin sides up, in vegetables. Add wine and just enough stock so that most of each leg is submerged but skins are not.

▶ Braise duck and vegetables, uncovered, switching position of pans halfway through braising, until duck is tender, 1½ to 2 hours total.

▶ Transfer vegetables and duck with a slotted spoon to a platter. Skim fat from pan juices and serve juices, seasoned with salt and pepper if necessary, on the side.

Cooks' note:

• Duck and vegetables can be browned and arranged in roasting pans (but not braised) 1 day ahead. Cool, uncovered, then chill, covered. Add wine and stock just before braising.

WILTED MUSTARD GREENS
SERVES 12
Active time: 45 min   Start to finish: 45 min

- 4 lb mustard greens, stems and coarse ribs discarded
- 2 large garlic cloves, minced
- 3 tablespoons unsalted butter
- ½ teaspoon salt, or to taste
- ¼ teaspoon black pepper, or to taste

▶ Cook mustard greens in 2 batches in a 6- to 8-quart pot of boiling salted water (see Tips, page 8), stirring to submerge, until wilted and tender, about 5 minutes. Transfer with tongs to a large bowl of cold water to stop cooking. Drain greens in a colander, pressing to squeeze out excess moisture, then coarsely chop.

▶ Cook garlic in butter in a 4- to 5-quart heavy pot over moderately low heat, stirring, until softened, about 2 minutes. Add boiled greens, salt, and pepper and cook, covered, stirring occasionally, until heated through, about 5 minutes.

Cooks' note:

• Greens can be boiled and chopped 1 day ahead and chilled in a sealed plastic bag. You will need to cook them in garlic butter about 10 minutes (instead of 5) when made ahead.

SAUTERNES-SOAKED GÉNOISE WITH CANDIED KUMQUATS

SERVES 12

Active time: 1¼ hr   Start to finish: 1¾ hr

For cake

1¼	cups cake flour (not self-rising)
⅛	teaspoon salt
5	large eggs
⅔	cup sugar
1	teaspoon vanilla
5	tablespoons unsalted butter, melted and cooled

For topping

1	cup water
1	cup sugar
⅛	teaspoon salt
3	cups fresh kumquats (¾ lb without leaves), 1 kumquat (left whole) reserved for Sauternes syrup and remainder halved lengthwise (quartered if large) and seeds discarded
2	tablespoons sliced blanched almonds, toasted (see Tips, page 8)

For Sauternes syrup

1½	cups Sauternes
6	tablespoons sugar
	Zest of 1 kumquat, removed with a vegetable peeler

Special equipment: a 10- by 2-inch round cake pan
Garnish: confectioners sugar

Make cake:

▶ Put oven rack in middle position and preheat oven to 350°F. Butter cake pan. Line bottom of pan with a round of wax paper or parchment, then butter paper. Dust pan with flour, knocking out excess.

▶ Sift together flour and salt. Beat together eggs, sugar, and vanilla with an electric mixer at high speed until tripled in volume and thick enough to form a ribbon that takes 2 seconds to dissolve when beater is lifted, 7 to 8 minutes in a stand mixer or 14 to 16 minutes with a handheld.

▶ Resift flour mixture, one third at a time, over batter, folding in gently but thoroughly with a rubber spatula after each addition. Stir together butter and about ¾ cup batter in a small bowl until combined, then fold butter mixture into batter gently but thoroughly.

▶ Pour batter into cake pan and bake until a wooden pick inserted in center comes out clean, 30 to 40 minutes.

▶ Transfer cake in pan to a rack, then run a thin knife between cake and side of pan and cool cake, about 20 minutes. Invert cake onto a platter with a lip and peel off paper.

Make candied kumquat topping while cake bakes:

▶ Bring water, sugar, and salt to a boil in a 2-quart heavy saucepan, stirring until sugar is dissolved. Reduce heat and simmer, uncovered, 2 minutes. Add kumquats and simmer, uncovered, stirring occasionally, until tender, 10 to 12 minutes. Transfer kumquats to a heatproof bowl using a slotted spoon, then boil syrup until reduced to about ⅔ cup, 3 to 7 minutes. Pour over kumquats.

Make Sauternes syrup while cake cools:

▶ Bring Sauternes, sugar, and zest to a boil in a 1-quart heavy saucepan, stirring until sugar is dissolved, then boil until reduced to about 1 cup, 5 to 8 minutes. Discard zest.

Assemble cake:

▶ Prick top of cake all over with wooden pick or skewer, then brush or pour Sauternes syrup, little by little, evenly over cake, letting syrup be absorbed before each new addition.

▶ Mound kumquats on cake using slotted spoon, then sprinkle with almonds. Serve remaining kumquat syrup on the side.

Cooks' notes:

• Cake can be made and cooled (but not soaked with syrup or topped with fruit and almonds) 1 day ahead and kept, wrapped in plastic wrap, at room temperature.

• Candied kumquats can be made 3 days ahead and chilled, covered. Bring to room temperature before serving.

• Sauternes syrup can be made 1 day ahead and chilled, covered.

• Cake can be soaked with syrup 6 hours before serving and kept at room temperature, covered with an inverted large bowl or a cake keeper.

TOAST OF THE TOWN

A MODERN IRISH SUPPER

SERVES 4 TO 6

POTTED CRAB

IRISH BROWN BREAD

SANTA CAROLINA BARRICA
SELECTION CHARDONNAY '02

POTATO CABBAGE BUNDLES

IRISH BACON

BECKMEN VINEYARDS CUVÉE
LE BEC '01

**RED ENDIVE AND
WATERCRESS SALAD**

COUNTRY RHUBARB CAKE

POTTED CRAB

SERVES 4 TO 6 (HORS D'OEUVRE)
Active time: 45 min   Start to finish: 3¾ hr (includes chilling and
bringing to room temperature)

*In manor-house cooking, meat, poultry, and fish were
preserved by being "potted"—minced and combined with
seasonings, then packed in a container and covered with a
layer of fat or butter. The fat was removed before serving, and
the contents of the container spread on toasts or crackers.*

  1   lb cooked king crab legs in shell, thawed if frozen and
       shells split lengthwise
  ½   lb lump crabmeat, picked over
  1   stick (½ cup) unsalted butter
  1   tablespoon medium-dry Sherry
  1   teaspoon finely grated fresh lemon zest
  1   teaspoon fresh lemon juice
  1   teaspoon minced shallot
  ¼   teaspoon ground mace
  ¼   teaspoon salt
  ⅛   teaspoon black pepper
       Pinch of cayenne

Special equipment: **a 2-cup glass or ceramic dish; or 4 to
6 (4-oz) ramekins**
Accompaniment: **Irish brown bread (recipe follows), thinly
sliced and toasted**

▶ Remove crabmeat from shell, discarding cartilage, then
finely chop all of crabmeat and transfer to a bowl.
▶ Melt butter in a 10-inch heavy skillet over low heat and stir
in remaining ingredients (except crabmeat). Cool 3 minutes,
then stir in crabmeat.
▶ Transfer mixture to dish and tamp down. Cover surface with
wax paper, then cover dish with plastic wrap and chill at least
2 hours. Bring to room temperature before serving.

Cooks' note:
• Potted crab is best when made at least 1 day ahead (to
allow flavors to develop) and can be kept chilled up to 3 days.

IRISH BROWN BREAD

MAKES 1 (9-INCH) ROUND LOAF
Active time: 15 min   Start to finish: 2 hr (includes cooling)

  2   cups whole-wheat flour
  2   cups all-purpose flour plus additional for kneading
  ½   cup toasted wheat germ
  2   teaspoons salt
  2   teaspoons sugar
  1   teaspoon baking soda
  ½   teaspoon cream of tartar
  1   stick (½ cup) cold unsalted butter, cut into
       ½-inch cubes
  2   cups well-shaken buttermilk

▶ Put oven rack in middle position and preheat oven to
400°F. Butter a 9- by 2-inch round cake pan.
▶ Whisk together flours, wheat germ, salt, sugar, baking
soda, and cream of tartar in a large bowl until combined well.
Blend in butter with a pastry blender or your fingertips until
mixture resembles coarse meal. Make a well in center and
add buttermilk, stirring until a dough forms. Gently knead on
a floured surface, sprinkling with just enough flour to keep
dough from sticking, until smooth, about 3 minutes.
▶ Transfer dough to cake pan and flatten to fill pan. With a
sharp knife, cut an X (½ inch deep) across top of dough
(5 inches long). Bake until loaf is lightly browned and sounds
hollow when bottom is tapped, 30 to 40 minutes. Cool in pan
on a rack 10 minutes, then turn out onto rack and cool,
right side up, about 1 hour.

Cooks' notes:
• Bread can be served the same day it is made, but it slices
more easily if kept, wrapped in plastic wrap, at room
temperature 1 day.
• Leftover bread keeps, wrapped in plastic wrap, at room
temperature 4 days.

POTATO CABBAGE BUNDLES

SERVES 4 TO 6 (MAIN COURSE)

Active time: 1½ hr   Start to finish: 2¼ hr

- 1 medium onion, halved lengthwise, then sliced crosswise (1 cup)
- 1 tablespoon vegetable oil
- 1 large head leafy green cabbage (3 lb)
- 1 teaspoon minced garlic
- ¾ teaspoon salt
- ¼ teaspoon black pepper
- ⅔ cup water
- 2 lb large boiling potatoes
- 1 cup well-shaken buttermilk
- 3 oz extra-sharp white Cheddar, coarsely grated (1 cup)
- 2 tablespoons drained bottled horseradish
- ¾ stick (6 tablespoons) unsalted butter
- ¾ cup coarse fresh bread crumbs from a country-style loaf

Special equipment: a nonstick muffin tin with 6 (1-cup) muffin cups; 12 (10- by 2-inch) strips of parchment paper
Accompaniment: Irish bacon (recipe follows)

▶ Cook onion in oil in a 10-inch heavy skillet over moderate heat, stirring occasionally, until golden, 6 to 8 minutes.

▶ Bring a 6- to 8-quart pot of salted water (see Tips, page 8) to a boil. Discard any discolored or damaged tough outer leaves from cabbage, then core cabbage and carefully lower into boiling water using a slotted spoon.

▶ Boil cabbage, pulling off 6 large leaves (to be used as decorative wrappers and eaten if desired) with tongs as they soften and leaving them with remaining cabbage, 5 minutes. Transfer large leaves to a bowl of ice water to stop cooking. Transfer remaining cabbage to a colander to drain. Transfer large leaves to paper towels to drain, then pat dry.

▶ Lightly butter muffin cups, then put 2 parchment strips in a crisscross pattern in each cup. (You will have a 2-inch overhang.) Line each cup with a large cabbage leaf. Coarsely chop enough remaining cabbage to measure 3 cups, then add to onion in skillet along with garlic, ¼ teaspoon salt, ⅛ teaspoon pepper, and water and cook over moderate heat, stirring occasionally, until cabbage is tender and browned, about 10 minutes.

▶ Put oven rack in middle position and preheat oven to 350°F.

▶ Peel potatoes and cut into 1-inch cubes, then cover with cold salted water (see Tips, page 8) by 1 inch in a 2- to 3-quart saucepan and bring to a boil. Cook potatoes until tender, about 15 minutes. Drain in colander, then set potatoes in colander over saucepan to steam-dry, uncovered, 5 minutes. Mash potatoes in a large bowl, then stir in buttermilk, cheese, horseradish, 4 tablespoons butter, remaining ½ teaspoon salt, and remaining ⅛ teaspoon pepper until combined well.

▶ Melt remaining 2 tablespoons butter in a cleaned 10-inch heavy skillet over moderate heat until foam subsides, then cook bread crumbs, stirring frequently, until golden, 5 to 7 minutes.

▶ Fill each cabbage leaf with about ½ cup potato mixture, then divide cabbage mixture among leaves. Top with remaining potato mixture, then sprinkle evenly with bread crumbs. Fold edges of cabbage in toward filling (do not completely cover). Bake until heated through and edges of cabbage are well browned, 25 to 30 minutes.

▶ Transfer stuffed leaves to plates using parchment overhangs.

Cooks' note:
• Stuffed cabbage leaves can be assembled (but not baked), 1 day ahead and chilled, covered. Bring to room temperature before baking.

IRISH BACON

SERVES 4 TO 6

Active time: 15 min   Start to finish: 15 min

Irish bacon, sliced and packaged, is increasingly available at supermarkets. If you find it at the butcher counter, ask the butcher to slice it into ¼-inch-thick slices.

- 1 lb sliced Irish bacon or Canadian bacon
- 2 tablespoons vegetable oil

▶ Pat bacon dry and cook in 2 batches in oil (1 tablespoon per batch) in a 12-inch heavy skillet over moderate heat, turning over once, until browned, about 4 minutes per batch (use caution; oil will splatter). Transfer with tongs to a paper-towel-lined platter and keep warm, loosely covered with foil.

RED ENDIVE AND WATERCRESS SALAD

SERVES 4 TO 6

Active time: 20 min   Start to finish: 1¼ hr

- 1 tablespoon malt vinegar or cider vinegar
- 1 teaspoon Dijon mustard
- ½ teaspoon finely chopped fresh thyme
- ¼ teaspoon minced garlic
- ¼ teaspoon salt
- ⅛ teaspoon black pepper
- ¼ cup extra-virgin olive oil
- 1 lb Belgian endives (4 large), cut crosswise into
    1-inch pieces
- 6 oz red endive or radicchio di Treviso, cut crosswise into
    1-inch pieces, or 1 medium round head radicchio, torn
    into bite-size pieces
- 2 cups loosely packed watercress sprigs (2 oz)

▶ Whisk together vinegar, mustard, thyme, garlic, salt, and
pepper in a large salad bowl until combined, then add oil in a
slow stream, whisking until emulsified. Cover vinaigrette and
let stand 1 hour.

▶ Add salad greens to vinaigrette and toss to coat.

Cooks' note:
• Greens can be washed, dried, and cut 4 hours ahead and
chilled in a sealed plastic bag.

COUNTRY RHUBARB CAKE

SERVES 6 TO 8

Active time: 35 min   Start to finish: 1¼ hr

For cake
- 1 lb fresh rhubarb stalks, cut into ½-inch pieces (3 cups),
    or 3 cups frozen rhubarb, thawed after measuring
- 1 cup packed light brown sugar
- 2 cups cake flour (not self-rising), sifted
- ¾ teaspoon baking powder
- ½ cup plus 2 tablespoons granulated sugar
- 1 stick (½ cup) cold unsalted butter, cut into
    ½-inch cubes
- ⅓ cup whole milk
- 2 large eggs (1 separated)

For whiskey cream
- 1 cup chilled heavy cream
- 2 tablespoons confectioners sugar
- 1 tablespoon whiskey (preferably Irish)
- ½ teaspoon vanilla

Make cake:
▶ Put oven rack in middle position and preheat oven to
400°F. Butter a 10-inch glass or ceramic pie plate or a
2½-quart oval gratin dish and chill.
▶ Toss rhubarb with brown sugar in a bowl until coated.
▶ Whisk together flour, baking powder, and ½ cup granulated
sugar in a large bowl until combined well. Blend in butter
with a pastry blender or your fingertips until mixture
resembles coarse meal. Whisk together milk, whole egg, and
yolk. Make a well in center of flour mixture and add milk
mixture, stirring with a wooden spoon to gradually
incorporate flour and form a soft, sticky dough.
▶ Transfer half of dough to chilled pie plate and pat out over
bottom and halfway up side with well-floured hands, then
spoon rhubarb and any juices onto dough. Using a
tablespoon, spoon remaining dough in small mounds evenly
over top. Lightly beat egg white with a few drops of water,
then lightly brush cake with egg wash. Sprinkle remaining
2 tablespoons granulated sugar over top.
▶ Bake cake until top crust is golden and rhubarb is tender,
30 to 40 minutes. Transfer to a rack to cool, about
30 minutes.
Make whiskey cream:
▶ Beat cream with confectioners sugar, whiskey, and vanilla
in a bowl with an electric mixer until it forms stiff peaks.
▶ Serve cake warm or at room temperature with whiskey
cream.

Cooks' notes:
• Cake can be made 4 hours ahead and cooled completely,
then kept, wrapped well in plastic wrap, at room temperature.
Reheat if desired.
• You can cut this cake into wedges or dish it out with a spoon
like a cobbler.

OPPOSITE: **potato cabbage bundles and Irish bacon**

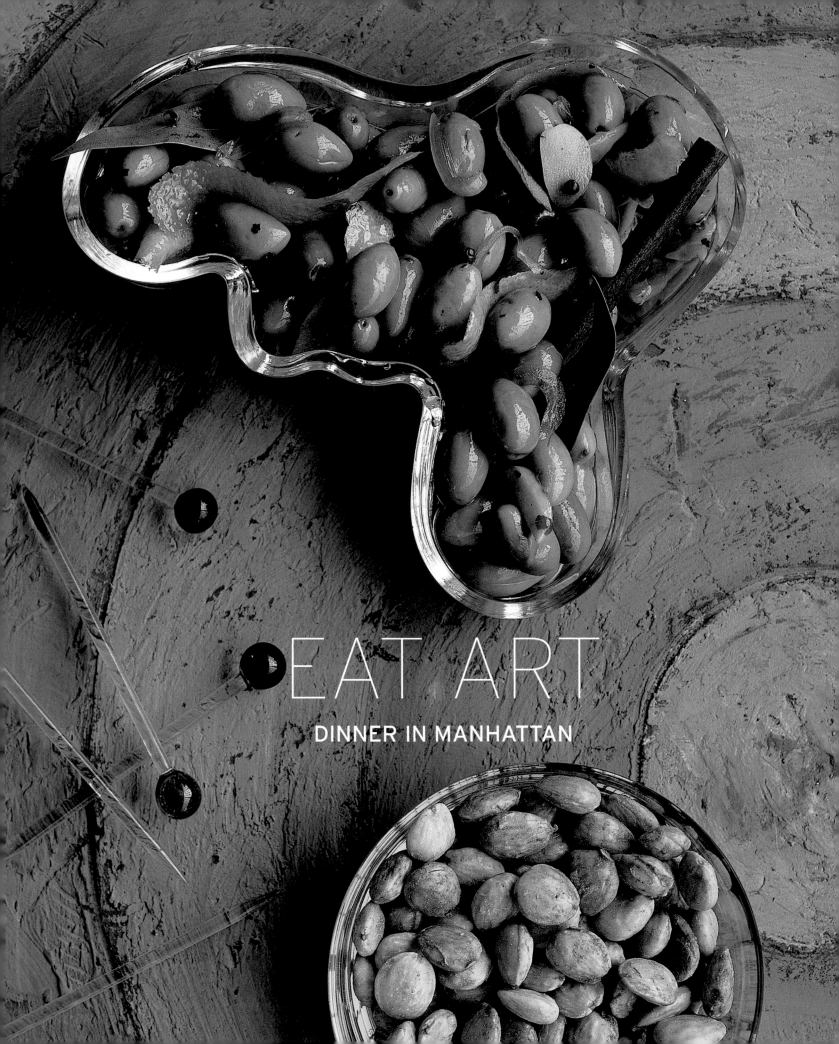

EAT ART

DINNER IN MANHATTAN

MANHATTANS

MAKES 2 DRINKS

Active time: 5 min   Start to finish: 5 min

4   oz blended whiskey (½ cup) such as Seagram's 7
2   oz sweet vermouth (¼ cup)
2   dashes Angostura bitters

Garnish: maraschino cherries

▶ Fill a cocktail shaker halfway with ice, then add all ingredients and shake or stir well. Strain into 2 Martini glasses.

SPICED MARCONA ALMONDS

MAKES ABOUT 2 CUPS

Active time: 10 min   Start to finish: 1 hr (includes cooling)

1   large egg white
1   teaspoon salt
½   teaspoon ground cumin
¼   teaspoon smoked hot or sweet Spanish paprika
2   cups blanched Marcona almonds (10 oz; see Sources)

Special equipment: parchment paper

▶ Put oven rack in middle position and preheat oven to 350°F. Line a large baking sheet with parchment.
▶ Whisk together egg white, salt, cumin, and paprika in a bowl, then add almonds and toss to coat. Spread almonds evenly on baking sheet and roast until golden, about 20 minutes.
▶ Transfer nuts on parchment to a rack and cool completely (almonds will crisp as they cool). Loosen nuts from parchment with a spatula and transfer to a bowl.

Cooks' notes:
• Almonds can be made 5 days ahead and kept in an airtight container at room temperature.
• If you have trouble finding Marcona almonds, you can substitute regular blanched almonds.

MARINATED PICHOLINE OLIVES

MAKES ABOUT 2 CUPS

Active time: 20 min   Start to finish: 24½ hr (includes marinating)

2   large garlic cloves, thinly sliced lengthwise
½   cup plus 2 tablespoons olive oil
½   cup white-wine vinegar
1   large shallot, thinly sliced lengthwise
1   tablespoon packed dark brown sugar
¼   teaspoon whole allspice, lightly crushed with flat side of a large heavy knife
1   teaspoon whole pink peppercorns, lightly crushed
1   (3-inch) cinnamon stick
2   Turkish bay leaves or 1 California
2   (3- by 1-inch) strips fresh lemon zest (see Tips, page 8)
2   (4- by 1-inch) strips fresh orange zest
2   cups whole *picholine* or other brine-cured small green olives (¾ lb)

▶ Cook garlic in 2 tablespoons oil in a small heavy skillet over moderate heat, stirring, until pale golden, about 30 seconds. Transfer garlic with a slotted spoon to a small bowl and reserve oil separately (to prevent garlic from continuing to brown in hot oil).
▶ Simmer ¼ cup vinegar with shallot and brown sugar in a 1-quart heavy saucepan, uncovered, stirring occasionally, until liquid is reduced to about 1 tablespoon, about 4 minutes.
▶ Add garlic, garlic oil, remaining ½ cup olive oil, remaining ¼ cup vinegar, spices, bay leaves, zests, and olives and bring to a simmer. Transfer mixture to a bowl and cool to warm. Marinate olives, covered and chilled, at least 24 hours.
▶ If desired, reheat in saucepan over low heat, stirring until warm. Transfer with a slotted spoon to a serving dish.

Cooks' notes:
• Olives can marinate up to 5 days.
• These olives can be served warm or at room temperature, but the flavor is brighter and the texture more tender when they're warm.

OPPOSITE: warm cucumber soup with scallop and sole mousseline

WARM CUCUMBER SOUP WITH SCALLOP AND SOLE MOUSSELINES

SERVES 10

Active time: 2½ hr   Start to finish: 12 hr (includes making mousselines)

Most people never think about cooking cucumber, but it acquires a wonderful velvety texture when cooked and puréed. The flavor and color of this soup are at their best when served warm, not hot, making it a great choice for a dinner party.

    3   large seedless cucumbers (usually plastic-wrapped;
         3 lb total), quartered lengthwise and cut crosswise into
         ¼-inch-thick slices
    1   small russet (baking) potato (¼ lb)
    1   medium onion, chopped
    1   medium carrot, chopped (½ cup)
   ½   celery rib, chopped
    1   large garlic clove, chopped
    1   Turkish or ½ California bay leaf
    1   (3-inch) fresh thyme sprig
    2   tablespoons unsalted butter

    4   cups water
   ¼   teaspoon black pepper
  1½   teaspoons salt
         Scallop and sole mousselines (recipe follows)

Garnish: **thinly sliced smoked sablefish (black cod); fresh chives or fresh dill sprigs**

▶ Cook cucumbers in a 4- to 5-quart pot of boiling salted water (see Tips, page 8), uncovered, just until water returns to a boil, about 1 minute, then immediately drain in a colander and transfer to a bowl of ice and cold water to stop cooking. Drain cucumbers well, then purée in 2 batches in a blender until as smooth as possible, about 1 minute, transferring to a bowl.

▶ Peel potato and cut into ½-inch cubes. Cook onion, carrot, celery, garlic, bay leaf, and thyme in butter in a 2-quart heavy saucepan over moderate heat, stirring occasionally, until vegetables are softened, about 3 minutes. Add potato, 4 cups water, pepper, and ½ teaspoon salt and simmer, partially covered, until potato is very tender, about 15 minutes. Discard bay leaf and thyme.

▶Purée mixture in batches in blender until very smooth, about 1 minute (use caution when blending hot liquids), transferring to a large bowl. Chill, uncovered, until completely cool, about 30 minutes.

▶Stir cucumber purée into potato purée and force soup through a fine-mesh sieve into a large bowl, pressing hard on and then discarding solids.

▶Stir remaining teaspoon salt into soup, then reheat in a bowl in a microwave or in a saucepan on stovetop over low heat (microwaving is best because it preserves the soup's bright green color). Put 1 mousseline in each of 10 shallow soup bowls and pour warm soup around each.

Cooks' note:
• Soup can be made 2 days ahead and chilled, covered.

SCALLOP AND SOLE MOUSSELINES
MAKES 10 (2-OZ) MOUSSELINES
Active time: 1½ hr   Start to finish: 10 hr (includes chilling)

If you're making this entire menu in a single oven, we recommend baking the mousselines a day ahead. On the day of the dinner, reheat them just before serving.

½ lb sea scallops, tough muscle removed from side
    of each if necessary
½ lb sole fillet, cut into 1-inch pieces
1 tablespoon lightly beaten egg white
1 cup chilled heavy cream
2 tablespoons unsalted butter, melted
¼ teaspoon salt
⅛ teaspoon black pepper
    Large pinch of freshly grated nutmeg
2 teaspoons chopped fresh chives
1 teaspoon chopped fresh dill

Special equipment: parchment paper; 10 (2-oz) metal timbale molds (2 inches in diameter)

▶Rinse scallops and sole and pat dry, then purée in a food processor until very smooth. Force purée through a fine-mesh sieve into a metal bowl, scraping bottom of sieve as needed.

▶Set metal bowl in a larger bowl of ice and cold water, then add egg white to purée and stir vigorously with a wooden

spoon or rubber spatula until well combined. Add cream 2 tablespoons at a time, stirring after each addition until incorporated. (Mousseline should be the consistency of soft mashed potatoes; if it becomes runny or separates, stop adding cream and chill mixture, covered—still in ice bath— until firmer, about 30 minutes. Then continue adding cream.) Cover bowl and chill mixture 8 hours.

▶Put oven rack in middle position and preheat oven to 350°F.

▶Cut out 10 rounds of parchment paper to line bottoms of molds and 10 rounds to line tops of molds, using 1 timbale mold as a guide. Brush molds with some melted butter and line bottom of each with a round of parchment. Chill molds 5 minutes (to set butter), then brush paper and sides of molds again with more melted butter.

▶Stir salt, pepper, nutmeg, chives, and dill into mousseline, then divide among molds (they will be about two-thirds full). Rap molds on counter once or twice to settle mixture, then put a buttered parchment round, buttered side down, on surface of each mousseline. Put molds in an 8-inch square or round baking pan (2 inches deep) and bake in a hot water bath (see Tips, page 8) in oven until mousselines are just set and springy to the touch, 20 to 25 minutes.

▶Cool mousselines in molds on a rack until warm, about 10 minutes, then invert onto a large plate and pat dry with paper towels before transferring to soup bowls.

Cooks' notes:
• Mousselines can be baked 1 day ahead and cooled completely in molds, then chilled in molds, covered. Bring to room temperature, then reheat in a hot water bath in oven about 15 minutes.
• The mousseline purée can also be spread and baked in a loaf pan and served as a fish pâté.

OPPOSITE: **vegetable-stuffed loin of veal with sweetbreads and orzo "risotto"; bibb lettuce and celery leaf salad**

VEGETABLE-STUFFED LOIN OF VEAL WITH SWEETBREADS

SERVES 10

Active time: 1½ hr   Start to finish: 19 hr (includes soaking and weighting sweetbreads)

For sweetbreads, stuffing, and sauce

- 4 lb veal sweetbreads
- 1 tablespoon plus 1 teaspoon salt
- ½ cup shelled pistachios (not dyed red; 2 oz)
- 1 tablespoon olive oil
- 5 tablespoons unsalted butter
- 2 oz thinly sliced lean pancetta, chopped
- 1 medium onion, finely chopped
- 1 medium carrot, cut into ¼-inch dice
- ½ celery rib, cut into ¼-inch dice
- 1 large garlic clove, chopped
- 1 Turkish or ½ California bay leaf
- 1 (3-inch) fresh thyme sprig
- 1 cup medium-dry Sherry
- 1 cup veal demi-glace
- 1 cup water
- ¾ teaspoon black pepper
- 6 oz spinach, coarse stems discarded (4 cups)
- ⅜ teaspoon freshly grated nutmeg

For veal

- 4 lb boneless veal strip loin roast or pork strip loin (not tied), completely trimmed of all fat, sinew, and silver membrane
- 2 tablespoons vegetable oil

Special equipment: **3 to 4 lb of weights such as large cans of soup or vegetables; parchment paper; kitchen string; an instant-read thermometer**

Prepare sweetbreads:

▶ Soak sweetbreads in a large bowl of ice and cold water in the refrigerator, changing water occasionally (2 or 3 times), at least 8 hours. Drain sweetbreads and transfer to a 4-quart heavy saucepan. Cover with cold water by 1 inch and add 1 tablespoon salt. Bring to a boil, then reduce heat and simmer, uncovered, until sweetbreads plump and feel slightly firmer to the touch, about 3 minutes. Drain in a colander and transfer to a bowl of cold water to stop cooking. Cut away any fat and pull away as much membrane and connective tissue as possible with a small paring knife without breaking up sweetbreads.

▶ Arrange sweetbreads in 1 layer in a baking dish, then cover with plastic wrap and top with another baking dish or plate holding weights. Chill sweetbreads, weighted, at least 8 hours.

▶ While sweetbreads chill, blanch pistachios in a small saucepan of boiling water 1 minute, then drain and peel.

▶ Pat sweetbreads dry and season with salt and pepper. Heat oil and 2 tablespoons butter in a deep 12-inch skillet over moderately high heat until foam subsides, then sauté half of sweetbreads, turning over once, until golden brown, about 4 minutes total, and transfer to a plate. Add 1 tablespoon butter to skillet and sauté remaining sweetbreads in same manner, transferring to plate.

▶ Add remaining 2 tablespoons butter to skillet, then reduce heat to moderate and cook pancetta, stirring occasionally, until beginning to brown, 2 to 3 minutes. Add onion, carrot, celery, garlic, bay leaf, and thyme, then reduce heat to moderately low and cook, stirring, until vegetables are softened, 3 to 5 minutes. Add Sherry and bring to a boil, then add demi-glace, water, ½ teaspoon salt, ¼ teaspoon pepper, pistachios, and sweetbreads and return to a boil. Reduce heat to low, then cover surface of mixture with a buttered round of parchment paper (buttered side down) and simmer sweetbreads, skillet partially covered with lid, until firm but still springy to the touch, 15 to 20 minutes.

▶ Transfer sweetbreads with a slotted spoon to a bowl and, when cool enough to handle, pull apart into 1- to 1½-inch pieces. Ladle cooking liquid through a sieve into a bowl, discarding bay leaf and thyme, and reserve. Reserve vegetables in another bowl for sauce and stuffing.

Make stuffing:

▶ Cook spinach in a large pot of boiling salted water (see Tips, page 8), uncovered, until wilted, about 20 seconds, then drain in colander. Transfer spinach to a bowl of cold water to stop cooking and drain again, squeezing handfuls of spinach to remove excess liquid. Chop spinach and stir into reserved vegetables along with ¼ teaspoon salt, ¼ teaspoon pepper, and ⅛ teaspoon nutmeg.

Stuff and roast veal loin:

▶ Put oven rack in middle position and preheat oven to 400°F.

▶ Make a hole for stuffing that runs lengthwise through veal: Beginning in middle of 1 end of roast, insert a sharp long thin knife lengthwise toward center, then repeat at opposite end of loin to complete an incision running through middle. Open up incision with your fingers, working from both ends, to create a 1½-inch-wide opening. Pack loin with all but

2 tablespoons vegetable stuffing, pushing from both ends toward center.

▶ Tie veal roast with kitchen string at 1-inch intervals along entire length of roast. Pat veal dry and season generously with salt and pepper.

▶ Heat oil in an ovenproof 12-inch heavy skillet over high heat until just smoking, then brown veal, turning with tongs, about 5 minutes.

▶ Transfer skillet to oven and roast veal until thermometer inserted diagonally 2 inches into meat (do not touch stuffing) registers 150°F, 45 to 50 minutes for veal; about 40 minutes for pork. Transfer roast with tongs to a platter and let stand 20 minutes.

Make sauce and reheat sweetbreads while veal stands:

▶ Skim fat from sweetbread cooking liquid and bring liquid to a boil in a 2½-quart heavy saucepan. Stir in remaining 2 tablespoons vegetables, remaining ¼ teaspoon salt, remaining ¼ teaspoon pepper, and remaining ¼ teaspoon nutmeg. Add sweetbreads along with any veal juices accumulated on platter and simmer until just heated through. Remove from heat and keep warm, covered.

▶ Discard string, then cut veal into 1-inch-thick slices and serve with sweetbreads and some sauce. Serve remaining sauce on the side.

Cooks' notes:

• Sweetbreads can be soaked in ice and cold water in refrigerator up to 24 hours.

• Weighted sweetbreads can be chilled up to 24 hours.

• Veal loin can be stuffed 1 day ahead and chilled, covered. Bring to room temperature before roasting. (Chill sweetbreads, cooking liquid, and remaining vegetables separately.)

• If you choose to omit the sweetbreads, simply begin recipe by sautéing the pancetta. In that case, you may also want to purchase a larger veal or pork loin—going up to a 5-pound veal loin or a 6-pound pork loin.

ORZO "RISOTTO"

SERVES 10 (SIDE DISH)

Active time: 10 min   Start to finish: 20 min

- 1 (1-lb) box orzo (rice-shaped pasta; not Greek)
- 2 cups chicken stock or reduced-sodium broth
- 1 packed teaspoon finely grated fresh orange zest
- ¼ teaspoon finely chopped fresh thyme
- 2 oz finely grated Parmigiano-Reggiano (1 cup; see Tips, page 8)
- 2 tablespoons unsalted butter
- ½ teaspoon salt
- ½ teaspoon black pepper

▶ Cook orzo in a large pot of boiling salted water (see Tips, page 8) until barely al dente, 5 to 6 minutes. Drain in a colander and rinse under cold water to stop cooking.

▶ Transfer orzo to a 2-quart heavy saucepan and add stock, zest, and thyme. Simmer over moderate heat, stirring constantly, until stock is absorbed, about 5 minutes.

▶ Stir in cheese, butter, salt, and pepper and serve immediately.

BIBB LETTUCE AND CELERY-LEAF SALAD

SERVES 10

Active time: 15 min   Start to finish: 15 min

- 2 tablespoons red-wine vinegar
- 1 tablespoon finely chopped shallot
- ¼ teaspoon salt
- ⅛ teaspoon black pepper
- 3 tablespoons olive oil
- 2 tablespoons hazelnut oil
- 2 lb Bibb lettuce (10 small heads), leaves separated
- 2 cups celery leaves (from 2 bunches celery; both top leaves and inner leaves from tender pale ribs)

▶ Whisk together vinegar, shallot, salt, and pepper in a small bowl, then add oils in a slow stream, whisking until emulsified. Toss lettuce and celery leaves with just enough vinaigrette to coat in a large bowl.

DARK-ROAST COFFEE GELÉE
MAKES ABOUT 3 CUPS
Active time: 20 min   Start to finish: 8½ hr (includes chilling)

For this recipe, the darker and richer the coffee, the better. We made cone-filtered coffee, but it's equally delicious with perked or plunged coffee. Don't use an electric drip coffeemaker for this recipe—too much yield is lost to evaporation.

Curry powder may seem like a strange addition to the whipped cream topping, but it's absolutely delicious. You won't perceive any curry flavor per se—when combined with the brown sugar it simply lends fullness and depth.

For gelée
- 6 tablespoons finely ground (for filter) dark-roast coffee
- 2¼ cups boiling-hot water plus 1 tablespoon cold water
- ½ cup granulated sugar
- 1½ teaspoons unflavored gelatin (from a ¼-oz envelope)
- 2 teaspoons vanilla

For topping
- ¼ cup packed dark brown sugar
- 1 cup chilled heavy cream
  Scant ¼ teaspoon curry powder

Make gelée:
▶ Brew ground coffee in a filter-style coffeemaker (not electric) or a sieve lined with a paper filter using 2 cups boiling-hot water.
▶ Meanwhile, bring granulated sugar and remaining ¼ cup hot water to a boil in a small saucepan, stirring until sugar is dissolved, then remove from heat.
▶ Sprinkle gelatin over 1 tablespoon cold water and let soften 1 minute. Stir together hot coffee, sugar syrup, and vanilla in a metal bowl, then add gelatin mixture, stirring until dissolved. Chill, covered, until softly set, at least 8 hours.
Make topping:
▶ Force brown sugar through a sieve into a bowl, then add cream and curry powder and beat with an electric mixer or a whisk until it just holds soft peaks.
▶ Divide gelée among 10 (2- to 4-ounce) cups (such as espresso cups) and top with dollops of whipped cream.

Cooks' note:
• Gelée can be chilled up to 1 day.

LEMON PEEL TUILES
MAKES ABOUT 6 DOZEN COOKIES
Active time: 45 min   Start to finish: 1½ hr

These thin cookies resemble the strip of lemon peel that's often served with a cup of espresso.

- ½ cup sugar
- 2 rounded tablespoons finely grated fresh lemon zest (from 4 lemons; see Tips, page 8)
- ½ stick (¼ cup) unsalted butter, softened
- ½ teaspoon vanilla
- 2 large egg whites
- ¼ cup all-purpose flour

Special equipment: a nonstick bakeware liner such as Silpat; a pastry bag fitted with a ¼-inch plain tip; a small offset spatula; a 1½- to 2-inch diameter rolling pin or wooden dowel

▶ Put oven rack in middle position and preheat oven to 350°F. Line a large baking sheet with nonstick liner.
▶ Grind sugar and zest in a food processor, pulsing 4 or 5 times, until combined well, then transfer to a bowl. Add butter and vanilla and beat with an electric mixer at medium speed until pale and fluffy, 3 to 5 minutes. Reduce speed to low, then add egg whites and mix until just combined, about 30 seconds. Add flour and mix until just combined, about 30 seconds.
▶ Transfer batter to pastry bag and pipe 12 (3-inch-long) lines, about 1 inch apart, on baking sheet. (Be careful not to squeeze bag too hard—lines should only be ¼ inch wide.)
▶ Bake *tuiles* until edges begin to brown, 7 to 9 minutes. Let *tuiles* stand on baking sheet 20 seconds (just long enough to allow them to firm up slightly), then transfer with offset spatula to rolling pin (stabilized on a cooling rack), draping them diagonally and wiping spatula clean before transferring next cookie. (If cookies become too crisp to drape, put them back in oven for a few seconds to soften.) Make more *tuiles* in same manner, using a cool baking sheet and wiping nonstick liner clean with paper towels between batches.

Cooks' note:
• *Tuiles* can be made 5 days ahead and kept, layered between sheets of wax paper, in an airtight container at room temperature.

PERECT HARMONY

A NORTHERN THAI FEAST

SERVES 8

ICED LEMONGRASS TEA

JUNGLE CURRY WITH PORK AND THAI EGGPLANT

STEAMED STICKY RICE

SPICY CHICKEN SOUP

TOMATO AND MINCED PORK RELISH WITH VEGETABLES

CUCUMBER SALAD

STEAMED CATFISH IN BANANA LEAVES

STIR-FRIED CHINESE BROCCOLI

FAIRVIEW COASTAL PINOTAGE '02

UÍTKYK STELLENBOSCH SAUVIGNON BLANC '03

PINEAPPLE ICE CREAM

MANGO COCONUT ICE CREAM

LACY RICE NOODLE CRISPS

KLEIN CONSTANTIA ESTATE VIN DE CONSTANCE '99

For help in finding specialty ingredients in this menu, see Sources.

ICED LEMONGRASS TEA
(Nahm Takrai)
MAKES 8 DRINKS
Active time: 10 min   Start to finish: 30 min

12   fresh lemongrass stalks, 1 or 2 outer leaves discarded
½   cup sugar
8   cups water

▶ Trim off bottom 6 inches of lemongrass stalks (reserve for Thai red curry paste, page 127). Cut enough lemongrass tops crosswise into ½-inch pieces (discard any discolored parts) to measure 1 cup. Bring lemongrass pieces, sugar, and 2 cups water to a boil in a 2-quart heavy saucepan, stirring until sugar is dissolved, then remove from heat and let steep, partially covered, 20 minutes.
▶ Put remaining 6 cups water in a pitcher. Blend lemongrass mixture in a blender until lemongrass is finely chopped (use caution when blending hot liquids), then pour through a fine-mesh sieve into water in pitcher, discarding solids. Serve over ice.

Cooks' note:
• Lemongrass tea can be made 1 day ahead and chilled, covered.

JUNGLE CURRY WITH PORK AND THAI EGGPLANT
(Gaeng Pah Muu)
SERVES 8 (AS PART OF LARGER MEAL)
Active time: 3¼ hr   Start to finish: 7¼ hr (includes making curry paste and stock)

Don't be intimidated by the start-to-finish time; the curry paste and chicken stock can be made days ahead. Once you have those components at hand, the recipe only takes about 1 hour to put together. If you prefer your food less spicy, use the smaller amounts of curry paste and vegetable oil.

1   lb Thai apple eggplants (see cooks' note, below)
2   tablespoons to ¼ cup vegetable oil
¼   to ½ cup Thai red curry paste (recipe follows)
1½   lb pork tenderloin, halved lengthwise, then sliced crosswise ¼ inch thick
⅓   cup julienne strips peeled fresh or frozen *grachai* (lesser galangal or wild ginger; thawed if frozen) or drained bottled *grachai*, rinsed, or ginger
3   oz Chinese long beans or green beans, cut into 1-inch pieces
8   canned baby corn, rinsed, drained, and halved lengthwise
1½   cups Thai chicken stock (page 127)
3   tablespoons *nam pla* (Asian fish sauce; preferably Thai)
5   (4-inch-long) fresh or frozen Kaffir lime leaves (sometimes called *bai makroot*)
1   fresh *chee fah* chile or 2 red jalapeño chiles, thinly sliced crosswise and seeds discarded
¼   teaspoon salt
1   cup loosely packed *bai grapao* (holy basil leaves)

Special equipment: **a large (6-qt) wok**
Accompaniment: **Thai pickled garlic (*gratiam dong*)**

▶ Trim eggplants and cut into 1-inch wedges (do this just before heating oil to avoid discoloration).
▶ Heat oil (see above) in wok over moderate heat until warm, about 30 seconds. Add curry paste (to taste) and cook, stirring constantly, until very fragrant and a shade darker, 2 to 3 minutes. Add pork and stir-fry over high heat until no longer pink on outside, 1 to 2 minutes. Add eggplant, *grachai*, beans, baby corn, and stock and simmer, stirring, until eggplant is crisp-tender, 3 to 5 minutes. Add fish sauce, lime leaves, chile, and salt and bring to a boil, then remove from heat. Stir in half of basil.
▶ Serve topped with remaining basil.

Cooks' notes:
• Long slender Asian eggplant can be substituted for Thai apple eggplant. Thai apple eggplant is traditionally eaten raw or crisp-tender, but Asian eggplant needs to be precooked. Cut Asian eggplant into 1-inch cubes and toss with 1 tablespoon vegetable oil, then bake in 1 layer in a shallow baking pan in a preheated 400°F oven until crisp-tender, about 12 minutes. Proceed with recipe.
• You can substitute bottled red curry paste for homemade. (We recommend Mae Ploy brand.)

THAI RED CURRY PASTE
MAKES ABOUT 1 CUP
Active time: 1½ hr   Start to finish: 1½ hr

There will be some curry paste left over after making the jungle curry (recipe precedes) and steamed catfish (page 131). Simply stir the remainder together with unsweetened coconut milk to give chicken, shrimp, or mussels a Thai spin.

17 to 20 (2- to 3-inch-long) *prik haeng* (dried hot red
      chiles), halved and seeds discarded
 4 teaspoons coriander seeds
 2 fresh lemongrass stalks, 1 or 2 outer leaves discarded
      (or use reserved bottoms from iced lemongrass tea,
      page 126)
 1 teaspoon whole black peppercorns
 4 teaspoons finely chopped peeled fresh or thawed
      frozen greater galangal (sometimes called *kha*)
 6 (4-inch-long) fresh or frozen Kaffir lime leaves
      (sometimes called *bai makroot*), finely chopped
 2 tablespoons chopped fresh cilantro roots or stems
 5 small shallots, chopped (6 tablespoons)
 ¼ cup chopped garlic
15 to 20 (1-inch-long) red *prik kii noo* (fresh bird's-eye
      chiles) or serrano chiles, finely chopped
 2 teaspoons *ga-pi* (Thai shrimp paste)
 ½ teaspoon salt

Special equipment: a large (2-cup) mortar and pestle (preferably granite) or a mini food processor

▶Cut dried chiles into ¼-inch pieces with kitchen shears and soak in warm water until softened, about 20 minutes. Drain well in a sieve.
▶While chiles soak, toast coriander in a dry small heavy skillet over moderate heat, shaking skillet, until fragrant, 3 to 4 minutes, then cool. Thinly slice lower 6 inches of lemongrass stalks and finely chop.
▶Finely grind coriander and peppercorns with mortar and pestle (or in mini food processor), about 2 minutes, then toss together with lemongrass, galangal, lime leaves, cilantro, shallot, garlic, fresh chiles, and soaked dried chiles in a bowl. Pound mixture in 3 batches with mortar and pestle until a fairly smooth paste is formed, 8 to

10 minutes per batch, transferring to cleaned bowl. (If using food processor, add about 1½ tablespoons water per batch.) Return all of curry paste to mortar, then add shrimp paste and salt and pound (or pulse) until combined well, about 1 minute.

Cooks' note:
• For the freshest flavor, curry paste is best used the same day it's made. It keeps 1 week, surface covered with plastic wrap, chilled.

THAI CHICKEN STOCK
MAKES ABOUT 10 CUPS
Active time: 45 min   Start to finish: 4 hr

 6 lb chicken wings, halved at joint
 4 qt cold water
 ½ cup coarsely chopped fresh cilantro stems
 3 garlic cloves, smashed
 3 (¼-inch-thick) fresh ginger slices, smashed
1½ teaspoons salt

Special equipment: cheesecloth

▶Crack chicken wing bones in several places with back of a cleaver or large knife on a cutting board. Bring all ingredients to a boil in an 8- to 10-quart pot, skimming froth as necessary, then reduce heat and gently simmer, partially covered, 2½ hours.
▶Remove pot from heat and cool stock to room temperature, about 1 hour. Pour stock through a large fine-mesh sieve lined with a triple thickness of cheesecloth into a large bowl and discard solids. Measure stock: If there is more than 10 cups, boil in cleaned pot until reduced; if there is less, add water.
▶If using stock right away, skim off and discard fat. If not, cool stock completely, uncovered, before skimming fat (it will be easier to remove when cool), then chill, covered.

Cooks' note:
• Stock can be chilled 3 days or frozen 1 month.

STEAMED STICKY RICE
(Kao Niaow)

SERVES 8 (AS PART OF LARGER MEAL)
Active time: 10 min   Start to finish: 3½ hr (includes soaking rice)

4 cups raw Thai sticky rice (26 oz)

Special equipment: **cheesecloth**

▶ Cover rice with 2 to 3 inches cold water in a large bowl and soak at room temperature at least 3 hours.
▶ Drain rice and put in a steamer basket (see cooks' note, below) lined with cheesecloth. Steam rice, covered with lid, over boiling water until shiny and tender, about 20 minutes. Remove from heat and let stand, covered, 5 minutes. Serve hot, warm, or at room temperature.

Cooks' notes:
• Rice can be soaked up to 12 hours.
• Thai cooks use a large conical steamer basket for steaming the rice, but we found that a footed colander or the steamer insert of a pasta pot also works well.

SPICY CHICKEN SOUP
(Yam Jin Gai)

SERVES 8 (AS PART OF LARGER MEAL; MAKES ABOUT 6½ CUPS)
Active time: 1½ hr   Start to finish: 5½ hr (includes making stock)

6 cups Thai chicken stock (page 127)
2 to 3 teaspoons northern Thai chile powder (recipe follows)
4 small shallots, thinly sliced (¼ cup)
¾ lb skinless boneless chicken breast, cut into 1½- by ¼-inch strips
1 to 2 tablespoons *nam pla* (Asian fish sauce; preferably Thai)
2 tablespoons soy sauce
½ cup coarsely chopped fresh mint
2 scallions, thinly sliced
1 cup loosely packed fresh cilantro leaves

▶ Bring stock to a simmer in a 3- to 4-quart saucepan, then stir in chile powder (to taste) and shallots and simmer, uncovered, 2 minutes. Add chicken and simmer until just cooked through, about 2 minutes. Stir in fish sauce (to taste) and soy sauce and simmer 1 minute. Remove from heat and stir in mint.
▶ Serve soup warm, topped with scallions and cilantro.

Cooks' note:
• Soup (without fish sauce, soy sauce, and mint) can be made 1 day ahead and cooled completely, uncovered, then chilled, covered.

NORTHERN THAI CHILE POWDER

MAKES ABOUT ½ CUP
Active time: 15 min   Start to finish: 20 min

Long pepper (sometimes called diplii diplii*) is a small, cylindrical pinecone-shaped spice that tastes like a cross between pepper and cassia. When toasted and crushed, it's delicious in any kind of Asian-inspired salad.*

About 16 *diplii diplii* (long peppers)
2 tablespoons coriander seeds
2 tablespoons cumin seeds
2 tablespoons Sichuan peppercorns (optional)
2 tablespoons torn *prik haeng* (dried hot red chiles), seeds discarded

Special equipment: **an electric coffee/spice grinder**

▶ Break enough *diplii diplii* in half to measure 2 tablespoons. Toast *diplii diplii*, coriander, cumin, peppercorns (if using), and chiles together in a 10- to 12-inch heavy skillet over moderately low heat, stirring, until fragrant and coriander seeds are a shade darker, 5 to 6 minutes. Transfer spices to a bowl to cool to room temperature, about 5 minutes, then finely grind in grinder.

Cooks' note:
• Chile powder can be made 3 days ahead and kept in an airtight container at room temperature.

OPPOSITE: spicy chicken soup

TOMATO AND MINCED PORK RELISH WITH VEGETABLES
(Nam Prik Ong)

SERVES 8 (AS PART OF LARGER MEAL)
Active time: 1½ hr   Start to finish: 1½ hr

Relishes are a cornerstone of Thai cooking, playing a crucial role in the balance of hot, salty, sour, and sweet. The vegetables are traditionally dipped into the relish and then eaten, but you might find it easier to use a plate. Because this dish is quite spicy even with just a few chiles, we suggest using the least amount the first time you make the recipe.

10   to 18 (2- to 3-inch-long) *prik haeng* (dried red chiles),
   halved and seeds discarded
 6   oz Chinese long beans, trimmed and cut into
   3-inch pieces
 6   small shallots, chopped (½ cup)
 4   garlic cloves, chopped
 ½   teaspoon salt
 ¼   teaspoon *ga-pi* (Thai shrimp paste)
 ⅛   teaspoon sugar
 ½   lb red cherry tomatoes, quartered
 ½   lb boneless pork shoulder, cut into ¼-inch pieces
 2   tablespoons vegetable oil
 1   tablespoon *nam pla* (Asian fish sauce; preferably Thai)
 4   carrots, cut diagonally into ¼-inch-thick slices
 ½   head cabbage (1½ lb), cut into 8 wedges
   (including core)

Special equipment: a large (2-cup) mortar and pestle
(preferably granite); a large (6-qt) wok

▶ Cut chiles into ¼-inch pieces with kitchen shears and soak in warm water until softened, about 20 minutes. Drain in a sieve.
▶ While chiles soak, blanch beans in a saucepan of boiling salted water (see Tips, page 8) 1 minute, then transfer to a bowl of ice and cold water to stop cooking. Drain well.
▶ Pound chiles, shallots, garlic, salt, shrimp paste, and sugar to a coarse paste with mortar and pestle, about 8 minutes. Transfer half of paste to a small bowl, then add half of tomatoes to mortar and pound until tomatoes begin to break up and form a chunky sauce. Transfer tomato mixture to another bowl and pound remaining chile paste and tomatoes in same manner.

▶ Pat pork dry. Heat oil in wok over moderate heat until hot but not smoking, then cook pork, stirring, until no longer pink, 3 to 4 minutes. Add tomato mixture and cook, stirring occasionally, until liquid is reduced and slightly thickened, 3 to 5 minutes. Add fish sauce and cook, stirring occasionally, 1 minute.
▶ Serve relish warm or at room temperature with vegetables on the side.

Cooks' notes:
• Chile paste (without tomatoes) can be made in a mini food processor, scraping down sides occasionally, instead of with a mortar and pestle.
• Relish (without fish sauce) can be made 1 day ahead and chilled, covered. Reheat relish over moderate heat, stirring, until hot before adding fish sauce.

CUCUMBER SALAD
(Yam Taeng Kwa)

SERVES 8 (AS PART OF LARGER MEAL)
Active time: 20 min   Start to finish: 20 min

 2   tablespoons fine-quality dried shrimp such as BDMP or
   Sea Emperor brands (optional)
 ½   cup fresh lime juice
 3   tablespoons sugar
 2   tablespoons *nam pla* (Asian fish sauce; preferably Thai)
 2   seedless cucumbers (usually plastic-wrapped; 1½ lb
   total), halved lengthwise and sliced crosswise
   ⅛ inch thick
 2   small shallots, thinly sliced (2 tablespoons)

▶ Finely grind shrimp (if using) in a blender until very fluffy, about 1 minute.
▶ Stir together lime juice, sugar, and fish sauce in a large bowl until sugar is dissolved, then add cucumber and shallot, tossing to coat.
▶ Serve salad sprinkled with dried shrimp.

Cooks' notes:
• Shrimp can be ground 1 day ahead and kept in an airtight container at room temperature.
• Salad (without shrimp) can be made 1 hour ahead and chilled, covered.

STEAMED CATFISH IN BANANA LEAVES
(Hor Neung Pla Duk)
SERVES 8 (AS PART OF LARGER MEAL)
Active time: 2 hr   Start to finish: 2¼ hr

- 1   lb banana leaves, thawed if frozen (see cooks' note, below)
- 3   tablespoons vegetable oil
- 2   tablespoons Thai red curry paste (page 127)
- 3   tablespoons Thai chicken stock (page 127) or canned reduced-sodium chicken broth
- 2   tablespoons *nam pla* (Asian fish sauce; preferably Thai)
- 1½   lb catfish fillets, cut into 1-inch cubes
- 1½   tablespoons toasted rice powder (recipe follows)
- 3   (4-inch-long) fresh or frozen Kaffir lime leaves (sometimes called *bai makroot*), very thinly sliced

Special equipment: a large (6-qt) wok with lid; a heatproof plate (just small enough to fit inside steamer rack); a large steamer rack

▸ Unfold banana leaves. Cut off and reserve tough center rib that runs along bottom edge of each leaf with kitchen shears. Cut ribs into 12-inch strips (you'll need 8) for tying packets. Gently cut leaves into 8 (10-inch) squares with shears, being careful not to split them (you may want to cut a few extra in case some split while folding). Gently wash banana leaf squares in a large pan of water, then pat dry.
▸ Heat oil in wok over moderate heat until warm, about 30 seconds, then cook curry paste, stirring constantly, until very fragrant and a shade darker, 1 to 2 minutes. Add stock and fish sauce and bring to a boil over high heat, stirring. Add fish and rice powder and stir-fry until outside of fish just turns white, 1 to 2 minutes, then transfer mixture to a bowl.
▸ Put a banana leaf square on a work surface, then put ⅓ cup fish curry in center of square and sprinkle with some of sliced Kaffir lime leaves. Fold 2 sides of banana leaf over fish to enclose it (be careful not to split leaf), then fold in opposite sides to form a packet. Tie packet with a strip of banana leaf rib and transfer to heatproof plate. Assemble 7 more packets in same manner, arranging in 1 layer on plate.
▸ Bring 1 inch water to a boil in wok fitted with steamer rack. Transfer plate with packets to steamer rack carefully and steam, covered with lid, 5 minutes. Serve packets warm or at room temperature.

Cooks' notes:
- Fish packets can be steamed 30 minutes ahead.
- You can substitute 8 large collard leaves for the banana leaves. Trim stems flush with leaves, then put leaves on pieces of foil cut to size. Mound fish curry on leaves, then fold up leaves and wrap packets in foil to catch any juices. Tie packets closed with kitchen string for steaming.
- You can substitute bottled red curry paste for homemade. (We recommend Mae Ploy brand.)

TOASTED RICE POWDER
(Kao Kua)
MAKES ¼ CUP
Active time: 10 min   Start to finish: 25 min

- ¼   cup raw Thai sticky rice

Special equipment: a mortar and pestle or an electric coffee/spice grinder

▸ Toast rice in a dry small heavy skillet over moderate heat, shaking skillet, until golden, 5 to 7 minutes (skillet will smoke), then cool. Grind to a powder with mortar and pestle.

Cooks' note:
- Rice powder is best when ground just before using to preserve the nutty flavor and aroma. Toasted whole rice keeps 3 weeks in an airtight container; powder keeps 4 days.

STIR-FRIED CHINESE BROCCOLI
(Pad Pak Khana)
SERVES 8 (AS PART OF LARGER MEAL)
Active time: 15 min   Start to finish: 15 min

This vegetable is more about leaves and stalks than its namesake cousin. It also has a sweeter flavor and juicier stems. All those green buds eventually blossom into white flowers, so when you're at the market, be sure to look for those with only a few open flowers—and the thinner the stalk, the better.

- 3 tablespoons vegetable oil
- 4 garlic cloves, smashed
- 2 lb Chinese broccoli (sometimes known as Chinese kale), ends of stems trimmed and broccoli cut into 1-inch pieces
- ½ cup Thai chicken stock (page 127) or canned reduced-sodium chicken broth
- 2 tablespoons Thai yellow bean sauce
- 2 tablespoons oyster sauce
- 2 teaspoons sugar

Special equipment: **a large (6-qt) wok**

▶ Heat oil in wok over high heat until hot but not smoking, then stir-fry garlic until pale golden, 10 to 15 seconds. Add broccoli and stock and stir-fry 2 minutes. Add bean sauce, oyster sauce, and sugar and stir-fry until broccoli is crisp-tender, 4 to 5 minutes.

Cooks' note:
• Broccoli can be trimmed and cut 6 hours ahead and chilled in a sealed plastic bag.

FROM TOP OF TABLE: **steamed sticky rice; steamed catfish in banana leaves; jungle curry with pork and Thai eggplant; cucumber salad; tomato and minced pork relish with vegetables**

PINEAPPLE ICE CREAM
MAKES ABOUT 1¼ QUARTS
Active time: 45 min   Start to finish: 17¾ hr (includes chilling and freezing)

- 1½ cups drained canned crushed pineapple in juice (from a 20-fl-oz can), reserving ½ cup plus 1 tablespoon juice
- ¾ cup plus 2 tablespoons sugar
- 2 teaspoons cornstarch
- 1¼ cups whole milk
- 2 large egg yolks
- ¼ teaspoon vanilla
- 1 cup chilled heavy cream

Special equipment: **an instant-read thermometer; an ice cream maker**
Accompaniment: **lacy rice noodle crisps (page 134)**

▶ Bring pineapple, ½ cup reserved pineapple juice, and ½ cup sugar to a boil in a 2- to 3-quart heavy saucepan, stirring until sugar is dissolved. Reduce heat and simmer, stirring occasionally, until pineapple is softened, about 5 minutes. Stir together cornstarch and remaining tablespoon pineapple juice in a small bowl until cornstarch is dissolved, then add to pineapple mixture and simmer, stirring frequently, until thickened, about 1 minute.
▶ Bring milk just to a boil in a 1½- to 2-quart heavy saucepan. Whisk together yolks, remaining ¼ cup plus 2 tablespoons sugar, and a large pinch of salt in a bowl, then add hot milk in a stream, whisking. Pour custard back into saucepan and cook over moderately low heat, stirring with a wooden spoon, until custard registers 170 to 175°F on thermometer, 2 to 3 minutes. Immediately pour custard through a very fine-mesh sieve into a bowl, then stir in pineapple mixture and vanilla and cool to room temperature, stirring occasionally. Stir in cream, then chill custard, covered, until very cold, about 4 hours.
▶ Freeze custard in ice cream maker. Transfer ice cream to an airtight container and put in freezer to harden, at least 12 hours.

Cooks' note:
• Ice cream can be made 3 days ahead.

MANGO COCONUT ICE CREAM

MAKES ABOUT 1½ QUARTS

Active time: 45 min   Start to finish: 17¾ hr (includes chilling and freezing)

If you can't get your hands on really good mangoes, you'll find that canned mango purée delivers the best flavor for this ice cream. We recommend Ratna brand, which uses Alphonso mangoes, an Indian cultivar renowned for its bright orange flesh and very intense flavor. Ka-Me brand is a runner-up.

1¼	cups canned mango purée
¾	cup well-stirred canned unsweetened coconut milk
½	cup heavy cream
2	tablespoons light corn syrup
1	tablespoon fresh lemon juice
¼	teaspoon vanilla
1	cup whole milk
2	large egg yolks
½	cup sugar

Special equipment: an instant-read thermometer; an ice cream maker

Accompaniment: lacy rice noodle crisps (recipe follows)

▶ Stir together mango purée, coconut milk, cream, corn syrup, lemon juice, and vanilla in a bowl until combined well.

▶ Bring milk just to a boil in a 2- to 3-quart heavy saucepan. Whisk together yolks, sugar, and a large pinch of salt in a bowl, then add hot milk in a stream, whisking. Pour custard into saucepan and cook over moderately low heat, stirring with a wooden spoon, until it registers 170 to 175°F on thermometer, 2 to 3 minutes. Remove from heat, then stir in mango mixture until combined well.

▶ Pour custard through a fine-mesh sieve into a large bowl (to remove any strings from mango), discarding solids, and cool to room temperature, stirring occasionally. Chill custard, covered, until very cold, about 4 hours.

▶ Freeze custard in ice cream maker. Transfer ice cream to an airtight container and put in freezer to harden, at least 12 hours.

Cooks' note:
• Ice cream can be made 3 days ahead.

LACY RICE NOODLE CRISPS

SERVES 8 (DESSERT TOPPING)

Active time: 20 min   Start to finish: 1¼ hr

> **About 1 oz dried rice vermicelli (rice-stick noodles)**
> **About 6 cups vegetable oil (48 fl oz)**
> **Confectioners sugar for dusting**

Special equipment: a deep-fat thermometer

▶ Soak noodles in cold water in a large bowl until very pliable, 15 to 20 minutes, then drain and pat dry. Spread noodles on several layers of paper towels and air-dry 30 minutes.

▶ Separate noodles into 1-tablespoon mounds, then gently pull each mound apart so it forms a loose tangle, about 3½ inches in diameter.

▶ Heat 1½ inches oil in a wide 4-quart heavy pot over moderately high heat until it registers 350°F on thermometer. Carefully drop (by hand) 2 noodle tangles about 2 inches apart into oil (noodles will sink to bottom and oil will immediately bubble up, then noodles will expand and rise to top) and fry until crisp, about 20 seconds (noodles will not turn golden). Transfer with a slotted spoon to paper towels to drain and immediately dust generously with confectioners sugar and season with salt. Fry remaining noodles, 2 tangles at a time, in same manner and dust with sugar and sprinkle with salt.

Cooks' notes:
• Noodle crisps can be made 1 day ahead and cooled completely, then kept in an airtight container at room temperature.
• If you'd like to make larger crisps for dramatic presentation, simply pull each noodle mound into a wider tangle, then fry crisps 1 at a time.

OPPOSITE: pineapple ice cream; mango coconut ice cream; lacy rice noodle crisp

HERE COMES THE SUN

LUNCH IN THE GARDEN

SERVES 6

MANGO SOURS

**BEET CHIPS WITH CURRIED
SOUR CREAM**

**MESCLUN SALAD WITH CONFIT
DUCK GIZZARDS AND MORELS**

LOBSTER "POTPIES"

SCHILD ESTATE BAROSSA VALLEY
SEMILLON '02

APRICOT CREAM TART

MOSCATEL TURIS VALENCIA
VINO DE LICOR

MANGO SOURS

MAKES 6 DRINKS
Active time: 5 min   Start to finish: 5 min

> 1   cup mango nectar
> ¾   cup vodka
> ½   cup fresh lemon juice
> 3   tablespoons superfine granulated sugar

Special equipment: **6 (12-oz) double Old Fashioned glasses**
Garnish: **fresh mango spears**

▶ Stir together nectar, vodka, lemon juice, and sugar in a
1-quart glass measure. Shake half of mixture in a cocktail
shaker half filled with ice cubes until cold, about
30 seconds. Strain into glasses half filled with ice cubes.
Shake and strain remaining nectar mixture in same manner.

BEET CHIPS WITH CURRIED SOUR CREAM

SERVES 6
Active time: 20 min   Start to finish: 2 hr

*Don't assemble these hors d'oeuvres until the last minute, or
the chips will get soggy.*

For chips
> 2   medium beets with stems trimmed to 1 inch (1 lb total,
>   including greens)
> 1   cup water
> 1   cup sugar

For curried sour cream
> 2   tablespoons finely chopped shallot
> 1   tablespoon olive oil
> ¾   teaspoon Madras curry powder
> ¾   cup sour cream
> 1½ tablespoons finely chopped fresh chives
> ¼   teaspoon salt
> ¼   teaspoon black pepper

Special equipment: **a Japanese Benriner (see Sources) or other adjustable-blade slicer; a nonstick bakeware liner such as Silpat**

Garnish: **fresh chives**

Make chips:

▶ Peel beets with a vegetable peeler, then slice paper-thin with slicer, using stems as handles.

▶ Bring water and sugar to a boil in a 3-quart heavy saucepan, stirring until sugar is dissolved. Add beets, then remove pan from heat and let stand 15 minutes. Drain beets in a colander, discarding liquid, then let stand in colander 15 minutes.

▶ Put oven rack in middle position and preheat oven to 225°F.

▶ Line a shallow baking pan with nonstick liner, then arrange beet slices snugly in 1 layer (it's not necessary to use any partial or broken slices) and season with salt and pepper. Bake beets until dry, about 1 hour. Immediately transfer chips to a rack to cool (chips will crisp as they cool).

Make curried cream while beets bake:

▶ Cook shallot in oil in a small skillet over moderate heat, stirring frequently, until golden, 3 to 4 minutes. Stir in curry powder and cook, stirring, 1 minute.

▶ Stir shallot into sour cream in a bowl along with chives, salt, and pepper. Serve curried cream with beet chips.

Cooks' notes:

• Beet chips can be made 5 days ahead and cooled completely, then kept in a sealed plastic bag at room temperature.

• Curried sour cream can be made 1 day ahead and chilled, covered.

OPPOSITE: **mesclun salad with confit duck gizzards and morels; beet chips with curried sour cream**

MESCLUN SALAD WITH CONFIT DUCK GIZZARDS AND MORELS

SERVES 6

Active time: 30 min   Start to finish: 30 min

For vinaigrette

  2 tablespoons finely chopped shallot

  2 tablespoons red-wine vinegar

  1 teaspoon whole- or coarse-grain mustard

  ¼ teaspoon salt

  3½ tablespoons extra-virgin olive oil

For salad

  2 tablespoons extra-virgin olive oil

  ½ lb confit duck gizzards (see Sources), each gizzard halved

  ½ lb small fresh morels (preferably 1 to 1½ inches), trimmed, halved lengthwise, and rinsed, or 1 oz small dried morels (1⅓ cups), soaked (see cooks' note, below)

  7 oz mesclun greens (12 cups loosely packed)

Make vinaigrette:

▶ Whisk together shallot, vinegar, mustard, salt, and pepper to taste in a small bowl. Add oil in a slow stream, whisking until combined. Let dressing stand 15 minutes (for flavors to develop).

Make salad:

▶ Heat 1 tablespoon oil in a 12-inch heavy skillet over high heat until just smoking, then sauté gizzards, stirring, until lightly browned, 2 to 3 minutes. Transfer to a bowl and season with salt and pepper. Whisk dressing, then pour half over gizzards, tossing to coat.

▶ Heat remaining tablespoon oil in skillet over high heat until hot but not smoking, then sauté morels, stirring, until lightly browned and tender, 3 to 4 minutes. Season with salt and pepper and add to gizzards, tossing to combine.

▶ Whisk remaining dressing, then pour over mesclun in a large bowl, tossing to coat.

▶ Divide mesclun among 6 plates and top with gizzards and morels.

Cooks' note:

• If using dried morels, soak in 2½ cups warm water until softened, 10 to 30 minutes. Lift from soaking liquid, then rinse well and pat dry.

LOBSTER "POTPIES"

SERVES 6
Active time: 2 hr   Start to finish: 3½ hr (includes making stock)

For lobsters and stock

- 4 qt water
- 4 (1¼- to 1½-lb) live lobsters
- 2 tablespoons unsalted butter
- 3 carrots, chopped (1 cup)
- 2 celery ribs, chopped (1 cup)
- ½ fennel bulb (sometimes called anise), stalks discarded and bulb chopped (1 cup)
- 3 large garlic cloves, minced
- 2 fresh tarragon sprigs
- 1½ teaspoons salt
- 1 cup dry white wine

For stew

- 2 medium tomatoes
- 2 tablespoons kosher salt
- 18 baby carrots (3 bunches), peeled, trimmed, and halved lengthwise if large
- 6 oz haricots verts, cut into 1½-inch pieces (1 cup)
- 1 cup shelled fresh peas (from ½ lb in pods) or thawed frozen baby peas

- ⅓ cup chopped shallot
- ¾ stick unsalted butter, cut into tablespoon pieces
- 1 fennel bulb (sometimes called anise), stalks discarded and bulb cut into 1-inch pieces (2 cups)
- 2 tablespoons cornstarch
- 1½ teaspoons fresh lemon juice
- 2 teaspoons chopped fresh tarragon
   Potato rosettes (recipe follows)

Special equipment: a 10- to 12-qt pot; cheesecloth

Cook lobsters and make stock:

▶ Bring water to a boil in pot, then plunge 2 lobsters headfirst into water and boil, covered, 8 minutes from time they enter water. Transfer with tongs to a shallow roasting pan to cool. Cook remaining 2 lobsters in same manner, reserving cooking liquid in pot.

▶ When lobsters are cool enough to handle, remove meat from tail and claws, catching juices in pan. Scrape off any coagulated white albumen from meat with point of a small knife, then cut meat into ½-inch pieces and chill in a bowl, covered. Cut lobster bodies in half lengthwise, then transfer to cooking liquid along with shells, tomalley, and any juices from roasting pan.

▶ Heat butter in a 12-inch heavy skillet over moderately high heat until foam subsides, then stir in carrots, celery, fennel, garlic, tarragon, and salt. Reduce heat to moderately low and cook vegetables, covered, stirring occasionally, until tender but not browned, about 15 minutes. Remove lid and add wine, then boil over high heat until most of liquid is evaporated, about 7 minutes. Add vegetable mixture to lobster-shell mixture and bring to a boil, skimming foam. Boil, uncovered, until stock is reduced to about 8 cups, 1 to 1½ hours.

▶ Discard lobster bodies, then pour stock through a cheesecloth-lined sieve into a large bowl, pressing on and then discarding solids. Set aside 3 cups stock for sauce and reserve remaining stock for another use (cool stock, uncovered, then chill, covered, or freeze).

Prepare vegetables for stew:

▶ Cut an X in end opposite stem of tomatoes and immerse in a pot of boiling water 10 seconds. Transfer tomatoes with a slotted spoon to a bowl of ice and cold water to stop cooking, reserving boiling water. Peel and seed tomatoes (reserve ice water) and cut into 2- by ¼-inch strips.

▶ Add kosher salt to boiling water, then add carrots and cook until just tender, about 5 minutes. Transfer with slotted spoon to bowl of ice water. Cook haricots verts and peas in boiling water until crisp-tender, about 4 minutes, then transfer with slotted spoon to ice water. Drain vegetables in a colander and pat dry.

Make sauce for stew:

▶ Cook shallot in 3 tablespoons butter in a 4- to 5-quart heavy pot over moderate heat, stirring occasionally, until shallot is softened, 4 to 5 minutes. Add fennel and salt and pepper to taste, then cook, stirring occasionally, until fennel is golden and tender, about 15 minutes.

▶ Add 2¾ cups lobster stock to fennel along with tomato strips and bring to a simmer. Whisk together cornstarch and remaining ¼ cup stock in a cup until smooth, then whisk into sauce. Simmer sauce, whisking, until slightly thickened, about 2 minutes, then whisk in remaining 3 tablespoons butter until incorporated. Stir in lemon juice and salt and pepper to taste. Add blanched vegetables, lobster, and tarragon and gently simmer, stirring occasionally, just until heated through, 4 to 5 minutes.

▶ Divide stew among 6 bowls and top with potato rosettes, upside down.

Cooks' notes:
• Lobster can be cooked and stock made 2 days ahead and chilled separately, covered.
• Carrots, haricots verts, and peas can be blanched 1 day ahead and chilled in a sealed plastic bag lined with paper towels.
• Sauce can be made 1 day ahead and cooled, uncovered, then chilled, covered. Bring to a simmer before proceeding.

POTATO ROSETTES
MAKES 6
Active time: 10 min   Start to finish: 30 min

2 large boiling potatoes (preferably white; 1¼ lb total)
2 tablespoons olive oil

Special equipment: **a Japanese Benriner (see Sources) or other adjustable-blade slicer**

▶ Put oven rack in middle position and preheat oven to 400°F.

▶ Peel potatoes, then cut crosswise into $\frac{1}{16}$-inch-thick slices with slicer and toss with oil.

▶ Oil a large baking sheet. Overlap 8 to 10 slices (use larger ones) in 1 corner of baking sheet to form a 5-inch rosette, then cover center of rosette with another potato slice. Make 5 more rosettes in same manner. Season with salt and pepper.

▶ Bake until well browned around edges, about 20 minutes. Immediately loosen from baking sheet with a thin metal spatula and flip over so browned bottom sides are on top.

APRICOT CREAM TART
SERVES 6 TO 8
Active time: 30 min   Start to finish: 3¾ hr

For tart shell
- ½ cup slivered almonds (2 oz), toasted (see Tips, page 8) and cooled
- 1 cup all-purpose flour
- ¼ cup sugar
- ¼ teaspoon salt
- ¾ stick (6 tablespoons) cold unsalted butter, cut into ½-inch cubes
- 1 large egg yolk
- ¼ teaspoon vanilla extract
- ⅛ teaspoon almond extract

For filling
- 1 lb firm-ripe apricots, halved, pitted, and each half cut into three wedges
- 1 tablespoon Disaronno Amaretto
- ¼ cup plus 2 tablespoons sugar
- ½ cup fine-quality apricot preserves
- 1 large egg
- 1 large egg yolk
- 2 tablespoons heavy cream
- ⅛ teaspoon almond extract

Special equipment: a pastry or bench scraper;
a 9- by 1-inch round tart pan with removable bottom;
pie weights or raw rice

Make dough:

▶ Pulse almonds, flour, sugar, and salt in a food processor until almonds are very finely chopped. Add butter and pulse until mixture resembles coarse meal with some small (roughly pea-size) butter lumps. Add yolk and extracts and pulse just until mixture begins to clump.

▶ Turn out dough onto a lightly floured surface and divide into 4 portions. With heel of your hand, smear each portion once or twice in a forward motion to distribute fat. Gather dough together into a ball with scraper and transfer to tart pan. Pat dough with floured fingers into tart pan in an even ¼-inch-thick layer, including side (side should be flush with top of rim). Chill until firm, about 30 minutes.

Make filling while dough chills:

▶ Toss apricots with Amaretto and ¼ cup sugar, then let macerate until juicy, at least 1 hour.

▶ Whisk together preserves, whole egg, yolk, cream, almond extract, a pinch of salt, and remaining 2 tablespoons sugar in another bowl until combined. Chill, covered, until ready to use.

Bake tart shell:

▶ Put oven rack in middle position and preheat oven to 375°F.

▶ Line tart shell with foil and fill with pie weights. Bake until side is set and edge is pale golden, 18 to 20 minutes. Carefully remove foil and weights and bake shell until bottom is pale golden, 5 to 7 minutes more. Cool completely in pan on a rack, about 15 minutes.

Fill and bake tart:

▶ Reduce oven temperature to 350°F.

▶ Lift apricots from liquid with a slotted spoon and arrange, skin sides down, in tart shell. Whisk remaining apricot liquid into egg mixture, then pour over apricots (fruit will poke through filling). Cover edge of tart shell with a pie shield or foil and bake tart until filling is set and slightly puffed, 45 to 50 minutes. Cool tart completely in pan on rack.

Cooks' notes:
• Tart can be made 6 hours ahead and kept, uncovered, at room temperature.
• Apricots can macerate up to 1 day, covered and chilled. Bring to room temperature before using.
• Egg mixture can be made 1 day ahead and chilled, covered. Bring to room temperature before using.
• Tart shell can be baked 1 day ahead and kept, loosely covered, at room temperature.

ALL WEEKEND
LONG

SATURDAY LUNCH

SERVES 6
TAHINI CHICKEN SALAD
BALSAMIC ZUCCHINI
WHEAT BERRY SALAD
HONEYDEW LIME POPSICLES

TAHINI CHICKEN SALAD

SERVES 6
Active time: 30 min   Start to finish: 2 hr

  6 chicken breast halves with skin and bones (4 to
       4½ lb total)
  2 tablespoons extra-virgin olive oil
  ½ teaspoon black pepper
  2 teaspoons salt
  ⅔ cup well-stirred tahini (Middle Eastern sesame paste)
  ½ cup water
  ½ cup fresh lemon juice
  4 garlic cloves, chopped
  ½ teaspoon sugar
  ½ lb sugar snap peas, trimmed
  1 red bell pepper, cut into ¼-inch-thick strips
  ¼ cup sesame seeds, toasted (see Tips, page 8)

▶ Put oven rack in middle position and preheat oven to
450°F.
▶ Rub chicken with oil in a shallow baking pan (1 inch deep)
and sprinkle with pepper and 1 teaspoon salt. Roast chicken
until just cooked through, 40 to 45 minutes.
▶ While chicken roasts, blend tahini, water, lemon juice,
garlic, sugar, and remaining teaspoon salt in a blender
until smooth.

▶ Blanch sugar snaps in a 2-quart saucepan of boiling salted
water (see Tips, page 8) 1 minute, then drain in a colander.
Rinse under cold water to stop cooking and drain well.
▶ When chicken is cool enough to handle, remove skin and
discard. Remove meat from bones in large pieces, discarding
bones, then pull meat into ⅓-inch-wide strips and transfer to
a large bowl. Add sugar snaps, bell pepper, and dressing and
toss to coat. Sprinkle with sesame seeds.

Cooks' notes:
• Chicken salad (without sugar snaps and sesame seeds) can
be made 1 day ahead. Add sugar snaps and sesame seeds just
before serving and thin dressing with warm water as needed.
• Sugar snaps can be blanched 1 day ahead and chilled in a
sealed plastic bag lined with dampened paper towels.
• Keep in mind that tahini can turn rancid rather quickly
(even in unopened cans, in our experience). We recommend
buying it from a place with a high turnover, such as a Middle
Eastern market or a natural foods store.

BALSAMIC ZUCCHINI

SERVES 6 (SIDE DISH)
Active time: 20 min   Start to finish: 45 min

- 4 lb medium zucchini, cut diagonally into ¾-inch-thick slices
- ¼ cup extra-virgin olive oil
- ¾ teaspoon salt
- ½ teaspoon coarsely ground black pepper
- ¼ cup balsamic vinegar
- 1½ oz finely grated Parmigiano-Reggiano (½ cup; see Tips, page 8)
- ⅓ cup pine nuts (1 oz), toasted (see Tips, page 8) and finely chopped

▶Preheat broiler.
▶Toss zucchini with oil, salt, and pepper in a large bowl. Arrange zucchini in 1 layer in 2 shallow baking pans (1 inch deep). Broil 1 pan of zucchini 3 to 5 inches from heat, without turning, until browned in spots and beginning to soften, 4 to 6 minutes. Drizzle 2 tablespoons vinegar over broiled zucchini and shake pan a few times, then continue to broil until most of vinegar is evaporated, about 2 minutes. Sprinkle ¼ cup cheese over broiled zucchini and broil until cheese is melted, about 1 minute more. Cook remaining pan of zucchini in same manner. Cool to room temperature and serve sprinkled with pine nuts.

Cooks' note:
• Balsamic zucchini (without pine nuts) can be made 3 hours ahead and kept at room temperature or chilled, covered. Sprinkle with pine nuts just before serving.

WHEAT BERRY SALAD

SERVES 6 (SIDE DISH)
Active time: 15 min   Start to finish: 1½ hr

- 2 cups hard wheat berries (¾ lb)
- 3 tablespoons red-wine vinegar
- ¾ teaspoon salt
- ½ teaspoon black pepper
- 3 tablespoons extra-virgin olive oil
- 1 small red onion, halved lengthwise, then very thinly sliced lengthwise
- ½ cup chopped fresh dill

▶Cook wheat berries in a 4-quart pot of boiling water (not salted), uncovered, until tender, 1 to 1¼ hours. Drain in a large sieve and rinse under cold water to cool, then drain well.
▶Whisk together vinegar, salt, and pepper in a large bowl. Add oil in a slow stream, whisking until combined. Add wheat berries, onion, and dill and stir to coat well.

Cooks' note:
• Salad can be made 1 day ahead and chilled, covered.

HONEYDEW LIME POPSICLES

MAKES 6 TO 10 POPSICLES
Active time: 20 min   Start to finish: 8½ hr (includes freezing)

The yield for these Popsicles depends on the size of your molds—you could use anything from paper cups to store-bought specialty molds.

- ¼ cup superfine or regular granulated sugar
- ¼ cup water
- 1 (3½-lb) ripe honeydew melon, peeled, seeded, and cut into ½-inch pieces (4 cups)
- ⅔ cup fresh lime juice

Special equipment: **6 to 10 Popsicle molds and sticks (see Sources)**

▶Dissolve sugar in water by stirring if using superfine or by heating in a small heavy saucepan if using regular granulated (then cool).
▶Blend half of melon and half of lime juice in a blender until smooth. Add syrup and remaining melon and lime juice and purée until smooth. Force purée through a fine-mesh sieve into a 2-quart glass measure or bowl, pressing on solids and then discarding them.
▶Pour mixture into molds and freeze until slushy, about 2 hours.
▶Insert sticks, then freeze Popsicles until completely hardened, at least 6 hours.

Cooks' note:
• Popsicles can be made 2 days ahead (flavor diminishes if made any earlier).

SATURDAY DINNER

SERVES 6

**GOLDEN BEET AND
SUNFLOWER SALAD**

**POACHED HALIBUT
WITH SAFFRON ORANGE AÏOLI**

**PROVENÇAL TOMATO
POTATO GRATIN**

VINE CLIFF BIEN NACIDO
CHARDONNAY '01

**POUND CAKE WITH BLUEBERRIES
AND LAVENDER SYRUP**

GOLDEN BEET AND SUNFLOWER SALAD

SERVES 6

Active time: 20 min   Start to finish: 1¼ hr

To maximize the flavor of this salad, toss the beets with the dressing while they're still warm, so they'll absorb more of it.

2½ lb medium golden beets (with greens)
½ cup raw (not roasted) sunflower seeds (2¼ oz)
2 tablespoons finely chopped shallot
2½ tablespoons cider vinegar
¾ teaspoon salt
¼ teaspoon black pepper
¼ teaspoon sugar
3 tablespoons extra-virgin olive oil
6 oz sunflower sprouts or baby mesclun (6 cups)

▸ Put oven racks in lower third and middle of oven and preheat oven to 425°F.
▸ Trim beet greens, leaving 1 inch of stems attached. Tightly wrap beets together in double layers of foil to make packages (2 or 3 per package) and roast in middle of oven until tender, 40 to 45 minutes. Unwrap beets and cool slightly.
▸ While beets roast, toast sunflower seeds in a pie plate or a small baking pan in lower third of oven, shaking occasionally, until seeds are golden, about 10 minutes.
▸ Whisk together shallot, vinegar, salt, pepper, and sugar in a small bowl, then add oil in a stream, whisking.
▸ When beets are cool enough to handle, slip off and discard skins. Cut beets lengthwise into ¼-inch-thick slices and gently toss with 3 tablespoons vinaigrette in a bowl.
▸ Toss sunflower sprouts and half of sunflower seeds with remaining vinaigrette in another bowl. Arrange beets on 6 salad plates and top with dressed sprouts. Sprinkle salads with remaining sunflower seeds.

Cooks' notes:
• Beets can be roasted, sliced, and dressed 1 day ahead and chilled, covered.
• Sunflower seeds turn rancid fairly quickly, so it's important to purchase them from a place with high turnover, such as a natural foods store.

POACHED HALIBUT WITH SAFFRON ORANGE AÏOLI

SERVES 6

Active time: 20 min   Start to finish: 40 min (includes making *aïoli*)

2 cups dry white wine
1 small onion, thinly sliced
2 Turkish bay leaves or 1 California
10 whole black peppercorns
2 (3-inch) fresh thyme sprigs
2½ teaspoons salt
6 (6-oz) halibut steaks with skin (1 inch thick)
Saffron orange *aïoli* (page 150)

▸ Bring 6 cups water with wine, onion, bay leaves, peppercorns, thyme, and salt to a boil in a deep 12-inch skillet, covered, over moderate heat, then reduce heat and simmer 10 minutes. Add halibut (liquid should barely cover fish; if not, add more water) and poach at a bare simmer, uncovered, until opaque and just cooked through, about 6 minutes.
▸ Transfer fish to a plate with a slotted spatula. Peel off and discard skin, then transfer fish to a platter or individual plates with slotted spatula. Serve warm or at room temperature, with *aïoli*.

SAFFRON ORANGE AÏOLI
MAKES ABOUT 1 CUP
Active time: 15 min   Start to finish: 15 min

If you're short on time or concerned about using raw egg (see cooks' note, below), you could substitute prepared mayo: Just omit the egg yolk and oil, and stir together with remaining ingredients until combined well.

- ⅛ teaspoon crumbled saffron threads
- 1 tablespoon hot water
- 1 garlic clove, chopped
- 1 teaspoon finely grated fresh orange zest
- ¼ cup fresh orange juice
- 1 tablespoon fresh lemon juice
- ¾ teaspoon salt
- ¼ teaspoon black pepper
- 1 large egg yolk
- ¾ cup olive oil

▶ Stir together saffron and water in a small bowl until saffron begins to dissolve (threads will still be intact). Transfer saffron mixture to a food processor along with remaining ingredients except oil, then pulse until combined. With motor running, add oil in a thin, steady stream until *aïoli* is thickened and emulsified. Transfer to a bowl and chill, covered, until ready to use.

Cooks' notes:
- The egg yolk in this recipe will not be cooked, which may be of concern if there is a problem with salmonella in your area.
- *Aïoli* can be made 1 day ahead and chilled, covered.

PROVENÇAL TOMATO POTATO GRATIN
SERVES 6
Active time: 25 min   Start to finish: 1¼ hr

- 10 tablespoons extra-virgin olive oil
- 2 lb medium tomatoes (about 6), cut crosswise into ½-inch-thick slices
  About 1¾ teaspoons salt
- 1 teaspoon black pepper
- 2 lb medium red potatoes, scrubbed well
- 1 garlic clove
- ½ cup plain fine dry bread crumbs
- ¼ cup finely chopped fresh basil
- 1½ teaspoons chopped fresh thyme

Special equipment: **a 3-quart shallow flameproof gratin or casserole dish (about 2 inches deep; not glass)**

▶ Put oven rack in middle position and preheat oven to 425°F.

▶ Brush a shallow baking pan (½ to 1 inch deep) with 2 tablespoons oil. Arrange tomato slices in 1 layer in baking pan and sprinkle with a scant ½ teaspoon salt and ¼ teaspoon pepper. Roast tomatoes until just tender (not falling apart), about 20 minutes.

▶ While tomatoes roast, cut potatoes crosswise into ¼-inch-thick slices and toss with 5 tablespoons oil in a large bowl.

▶ Remove tomatoes from oven and put oven racks in upper and lower thirds of oven. Arrange potato slices in 1 layer in 2 shallow baking pans (½ to 1 inch deep) and sprinkle each pan with a scant ½ teaspoon salt and ¼ teaspoon pepper. Roast potatoes, switching position of pans halfway through roasting, until tender, about 16 minutes total.

▶ While potatoes roast, mince garlic and mash to a paste with a pinch of salt using a large heavy knife. Transfer paste to a bowl and stir in bread crumbs, basil, thyme, remaining 3 tablespoons oil, remaining ¼ teaspoon salt, and remaining ¼ teaspoon pepper.

▶ Preheat broiler.

▶ Arrange tomatoes and potatoes in 1 layer in gratin dish, alternating slices and overlapping them, and spoon any juices from tomatoes into dish. Sprinkle top with bread crumbs and broil 5 to 7 inches from heat, checking frequently after 1 minute (crumbs can brown quickly), until golden brown, about 2 minutes. Serve warm or at room temperature.

Cooks' note:
• Gratin can be assembled (but not broiled) 1 hour ahead and kept at room temperature.

POUND CAKE WITH BLUEBERRIES AND LAVENDER SYRUP

SERVES 6 TO 8
Active time: 20 min   Start to finish: 2¾ hr

For cake
- 2 cups all-purpose flour
- ½ teaspoon baking powder
- ¼ teaspoon salt
- 2 sticks (1 cup) unsalted butter, softened
- 1½ cups sugar
- 3 large eggs, at room temperature for 30 minutes

- 1 teaspoon finely grated fresh lemon zest
- 1 teaspoon vanilla
- ½ cup whole milk, at room temperature

For blueberries in syrup
- ¾ cup water
- ½ cup sugar
- 4 teaspoons dried edible lavender flowers (see Sources) or 2 tablespoons fresh edible lavender flowers
- 2 teaspoons fresh lemon juice
- 10 oz blueberries (1 pt)

Special equipment: **a 9- by 5- by 3-inch metal loaf pan**

Make cake:
▶ Put oven rack in middle position and preheat oven to 350°F. Generously butter and flour loaf pan, knocking out excess flour.

▶ Whisk together flour, baking powder, and salt. Beat together butter and sugar in a large bowl with an electric mixer at medium-high speed until light and fluffy, about 3 minutes in a stand mixer or 5 with a handheld. Add eggs 1 at a time, beating well after each addition, then beat in zest and vanilla. Reduce speed to low and add flour mixture and milk alternately in batches, beginning and ending with flour and mixing until just incorporated.

▶ Spoon batter into loaf pan and bake until golden and a wooden pick or skewer inserted in center comes out with crumbs adhering, 1 to 1¼ hours. Cool cake in pan on a rack 30 minutes, then invert onto rack and cool completely.

Prepare blueberries in syrup:
▶ Bring water and sugar to a boil in a small saucepan, stirring until sugar is dissolved. Remove from heat and stir in lavender, then steep 30 minutes for dried lavender or 40 minutes for fresh. Pour syrup through a fine-mesh sieve into a bowl, discarding lavender. Stir in lemon juice and blueberries.

▶ Spoon blueberries and syrup over slices of cake just before serving.

Cooks' notes:
• Cake can be made 1 day ahead and cooled completely, then wrapped tightly in plastic wrap or kept in an airtight container at room temperature.
• Lavender syrup (without berries) can be made 2 hours ahead and kept, covered, at room temperature. Add berries just before serving.

SUNDAY BRUNCH

SERVES 6

CARROT, GRANNY SMITH, AND GINGER JUICE

CORNMEAL CRÊPES WITH RICOTTA AND HAM

SUMMER FRUIT SALAD WITH MINT SUGAR

CARROT, GRANNY SMITH, AND GINGER JUICE

MAKES ABOUT 7½ CUPS
Active time: 20 min   Start to finish: 2¼ hr (includes chilling)

Not all juicers are created equal—the amount of juice extracted varies from brand to brand. The weight ranges for the ingredients below will ensure that you have enough juice.

  4 to 5 lb Granny Smith apples
  3 to 4 lb carrots, peeled and trimmed
  1 (6-inch) piece peeled fresh ginger

Special equipment: **a juicer (see cooks' note, below)**

▸Slice apples. Process enough slices in juicer, skimming and discarding any foam, to measure 4 cups juice, then transfer juice to a pitcher. Process enough carrots, skimming and discarding any foam, to measure 3½ cups juice, then add to pitcher with apple juice. Process ginger, then stir 2½ tablespoons ginger juice into pitcher. Chill until cold, about 2 hours.
▸Serve over ice, if desired.

Cooks' note:
• If you don't have a juicer, you can substitute 3 cups nonalcoholic sparkling cider for homemade apple juice (flavor will be sweeter than Granny Smith apple juice). Increase carrot juice to 4 cups and use a good-quality fresh juice (not canned). Juice ginger by finely grating, then forcing pulp through a fine-mesh sieve.

ABOVE: **carrot, Granny Smith, and ginger juice; summer fruit salad**

CORNMEAL CRÊPES WITH RICOTTA AND HAM

SERVES 6

Active time: 45 min   Start to finish: 1¾ hr

For crepes

1¼ cups all-purpose flour
¾   cup yellow cornmeal
¾   teaspoon ground cumin
½   teaspoon salt
2   cups whole milk
3   large eggs
2   tablespoons unsalted butter, melted, plus additional
     for brushing skillet

For filling

3⅓ cups whole-milk or part-skim ricotta (30 oz)
1   (6-oz) piece Black Forest or Virginia ham, cut into
     ¼-inch dice
1   large egg, lightly beaten
½   teaspoon salt
½   teaspoon coarsely ground black pepper
¼   cup hot pepper jelly

For topping

3   tablespoons unsalted butter
6   scallions, thinly sliced and white and pale green parts
     reserved separately from greens
2   cups corn (from 4 ears)
½   teaspoon salt
¼   teaspoon black pepper

Make crêpes:

▶ Blend flour, cornmeal, cumin, salt, milk, eggs, and
2 tablespoons butter in a blender until smooth. Let batter
stand at room temperature 30 minutes.

▶ Lightly brush a 10-inch nonstick skillet with butter and
heat over moderately high heat until hot but not smoking.
Stir batter, then, holding skillet off heat, pour in ⅓ cup
batter, immediately tilting and rotating skillet to coat bottom.
(If batter sets before skillet is coated, reduce heat slightly for
next crêpe.) Return skillet to heat and cook until just set and
pale golden around edges, 10 to 15 seconds. Loosen edge of
crêpe with a heatproof silicone spatula, then flip crêpe over
carefully with your fingertips. Cook until underside is set,
about 20 seconds more, and transfer crêpe to a plate. Make
11 more crêpes in same manner, brushing skillet lightly with
butter for each and stacking crêpes on plate as cooked.

Make filling and bake crepes:

▶ Put oven rack in middle position and preheat oven to
375°F. Lightly butter a 13- by 9-inch (or 15- by 10-inch)
shallow baking dish.

▶ Stir together ricotta, ham, egg, salt, and pepper. Put
1 crêpe, paler side up, on a work surface and spread
1 teaspoon pepper jelly in a horizontal line just below center
of crêpe (toward end nearest you), leaving a 1-inch border on
each side. Spoon ⅓ cup ricotta filling over jelly and fold in
sides of crêpe over filling, then, beginning at bottom, roll up
to enclose filling. Arrange crêpe, seam side down, in baking
dish. Assemble 11 more crêpes in same manner, arranging
them in 1 layer in baking dish.

▶ Bake, covered with foil, until filling is hot, about
30 minutes.

Make topping just before serving:

▶ Melt butter in 10-inch skillet over moderate heat until
foam subsides, then cook white and pale green scallions,
stirring, until softened, about 2 minutes. Add corn, salt, and
pepper and cook, stirring, until crisp-tender, 2 to 3 minutes.
Add scallion greens and cook, stirring, until softened, about
1 minute. Spoon topping over crêpes.

Cooks' note:

• Crêpes can be filled (but not baked) 1 day ahead and
chilled, covered. Bring to room temperature before baking.

SUMMER FRUIT SALAD WITH MINT SUGAR

SERVES 6

Active time: 20 min   Start to finish: 25 min

¼   cup loosely packed fresh mint leaves
3   tablespoons sugar
1¼ lb blackberries, left whole, or 1½ lb sweet cherries,
     pitted and halved
3   firm-ripe medium peaches or nectarines, halved
     lengthwise, pitted, and cut into ⅓-inch-thick wedges
½   lb seedless green grapes (1½ cups), halved

▶ Pulse mint and sugar in a food processor until finely
ground. Sprinkle mint sugar over fruit in a large bowl and
toss gently to combine. Let stand 5 minutes before serving.

SUNDAY DINNER

SERVES 6

LIMONCELLO AND MINT SPARKLERS

CAPONATINA TOASTS

CHILLED TOMATO CONSOMMÉ

GRILLED LEG OF LAMB WITH ROSEMARY SALT

WAX BEANS AND CELERY WITH ANCHOVY VINAIGRETTE

MARINATED MUSHROOM SALAD

BLACK OLIVE TWISTS

SEVEN HILLS, SEVEN HILLS VINEYARD WALLA WALLA MERLOT '01

PASSION-FRUIT AND BLACKBERRY JELLIES WITH LEMON VERBENA CREAM

MARENCO PINETO BRACHETTO D'ACQUI '03

LIMONCELLO AND MINT SPARKLERS

SERVES 6
Active time: 15 min   Start to finish: 1¼ hr (includes chilling)

1   cup loosely packed fresh mint leaves
1   cup chilled *limoncello*
½   cup fresh lemon juice
3   cups chilled sparkling water

Garnish: fresh mint sprigs; lemon slices

▶ Combine mint and *limoncello* in a bowl, then gently bruise mint with a pestle or wooden spoon (to release flavor). Chill, covered, 1 hour.
▶ Pour *limoncello* through a fine-mesh sieve into a pitcher, pressing firmly on mint and then discarding it.
▶ Just before serving, stir in lemon juice, sparkling water, and enough ice to fill pitcher.

ABOVE: grilled leg of lamb with rosemary salt, wax beans and celery with anchovy vinaigrette, and marinated mushroom salad; chilled tomato consommé

CAPONATINA TOASTS

MAKES 18 HORS D'OEUVRES
Active time: 45 min   Start to finish: 1 hr

Caponata *is a Sicilian antipasto; its bold flavors usually include eggplant, anchovy, olives, and capers. We call our version a "caponatina," because we've finely diced the ingredients for a more refined hors d'oeuvre.*

18   (⅛-inch-thick) slices *ficelle* or baguette
1½   cups vegetable oil
1   (6-oz) baby Italian eggplant, cut into ¼-inch cubes
¼   cup finely diced onion
1   tablespoon olive oil
1   tablespoon tomato paste
⅛   teaspoon cinnamon
2   tablespoons water
1   teaspoon red-wine vinegar
Pinch of sugar
2   tablespoons finely diced pitted green olives (preferably Sicilian)
1   tablespoon drained bottled small (nonpareil) capers, rinsed
¼   teaspoon salt
⅛   teaspoon black pepper
2   tablespoons finely diced celery

Special equipment: **a deep-fat thermometer**
Garnish: **small fresh basil leaves**

▶ Put oven rack in middle position and preheat oven to 350°F.
▶ Toast bread on a baking sheet until crisp and pale golden, 12 to 15 minutes, then transfer to a rack to cool.
▶ Heat vegetable oil in a 1- to 1½-quart heavy saucepan over high heat until it registers 375°F on thermometer. Fry eggplant in 4 batches, stirring frequently, until pale golden, about 3 minutes per batch, transferring with a slotted spoon to paper towels to drain. (Return oil to 375°F between batches.)
▶ Cook onion in olive oil in a 10-inch heavy skillet over moderate heat, stirring occasionally, until softened, about 5 minutes. Add tomato paste and cinnamon and cook, stirring, 1 minute. Stir in water, vinegar, and sugar until combined, then add olives, capers, salt, and pepper and cook, stirring, 1 minute. Add eggplant and celery and cook, stirring gently, 1 minute. Transfer *caponatina* to a bowl and cool to room temperature.
▶ Serve toasts topped with *caponatina*.

Cooks' notes:
• Toasts can be made 1 week ahead and cooled completely, then kept in an airtight container at room temperature.
• *Caponatina* can be made 1 day ahead and chilled, covered. Bring to room temperature before serving.

CHILLED TOMATO CONSOMMÉ
SERVES 6 (MAKES ABOUT 1 QUART)
Active time: 1¼ hr   Start to finish: 3½ hr (includes chilling)

The riper the tomatoes, the better the flavor of this delicate consommé. To clarify it, we've used the traditional French method of creating an egg-white "raft," which attracts particles from the simmering broth and is then discarded.

1½ lb fennel (sometimes called anise; 1 large bulb or
       2 small)
 2 medium onions, coarsely chopped
 2 garlic cloves, coarsely chopped
 2 tablespoons olive oil
 5 lb tomatoes (preferably plum), quartered and puréed
       in a food processor

1½ teaspoons fine sea salt
 1 teaspoon black pepper
 8 large egg whites, chilled
 ¼ cup coarsely chopped fresh flat-leaf parsley
 2 tablespoons coarsely chopped fresh basil
 1 tablespoon coarsely chopped fresh tarragon
 ½ cup ice, lightly crushed if cubes are large
10 oz mixed yellow and red pear tomatoes, halved
       lengthwise
1½ teaspoons Sherry vinegar

▶ Cut fronds from fennel stalks and reserve. Cut whole fennel (with stalks) in half lengthwise and core. Separate layers, reserving 3 or 4 tender inner pieces, and coarsely chop remaining fennel, including stalks.
▶ Cook onions, garlic, and chopped fennel in oil in a 5- to 6-quart heavy pot over moderate heat, stirring frequently, until softened, 10 to 12 minutes. Stir in puréed tomato, 1 teaspoon sea salt, and ½ teaspoon pepper and simmer, uncovered, stirring occasionally, 20 minutes.
▶ Pour tomato mixture through a fine-mesh sieve into a 4-quart saucepan, pressing hard on solids and then discarding them, and bring tomato broth to a full boil.
▶ Whisk together egg whites, herbs, ice, remaining ½ teaspoon sea salt, and remaining ½ teaspoon pepper in a bowl until frothy, then quickly pour into boiling broth, whisking vigorously 2 or 3 times. (Egg mixture will form a "raft.") When broth returns to a simmer, find a place where bubbles break through raft and gently enlarge hole to the size of a ladle. Cook broth at a bare simmer, uncovered, without stirring (keep raft opening clear by gently spooning out any froth), until broth is clear, 15 to 20 minutes.
▶ Remove saucepan from heat and, disturbing raft as little as possible, carefully ladle out consommé through opening in raft, tilting saucepan as necessary, and transfer to cleaned fine-mesh sieve lined with a double layer of dampened paper towels set over a bowl or large glass measure. Discard raft. Chill consommé, uncovered, until cold, about 1½ hours.
▶ Just before serving, season consommé with salt. Slice reserved tender fennel into thin slivers and toss with fennel fronds, pear tomatoes, and vinegar. Divide consommé and tomato salad among chilled bowls.

Cooks' note:
• Consommé (without tomato salad) can be made 3 days ahead and cooled, uncovered, then chilled, covered.

GRILLED LEG OF LAMB WITH ROSEMARY SALT

SERVES 6 GENEROUSLY

Active time: 45 min   Start to finish: 7 hr (includes marinating)

For lamb

1½ cups plain whole-milk yogurt
7 garlic cloves, thinly sliced
2½ tablespoons coarsely chopped fresh rosemary
½ teaspoon coarsely ground black pepper
1 (5½-lb) piece boneless butterflied leg of lamb
1½ tablespoons kosher salt

For rosemary salt

1 teaspoon finely chopped fresh rosemary
1 tablespoon Maldon sea salt or other flaky sea salt

Special equipment: **8 to 10 (12-inch) wooden or metal skewers; an instant-read thermometer**

Marinate lamb:

▶ Stir together yogurt, garlic, rosemary, and pepper in a 13- by 9-inch glass baking dish or 2-gallon sealable plastic bag. Add lamb, turning to coat completely, and marinate, covered and chilled, turning over once or twice, 5 hours.
▶ Bring lamb to room temperature, about 1 hour.
▶ Remove lamb from marinade, discarding marinade, and put on a work surface. Run skewers horizontally through meat, about 1½ inches apart, first lengthwise (4 or 5 skewers), then crosswise (4 or 5 more) to form a grid. (Skewering makes meat easier to move and turn over.) Sprinkle with kosher salt.
▶ Prepare grill for cooking. If using a charcoal grill, open vents on bottom of grill, then light charcoal. Charcoal fire is medium-hot when you can hold your hand 5 inches above rack for 3 to 4 seconds. If using a gas grill, preheat burners on high, covered, 10 minutes, then reduce to moderate.
▶ Grill lamb, covered only if using a gas grill, on lightly oiled grill rack, turning occasionally, until thermometer inserted diagonally into thickest part of meat registers 125°F for medium-rare (thinner parts will register higher), 25 to 30 minutes if using charcoal or 20 to 25 minutes if using gas. Transfer lamb to a cutting board and let stand 10 minutes before thinly slicing.

Make rosemary salt:

▶ Stir together rosemary and sea salt and serve with lamb.

Cooks' note:
• If you aren't able to grill outdoors, you can cook lamb in a well-seasoned double-burner grill pan. Omit skewering and cut lamb into 3 or 4 pieces to fit in pan, then grill over moderately high heat, turning over once, 20 to 25 minutes.

WAX BEANS AND CELERY WITH ANCHOVY VINAIGRETTE

SERVES 6

Active time: 20 min   Start to finish: 25 min

5 flat anchovy fillets
2 small garlic cloves
2 tablespoons fresh lemon juice
1 teaspoon white-wine vinegar
¼ teaspoon salt
⅛ teaspoon black pepper
¼ cup extra-virgin olive oil
2 celery ribs plus 1 tablespoon coarsely chopped celery leaves
1½ lb wax beans, trimmed

▶ Purée anchovies, garlic, lemon juice, vinegar, salt, and pepper in a blender until smooth. With motor running, add oil in a stream.
▶ Peel outer strings from celery ribs with a vegetable peeler, then halve ribs crosswise. Thinly shave ribs along a thin edge with peeler into narrow ribbons and transfer to a large bowl of ice and cold water to crisp.
▶ Cook beans in a 6- to 8-quart pot of boiling salted water (see Tips, page 8), uncovered, until just tender, 5 to 6 minutes, then drain.
▶ Toss warm beans, celery ribbons, and celery leaves with vinaigrette in a large bowl. Serve immediately.

Cooks' notes:
• Vinaigrette can be made 1 day ahead and chilled, covered. Bring to room temperature before using.
• Celery can be ribboned 3 hours ahead and kept in ice water.
• Beans are best when cooked just before serving but can be boiled 1 day ahead and chilled, covered. Bring to room temperature before dressing.

MARINATED MUSHROOM SALAD

SERVES 6

Active time: 30 min   Start to finish: 1¾ hr

This salad is prepared in the French style known as à la grecque, *in which vegetables are cooked in a lemon and olive-oil marinade (often infused with coriander and pepper) and then served cold.*

- ¼ teaspoon whole white peppercorns
- ¼ teaspoon whole black peppercorns
- ¼ teaspoon fennel seeds
- ¼ teaspoon coriander seeds
- 1½ cups water
- ¼ cup extra-virgin olive oil
- 3 (4- by ½-inch) strips fresh lemon zest (see Tips, page 8)
- 3½ tablespoons fresh lemon juice
- 3 small shallots, sliced crosswise
- 1 lb mixed fresh mushrooms such as chanterelle, oyster, and cremini, trimmed and quartered if large
- ¾ teaspoon salt
- ⅛ teaspoon ground black pepper
- 3 tablespoons coarsely chopped fresh flat-leaf parsley

Special equipment: **cheesecloth; kitchen string**

▶ Wrap whole peppercorns and seeds in a small square of cheesecloth and tie into a bundle with string, then put in a 3-quart saucepan along with water, oil, zest, 2 tablespoons lemon juice, and shallots. Bring to a simmer over moderate heat, then reduce heat to moderately low and simmer, covered, 10 minutes. Add mushrooms and bring to a boil, then reduce heat and simmer, covered, stirring occasionally, until tender, about 12 minutes. Transfer mushrooms to a bowl with a slotted spoon, then increase heat and boil cooking liquid until reduced to about ¾ cup.
▶ Discard cheesecloth bag and zest, then stir salt and ground pepper into broth. Pour through a fine-mesh sieve into bowl with mushrooms. Cool to room temperature and stir in parsley and remaining 1½ tablespoons lemon juice.

BLACK OLIVE TWISTS

MAKES 12 SOFT BREADSTICKS

Active time: 30 min   Start to finish: 4¾ hr (includes thawing dough)

- 1 lb frozen pizza dough, thawed
- 2 tablespoons prepared black olive paste (preferably not tapenade)
- 1 large egg white, lightly beaten
- ¾ teaspoon fennel seeds
- ¼ teaspoon cumin seeds
- 1 teaspoon kosher salt

Special equipment: **parchment paper**

▶ Put oven racks in upper and lower thirds of oven and preheat oven to 400°F. Line 2 large baking sheets with parchment.
▶ Cut dough into 12 equal pieces. Roll each piece into a 10-inch-long rope on a lightly floured surface with lightly floured hands, stretching as needed, then pat lightly to flatten slightly.
▶ Spread top of each rope with ½ teaspoon olive paste, then fold in half. Let stand, uncovered, 10 minutes.
▶ Working with 1 piece at a time, twist folded dough, stretching it slightly, into a 6-inch twist, then transfer to 1 of 2 baking sheets, pressing ends lightly onto parchment to keep twists from untwisting.
▶ Brush twists generously with egg white and sprinkle with fennel, cumin, and kosher salt, pressing to help adhere.
▶ Bake twists, switching position of sheets halfway through baking, until golden, 22 to 24 minutes total. Transfer twists to a rack and cool to just warm.

Cooks' note:
• Twists (without egg white and seeds) can be prepared 2 hours ahead and chilled, covered. Let stand at room temperature 15 minutes before coating with egg white and seeds and baking.

PASSION-FRUIT AND BLACKBERRY JELLIES WITH LEMON VERBENA CREAM

SERVES 6

Active time: 1½ hr   **Start to finish:** 17 hr (includes chilling)

These soft jellies, layered with tart passion-fruit and sweet blackberry purées, are a wonderful summer dessert. Unbelievably cool and delicious, they're well worth the extra time it takes to make them.

For passion-fruit mixture

- 1½ teaspoons unflavored gelatin (from a ¼-oz envelope)
- 1¼ cups water
- ½ cup sugar
- 1 cup thawed passion-fruit purée (from a 14-oz frozen package; see Sources)

For blackberry mixture

- 1½ teaspoons unflavored gelatin (from a ¼-oz envelope)
- 1 cup water
- 1 cup sugar
- 11 to 12 oz blackberries (2½ cups)
- 2 tablespoons fresh lemon juice

For lemon verbena cream

- 3 tablespoons chopped fresh lemon verbena or lemon balm (see Sources)
- ½ tablespoon sugar
- ½ cup heavy cream

Special equipment: 6 (6- to 8-oz) juice glasses
Garnish: fresh lemon verbena sprigs

Make passion-fruit mixture:

▶ Sprinkle gelatin over ¼ cup water and let stand 2 minutes to soften.

▶ Heat sugar and remaining cup water in a 1-quart heavy saucepan over moderately high heat, stirring, until sugar is dissolved. Add gelatin mixture and stir until dissolved. Transfer mixture to a 1-quart glass measure or bowl, then set in a large bowl of ice and cold water and stir frequently until cold but not set, about 15 minutes. Stir in passion-fruit purée, then chill in refrigerator until ready to use.

Make blackberry mixture:

▶ Sprinkle gelatin over ¼ cup water and let stand 2 minutes to soften.

▶ Heat sugar and remaining ¾ cup water in 1-quart saucepan over moderately high heat, stirring, until sugar is dissolved. Add gelatin mixture and stir until dissolved. Transfer mixture to another 1-quart glass measure or bowl, then set in a large bowl of ice and cold water and stir frequently until cold but not set, about 15 minutes.

▶ While gelatin mixture chills, purée blackberries in a food processor, then force through a fine-mesh sieve into a bowl, discarding seeds.

▶ Stir lemon juice and 1 cup purée into chilled gelatin mixture, then chill in refrigerator until ready to use.

Assemble jellies:

▶ Pour a scant ¼ cup passion-fruit mixture into each glass, then stand all 6 glasses in a wide pot. Fill pot with enough ice and cold water to reach level of jelly and chill in refrigerator until jelly is just set, about 2 hours. (Keep unused portion of jellies in refrigerator, stirring once or twice to slow setting.)

▶ Pour a scant ¼ cup blackberry mixture on top of set passion-fruit jelly (pouring mixture gently over back of a spoon held just over set jelly helps to keep new layer from damaging layer beneath). Add enough ice to pot to reach level of jelly and chill in refrigerator until jelly is set, about 2 hours.

▶ Make another layer of passion-fruit jelly and another layer of blackberry jelly in same manner, adding ice to pot and chilling in refrigerator until jellies are set (last two layers will take only about 1½ hours each to chill).

▶ When all layers are set, remove glasses from ice bath and chill, loosely covered with plastic wrap, 8 hours (or overnight).

Make cream 2 hours before serving:

▶ Combine lemon verbena with sugar in a small bowl, then gently bruise verbena with a pestle or wooden spoon (to release flavor). Stir in cream and chill, stirring occasionally, 1 hour.

▶ Pour through cleaned fine-mesh sieve into a larger bowl, pressing gently on solids and then discarding them, then chill cream, covered, until ready to serve.

▶ Just before serving, beat cream with an electric mixer until it just holds soft peaks and spoon dollops over jellies.

Cooks' note:

• Jellies (without cream topping) can be layered 2 days ahead and chilled, loosely covered.

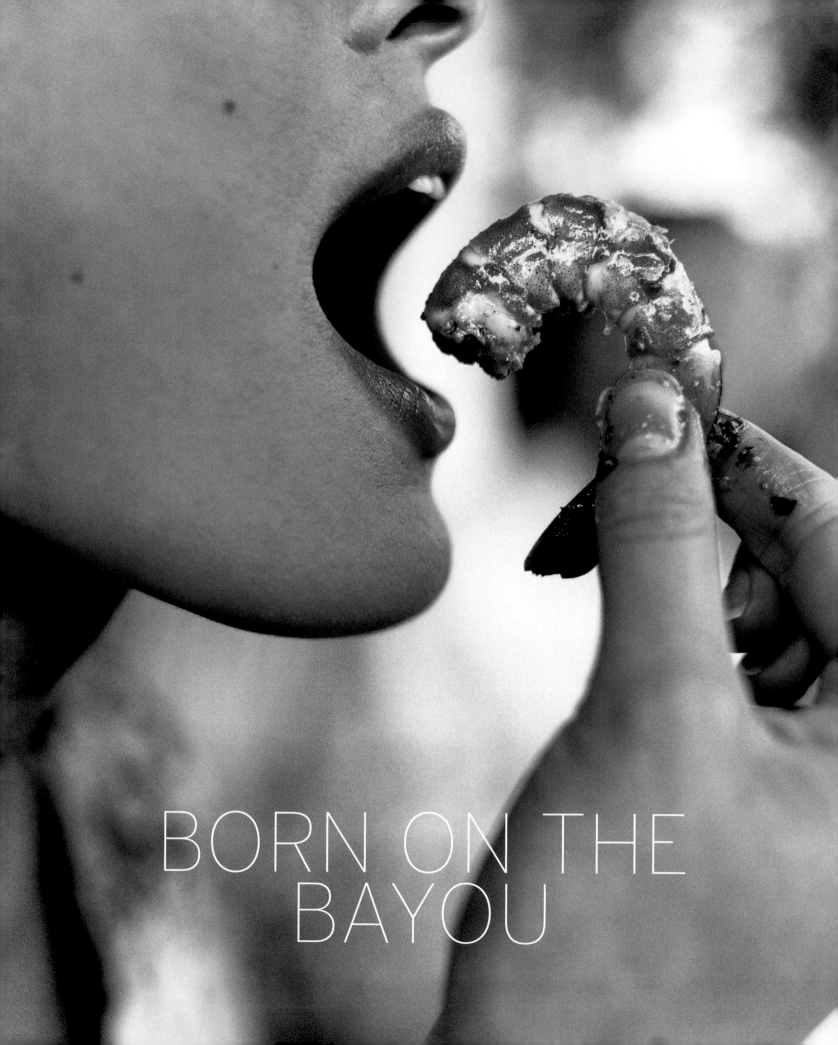

BORN ON THE
BAYOU

SERVES 8

SCREWDRIVER HIGHBALLS

**CHERRY TOMATOES AND
CUCUMBER SPEARS WITH SPICED SALT**

GRILLED SHRIMP RÉMOULADE

CREAMY COLESLAW

**SMOKED-SAUSAGE AND OKRA
DIRTY RICE**

TRAMIN UNTEREBNER ALTO ADIGE
PINOT GRIGIO '02

**PEACHES "FOSTER"
WITH CANE SYRUP PECAN ICE CREAM**

SCREWDRIVER HIGHBALLS
MAKES 8 DRINKS
Active time: 5 min   Start to finish: 5 min

12   oz vodka (1½ cups)
 6   cups fresh orange juice, chilled

Garnish: **orange slices**

▸ Stir together vodka and juice in a large pitcher, then serve over ice.

CHERRY TOMATOES AND CUCUMBER SPEARS WITH SPICED SALT
SERVES 8 (HORS D'OEUVRE)
Active time: 10 min   Start to finish: 20 min

 3   seedless cucumbers (usually plastic-wrapped), halved
     crosswise, then each half cut lengthwise into 8 spears
¼   cup kosher salt
 1   teaspoon cayenne
½   teaspoon black pepper
 2   pt cherry tomatoes
 1   lime, halved

▸ Chill cucumber spears in a large bowl of ice and cold water 15 minutes, then arrange in a serving bowl filled with ice.
▸ Stir together kosher salt, cayenne, and black pepper in a small serving bowl for dipping vegetables.
▸ Arrange cherry tomatoes in serving bowls, then squeeze lime over them just before serving (juice helps salt adhere to tomatoes).

Cooks' note:
• Spiced salt can be made 1 day ahead and kept, covered, at room temperature.

GRILLED SHRIMP RÉMOULADE
SERVES 8 (MAIN COURSE)
Active time: 1¼ hr   Start to finish: 1½ hr

¼   cup Creole mustard (see Sources) or other
     coarse-grain mustard
¼   cup white-wine vinegar
⅔   cup plus ¼ cup vegetable oil
 3   tablespoons minced fresh flat-leaf parsley
2½   tablespoons drained bottled horseradish
2½   tablespoons minced dill pickle
 2   tablespoons minced scallion greens
 2   teaspoons paprika (not hot)
1½   teaspoons cayenne
2¼   teaspoons salt
 1   teaspoon black pepper
 3   lb large shrimp in shell (21 to 25 per lb)

Special equipment: **14 (12-inch) wooden skewers**

▸ To make rémoulade, whisk together mustard and vinegar in a large bowl until combined well, then whisk in ⅔ cup oil with parsley, horseradish, pickle, scallion, paprika, cayenne, 1¼ teaspoons salt, and ½ teaspoon black pepper.
▸ Snip through shells of shrimp down middle of back using scissors, exposing vein and leaving tail and first segment of shell intact. Devein shrimp, leaving shells in place. (Shells will prevent shrimp from becoming tough on outside when grilled.) Toss shrimp with remaining ¼ cup oil, remaining teaspoon salt, and remaining ½ teaspoon black pepper in a large bowl, then thread about 6 shrimp (through top and tail, leaving shrimp curled) onto each skewer.
▸ Prepare grill for cooking. If using a charcoal grill, open vents on bottom of grill, then light charcoal. Charcoal fire is medium-hot when you can hold your hand 5 inches above rack for 3 to 4 seconds. If using a gas grill, preheat burners on high, covered, 10 minutes, then reduce heat to moderately high.
▸ Grill shrimp on lightly oiled grill rack, covered only if using a gas grill, turning over once, until just cooked through, 3 to 4 minutes total.
▸ When just cool enough to handle, push shrimp off skewers into rémoulade, then toss to combine well and cool at least 15 minutes. Serve warm or at room temperature.

CREAMY COLESLAW

SERVES 8

Active time: 15 min   Start to finish: 45 min

½   cup mayonnaise
¼   cup sour cream
 2   tablespoons cider vinegar
¾   teaspoon sugar
½   teaspoon salt
½   teaspoon black pepper
 2   lb green cabbage, quartered, cored, and thinly sliced
     (8 cups)
 3   medium carrots, shredded

▶ Whisk together mayonnaise, sour cream, vinegar, sugar, salt, and pepper in a large bowl until combined well, then toss with cabbage and carrots. Let stand, uncovered, at room temperature, tossing occasionally, until wilted, about 30 minutes. Serve at room temperature or chilled.

Cooks' note:
- Coleslaw can be made 1 day ahead and chilled, covered.

SMOKED-SAUSAGE AND OKRA DIRTY RICE

SERVES 8

Active time: 45 min   Start to finish: 1 hr

Any type of hot smoked pork sausage such as andouille or kielbasa will do for this Louisiana dirty rice takeoff.

4¼   cups water
2½   cups long-grain white rice
1½   teaspoons salt
 2   tablespoons vegetable oil
 1   lb smoked hot pork sausage links, quartered lengthwise
     and cut crosswise into ½-inch pieces
½   lb okra, trimmed (discarding stem and blossom end) and
     thinly sliced crosswise
 2   medium onions, chopped
 1   medium green bell pepper, chopped
 1   medium red bell pepper, chopped
 2   large garlic cloves, finely chopped
1¾   cups reduced-sodium chicken broth
½   teaspoon black pepper
 6   scallions, thinly sliced

▶ Bring 4 cups water to a boil in a 4-quart heavy saucepan, then add rice and ½ teaspoon salt and cook, covered tightly, over low heat until water is absorbed and rice is tender, about 20 minutes. Remove from heat and let stand, covered and undisturbed, 10 minutes. Fluff rice with a fork and keep covered.

▶ While rice cooks, heat 1 tablespoon oil in a 10- to 12-inch heavy skillet (preferably cast-iron) over moderately high heat until hot but not smoking, then sauté sausage in 2 batches, stirring occasionally, until browned, 2 to 3 minutes per batch, transferring with a slotted spoon to a bowl. Add okra to skillet and sauté, stirring occasionally, until browned, 2 to 3 minutes. Transfer to another bowl.

▶ Heat remaining tablespoon oil in skillet over moderately high heat until hot but not smoking, then sauté onions and bell peppers, stirring occasionally, until softened and browned, about 5 minutes. Add garlic and sauté, stirring, 1 minute. Add okra, broth, black pepper, remaining ¼ cup water, and remaining teaspoon salt and simmer, uncovered, stirring occasionally, until slightly thickened and level of liquid is evaporated to just below surface of solids, 10 to 15 minutes. Stir in sausage.

▶ Toss sausage mixture with rice, scallions, and salt and pepper to taste.

Cooks' note:
- Sausage mixture and rice (not combined) can be made 1 day ahead and cooled completely, then chilled separately, covered. Reheat rice in a steamer rack or large sieve set over simmering water, covered, until hot, about 15 minutes. Heat sausage mixture in a large saucepan over moderate heat, covered, stirring occasionally, until hot, then toss with rice and scallions.

PEACHES "FOSTER" WITH CANE SYRUP PECAN ICE CREAM

SERVES 8

Active time: 1 hr   Start to finish: 5 hr (includes making ice cream)

  4 large ripe peaches (2 lb total)
  ½ stick (¼ cup) unsalted butter
  6 tablespoons packed light brown sugar
  ⅓ cup dark rum
  ¼ teaspoon cinnamon
  ⅛ teaspoon salt
     Cane syrup pecan ice cream (recipe follows)

Garnish: **chopped toasted pecans**

▶ Have ready a large bowl of ice and cold water. Bring a 6-quart pot three-fourths full of water to a boil, then gently drop peaches into water and cook 15 seconds. Transfer with a slotted spoon to ice water and cool completely to stop cooking. Remove skin with a paring knife and cut peaches into ½-inch-thick wedges, discarding pits.
▶ Melt butter in a 10- to 12-inch heavy skillet over moderate heat, then stir in brown sugar, rum, cinnamon, and salt until smooth. Add peaches and simmer, stirring and turning peaches over occasionally, until tender, 3 to 5 minutes. Cool until warm and serve over scoops of ice cream.

Cooks' notes:
• Peaches in sauce can be made 2 hours ahead. Reheat to warm before serving.
• To save time, you can use store-bought premium vanilla or butter pecan ice cream instead of homemade.

CLOCKWISE FROM TOP LEFT: screwdriver highballs; cherry tomatoes and cucumber spears with spiced salt; peaches "Foster" with cane syrup pecan ice cream; smoked sausage and okra dirty rice

CANE SYRUP PECAN ICE CREAM

MAKES ABOUT 2 QUARTS

Active time: 20 min   Start to finish: 5 hr (includes freezing)

  ⅔ cup cane syrup (see Sources), or ¼ cup dark corn syrup mixed with ¾ cup mild molasses (not robust or blackstrap)
  ¼ cup sugar
  2 teaspoons cornstarch
  4 large eggs
  2 cups whole milk
  2 cups heavy cream
  ¾ teaspoon vanilla
1⅓ cups pecans (5½ oz), coarsely chopped, toasted (see Tips, page 8), and cooled

Special equipment: **an instant-read thermometer; an ice cream maker**

▶ Whisk together cane syrup, sugar, cornstarch, and a pinch of salt in a large bowl, then add eggs, whisking until combined. Bring milk and cream just to a boil in a 4-quart heavy saucepan over moderately high heat, stirring occasionally, then add to egg mixture in a stream, whisking constantly. Transfer custard to saucepan.
▶ Cook custard over moderately low heat, stirring constantly with a wooden spoon, until thick enough to coat back of spoon and registers 170°F on thermometer, 5 to 8 minutes (custard may look slightly curdled; do not let boil).
▶ Immediately pour custard through a fine-mesh sieve into a bowl, then stir in vanilla and cool, stirring occasionally. Chill custard, its surface covered with wax paper, until cold, at least 3 hours.
▶ Freeze half of custard in ice cream maker until almost firm, then stir together ice cream and half of pecans in a large bowl. Transfer to an airtight container and put in freezer to harden. Repeat with remaining custard and pecans.

Cooks' notes:
• It's really worth seeking out the cane syrup for this recipe—it makes for a much more complex-flavored ice cream.
• To cool custard quickly after straining, set bowl in a larger bowl of ice and cold water and stir until chilled.
• Custard can be chilled up to 1 day.
• Ice cream keeps 5 days.

KEEP YOUR COOL

A BREEZY SUMMER DINNER

SERVES 4

**VEGETABLE COUSCOUS,
GOAT CHEESE, AND BEETS**

DOMAINE TSELEPOS MANTINEA '02

**POACHED CHICKEN WITH
TOMATOES, OLIVES, AND
GREEN BEANS**

DOMAINE SKOURAS ST. GEORGE '01

**CANTALOUPE CURLS WITH
SPICED WINE**

SIGALAS SANTORINI MEZZO '00

VEGETABLE COUSCOUS, GOAT CHEESE, AND BEETS

SERVES 4
Active time: 30 min   Start to finish: 30 min

1   teaspoon chopped fresh dill
1   teaspoon finely chopped fresh chives
⅛   teaspoon black pepper
1   (4-oz) piece soft mild goat cheese from a log
⅔   cup water
½   teaspoon salt
4   tablespoons olive oil
½   cup couscous (3 oz)
¼   cup diced (¼ inch) red onion
½   cup diced (¼ inch) zucchini
½   cup diced (¼ inch) red bell pepper
¼   cup fresh corn kernels
1   small beet (about 2 inches in diameter), trimmed
1   tablespoon Sherry vinegar
4   thin prosciutto slices (optional)

Special equipment: a Japanese Benriner (see Sources) or other adjustable-blade slicer; a 4-oz ramekin
Accompaniment: *grissini* (long thin breadsticks) or flatbread

► Stir together dill, chives, and pepper on a plate, then roll cheese in herb mixture to coat sides (not ends). Wrap cheese in plastic wrap and chill.
► Bring water, salt, and 1 tablespoon oil to a boil in a 1-quart heavy saucepan. Stir in couscous, then cover pan and remove from heat. Let stand, covered, 5 minutes.
► Heat 1 tablespoon oil in a 12-inch heavy skillet over moderate heat until hot but not smoking, then cook onion, stirring, 1 minute. Add zucchini, bell pepper, and corn and cook, stirring, until zucchini is bright green, about 3 minutes. Season with salt and pepper and transfer to a bowl.
► Fluff couscous with a fork and stir into vegetables, then season with salt and pepper.
► Peel beet and cut half of beet into very thin slices (less than ⅛ inch thick) with slicer (discard remainder), then stack slices and cut into thin matchsticks. Rinse beets and pat dry, then transfer to a bowl.

▶ Whisk together vinegar, remaining 2 tablespoons oil, and salt and pepper to taste. Add ½ tablespoon dressing to beets and toss to coat.

▶ Fill ramekin with couscous, pressing it firmly into mold with a rubber spatula. Invert ramekin onto a salad plate and carefully unmold couscous, then make 3 more couscous mounds on 3 more plates.

▶ Drape each couscous mound with 1 prosciutto slice (if using), then top with some of beets.

▶ Unwrap cheese and cut crosswise into 4 equal slices with a lightly oiled knife, then arrange 1 cheese slice alongside each couscous mound and spoon remaining dressing around mounds.

Cooks' note:

• Couscous can be made 1 day ahead and chilled, covered. Bring to room temperature before stirring into vegetables.

POACHED CHICKEN WITH TOMATOES, OLIVES, AND GREEN BEANS

SERVES 4

Active time: 40 min Start to finish: 40 min

4	skinless boneless chicken breast halves (1¾ lb total)
1	tablespoon plus ¼ teaspoon kosher salt
5	cups water
1¾	cups reduced-sodium chicken broth (14 fl oz)
1	fresh thyme sprig
¾	lb haricots verts or other thin green beans, trimmed
5	tablespoons extra-virgin olive oil
1	lb tomatoes, cut into ¼-inch dice (3 cups)
½	cup brine-cured green and black olives such as *picholine* and Kalamata, pitted and chopped
1	tablespoon torn fresh oregano leaves
⅛	teaspoon black pepper

▶ Sprinkle chicken all over with 1 tablespoon kosher salt and let stand.

▶ While chicken stands, bring water, broth, and thyme to a boil in a 4- to 6-quart heavy pot, then add beans and cook, uncovered, until crisp-tender, 3 to 6 minutes. Transfer beans with a slotted spoon to a bowl and toss with 1 tablespoon oil and salt and pepper to taste.

▶ Add salted chicken to broth and cook at a bare simmer, uncovered, 6 minutes. Remove pot from heat and let chicken stand, covered, until cooked through, about 15 minutes .

▶ Transfer chicken with tongs to a cutting board and cool, about 5 minutes.

▶ While chicken cools, stir together tomatoes, olives, oregano, pepper, remaining ¼ teaspoon salt, and remaining 4 tablespoons oil in a bowl.

▶ Holding a knife at a 45-degree angle, cut chicken across the grain into 1-inch-thick slices.

▶ Divide green beans among 4 plates, then arrange sliced chicken over beans and top with tomato olive mixture.

Cook's note:

• Beans, chicken, and tomato olive mixture can be made 2 hours ahead and chilled separately, covered.

CANTALOUPE CURLS WITH SPICED WINE

SERVES 4

Active time: 20 min Start to finish: 30 min

1	cup dry red wine
2	tablespoons sugar
1	Turkish or ½ California bay leaf
1	teaspoon mustard seeds
1	teaspoon pink peppercorns (optional), crushed
2	ripe cantaloupes, chilled

▶ Simmer wine, sugar, bay leaf, mustard seeds, and peppercorns (if using) in a 1-quart heavy saucepan until liquid is reduced to about ¼ cup, 10 to 15 minutes. Remove from heat and cool in saucepan set in a bowl of ice and cold water. Discard bay leaf.

▶ Halve each cantaloupe and discard seeds. Scoop out curls from melon halves with an ice cream scoop (not one with a lever), then divide curls among 4 bowls along with any juices. Just before serving, drizzle each serving with about 1 tablespoon cooled spiced wine.

Cooks' note:

• Spiced wine can be made 1 week ahead and chilled in an airtight container.

OPPOSITE: **poached chicken with tomatoes, olives, and green beans; cantaloupe curls with spiced wine**

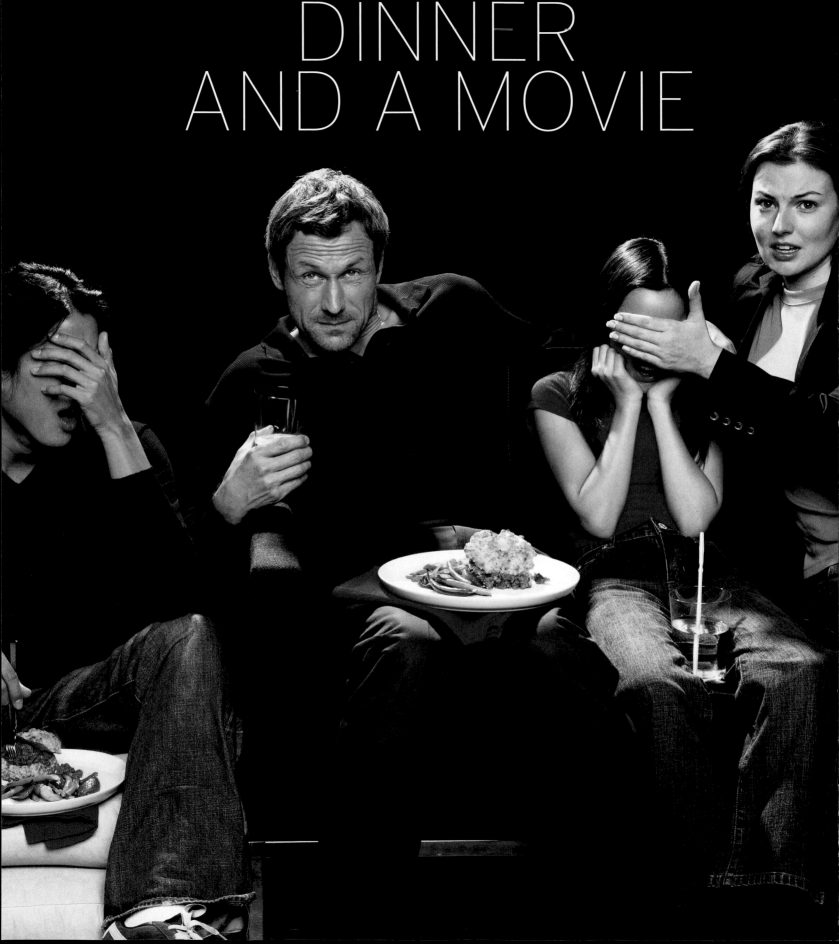

DINNER
AND A MOVIE

SERVES 8

TURKEY SLOPPY JOES ON CHEDDAR BUTTERMILK BISCUITS

GREEN BEANS AND ROASTED RED ONIONS

SHIPYARD BREWING COMPANY OLD THUMPER EXTRA SPECIAL ALE

CHOCOLATE PEANUT BUTTER BARS WITH HOT FUDGE SAUCE

TURKEY SLOPPY JOES ON CHEDDAR BUTTERMILK BISCUITS

SERVES 8
Active time: 40 min   Start to finish: 1¾ hr (includes making biscuits)

- 3 tablespoons olive oil
- 1 large onion, chopped
- 2 celery ribs, chopped
- 1 red bell pepper, chopped
- 4 garlic cloves, finely chopped
- 2½ lb ground turkey (with at least 7 percent fat; not labeled "all breast meat")
- 1 teaspoon salt
- ½ teaspoon black pepper
- 1 (28- to 32-oz) can whole tomatoes in juice
- ½ cup ketchup
- 2 tablespoons molasses (not blackstrap)
- 2 tablespoons cider vinegar
- 1½ tablespoons Worcestershire sauce
- 1¼ teaspoons Tabasco, or to taste
  Cheddar buttermilk biscuits (recipe follows)

▶ Heat oil in a wide 8-quart heavy pot over moderately high heat until hot but not smoking, then sauté onion, celery, bell pepper, and garlic, stirring occasionally, until golden, 10 to 12 minutes. Add turkey and sauté, stirring occasionally and breaking up large lumps with a wooden spoon, until meat is no longer pink, about 5 minutes. Stir in salt and pepper.
▶ Purée tomatoes with juice, ketchup, molasses, vinegar, Worcestershire sauce, and Tabasco in a blender until smooth. Add to turkey and simmer, uncovered, stirring occasionally, until sauce is thickened, 25 to 30 minutes.
▶ Serve turkey sloppy joes on split Cheddar buttermilk biscuits.

CHEDDAR BUTTERMILK BISCUITS

MAKES 8 BISCUITS
Active time: 15 min   Start to finish: 40 min

- 1¾ cups all-purpose flour
- ¾ cup cornmeal (preferably stone-ground; not coarse)
- 4 teaspoons baking powder
- 1 teaspoon baking soda
- 1 teaspoon salt
- ½ stick (¼ cup) cold unsalted butter, cut into ½-inch cubes
- 6 oz extra-sharp Cheddar, coarsely grated (2 cups)
- 3 tablespoons finely grated Parmigiano-Reggiano (see Tips, page 8)
- 3 scallions, finely chopped
- 1⅓ cups well-shaken buttermilk

▶ Put oven rack in middle position and preheat oven to 450°F. Butter a large baking sheet.
▶ Whisk together flour, cornmeal, baking powder, baking soda, and salt in a bowl, then blend in butter with your fingertips or a pastry blender until mixture resembles coarse meal. Stir in cheeses and scallions with a wooden spoon, then add buttermilk and stir until just combined.
▶ Drop dough in 8 equal mounds about 2 inches apart on baking sheet. Bake until golden, about 15 minutes. Transfer to a rack and cool to warm, about 10 minutes, then cut in half horizontally.

Cooks' notes:
• You can use 2 small baking sheets instead of 1 large. Bake biscuits in upper and lower thirds of oven, switching position of sheets halfway through baking.
• Biscuits can be made 1 day ahead and cooled completely, then kept in an airtight container at room temperature. Reheat in a preheated 350°F oven 10 minutes.

GREEN BEANS AND ROASTED RED ONIONS

SERVES 8
Active time: 15 min   Start to finish: 1 hr

- 2¼ lb medium red onions (about 5)
- ¼ cup olive oil
- 2 tablespoons balsamic vinegar
- 1 teaspoon kosher salt
- ¼ teaspoon black pepper
- ¼ cup water
- 1½ lb green beans, trimmed and cut diagonally into 2-inch pieces

▶ Put oven rack in middle position and preheat oven to 450°F. Oil a 13- by 9-inch baking pan.
▶ Peel onions, trimming root ends but leaving onions whole,

then quarter onions lengthwise. Put in baking pan, then drizzle with oil and vinegar, tossing to coat. Arrange onions with a cut side down and sprinkle with kosher salt and pepper.

▶ Roast, uncovered, turning over once and basting with pan juices twice during baking, until deep golden, about 30 minutes. Add water to pan and roast until onions are tender and caramelized, about 20 minutes more. Transfer onions with pan juices to a large bowl.

▶ While onions roast, cook beans in a 5- to 6-quart pot of boiling salted water (see Tips, page 8), uncovered, until crisp-tender, about 5 minutes. Drain beans in a colander, then add to onions and toss. Season with salt and pepper.

CHOCOLATE PEANUT BUTTER BARS WITH HOT FUDGE SAUCE

SERVES 8 GENEROUSLY

Active time: 35 min   Start to finish: 3 hr

For chocolate layer

    Vegetable oil for greasing pan

7 oz fine-quality bittersweet chocolate (not unsweetened), chopped

1 stick (½ cup) cold unsalted butter, cut into tablespoon pieces

¼ cup granulated sugar

¼ teaspoon salt

3 large eggs, lightly beaten

1 teaspoon vanilla

1 cup salted dry-roasted peanuts (4 oz)

For peanut butter layer

4 oz cream cheese, softened

½ cup creamy peanut butter (not "natural")

¾ cup confectioners sugar

¼ teaspoon salt

½ cup chilled heavy cream

1 teaspoon vanilla

For hot fudge sauce

⅓ cup heavy cream

3 tablespoons light corn syrup

3 tablespoons packed brown sugar

2 tablespoons Dutch-process unsweetened cocoa powder

¼ teaspoon salt

3½ oz fine-quality bittersweet chocolate (not unsweetened), chopped

½ teaspoon vanilla

Make chocolate layer:

▶ Put oven rack in middle position and preheat oven to 350°F. Line a 9-inch square baking pan with foil, allowing 2 inches of foil to hang over 2 opposite ends of pan, and lightly brush foil (except overhang) with oil.

▶ Melt chocolate with butter, sugar, and salt in a double boiler or a large metal bowl set over a pan of barely simmering water, whisking occasionally, until smooth. Remove top of double boiler or bowl from heat and whisk in eggs and vanilla, then stir in peanuts.

▶ Pour batter into baking pan and bake until set and edges are slightly puffed, about 15 minutes. Transfer cake in pan to a rack to cool completely.

Make peanut butter layer:

▶ Beat cream cheese, peanut butter, confectioners sugar, and salt in a bowl with an electric mixer at medium speed until combined well, about 4 minutes.

▶ Beat cream with vanilla in another bowl with cleaned beaters at medium-high speed until it just holds stiff peaks, then fold into peanut butter mixture gently but thoroughly.

▶ Spread mixture evenly on top of chocolate layer and freeze, pan covered with foil, until firm, about 2 hours.

Make hot fudge sauce:

▶ Bring cream, syrup, brown sugar, cocoa, salt, and chocolate to a boil in a 1-quart heavy saucepan over moderate heat, stirring until chocolate is melted. Reduce heat and simmer, stirring frequently, until thickened, about 3 minutes, then remove from heat. Stir in vanilla until incorporated. Cool sauce to warm.

To serve:

▶ Carefully lift cake from pan using foil overhang. Trim ¼ inch from edges of cake and discard, then cut into 8 bars. Peel off foil and serve bars with sauce.

Cooks' notes:

• These frozen dessert bars are very large. Don't worry about them melting—they're just as delicious when they soften.

• Sauce can be made 1 week ahead and cooled completely, then chilled in an airtight container. Reheat before using.

• Leftover bars can be frozen, individually wrapped in plastic wrap, up to 4 days.

REIMAGINING GIGI

A GRAND CINEMATIC DINNER

SERVES 6

**SCRAMBLED EGGS EN COQUE
WITH CAVIAR**

PERRIER-JOUËT FLEUR DE
CHAMPAGNE '96

ROAST QUAIL WITH FRESH FIGS

POMMES ALLUMETTES

CHÂTEAU GRUAUD-LAROSE
ST.-JULIEN '99

**SALADE AUX FINES HERBES
WITH CAMEMBERT**

OPÉRA CAKE

DOMAINE DE MONTAHUC, MUSCAT
DE ST. JEAN DE MINERVOIS '02

SCRAMBLED EGGS EN COQUE WITH CAVIAR

SERVES 6 (FIRST COURSE)
Active time: 45 min   Start to finish: 45 min

  6 large eggs (in shells)
  2 tablespoons heavy cream
  5 tablespoons unsalted butter
  ¼ teaspoon salt
  ¼ teaspoon black pepper
  3 (½-inch-thick) slices firm white bread such as
      pain de mie or Pullman loaf, crusts discarded
 50 g caviar (preferably osetra)

Special equipment: **an egg topper (see Sources) or a sharp paring knife; 6 eggcups; 6 demitasse spoons**

▶ Holding 1 egg narrow end up, remove top half inch of shell with egg topper or knife and discard. Pour egg into a bowl and reserve shell. Repeat with remaining eggs.
▶ Rinse eggshells gently in water, then submerge in a 2-quart saucepan of water and bring to a boil, covered. Remove from heat, leaving shells in water to keep warm.
▶ While shells come to a boil, add cream to eggs and whisk until well combined.
▶ Melt 4 tablespoons butter in a double boiler or in a metal bowl set over a saucepan of barely simmering water, then cook egg mixture, gently whisking constantly, until the consistency of pudding (thick enough to mound), 15 to 20 minutes. Remove from heat and whisk in salt, pepper, and remaining tablespoon butter. Transfer to a 2-cup glass measure and keep warm, covered.
▶ Toast bread and cut into long ½-inch-thick sticks.
▶ While bread toasts, drain eggshells upside down on paper towels.
▶ Put shells in eggcups, then pour egg mixture into shells, guiding flow with a small spoon. (Alternatively, put shells in an empty egg carton to stabilize while filling, then wipe shells clean before transferring to eggcups.) Spoon some caviar on top of each and serve with toast fingers and demitasse spoons.

ROAST QUAIL WITH FRESH FIGS

SERVES 6
Active time: 1¾ hr   Start to finish: 2 hr

If you're making this entire menu, you'll want to brown the quail and figs before starting the eggs; then you can simply pop them in the oven when serving the first course.

For stuffing
  1 medium onion, finely chopped
  2 celery ribs, finely chopped
  1 large garlic clove, finely chopped

½ stick (¼ cup) unsalted butter

⅓ cup veal demi-glace (see Sources)

2 tablespoons chopped fresh tarragon

1 tablespoon fig balsamic vinegar (see Sources)

¾ cup chopped walnuts (2 oz)

⅔ cup soft dried Mission figs (¼ lb), stems discarded and figs finely chopped

1 cup coarse fresh bread crumbs

½ teaspoon salt

¼ teaspoon black pepper

For figs and sauce

½ stick (¼ cup) unsalted butter

1 pt fresh figs, stems discarded and figs halved lengthwise

¼ cup finely chopped shallot

¼ cup finely chopped celery

1 cup dry red wine

1⅓ cups veal demi-glace

1 teaspoon arrowroot or cornstarch

2 tablespoons fig balsamic vinegar

1 tablespoon chopped fresh tarragon

½ teaspoon salt

¼ teaspoon black pepper

For quail

12 semiboneless quail (see Sources)

½ teaspoon salt

¼ teaspoon black pepper

2 tablespoons unsalted butter

2 tablespoons vegetable oil

Special equipment: kitchen string; wooden picks

Make stuffing:

▶ Cook onion, celery, and garlic in butter in a 10-inch heavy skillet over moderate heat, stirring, until pale golden, about 10 minutes. Add demi-glace and boil, stirring occasionally, until most of liquid is evaporated, about 3 minutes. Stir in tarragon, vinegar, walnuts, dried figs, bread crumbs, salt, and pepper, then spread stuffing on a plate to cool.

Prepare figs and make sauce:

▶ Heat 2 tablespoons butter in a 12-inch heavy skillet over moderately high heat until foam subsides, then brown figs, cut sides down, without stirring, about 3 minutes. Transfer figs to a bowl with a slotted spatula. Add shallot and celery to skillet and sauté, stirring, until golden, 3 to 5 minutes. Add wine and 8 to 10 browned fig halves (reserve remainder) and boil, stirring and mashing figs, until wine is reduced to a

syrup, about 5 minutes. Stir in demi-glace and bring to a boil. Stir arrowroot into vinegar until dissolved, then add to skillet, whisking to incorporate. Boil sauce 2 minutes, then pour through a fine-mesh sieve into a 2-quart heavy saucepan, pressing on and then discarding solids. Stir in tarragon, salt, and pepper.

Prepare quail and finish sauce:

▶ Discard any disposable metal skewers from cavity of each quail, then rinse quail inside and out and pat dry. Stuff 1 quail with a scant ¼ cup stuffing, pressing and shaping it to fill out breast. Tie legs together with string and push legs up against body. Thread cavity closed with a wooden pick. Repeat with remaining quail.

▶ Put oven rack in middle position and preheat oven to 350°F.

▶ Sprinkle quail all over with salt and pepper. Heat 1 tablespoon each butter and oil in cleaned 10-inch heavy skillet over moderately high heat until foam subsides, then brown 6 quail on all sides, about 10 minutes total. Transfer with tongs to a large shallow baking pan. Wipe skillet clean and brown remaining 6 quail in same manner in remaining tablespoon each of butter and oil.

▶ Remove strings and picks from all quail, then roast quail, breast sides up, until just cooked through (check inner thigh—meat will still be slightly pink), 10 to 15 minutes. Add reserved browned figs to pan for last 2 to 3 minutes of roasting.

▶ While quail roast, return sauce to a simmer, then add remaining 2 tablespoons butter, whisking until incorporated.

▶ Transfer quail and figs to a serving dish and pour any juices from baking pan into sauce. Serve quail with sauce.

Cooks' notes:

• Stuffing can be made 1 day ahead and cooled completely, uncovered, then chilled, covered. Bring to room temperature before proceeding.

• Figs and sauce (without remaining 2 tablespoons butter) can be prepared 1 day ahead and cooled, uncovered, then chilled separately, covered. Bring sauce to a simmer before adding butter.

• Quail can be browned 1 hour before roasting. Keep quail, uncovered, at room temperature.

POMMES ALLUMETTES
(Matchstick Potatoes)
SERVES 6
Active time: 20 min   Start to finish: 50 min

There are two temptations in this recipe that you need to resist: Do not use a small pot for frying the potatoes—the oil will bubble up and overflow, which is extremely dangerous. And do not try to cook the potatoes in fewer than 6 batches or they won't get crisp enough.

Because the timing for this menu can be complicated, we recommend that you make the potatoes ahead. They are just as delicious at room temperature as they are when hot.

 2 large russet (baking) potatoes (1½ lb total)
    About 6 cups vegetable oil

Special equipment: **a food processor fitted with fine (2-mm) julienne disk or a *mandoline* fitted with julienne cutter; a deep-fat thermometer**

▶ Peel potatoes and cut lengthwise into ⅛-inch-thick julienne in processor or with *mandoline*. Transfer as cut to a bowl of ice and cold water and let chill in water at least 30 minutes.
▶ Heat 1¼ inches oil in a 6- to 7-quart heavy pot over moderately high heat until thermometer registers 375°F.
▶ While oil heats, drain potatoes and pat completely dry between several layers of paper towels. Fry potatoes in 6 batches, gently stirring once or twice with a slotted spoon or skimmer, until golden and crisp, 1 to 1½ minutes per batch. Transfer potatoes with slotted spoon to paper towels to drain and season with salt. (Return oil to 375°F between batches.)

Cooks' notes:
• Raw julienne potatoes can chill in water in refrigerator up to 4 hours.
• Potatoes can be fried and salted 6 hours ahead and kept, uncovered, at room temperature.

SALADE AUX FINES HERBES WITH CAMEMBERT
SERVES 6
Active time: 15 min   Start to finish: 15 min

The term fines herbes *refers to a blend of aromatic herbs that usually includes parsley, chervil, chives, and tarragon. The combination is used in sauces, vegetables, and meat dishes, but it also adds subtle freshness to green salads.*

 2   teaspoons Champagne vinegar
 ½   tablespoon minced shallot
 ½   teaspoon whole-grain mustard
 ¼   teaspoon salt
 ⅛   teaspoon black pepper
 2   tablespoons mild olive oil
 4   cups loosely packed *mâche* (lambs' lettuce; 1 to 2 oz), trimmed
 2   Belgian endives, cut crosswise into ⅛-inch-thick slices
 4   cups torn Boston lettuce (from 1 small head)
 ¼   cup loosely packed chervil sprigs or 1 tablespoon chopped fresh tarragon
 1   tablespoon finely chopped fresh chives

Accompaniments: **Camembert cheese at room temperature and sliced baguette**

▶ Whisk together vinegar, shallot, mustard, salt, and pepper in a small bowl, then add oil in a slow stream, whisking until emulsified.
▶ Toss salad greens and herbs with dressing in a large bowl.

Cooks' notes:
• Dressing can be made 2 hours ahead and kept at room temperature.
• Lettuces and herbs can be washed, dried, and torn or cut 2 hours ahead and chilled in sealed plastic bags lined with paper towels.

OPÉRA CAKE

SERVES 6 TO 8

Active time: 2 hr   Start to finish: 3½ hr (includes chilling buttercream and glaze)

There are many stories about the origins of this cake. Many believe that Louis Clichy was its creator because he premiered the gâteau, with his name written across the top, at the 1903 Exposition Culinaire in Paris. It became the signature cake of Clichy's shop on the Boulevard Beaumarchais. However, another pastry shop, Dalloyau, sold a very similar dessert, known as L'Opéra (in honor of the Paris Opera), and some claim that theirs was the original.

For almond sponge cake

- 3 tablespoons cake flour (not self-rising), sifted after measuring, plus additional for dusting pan
- 2 whole large eggs at room temperature for 30 minutes
- 1 cup almond flour (3½ oz) or ⅔ cup blanched whole almonds (see cooks' note, below)
- ½ cup confectioners sugar, sifted after measuring
- 2 large egg whites at room temperature for 30 minutes
- ⅛ teaspoon cream of tartar

- ⅛ teaspoon salt
- 1 tablespoon granulated sugar
- 2 tablespoons unsalted butter, melted, foam discarded, and butter cooled

For coffee syrup

- 1 teaspoon instant-espresso powder
- ½ cup plus 1 tablespoon water
- ½ cup granulated sugar
- ¼ cup Cognac or other brandy

For coffee buttercream

- 2 teaspoons instant-espresso powder
- ¼ cup plus 1 tablespoon water
- 6 tablespoons granulated sugar
- 2 large egg yolks
- 1 stick (½ cup) unsalted butter, cut into ½-inch cubes and softened

For chocolate glaze

- ¾ stick (6 tablespoons) unsalted butter
- 7 oz fine-quality bittersweet chocolate (not unsweetened; preferably 70 to 71% cacao), coarsely chopped

Special equipment: a 15- by 10-inch shallow baking pan; an offset metal spatula; a candy thermometer; a small sealable plastic bag

Make sponge cake:

▶ Put oven rack in middle position and preheat oven to 425°F. Butter baking pan, then line bottom with a sheet of parchment or wax paper, leaving a 1-inch overhang on short sides, and generously butter paper. Dust pan with cake flour, knocking out excess.

▶ Beat whole eggs in a large bowl with a handheld electric mixer at high speed until eggs have tripled in volume and form a ribbon when beaters are lifted, 2 to 3 minutes. Reduce speed to low, then add almond flour and confectioners sugar and mix until just combined. Resift cake flour over batter and gently fold in.

▶ Beat egg whites in a bowl with cleaned beaters at medium speed until foamy. Add cream of tartar and salt and beat until whites just hold soft peaks. Add granulated sugar, then increase speed to high and beat until whites just hold stiff peaks.

▶ Fold one third of whites into almond mixture to lighten, then fold in remaining whites gently but thoroughly. Fold in butter, then pour batter evenly into baking pan, spreading gently and evenly with offset spatula and being careful not to deflate (batter will be about ¼ inch thick).

▶ Bake until very pale golden, 8 to 10 minutes, then cool in pan on a rack 10 minutes.

▶ Loosen edges of cake with spatula, then transfer cake (on paper) to a cutting board. Halve cake crosswise, cutting through paper. Cut off a 3¼-inch-wide strip from bottom of each half for a total of 2 (roughly 7-inch) squares and 2 (roughly 3- by 7-inch) rectangles. Put two rectangles together to make the square middle layer. Trim outside edges slightly, then carefully peel paper from strips and squares and set back on paper.

Make coffee syrup:

▶ Stir together espresso powder and 1 tablespoon water until powder is dissolved. Bring sugar and remaining ½ cup water to a boil in a 1- to 2-quart heavy saucepan, stirring until sugar is dissolved. Reduce heat and simmer syrup, without stirring, 5 minutes. Remove from heat and stir in Cognac and coffee mixture.

Make coffee buttercream:

▶ Stir together espresso powder and 1 tablespoon water until powder is dissolved. Bring sugar and remaining ¼ cup water to a boil in a very small heavy saucepan, stirring until sugar is dissolved. Boil, without stirring, washing down any sugar crystals on side of pan with a pastry brush dipped in cold water, until syrup registers 234 to 240°F on thermometer (soft-ball stage; see cooks' note, below).

▶ While syrup boils, beat yolks in a large bowl with cleaned beaters at medium speed 1 minute.

▶ Add hot syrup to yolks in a slow stream (try to avoid beaters and side of bowl), beating, then add coffee mixture and beat until completely cool, 3 to 5 minutes. Beat in butter, 1 piece at a time, and beat until thickened and smooth.

Make glaze:

▶ Melt butter and all but 2 tablespoons chopped chocolate in a double boiler or in a metal bowl set over a saucepan of barely simmering water, stirring occasionally, until smooth. Remove top of double boiler and stir in remaining 2 tablespoons chocolate until smooth, then cool glaze until room temperature but still liquid.

Assemble cake:

▶ Put 1 cake square on a plate, then brush generously with one third of coffee syrup. Spread half of buttercream evenly over top with cleaned offset spatula, spreading to edges.

▶ Arrange both cake strips side by side on top of first layer (seam will be hidden by next layer), then brush with half of remaining coffee syrup. Spread half of glaze evenly over top, spreading just to edges.

▶ Top with remaining cake square and brush with remaining coffee syrup. Spread remaining buttercream evenly over top, spreading just to edges. Chill cake until buttercream is firm, about 30 minutes.

▶ Reheat remaining glaze over barely simmering water just until shiny and spreadable (but not warm to the touch), about 1 minute. Pour all but 1 tablespoon glaze over top layer of cake and spread evenly just to edges. Scrape remaining tablespoon glaze into sealable plastic bag and twist bag so glaze is in 1 corner. Snip a tiny hole in corner and decorate cake (leave a ½-inch border around edges). Chill cake until glaze is set, about 30 minutes, then trim edges slightly with a sharp serrated knife.

Cooks' notes:

• If you can't find almond flour, you can pulse whole almonds with the confectioners sugar in a food processor until powdery (be careful not to grind to a paste).

• To take the temperature of a shallow amount of syrup, put bulb in saucepan and turn thermometer facedown, resting other end against rim of saucepan. Check temperature frequently.

• Opéra cake can be made 2 days ahead. Cover sides with strips of plastic wrap and top of cake loosely with plastic wrap (once glaze is set) and chill cake. Remove plastic wrap from top immediately after removing cake from refrigerator and bring cake to room temperature, 30 minutes to 1 hour.

BRINGING IT ALL BACK HOME

A TRAVEL-INSPIRED DINNER

SERVES 6

POTATO CROQUETAS WITH SAFFRON ALIOLI

PORCINI AND CELERY SALAD

FEUDI DI SAN GREGORIO FIANO DI AVELLINO '03

**SEA SCALLOPS WITH HAM-BRAISED
CABBAGE AND KALE**

CREAMY STONE-GROUND GRITS

SANFORD SANTA RITA HILLS
PINOT NOIR-VIN GRIS '03

**HIBISCUS TEA SORBET, BASIL ICE CREAM,
AND ORANGE ICE CREAM**

SPICED MADELEINES

POTATO CROQUETAS WITH SAFFRON ALIOLI

MAKES 24 TO 28 HORS D'OEUVRES

Active time: 1½ hr   Start to finish: 2 hr (includes making *alioli*)

In the past two years, half of our food editors have traveled to Spain, where they tried a variety of croquetas *(ham, fish, and vegetable) that left a very positive impression. Serve these* potato croquetas *with any combination of dried sausage, olives, nuts, and cheese.*

- 1 lb large boiling potatoes (2)
- 3 large eggs
- 1 tablespoon chopped fresh flat-leaf parsley
- 1 tablespoon finely chopped fresh chives
- ¼ teaspoon chopped fresh tarragon
- 2 tablespoons unsalted butter, softened
- ½ teaspoon salt
- ⅛ teaspoon black pepper
- ¾ cup all-purpose flour
- ¾ cup fine dry bread crumbs
  - About 4 cups olive oil (not extra-virgin) for frying

Special equipment: **a potato ricer; a deep-fat thermometer**
Accompaniment: **saffron *alioli* (recipe follows)**

▶ Peel potatoes and cut into 1-inch pieces. Cover with salted cold water (see Tips, page 8) by 1 inch in a 2-quart saucepan, then boil until tender, about 8 minutes. Drain in a colander, then force potatoes through ricer into a bowl and cool.

▶ Lightly beat 1 egg in a small bowl with a fork. Add to cooled potatoes along with herbs, butter, salt, and pepper and stir just until combined.

▶ Spoon tablespoons of potato mixture onto a tray, then lightly roll each into a ball between palms of your hands and return to tray.

▶ Lightly beat remaining 2 eggs in a small bowl. Spread flour in a shallow bowl, then spread bread crumbs in another shallow bowl.

▶ Working in 4 batches (of 6 or 7), roll balls in flour to coat, gently shaking off excess flour. Dip balls in egg, turning to coat and letting excess drip off, then roll in bread crumbs and return to tray. Chill, covered, 30 minutes.

▶ Preheat oven to 200°F.

▶ Heat 1½ inches oil in a 3-quart pot until it registers 360°F

on thermometer. Working in 4 batches, fry *croquetas*, turning if necessary, until browned, about 1½ minutes per batch. Transfer with a slotted spoon to paper towels to drain, then transfer to a baking pan and keep warm in oven while frying remaining *croquetas*. (Return oil to 360°F between batches.)

Cooks' note:
• *Croquetas* can be fried 3 hours ahead and kept at room temperature. Reheat in a preheated 400°F oven 8 minutes.

SAFFRON ALIOLI

MAKES ABOUT ⅔ CUP

Active time: 10 min   Start to finish: 10 min

Alioli, a very popular Spanish sauce, goes well with almost anything—from grilled meat to vegetables to seafood. Although the authentic version is an emulsion of garlic and oil, eggs are commonly added (especially in restaurants) because they make the sauce less fragile and easier to whip up. We've made ours even easier by using store-bought mayonnaise.

- Pinch of saffron threads, crumbled
- ½ teaspoon hot water
- ½ cup mayonnaise
- 1 garlic clove, chopped
- 1 teaspoon Dijon mustard
- 1 tablespoon extra-virgin olive oil
- 1 teaspoon fresh lemon juice
- ¼ teaspoon tomato paste
- ⅛ teaspoon salt
- ⅛ teaspoon black pepper

▶ Put saffron threads in a small cup, then add hot water and let stand 5 minutes.

▶ Purée saffron mixture with remaining ingredients in a mini food processor or a blender until smooth.

Cooks' note:
• *Alioli* can be made 2 days ahead and chilled, covered. Bring to room temperature before serving (this will take about 1 hour).

OPPOSITE: **sea scallops with ham-braised cabbage and kale; creamy stone-ground grits**

PORCINI AND CELERY SALAD

SERVES 6

Active time: 20 min   Start to finish: 40 min

This delicate salad grew out of the memories of two food editors—Zanne Stewart and Alexis Touchet—of similar ones they had at restaurants in Italy. (Surprisingly, they were in different regions and traveling 20 years apart.)

- 5   large celery ribs
- 1   tablespoon plus ¼ teaspoon salt
- ½   lb fresh porcini mushrooms (sometimes called cèpes)
- 1   tablespoon fresh lemon juice
- 1   tablespoon plus 1 teaspoon extra-virgin olive oil
- ⅛   teaspoon black pepper
- 1   (6-oz) piece Parmigiano-Reggiano

Special equipment: **a Japanese Benriner or other adjustable-blade slicer**

▶ Peel outer strings from celery ribs with a sharp paring knife, then cut ribs on a 45-degree angle into paper-thin slices with slicer.
▶ Stir together 1 quart water and 1 tablespoon salt in a bowl until salt is dissolved. Add celery and soak 15 minutes, then drain in a colander. Spread celery evenly on a clean kitchen towel. Gently roll up towel and let stand 5 minutes.
▶ Wipe mushrooms with paper towels to remove any dirt or grit. Keeping stems attached, trim any discoloration from stems with paring knife.
▶ Cut mushrooms into paper-thin slices with slicer and transfer to a large bowl. Add celery, lemon juice, oil, pepper, and remaining ¼ teaspoon salt and gently toss with hands.
▶ Divide salad among 6 plates. Just before serving, use a vegetable peeler to shave cheese to taste over each salad.

SEA SCALLOPS WITH HAM-BRAISED CABBAGE AND KALE

SERVES 6

Active time: 1 hr   Start to finish: 3¾ hr (includes making ham stock)

This dish—the result of a conversation between two food editors who had just returned from opposite parts of the country—almost made itself. Paul Grimes came back from Charleston talking about the creamy stone-ground grits, shrimp, and collard greens of chef Kevin Johnson at Anson, and Kemp Minifie returned from Seattle to tell us about the scallops over braised cabbage with foie gras vinaigrette that Johnathan Sundstrom serves at Lark.

- 1   large onion, chopped
- 5   tablespoons extra-virgin olive oil
- 1   Turkish or ½ California bay leaf
- 1   tablespoon finely chopped garlic
- 1   large head Savoy cabbage (2 to 2½ lb), quartered, cored, and coarsely chopped
     Ham stock including meat (recipe follows)
- 1¼   lb tender green kale (1 large bunch), stems and center ribs cut out and discarded and leaves coarsely chopped
- 1   teaspoon salt
- ½   teaspoon black pepper
- 30   large sea scallops (2 to 2½ lb total), tough muscle removed from side of each if necessary
- 1   cup dry white wine
- 1   teaspoon fresh lemon juice, or to taste

Accompaniment: **creamy stone-ground grits (recipe follows)**

▶ Cook onion in 3 tablespoons oil with bay leaf in a 6- to 8-quart heavy pot over moderate heat, stirring occasionally, until beginning to soften, about 3 minutes. Add garlic and cook, stirring occasionally, 1 minute. Add cabbage and increase heat to moderately high, then sauté, stirring occasionally, until cabbage starts to wilt, about 5 minutes. Add stock (with meat from ham hocks) and simmer, partially covered, stirring occasionally, until cabbage is tender, about 30 minutes. Stir in kale, ½ teaspoon salt, and ¼ teaspoon pepper and simmer, partially covered, stirring occasionally, until kale is tender, about 15 minutes.
▶ Preheat oven to 200°F.

▶ Pat scallops dry and sprinkle both sides with remaining ½ teaspoon salt and remaining ¼ teaspoon pepper (total). Heat remaining 2 tablespoons oil in a 12-inch heavy nonstick skillet over moderately high heat until hot but not smoking, then sauté scallops (without crowding), in 2 batches if necessary, turning over once, until golden and just cooked through, about 5 minutes per batch. Transfer scallops to a shallow baking dish and keep warm in oven.
▶ Add wine to skillet and deglaze by boiling, stirring and scraping up any brown bits, until liquid is reduced to about ⅔ cup. Stir in 1 teaspoon lemon juice, then add sauce to cabbage mixture. Season with salt, pepper, and additional lemon juice if desired. Pour any scallop juices accumulated in baking dish into cabbage mixture.
▶ Serve mixture spooned over grits and topped with scallops.

HAM STOCK
MAKES ABOUT 3½ CUPS (NOT INCLUDING MEAT)
Active time: 15 min   Start to finish: 2¼ hr

The quantity of meat you'll have in your finished stock will vary depending on whether you use shanks or hocks. Although shanks from the butcher yield more meat, they are not as widely available as hocks, which can be found at most supermarkets.

2½   lb meaty smoked ham shanks or ham hocks
2   qt cold water
1   large onion, chopped
2   carrots, cut crosswise into ½-inch-thick slices
2   celery ribs, cut crosswise into ½-inch-thick slices
3   large garlic cloves, crushed
1   Turkish or ½ California bay leaf
2   teaspoons dried thyme, crumbled
3   whole cloves
¼   teaspoon whole black peppercorns

▶ Combine ham shanks and cold water in a 4- to 5-quart heavy pot and bring to a boil, skimming any foam. Add remaining ingredients and simmer, partially covered, until shanks are tender, about 2 hours.
▶ Pour stock through a fine-mesh sieve into a large metal bowl, reserving shanks and discarding remaining solids.
▶ Discard skin and bones from shanks. Trim and coarsely shred meat, then return to stock.

Cooks' note:
• Stock can be made 1 week ahead and cooled completely, uncovered, then chilled, covered, or frozen in an airtight container 1 month.

CREAMY STONE-GROUND GRITS
SERVES 6
Active time: 20 min   Start to finish: 1¼ hr

Hand-milled grits are far more complex in both flavor and texture than their supermarket counterpart, which we don't recommend for this particular recipe.

4   cups water
¾   teaspoon salt
2   tablespoons unsalted butter
1   cup coarse stone-ground white grits (see Sources)
1   cup whole milk
¼   teaspoon black pepper

▶ Bring water, salt, and 1 tablespoon butter to a boil in a 3- to 4-quart heavy saucepan, then add grits gradually, stirring constantly with a wooden spoon. Reduce heat and cook at a bare simmer, covered, stirring frequently, until water is absorbed and grits are thickened, about 15 minutes.
▶ Stir in ½ cup milk and simmer, partially covered, stirring occasionally to keep grits from sticking to bottom of pan, 10 minutes. Stir in remaining ½ cup milk and simmer, partially covered, stirring occasionally, until liquid is absorbed and grits are thick and tender, about 35 minutes more. (Grits will have a soft, mashed-potato-like consistency.)
▶ Stir in pepper and remaining tablespoon butter.

Cooks' note:
• Grits can be made 1 day ahead and chilled, their surface covered with lightly buttered wax paper. Reheat in a 3-quart saucepan with 1 to 1¼ cups additional water, uncovered, stirring occasionally, until heated through.

> Stir in lemon and lime juices and freeze in ice cream maker. Transfer sorbet to an airtight container and put in freezer to harden, at least 2 hours.

Cooks' note:
• Sorbet can be made 2 days ahead.

BASIL ICE CREAM
MAKES ABOUT 3 CUPS
Active time: 25 min   Start to finish: 3½ hr

When food editor Shelley Wiseman remarked on the basil ice cream she had at JoJo, Jean-Georges Vongerichten's Manhattan bistro, other editors recalled tasting herb-flavored custards in Milan years ago.

  2 cups whole milk
  3 tablespoons chopped fresh basil
 ½ cup sugar
  4 large egg yolks
 ½ cup well-chilled heavy cream

Special equipment: **an instant-read thermometer; an ice cream maker**

> Bring milk, basil, ¼ cup sugar, and a pinch of salt to a boil in a 2-quart heavy saucepan, stirring, then remove from heat and steep 30 minutes. Transfer to a blender (reserve saucepan) and blend until basil is finely ground, about 1 minute.
> Beat together yolks and remaining ¼ cup sugar in a bowl with an electric mixer until thick and pale, about 1 minute. Add milk mixture in a stream, beating until combined well. Pour mixture into reserved saucepan and cook over moderate heat, stirring constantly with a wooden spoon, until mixture coats back of spoon and registers 175°F on thermometer (do not let boil). Immediately remove from heat and pour through a fine-mesh sieve into a metal bowl. Set bowl in a larger bowl of ice and cold water and stir until cold, 10 to 15 minutes.
> Stir in cream and freeze in ice cream maker. Transfer ice cream to an airtight container and put in freezer to harden, at least 2 hours.

Cooks' note:
• Ice cream can be made 2 days ahead.

HIBISCUS TEA SORBET
MAKES ABOUT 1 QUART
Active time: 25 min   Start to finish: 3 hr

The prototype for this wonderfully tangy sorbet was discovered in Hua Hin, Thailand, where we tasted a hibiscus sorbet made by chef David Bedinghaus at the Anantara Resort & Spa.

  2 cups water
  1 cup unsprayed dried hibiscus flowers (see Sources)
  1 cup sugar
  1 tablespoon fresh lemon juice
  1 tablespoon fresh lime juice

Special equipment: **an ice cream maker**

> Bring water to a boil in a small saucepan. Stir in hibiscus and remove from heat, then steep 15 minutes.
> Pour hibiscus tea through a fine-mesh sieve into a metal bowl, pressing hard on and then discarding solids. Return tea to saucepan and bring to a boil with sugar and a pinch of salt, stirring until sugar is dissolved. Transfer mixture to a metal bowl, then set bowl in a larger bowl of ice and cold water and stir until cold, 10 to 15 minutes.

ORANGE ICE CREAM

MAKES ABOUT 3 CUPS
Active time: 25 min   Start to finish: 3½ hr

This recipe was inspired by an unforgettable blood-orange ice cream made by chef Greg Malouf of Mo Mo restaurant in Melbourne, Australia. We've used navel oranges, available all year long.

- 2   large navel oranges
- 2   cups whole milk
- ½   cup sugar
- 4   large egg yolks

Special equipment: an instant-read thermometer; an ice cream maker

▶ Finely grate 2 tablespoons zest from oranges, then halve oranges and squeeze enough juice to measure ½ cup. Discard oranges.

▶ Bring milk, ¼ cup sugar, a pinch of salt, and 1 tablespoon zest to a boil in a 2-quart heavy saucepan, then remove from heat and steep 30 minutes.

▶ Beat together yolks and remaining ¼ cup sugar in a bowl with an electric mixer until thick and pale, about 1 minute. Add milk mixture in a stream, whisking constantly until combined well. Pour mixture into saucepan and cook over moderate heat, stirring constantly with a wooden spoon, until mixture coats back of spoon and registers 175°F on thermometer (do not let boil). Immediately remove from heat and pour through a fine-mesh sieve into a metal bowl. Set bowl in a larger bowl of ice and cold water and stir until cold, 10 to 15 minutes.

▶ Stir in orange juice and remaining tablespoon zest and freeze in ice cream maker. Transfer ice cream to an airtight container and put in freezer to harden, at least 2 hours.

Cooks' note:
• Ice cream can be made 2 days ahead.

OPPOSITE: basil ice cream; hibiscus tea sorbet; orange ice cream

SPICED MADELEINES

MAKES 12 MADELEINES
Active time: 35 min   Start to finish: 1 hr

Spiced cakes, like the warm miniature madeleines served at Aix, in Manhattan, seemed the perfect pairing for the hibiscus tea sorbet and basil and orange ice creams. Unlike the madeleines that Aix pastry chef Jehangir Mehta makes, ours are the traditional size.

- ¾   stick (6 tablespoons) unsalted butter, melted, plus
       1 tablespoon (melted) for greasing molds
- ¾   cup all-purpose flour
- 1   teaspoon baking powder
- ½   teaspoon cinnamon
- ½   teaspoon ground coriander
- ¼   teaspoon freshly grated nutmeg
- ⅛   teaspoon ground allspice
- ¼   cup granulated sugar
- 3   tablespoons packed light brown sugar
- 2   large eggs
      Confectioners sugar for dusting

Special equipment: a madeleine pan with 12 (3- by 2-inch) molds (see Sources)

▶ Put oven rack in middle position and preheat oven to 400°F. Brush molds with some melted butter, then chill until set, about 5 minutes. Brush molds again with some melted butter and chill pan.

▶ Sift together flour, baking powder, spices, and a pinch of salt.

▶ Whisk together sugars and eggs until combined well. Add flour mixture and whisk until just combined, then stir in remaining butter (6 tablespoons) until just incorporated.

▶ Spoon batter into molds, filling them about two thirds full. Bake 5 minutes, then reduce oven temperature to 350°F and bake until springy to the touch and edges are lightly browned, 4 to 6 minutes. Turn out onto a rack and cool 15 minutes. Just before serving, dust with confectioners sugar.

Cooks' note:
• Madeleines can be made 6 hours ahead and are best eaten the same day.

FLAVORS OF SUMMER

LOW-FAT MENU

SERVES 6

RIBBONED ZUCCHINI SALAD

SEA SCALLOPS WITH CORN COULIS AND TOMATOES

CARAMELIZED PEACH UPSIDE-DOWN CAKES

EACH SERVING ABOUT 503 CALORIES AND 16 GRAMS FAT

RIBBONED ZUCCHINI SALAD

SERVES 6

Active time: 30 min   Start to finish: 30 min

Preparing the zucchini for this dish won't heat up your kitchen—simply salting thin slices is enough to tenderize them.

- 2 lb small zucchini, trimmed
- 1 teaspoon salt
- 2 tablespoons extra-virgin olive oil
- 2 teaspoons finely grated fresh lemon zest
- 2 teaspoons fresh lemon juice
- 2 teaspoons Dijon mustard
- 1 teaspoon anchovy paste
- ¼ teaspoon black pepper
- 3 oz frisée (French curly endive), trimmed and torn into small pieces (4 cups loosely packed)
- ½ cup loosely packed fresh flat-leaf parsley leaves
- ½ cup loosely packed fresh mint leaves, torn in half lengthwise if large
- ½ cup loosely packed fresh basil leaves, torn into small pieces
- 12 Kalamata or other brine-cured black olives, pitted and thinly sliced lengthwise
- 1 small red onion, halved lengthwise and thinly sliced crosswise (½ cup)

Special equipment: **a Japanese Benriner (see Sources) or other adjustable-blade slicer**

▶ Cut zucchini lengthwise into ⅛-inch-thick slices with slicer and transfer to a colander set over a bowl. Sprinkle zucchini with salt and toss to coat. Let stand 5 minutes, then rinse under cold water. Transfer zucchini to a clean kitchen towel and spread in 1 layer, then gently roll up towel to absorb excess water and let stand 5 minutes more.

▶ Whisk together oil, zest, juice, mustard, anchovy paste, and pepper in a large bowl.

▶ Add zucchini, frisée, herbs, olives, and onion and toss to coat. Serve immediately.

EACH SERVING ABOUT 112 CALORIES AND 6 GRAMS FAT

SEA SCALLOPS WITH CORN COULIS AND TOMATOES

SERVES 6

Active time: 35 min   Start to finish: 45 min

- 1 teaspoon finely chopped shallot
- ¼ teaspoon finely chopped garlic
- 4 teaspoons olive oil
- ¾ cup corn (from 2 large ears)
- 1 teaspoon finely chopped fresh basil
- ¼ teaspoon salt
- ⅛ teaspoon black pepper
- ½ cup 1% milk
- ½ lb plum tomatoes, seeded and cut into ¼-inch dice (1 cup)
- 1 tablespoon chopped fresh flat-leaf parsley
- 30 large sea scallops (2½ lb total), tough muscle removed from side of each if necessary

▶ Cook shallot and garlic in 2 teaspoons oil in a small skillet over moderately low heat, stirring, until softened, about 1 minute. Add corn, basil, salt, and pepper and cook, stirring occasionally, until corn is tender and beginning to lightly brown on edges, about 4 minutes. Add milk, stirring and scraping up any brown bits from bottom of skillet, then remove from heat.

▶ Purée corn mixture in a blender at medium speed until very smooth, about 1 minute. Force purée through a fine-mesh sieve into a small saucepan, pressing hard on and then discarding solids. Cover coulis until ready to serve.

▶ Toss tomatoes with parsley and salt and pepper to taste in a bowl.

▶ Pat scallops dry and season with salt and pepper. Heat remaining 2 teaspoons oil in a 12-inch nonstick heavy skillet over moderately high heat until hot but not smoking, then sauté half of scallops, turning over once, until golden and just cooked through, 4 to 5 minutes total. Transfer to a platter and keep warm, loosely covered with foil. Sauté remaining scallops in same manner.

▶ Reheat coulis over low heat, covered, then spoon 2 tablespoons onto center of each of 6 plates. Arrange 5 scallops per plate in a circle on coulis, then spoon tomatoes into center.

EACH SERVING ABOUT 222 CALORIES AND 5 GRAMS FAT

CARAMELIZED PEACH UPSIDE-DOWN CAKES

SERVES 6

Active time: 50 min   Start to finish: 1¼ hr

To prevent the caramelized peaches from sticking to the parchment paper, unmold these flavorful little cakes while they're still warm.

1	tablespoon plus 2 teaspoons unsalted butter
6	tablespoons plus 1 teaspoon cake flour (not self-rising)
1¼	lb medium peaches (about 4)
9	tablespoons packed light brown sugar
2	large eggs
¼	teaspoon salt
⅛	teaspoon almond extract

Special equipment: **a muffin tin with 6 large (1-cup) muffin cups; parchment paper**

▸ Put oven rack in middle position and preheat oven to 400°F.

▸ Melt 2 teaspoons butter, then brush muffin cups with some of it. Chill muffin tin 2 minutes to set butter. Line bottom of each muffin cup with a round of parchment, then brush cups and parchment with remaining melted butter and chill 2 minutes more. Divide 1 teaspoon flour among muffin cups and shake to coat, knocking out excess flour.

▸ Cut an X in bottom of each peach and immerse peaches in a large pot of boiling water until skins loosen, about 15 seconds. Transfer peaches with a slotted spoon to a large bowl of ice and cold water to cool. Peel peaches, then halve lengthwise and pit. Cut peach halves lengthwise into ½-inch-thick slices, then cut slices crosswise into ½-inch pieces.

▸ Melt remaining tablespoon butter in a 10-inch heavy skillet over moderate heat, then stir in 3 tablespoons brown sugar and cook, stirring occasionally, until sugar is melted and bubbling, about 2 minutes. Carefully add a scant 2 cups peaches (caramel will splatter and sugar will seize), reserving remaining ⅓ cup peaches, then reduce heat and simmer, stirring occasionally, until peaches are tender and caramel is syrupy, 6 to 8 minutes. Spoon cooked peaches and caramel evenly into muffin cups.

▸ Purée reserved peaches in a blender until smooth.

Beat together eggs, salt, almond extract, and remaining 6 tablespoons brown sugar in a bowl with an electric mixer at high speed until mixture is creamy and tripled in volume, 3 to 5 minutes in a stand mixer or 6 to 8 minutes with a handheld. Reduce speed to low, then add puréed peaches and mix until just combined. Sift remaining 6 tablespoons flour evenly over egg mixture and fold in gently but thoroughly.

▸ Spoon batter over caramelized peaches and bake until golden brown and a wooden pick or skewer inserted in center of a cake comes out clean, 10 to 12 minutes. Cool in muffin tin on a rack 2 to 3 minutes, then invert a platter over muffin tin and flip cakes onto platter while still warm. Reposition any peaches that have stuck to parchment and serve cakes warm or at room temperature.

Cooks' note:
• Cakes can be made 2 hours ahead and kept at room temperature.

EACH SERVING ABOUT 169 CALORIES AND 5 GRAMS FAT

AN AUTUMNAL DINNER

LOW-FAT MENU

SLOW-COOKED ONION SALAD

**STEAMED COD WITH CAULIFLOWER
IN SAFFRON BROTH**

CHOCOLATE MACAROONS

EACH SERVING ABOUT 527 CALORIES AND 18 GRAMS FAT

SLOW-COOKED ONION SALAD
SERVES 6
Active time: 35 min   Start to finish: 1½ hr

For meltingly tender results, be sure to peel off the papery outer layer, the leathery second layer, and any paper-thin membranes from the onions, shallots, and leeks.

For onion mixture

- 4 medium leeks (1 lb total; white and pale green parts only), trimmed and cut crosswise into 1-inch pieces
- 2 tablespoons mild honey
- 1 tablespoon olive oil
- ½ teaspoon salt
- ½ teaspoon black pepper
- 1 sweet onion such as Vidalia (½ lb), trimmed and cut crosswise into 6 slices
- 1 large red onion (½ lb), trimmed and cut lengthwise into 6 wedges
- 1 large white onion (10 oz), trimmed and cut lengthwise into 6 wedges
- 6 medium shallots (10 oz total), trimmed
- 8 fresh thyme sprigs

For salad

- 1 tablespoon olive oil
- 2 teaspoons fresh lemon juice
- 1 teaspoon finely chopped garlic
- 1 teaspoon coarse-grain mustard
- ½ teaspoon salt
- ½ teaspoon black pepper
- 2 Belgian endives
- 5 cups loosely packed baby spinach (5 oz)
- ¼ cup chopped fresh chives or scallions

Accompaniment: lemon wedges

Make onion mixture:
▶ Put oven rack in upper third of oven and preheat oven to 400°F. Line a large shallow baking pan with foil, allowing 2 inches to hang over each end of pan.
▶ Wash leek pieces well in a bowl of cold water, then lift out and drain well.
▶ Whisk together honey, oil, salt, and pepper and add onions, shallots, and leeks, tossing to coat. Spread onion mixture in an even layer in baking pan. Scatter thyme on top, then cover with another large sheet of foil and crimp edges all around to seal, forming a package.

▶ Roast until very tender, about 1 hour. Carefully remove top sheet of foil (steam will emerge) and turn on broiler. Broil onion mixture 5 to 6 inches from heat until tops of onions are browned and caramelized, 2 to 5 minutes. (Check frequently, removing pieces as they brown.) Discard thyme.
Make salad while onion mixture roasts:
▶ Whisk together oil, lemon juice, garlic, mustard, salt, and pepper in a large bowl.
▶ Trim endives and halve lengthwise. Cut in half crosswise, then cut lengthwise into ¼-inch-wide strips.
▶ Just before serving, add endives to dressing along with spinach and chives and toss until lightly coated. Season with salt and pepper.
▶ Divide salad among 6 plates and top with warm onion mixture.

Cooks' notes:
• Onions, shallots, and leeks can be roasted 1 day ahead and cooled completely, then chilled, covered. Reheat in a preheated 350°F oven 5 to 10 minutes.
• Dressing can be made 3 hours ahead and chilled, covered.
EACH SERVING ABOUT 179 CALORIES AND 5 GRAMS FAT

STEAMED COD WITH CAULIFLOWER IN SAFFRON BROTH
SERVES 6
Active time: 25 min   Start to finish: 45 min

- 1 large pinch of saffron threads, crumbled
- 1 cup lukewarm water
- 1 (2-lb) head cauliflower
- 1 tablespoon olive oil
- 1 garlic clove, crushed
- 1 small carrot, cut into ¼-inch dice (⅓ cup)
- ½ cup dry white wine
- 1 cup fat-free reduced-sodium chicken broth
- 1¼ teaspoons salt
- ½ teaspoon white pepper
- 6 (¼-lb) pieces cod or scrod fillet (1 inch thick), skinned and pin bones removed
- 1½ lb small to medium mussels (preferably cultivated; 3 dozen), scrubbed and beards removed
- 3 scallions, chopped
- 2 tablespoons chopped fresh flat-leaf parsley

▸ Put saffron threads in a small bowl, then stir in lukewarm water and let stand.

▸ Trim cauliflower stalk flush with base of crown, discarding stalk, then quarter cauliflower lengthwise. Cut each quarter lengthwise into ½-inch-thick slices. Set aside large slices and reserve small pieces without any stem for another use.

▸ Swirl oil with garlic in a deep 12-inch heavy skillet to coat, then heat over moderately high heat until oil is just smoking. Discard garlic. Carefully arrange cauliflower slices in 1 layer in skillet and cook until undersides are lightly browned, about 2 minutes. Turn over with tongs and cook until other sides are lightly browned, about 2 minutes.

▸ Add carrot and wine and swirl skillet to combine, then boil until liquid is reduced by about half, about 30 seconds. Add saffron water, broth, ¾ teaspoon salt, and ¼ teaspoon white pepper and simmer, covered, until cauliflower and carrot are crisp-tender, 5 to 8 minutes.

▸ While cauliflower simmers, pat fish dry and sprinkle both sides with remaining ½ teaspoon salt and ¼ teaspoon white pepper.

▸ Increase heat to moderately high, then add mussels to skillet and steam, covered, checking frequently after 3 to 4 minutes, until mussels just open wide, about 8 minutes. (Discard any unopened mussels after 8 minutes.) Divide mussels among 6 shallow serving bowls using a slotted spoon.

▸ Place cod on top of cauliflower, arranging fillets in 1 layer. Sprinkle with scallions and parsley and steam, covered, over moderately high heat until fish is cooked through, 7 to 10 minutes.

▸ Transfer some of cauliflower along with 1 piece of cod to each bowl using slotted spoon. Season broth with salt and white pepper, then ladle broth (with carrots) over each serving.

EACH SERVING ABOUT 193 CALORIES AND 4 GRAMS FAT

CHOCOLATE MACAROONS
MAKES 12 SANDWICH COOKIES
Active time: 25 min   Start to finish: 1 hr

- ½ cup sliced blanched almonds (1¾ oz)
- 1 tablespoon unsweetened cocoa powder
- ½ cup plus 2 tablespoons confectioners sugar
- 2 large egg whites
- 2 oz fine-quality bittersweet chocolate (not unsweetened), finely chopped
- 2 tablespoons half-and-half

Special equipment: **parchment paper; a pastry bag fitted with a ½-inch plain tip**

▸ Put oven rack in middle position and preheat oven to 350°F. Line a large baking sheet with parchment.

▸ Pulse almonds with cocoa and ½ cup confectioners sugar in a food processor until very fine and powdery.

▸ Beat egg whites with a pinch of salt in a large bowl with an electric mixer at medium-high speed until they hold soft peaks, then add remaining 2 tablespoons sugar, a little at a time, beating until whites just hold stiff peaks.

▸ Fold one third of almond mixture into whites with a rubber spatula, then fold in remaining almond mixture gently but thoroughly.

▸ Transfer batter to pastry bag and pipe 24 (1½-inch-wide) rounds (⅓ inch thick) about 1 inch apart onto baking sheet. Tap down any peaks with a finger dipped in cold water. Bake until macaroons are puffed and edges are slightly darker, 15 to 18 minutes. Cool on baking sheet on a rack 20 minutes.

▸ While macaroons bake, heat chocolate and half-and-half in a 1-quart heavy saucepan over low heat, stirring constantly, until mixture is smooth and chocolate is completely melted. Cool to room temperature.

▸ When macaroons are cool, spoon chocolate filling into a small resealable plastic bag and seal bag, forcing out excess air. Snip off 1 bottom corner of bag with scissors to form a ⅛-inch hole.

▸ Pipe a small mound (1 teaspoon) of chocolate filling onto flat sides of 12 macaroons, then top with remaining 12 macaroons to form sandwich cookies, pressing flat sides together gently. (You may have some filling left over.)

EACH SERVING (2 SANDWICH COOKIES) ABOUT 155 CALORIES AND 9 GRAMS FAT

THE RECIPE COMPENDIUM

Here you'll find scores of recipes, culled from *Gourmet*'s regular food columns. All of these delicious ideas–from hors d'oeuvres to desserts and everything in between–have been created, tested, and cross-tested by our eleven food editors. Not sure what to do with the mint that's running riot in your garden? Whip up a sprightly potato salad with mint and peas or consider a fresh mint chutney. Need a casual, quick meal for friends? We have dozens of delicious solutions, whether it's a fragrant pot of soup, grilled skirt steak with cilantro garlic sauce, or colorful shrimp and mango wraps. And if you're searching for sweets, look no further.

What all these recipes have in common is unsurpassed flavor. Every month, the Seasonal Kitchen column highlights a particular vegetable or fruit at its peak or a favorite pantry item. Throughout the year, we focused on eggplant, watermelon, and matzo, and even teased your sweet tooth with to-die-for chocolate desserts, including a dreamy chocolate cream pie and the gorgeous layer cake on our front jacket. In our New York issue, we got cooking with onions, the ingredient that gives so many famous Big Apple dishes their oomph. Our Alsace onion tart and addictive onion rings whisk this unassuming bulb out of the wings and into the spotlight.

Another monthly column, Gourmet Every Day, transforms supermarket ingredients into something special, such as shrimp with Napa cabbage and ginger and warm broccoli salad with Sherry vinaigrette. Mix and match your favorite recipes to create a wonderful midweek dinner: Think hoison and honey glazed pork chops paired with tangy hot and sour coleslaw, followed by a scoop of lychee coconut sorbet with fresh mango.

We've also included recipes from Five Ingredients, a special feature of Gourmet Every Day, such as watercress vichyssoise, roasted red snapper with artichokes and lemon, and a decadent espresso and mascarpone icebox cake. Why not combine these three dishes into a casual dinner party menu? It just might be the shortest shopping trip you ever make, and your guests will never guess how easy it was to pull off.

Finally, there is Last Touch. The magazine's closing page is what many readers turn to first, and for good reason– you'll discover things like smoked chicken and cranberry salad, buttery *fleur de sel* caramels, and a cunning coconut rice pudding made with leftover rice from last night's takeout. These quick, simple recipes offer maximum flavor for minimal effort.

It's a pleasure to peruse these pages and earmark dishes that catch your fancy, but if you're in a hurry, flip to the comprehensive index. Quick recipes–those that take 30 minutes active time or less to prepare–are denoted by a clock symbol. Lighter/leaner dishes are marked with a feather.

Indeed, *quick* and *simple* are the catchwords of this year's *Best of Gourmet* Recipe Compendium, but so too are *satisfying*, *impressive*, and *absolutely delicious*.

APPETIZERS

HORS D'OEUVRES

NEGIMAKI
(Japanese Beef and Scallion Rolls)
SERVES 6 (HORS D'OEUVRE) OR 4 (MAIN COURSE)
Active time: 40 min   Start to finish: 1 hr

These beautiful rolls aren't raw—they're seared to create a flavorful brown crust and a medium-rare center.

12 small scallions, trimmed to 6-inch lengths
1 (1-lb) piece flank steak (roughly 6 to 7 inches square)
¼ cup sake (Japanese rice wine)
¼ cup mirin (Japanese sweet rice wine; see Sources)
3 tablespoons soy sauce
1 tablespoon sugar
1 tablespoon vegetable oil

Special equipment: **a meat pounder; kitchen string**

Prepare scallions:
▶ Blanch scallions in a pot of boiling salted water (see Tips, page 8) 45 seconds, then transfer with a slotted spoon to a bowl of ice and cold water to stop cooking. Transfer scallions to paper towels to drain and pat dry.

Prepare beef:
▶ Cut flank steak with the grain holding a large knife at a 30-degree angle to cutting board into 12 (⅛-inch-thick) slices (1½ to 2 inches wide). Arrange slices 1 inch apart on a very lightly oiled sheet of parchment paper or plastic wrap, then cover with another very lightly oiled sheet of parchment or plastic wrap (oiled side down) and pound slices with flat side of meat pounder until about ¹⁄₁₆ inch thick.

Assemble rolls:
▶ Arrange 3 beef slices side by side on a fresh sheet of plastic wrap, overlapping slices slightly to form a 6-inch square with short ends of slices nearest you. Sprinkle square lightly with a pinch of salt, then lay 3 scallions (with some white parts at both ends) across slices at end closest to you and tightly roll up meat around scallions to form a log, using

plastic wrap as an aid. Tie log with kitchen string at ends and where meat slices overlap. Make 3 more *negimaki* rolls in same manner.

Marinate rolls:
▶ Stir together sake, mirin, soy sauce, and sugar in a small bowl until sugar is dissolved.
▶ Put rolls in a small baking dish and pour marinade over them, turning to coat. Marinate, loosely covered with plastic wrap, turning occasionally, 15 minutes.

Cook rolls:
▶ Heat a 10-inch heavy skillet over moderately high heat until hot, 1 to 2 minutes. While skillet heats, lift rolls out of marinade, letting excess drip off, and pat dry (reserve marinade). Add oil to skillet, swirling to coat bottom, then cook rolls, turning with tongs, until well browned on all sides, 4 to 5 minutes total for medium-rare. Transfer rolls to cutting board. Add marinade to skillet and boil until slightly syrupy, 1 to 2 minutes, then remove from heat.
▶ Cut off and discard strings, then cut each roll crosswise into 6 slices. Pour sauce into a shallow serving dish and arrange *negimaki* in sauce.

Cooks' note:
• *Negimaki* can be rolled and tied (but not marinated or cooked) 4 hours ahead and chilled, wrapped in plastic wrap.

PA AMB TOMÀQUET
(Grilled Catalan Tomato Bread)
MAKES ABOUT 10 LARGE TOASTS
Active time: 15 min   Start to finish: 30 min

1 (8-inch) sourdough round or a 20-inch-long sourdough baguette
2 large garlic cloves, halved crosswise
3 to 4 ripe small tomatoes, halved crosswise
3 to 4 tablespoons extra-virgin olive oil
   Coarse salt to taste

▶ Prepare grill for cooking. If using a charcoal grill, open vents on bottom of grill, then light charcoal. Charcoal fire is medium-hot when you can hold your hand 5 inches above rack for 3 to 4 seconds. If using a gas grill, preheat burners on high, covered, 10 minutes, then reduce heat to moderate.

▶ Cut bread into ¾-inch-thick slices (cut baguette on a long diagonal for 6-inch-long slices).

▶ Working in batches of 3 or 4 slices, grill bread on lightly oiled grill rack, covered only if using a gas grill, turning over once, until grill marks appear, 1 to 2 minutes total per batch. Remove bread from heat and immediately rub 1 side of each slice with cut side of a garlic half, then rub with cut side of a tomato half, using 1 tomato half for 1 to 2 slices of bread and allowing most of pulp to be absorbed by bread (discard remainder of garlic and tomato halves). Brush bread with oil, then sprinkle with salt and serve immediately.

Cooks' notes:

• If you aren't able to grill outdoors, bread can be grilled in a hot lightly oiled well-seasoned ridged grill pan over moderately high heat.

• If your salt is very coarse, crush it using the flat side of a large heavy knife.

KITCHEN NOTE

MIRIN, A JAPANESE COOKING WINE MADE FROM GLUTINOUS RICE, ADDS SWEETNESS AND FLAVOR TO MANY JAPANESE DISHES. WE PREFER *HON-MIRIN* (NATURALLY BREWED MIRIN) TO *AJI-MIRIN,* WHICH CONTAINS ADDITIVES SUCH AS CORN SYRUP AND SALT. MIRIN WILL LAST FOR MONTHS IF KEPT IN A COOL, DRY, DARK PLACE.

BACON AND CHEDDAR TOASTS

MAKES 56 HORS D'OEUVRES
Active time: 25 min   Start to finish: 1 hr

½   lb extra-sharp white Cheddar, coarsely grated (2 cups)
½   lb cold sliced lean bacon, finely chopped
1   small onion, finely chopped (⅓ cup)
1½ tablespoons drained bottled horseradish
½   teaspoon salt
¼   teaspoon black pepper
14   very thin slices firm white sandwich bread

▶ Put oven rack in middle position and preheat oven to 375°F.

▶ Stir together cheese, bacon, onion, horseradish, salt, and pepper in a bowl with a rubber spatula until blended well.

▶ Spread about 1½ tablespoons mixture evenly to edges of each slice of bread with a small offset spatula or butter knife. Arrange slices in 1 layer on a large baking sheet and freeze, covered with wax paper, until firm, about 15 minutes.

▶ Trim crusts off bread and discard, then cut each slice into 4 squares. Bake toasts on baking sheet until beginning to brown on edges, about 20 minutes.

Cooks' note:

• Toasts can be prepared and cut 2 weeks ahead and frozen, layered between sheets of wax paper in an airtight container. Thaw before baking.

CHICKEN SATAY BITES

MAKES 32 HORS D'OEUVRES
Active time: 30 min   Start to finish: 45 min

2   (6-inch) pita loaves with pockets, each cut into 8 wedges
2   tablespoons vegetable oil
¼   cup crunchy peanut butter
¼   cup chopped fresh cilantro plus 32 whole fresh cilantro leaves
3   tablespoons fresh lime juice
3   tablespoons water
1   tablespoon chopped peeled fresh ginger
½   teaspoon Tabasco
¼   teaspoon salt
2   cups shredded cooked chicken, warm (½ lb; preferably dark meat with skin)

▶ Put oven rack in middle position and preheat oven to 400°F.

▶ Tear each pita wedge at fold to form 2 triangles. Brush rough sides of pita triangles with 1 tablespoon oil (total) and toast on a baking sheet until crisp and golden, 8 to 10 minutes.

▶ Pulse peanut butter, chopped cilantro, lime juice, water, ginger, Tabasco, salt, and remaining tablespoon oil in a food processor until combined well but still slightly chunky. Toss chicken with peanut sauce and season with salt. Mound on pita toasts and top with cilantro leaves.

POTATO, PEPPER, AND CHORIZO EMPANADAS

MAKES 12 PASTRIES
Active time: 1½ hr   Start to finish: 3 hr (includes making dough)

- ¾ cup finely chopped Spanish chorizo (cured spiced pork sausage; 3 oz)
- 2 tablespoons olive oil
- 2 onions, finely chopped
- 3 garlic cloves, finely chopped
- 1 red bell pepper, finely chopped
- ½ green bell pepper, finely chopped (½ cup)
- 1 Turkish or ½ California bay leaf
- ½ teaspoon salt
- ¼ teaspoon dried oregano, crumbled
- ½ lb yellow-fleshed potato such as Yukon Gold (1 large) Empanada dough (recipe follows)
- 1 egg, lightly beaten with 1 tablespoon water

Make filling:
▶ Cook chorizo in oil in a 2½- to 3-quart heavy saucepan over moderate heat, stirring, 2 minutes, then transfer to a bowl with a slotted spoon. Add onions to saucepan and cook, stirring frequently, until golden and very soft, about 15 minutes. Add garlic, bell peppers, bay leaf, salt, and oregano and cook, stirring frequently, until peppers are very soft, about 15 minutes. Peel potato and cut into ½-inch pieces, then stir into onion mixture and cook over moderately low heat, covered, stirring frequently, until potato is just barely tender, 10 to 12 minutes. Add potato mixture to chorizo and stir to combine. Cool filling to room temperature and discard bay leaf.

Form and bake empanadas:
▶ Put oven racks in upper and lower thirds of oven and preheat oven to 400°F.

▶ Divide dough into 12 equal pieces and form each into a disk. Keeping remaining pieces covered, roll out 1 piece on a lightly floured surface with a lightly floured rolling pin into a 5-inch round (⅛ inch thick).

▶ Spoon about 2 tablespoons filling onto center and fold dough in half, enclosing filling. Press edges together to seal, then crimp decoratively with your fingers or tines of a fork. Transfer empanada to a baking sheet. Make 11 more empanadas in same manner, arranging on 2 baking sheets.

▶ Lightly brush empanadas with some egg wash and bake, switching position of sheets halfway through baking, until golden, about 25 minutes. Transfer empanadas to a rack to cool at least 5 minutes. Serve warm or at room temperature.

EMPANADA DOUGH

MAKES ENOUGH FOR 12 PASTRIES
Active time: 20 min   Start to finish: 1¼ hr

- 2¼ cups unbleached all-purpose flour
- 1½ teaspoons salt
- 1 stick (½ cup) cold unsalted butter, cut into ½-inch cubes
- 1 large egg
- ⅓ cup ice water
- 1 tablespoon distilled white vinegar

▶ Sift flour with salt into a large bowl and blend in butter with your fingertips or a pastry blender until mixture resembles coarse meal with some (roughly pea-size) butter lumps.

▶ Beat together egg, water, and vinegar in a small bowl with a fork. Add to flour mixture, stirring with fork until just incorporated. (Mixture will look shaggy.)

▶ Turn out mixture onto a lightly floured surface and gather together, then knead gently with heel of your hand once or twice, just enough to bring dough together. Form dough into a flat rectangle and chill, wrapped in plastic wrap, at least 1 hour.

Cooks' note:
• Dough can be chilled up to 6 hours.

MINI SHRIMP CORNETS

MAKES 48 HORS D'OEUVRES
Active time: 45 min   Start to finish: 1¼ hr

  1 tablespoon unsalted butter
  ¼ cup finely chopped onion
  1 lb large shrimp in shell (21 to 25 per lb), peeled, deveined, and coarsely chopped
  2 tablespoons medium-dry Sherry
  1 tablespoon chopped fresh tarragon
  ½ teaspoon salt
  ¼ teaspoon black pepper
  1 (17¼-oz) package frozen puff pastry sheets, thawed
    All-purpose flour for dusting
  1 large egg
  1 tablespoon milk

Special equipment: **parchment paper**

▸ Put oven racks in upper and lower thirds of oven and preheat oven to 400°F. Line 2 large baking sheets with parchment.

▸ Heat butter in an 8-inch skillet over moderately low heat until foam subsides, then cook onion, stirring occasionally, until softened but not browned, about 2 minutes. Transfer to a bowl to cool.

▸ When onion is cool, add shrimp, Sherry, tarragon, salt, and pepper and stir until combined well.

▸ Roll out 1 sheet of pastry on a lightly floured surface into a 12-inch square. Cut into thirds in one direction, then into fourths in the other direction to make 12 (3- by 4-inch) rectangles. Cut each rectangle in half diagonally to form 2 triangles. Place 1 triangle on a work surface with longest edge nearest you, then put 1 teaspoon shrimp filling in center of triangle. Bring bottom corner of shortest side up to top point, then wrap remaining corner around resulting cone. Pinch to seal, then transfer to a baking sheet. Form more *cornets*, then repeat with remaining sheet of pastry. Chill first sheet of *cornets*, loosely covered, while making second.

▸ Whisk together egg and milk and lightly brush some of egg wash over top of pastries.

▸ Bake, switching position of sheets halfway through baking, until golden, 18 to 20 minutes total.

▸ Cool *cornets* on sheets on racks 5 minutes, then gently loosen from parchment with a spatula. Serve warm.

Cooks' note:
• *Cornets* can be formed (but not brushed with egg wash) 3 days ahead. Freeze on baking sheets in 1 layer, then remove from sheets and keep in a sealed plastic bag. Do not thaw before brushing with egg wash and baking as directed.

SMOKED WHITEFISH ON CUCUMBER ROUNDS

MAKES 36 HORS D'OEUVRES
Active time: 20 min   Start to finish: 20 min

  2 large seedless cucumbers (usually plastic-wrapped)
  ½ cup diced (¼-inch) Granny Smith apple
  ⅓ cup sour cream
1½ tablespoons finely chopped shallot
1½ teaspoons finely grated fresh lemon zest
  1 teaspoon fresh lemon juice
  ½ teaspoon black pepper
  2 teaspoons finely chopped fresh dill plus 36 whole small fresh dill sprigs
1¼ cups flaked smoked whitefish (½ lb)

▸ Cut 36 (⅓-inch-thick) slices from cucumbers, reserving remaining cucumber. Scoop out and discard some cucumber from center of each round with a melon-ball cutter or a small spoon to create an indentation (leaving bottom intact).

▸ Cut enough of remaining cucumber into ¼-inch dice to measure ½ cup.

▸ Toss diced cucumber with apple, sour cream, shallot, zest, juice, pepper, chopped dill, and salt to taste. Fold in fish.

▸ Mound 1 to 1½ teaspoons fish mixture onto each cucumber round and top with dill sprigs.

KITCHEN NOTE

WHEN PLANNING A COCKTAIL PARTY, KEEP THE VARIETY OF **HORS D'OEUVRES** AND RICHNESS OF EACH IN MIND. FOR EIGHT TO TEN GUESTS, SERVE AT LEAST FOUR DIFFERENT HORS D'OEUVRES (EACH PERSON WILL EAT THREE OR FOUR OF EACH TYPE). FOR 14 TO 16 GUESTS, YOU'LL WANT FIVE OR SIX HORS D'OEUVRES (EACH GUEST WILL HAVE TWO OR THREE OF EACH).

WASABI SHRIMP CRACKERS

MAKES 30 HORS D'OEUVRES

Active time: 20 min   Start to finish: 20 min

- 8 oz cream cheese, softened
- 3 to 4 teaspoons wasabi paste (Japanese horseradish paste)
- 30 (2-inch) thin rice crackers
- 30 peeled cooked medium shrimp (about 1 lb), halved lengthwise
- 1 scallion green, thinly sliced

▶ Purée cream cheese with wasabi (to taste) in a food processor until smooth. Mound 1 teaspoon cream cheese mixture on each cracker and top with 2 shrimp halves. Sprinkle with scallion and serve immediately.

DIPS AND SPREADS

SUN-DRIED TOMATO DIP

MAKES ABOUT 1 CUP

Active time: 15 min   Start to finish: 20 min

This dip is great with crudités or crackers, on sandwiches, or with cold meats.

- ¼ cup drained oil-packed sun-dried tomatoes
- 2 tablespoons chopped drained bottled roasted red peppers (1 oz)
- ½ cup walnuts (1¾ oz), toasted (see Tips, page 8)
- 1 teaspoon finely chopped shallot
- 1½ tablespoons red-wine vinegar
- 2 tablespoons water
- ¼ cup olive oil

▶ Purée all ingredients except oil in a food processor. With motor running, add oil in a slow stream, blending until incorporated. Season with salt.

PARMESAN DIP

MAKES ABOUT 1½ CUPS

Active time: 10 min   Start to finish: 10 min

- 1 cup sour cream
- ¼ cup mayonnaise
- 2 oz finely grated Parmigiano-Reggiano (1 cup)
- 2 tablespoons fresh lemon juice
- 1 teaspoon black pepper
- ½ teaspoon salt

Accompaniment: **crudités, crackers, or toasts**

▶ Whisk together all ingredients in a bowl.

ROASTED FETA WITH OLIVES AND RED PEPPERS

SERVES 4

Active time: 15 min   Start to finish: 15 min

- ½ lb feta (preferably Greek), rinsed and drained
- ¼ teaspoon dried oregano, crumbled
- ¼ teaspoon black pepper
- ¼ cup drained bottled roasted red peppers, chopped
- 10 Kalamata or other brine-cured black olives, pitted, rinsed, and coarsely chopped (¼ cup)
- 2 tablespoons extra-virgin olive oil

Accompaniment: **lemon wedges; toasted pita wedges or crusty bread**
Garnish: **chopped fresh flat-leaf parsley**

▶ Preheat broiler.
▶ Cut cheese into ½-inch-thick slices and arrange in 1 layer in a large flameproof baking dish, then sprinkle with oregano and pepper. Stir together roasted peppers, olives, and oil in a small bowl, then spoon mixture over and around cheese.
▶ Broil 2 to 4 inches from heat until edges of cheese are golden, about 5 minutes.

FIRST COURSES

ALSACE ONION TART
SERVES 10 (FIRST COURSE) OR 6 (MAIN COURSE)
Active time: 1¼ hr   Start to finish: 3½ hr (includes chilling dough)

For pastry
- 2 cups all-purpose flour
- 1 stick (½ cup) cold unsalted butter, cut into ½-inch cubes
- ¼ cup vegetable shortening
- ½ teaspoon salt
- 4 to 5 tablespoons ice water

For filling
- 4 bacon slices (¼ lb), cut crosswise into ⅛- to 1/16-inch-wide strips
- 3 tablespoons unsalted butter
- 2 lb onions, halved lengthwise and very thinly sliced crosswise (10 cups)
- 1¼ teaspoons salt
- 1 teaspoon black pepper
- 1 cup crème fraîche or heavy cream
- 4 large eggs
- ½ teaspoon freshly grated nutmeg

Special equipment: **a pastry or bench scraper; an 11-inch tart pan (1¼ inches deep) with a removable bottom; pie weights or raw rice**

Make pastry:
▶ Blend together flour, butter, shortening, and salt in a bowl with your fingertips or a pastry blender (or pulse in a food processor) just until most of mixture resembles coarse meal with some small (roughly pea-size) butter lumps. Drizzle evenly with 4 tablespoons ice water and gently stir with a fork (or pulse in processor) until incorporated.
▶ Squeeze a small handful: If it doesn't hold together, add more ice water, ½ tablespoon at a time, stirring (or pulsing) until just incorporated, then test again. (Do not overwork mixture, or pastry will be tough.)
▶ Turn out mixture onto a lightly floured surface and divide into 6 equal portions. With heel of your hand, smear each portion once or twice in a forward motion. Gather dough together with scraper and press into a ball, then flatten into

a disk. Chill dough, wrapped in plastic wrap, until firm, at least 1 hour.
▶ Roll out dough on a floured surface with a floured rolling pin into a 14-inch round and fit into tart pan. Trim excess dough, leaving a ½-inch overhang, then fold overhang over pastry and press against side to reinforce edge. Lightly prick bottom with a fork and chill until firm, about 30 minutes.
▶ Put oven rack in middle position and preheat oven to 400°F.
▶ Line chilled shell with foil and fill with pie weights. Bake until pastry is set and pale golden along rim, 15 to 20 minutes. Carefully remove foil and weights and bake shell until golden all over, 10 to 15 minutes more. Transfer shell to a rack. (Leave oven on.)

Prepare filling while shell bakes:
▶ Cook bacon in a 12-inch nonstick skillet over moderate heat, stirring occasionally, until crisp, 6 to 8 minutes. Transfer bacon with a slotted spatula to paper towels to drain and pour off bacon fat. Add butter to skillet and cook onions with ¾ teaspoon salt and ½ teaspoon pepper over moderate heat, stirring, until just wilted, about 2 minutes. Cover surface of onions with a round of parchment or wax paper (or cover skillet with a tight-fitting lid) and continue to cook, lifting parchment to stir frequently, until onions are very soft and pale golden, about 20 minutes. Stir in bacon, then remove from heat and cool 10 minutes.
▶ Whisk together crème fraîche, eggs, nutmeg, remaining ½ teaspoon salt, and remaining ½ teaspoon pepper in a large bowl, then stir in onions.

Fill and bake tart:
▶ Pour filling into tart shell, spreading onions evenly, and bake until filling is set and top is golden, 25 to 35 minutes. Serve warm or at room temperature.

Cooks' notes:
• Dough (as a disk or fitted into tart shell) can be chilled, wrapped in plastic wrap, up to 1 day. Let disk stand at room temperature 20 minutes before rolling out.
• Tart can be baked 1 day ahead and cooled, uncovered, then chilled, covered. Bring to room temperature before serving.

BUTTERNUT SQUASH FLAN WITH PARMESAN SAGE SAUCE

SERVES 8 TO 10

Active time: 25 min   Start to finish: 2½ hr

- 1 (2½-lb) butternut squash, halved lengthwise and seeded
- 4 large eggs plus 2 yolks
- 2 cups half-and-half
- 1⅛ oz finely grated Parmigiano-Reggiano (½ cup plus 2 tablespoons; see Tips, page 8)
- 1½ teaspoons salt
- 1 teaspoon black pepper
- 4 large fresh sage leaves plus 2 teaspoons finely chopped sage
- 2 large egg yolks

Special equipment: an 8- by 2-inch round cake pan; a candy or instant-read thermometer
Garnish: fresh sage leaves

▶ Put oven rack in middle position and preheat oven to 400°F.
▶ Roast squash, cut sides down, in a lightly oiled shallow baking pan until neck is tender, about 1 hour. Remove from oven, then reduce oven temperature to 325°F. Cool squash to warm.
▶ Butter cake pan. Line bottom with a round of parchment or wax paper and butter paper.
▶ Scoop flesh from squash, discarding skin, and purée in a food processor until smooth, about 45 seconds. Put 2 cups purée in a bowl, then whisk in whole eggs, 1 cup half-and-half, 2 tablespoons cheese, 1¼ teaspoons salt, and ½ teaspoon pepper until combined.
▶ Pour squash mixture into cake pan and bake in a water bath (see Tips, page 8) until just set and a wooden pick or skewer comes out almost clean, 45 minutes to 1 hour. Remove from water bath and cool flan in pan on a rack 15 minutes. Invert a flat plate over flan, then invert flan onto plate and carefully remove parchment.
▶ Meanwhile, bring whole sage leaves and remaining cup half-and-half just to a simmer in a 1- to 2-quart heavy saucepan, then remove from heat and let steep, covered, 10 minutes.
▶ Remove sage, carefully squeezing leaves to extract liquid, and discard leaves.

▶ Whisk yolks into half-and-half and cook over moderately low heat, stirring constantly with a wooden spoon, until sauce coats back of spoon and registers 170 to 175°F on thermometer, about 4 minutes (do not let boil).
▶ Immediately pour sauce through a fine-mesh sieve into a bowl, then add remaining ½ cup cheese and chopped sage, stirring until cheese is melted. Stir in remaining ¼ teaspoon salt and remaining ½ teaspoon pepper.
▶ Cut flan into wedges with a thin knife, wiping knife clean after each slice. Serve flan with sauce.

Cooks' note:
• Flan can be made 2 days ahead and chilled, loosely covered with plastic wrap. Bring to room temperature, then warm on an ovenproof serving platter in a preheated 325°F oven, about 10 minutes.

WILD MUSHROOM TART

SERVES 8 (FIRST COURSE) OR 6 (MAIN COURSE)

Active time: 1 hr   Start to finish: 3¾ hr (includes making dough)

- Pastry dough (recipe follows)
- 1 tablespoon unsalted butter
- 1 tablespoon vegetable oil
- ¾ lb mixed fresh wild mushrooms such as cremini, oyster, and chanterelle, trimmed and quartered lengthwise
- 2 tablespoons finely chopped shallot
- 1 teaspoon chopped fresh thyme
- ¾ teaspoon salt
- ⅜ teaspoon black pepper
- ½ cup crème fraîche
- ½ cup heavy cream
- 1 large whole egg
- 1 large egg yolk

Special equipment: a 9- by 1-inch round fluted tart pan with a removable bottom; pie weights or raw rice

Make shell:
▶ Roll out dough on a lightly floured surface with a lightly floured rolling pin into an 11-inch round and fit into tart pan, trimming excess dough. Chill until firm, about 30 minutes.
▶ Put oven rack in middle position and preheat oven to 375°F.
▶ Lightly prick bottom of shell all over with a fork, then line

with foil and fill with pie weights. Bake until side is set and edge is pale golden, 18 to 20 minutes. Carefully remove foil and weights and bake shell until bottom is golden, 10 to 15 minutes more.

▶ Cool completely in pan on a rack, about 15 minutes. (Leave oven on.)

Make filling while shell bakes:

▶ Heat butter and oil in a 12-inch heavy skillet over moderately high heat until foam subsides, then sauté mushrooms, shallot, thyme, ½ teaspoon salt, and ¼ teaspoon pepper, stirring frequently, until mushrooms are tender and any liquid given off is evaporated, 8 to 10 minutes. Transfer to a bowl and cool to room temperature.

▶ Whisk together crème fraîche, heavy cream, whole egg, yolk, remaining ¼ teaspoon salt, and remaining ⅛ teaspoon pepper in a bowl until combined.

Fill and bake tart:

▶ Reduce oven temperature to 325°F.

▶ Scatter mushrooms evenly in tart shell and pour custard over them. Bake tart in pan on a baking sheet until custard is just set and slightly puffed, 35 to 45 minutes.

▶ Cool tart in pan on rack at least 20 minutes, then remove side of pan. Serve tart warm or at room temperature.

Cooks' notes:

• Tart shell can be baked 1 day ahead and cooled completely, then kept in pan, wrapped well in plastic wrap, at room temperature.

• Baked tart can be made 2 hours ahead and kept, uncovered, at room temperature. Serve at room temperature.

PASTRY DOUGH

MAKES ENOUGH DOUGH FOR A 9- TO 10-INCH ROUND SHELL
Active time: 15 min   Start to finish: 1¼ hr

1¼   cups all-purpose flour
¼   teaspoon salt
¾   stick (6 tablespoons) cold unsalted butter, cut into
      ½-inch cubes
2   tablespoons cold vegetable shortening (preferably
      trans-fat-free)
3   to 4 tablespoons ice water

Special equipment: a pastry or bench scraper

▶ Sift together flour and salt in a large bowl. Blend in butter and shortening with your fingertips or a pastry blender (or pulse in a food processor) until most of mixture resembles coarse meal with some small (roughly pea-size) butter lumps. Drizzle evenly with 3 tablespoons ice water and gently stir with a fork (or pulse in processor) until incorporated.

▶ Squeeze a small handful: If it doesn't hold together, add more ice water, ½ tablespoon at a time, stirring (or pulsing) until just incorporated, then test again. (Do not overwork, or pastry will be tough.)

▶ Turn out mixture onto a lightly floured surface and divide into 4 portions. With heel of your hand, smear each portion once or twice in a forward motion to help distribute fat. Gather dough together with scraper and press into a ball, then flatten into a 5-inch disk. Chill dough, wrapped tightly in plastic wrap, until firm, at least 1 hour.

Cooks' notes:

• Dough can be chilled up to 1 day.

• This classic pastry dough works well for both savory and sweet pies.

CAVIAR PANCAKES

SERVES 2
Active time: 30 min   Start to finish: 30 min (includes making pancakes)

2   tablespoons unsalted butter
6   buttermilk pancakes (page 212)
      About ⅓ cup sour cream
      About 2 tablespoons caviar (2 oz)
1   hard-boiled large egg yolk, forced through a sieve
½   scallion, minced

▶ Cook butter in a very small saucepan over moderate heat, swirling pan occasionally, until golden brown (be careful not to let it burn). Remove from heat and keep warm, covered.

▶ Spread each pancake with about 1 tablespoon sour cream (to taste) and top with about 1 teaspoon caviar. Sprinkle with some of yolk and scallion. Stack 3 pancakes on each of 2 plates and drizzle with brown butter.

KITCHEN NOTE

THERE ARE TIMES WHEN ONLY THE BEST **CAVIAR** WILL DO, BUT SUPERMARKET ROE WORKS FINE FOR OUR CAVIAR PANCAKES.

BUTTERMILK PANCAKES
MAKES 14 (3-INCH) PANCAKES
Active time: 15 min   Start to finish: 15 min

  1   cup all-purpose flour
  1   teaspoon baking soda
 ½   teaspoon salt
  1   large egg, lightly beaten
  1   cup well-shaken buttermilk
      Vegetable oil for brushing griddle

▶ Preheat oven to 200°F.
▶ Whisk together flour, baking soda, salt, egg, and buttermilk until smooth.
▶ Heat a griddle or a large heavy skillet over moderate heat until hot enough to make drops of water scatter over its surface, then brush with oil. Working in batches and using a ¼-cup measure filled halfway, pour batter onto griddle and cook pancakes, turning over once, until golden, about 2 minutes per batch. Transfer to a heatproof plate and keep warm, covered, in oven.

Cooks' notes:
• Batter keeps, chilled and covered, 3 days. Thin as necessary with additional buttermilk or water, 1 tablespoon at a time, before using.
• You can use these pancakes for the caviar pancakes (recipe on page 211) and save the remaining batter for breakfast.

STEAMED COCKLES IN GINGER CILANTRO BROTH
SERVES 6
Active time: 15 min   Start to finish: 20 min

  2   lb small cockles (sometimes labeled New Zealand clams; about 1 inch in diameter; 5 to 6 dozen)
  3   cups water
 ½   cup medium-dry Sherry
  1   (1½-inch) piece fresh ginger, peeled, thinly sliced, and cut into very thin matchsticks (¼ cup)
 ½   cup (1-inch) pieces of fresh cilantro stems, plus ¼ cup loosely packed fresh cilantro leaves
  1   bunch scallions (white and pale green parts only), coarsely chopped
 ½   teaspoon fine sea salt

▶ Rinse cockles in a colander under cold water.
▶ Bring water to a boil in a 12-inch heavy skillet over high heat, then add Sherry, ginger, cilantro stems, scallions, and sea salt and return to a boil. Add cockles and cook, covered, until shells open wide, 3 to 5 minutes. (Discard any unopened cockles after 5 minutes.)
▶ Divide cockles among 6 bowls using tongs or a slotted spoon, then ladle out broth into a fine-mesh sieve lined with a paper towel set over a bowl, working from top, leaving any silt in bottom of skillet. Ladle strained broth over cockles and top with cilantro leaves.

Cooks' note:
• If cockles are hard to find in your area, you can substitute other small hard-shelled clams (though steaming time will vary with the type and size).

BREADS

PLETZEL
(Jewish Onion Bread)

MAKES ABOUT 15 (3-INCH) SQUARES
Active time: 1 hr Start to finish: 3¾ hr

This onion bread—whether formed into individual rolls or, as we did here, into a flat loaf (similar to Italian focaccia)—can be found in Jewish bakeries all over New York City's Lower East Side. We used nigella seeds (often called black onion seeds, although that's a misnomer), with their subtle nutty flavor, for the topping instead of the more typical poppy seeds.

1	cup warm water (105–115°F)
1	(¼-oz) package active dry yeast (2½ teaspoons)
2	teaspoons sugar
3½	cups all-purpose flour
2½	teaspoons salt
3	tablespoons vegetable oil
2	medium onions, finely chopped (2 cups)
1	large egg, lightly beaten with 1 tablespoon water
1	teaspoon nigella seeds (see Sources) or poppy seeds

Make dough:

▶ Stir together water, yeast, and sugar in a small bowl until sugar is dissolved, then let stand until foamy, about 5 minutes. (If mixture doesn't foam, discard and start over with new yeast.)

▶ Stir together 2½ cups flour and 1½ teaspoons salt in a large bowl, then add yeast mixture and 2 tablespoons oil and stir until a dough forms. Turn out dough onto a floured surface and knead, adding just enough of remaining cup flour as needed to prevent stickiness, until smooth and elastic, about 8 minutes.

▶ Form dough into a ball and transfer to an oiled large bowl, turning to coat with oil. Cover bowl with plastic wrap and let dough rise in a draft-free place at warm room temperature until doubled in bulk, about 2 hours.

Cook onions while dough rises:

▶ Cook onions in remaining tablespoon oil with remaining teaspoon salt in an 8- to 9-inch nonstick skillet over moderately low heat, stirring, until slightly softened, about 2 minutes. Cover surface of onions with a round of parchment or wax paper (or cover skillet with a tight-fitting lid) and cook onions, lifting parchment to stir frequently, until very soft and pale golden, 12 to 15 minutes.

Shape and bake bread:

▶ Transfer dough to a 15- by 10- by 1-inch baking pan and stretch dough, first by pulling with your hands, then by pressing your fingertips into dough and working outward from center, until dough fills pan. Prick dough all over at 1-inch intervals with a fork, leaving a 1-inch border all around sides, and cover loosely with oiled plastic wrap (oiled side down). Let dough rise slightly in draft-free place at warm room temperature, 30 minutes.

▶ While dough rises, put oven rack in middle position and preheat oven to 400°F.

▶ Gently brush dough with some egg wash, being careful not to deflate dough. Scatter onions evenly over dough, leaving a 1-inch border, then sprinkle with nigella seeds. Bake until top is golden and bottom sounds hollow when tapped, about 30 minutes. Lift bread from pan and transfer to a rack to cool slightly.

▶ Cut into roughly 3-inch squares before serving.

Cooks' note:

• Dough can be formed into a ball 1 day ahead and allowed to rise, chilled. Bring to room temperature before shaping.

KITCHEN NOTE

OFTEN MISTAKEN FOR AND INCORRECTLY LABELED AS ONION SEEDS OR BLACK SESAME SEEDS, PEPPERY **NIGELLA SEEDS** ARE A POPULAR FLAVORING IN TURKEY, RUSSIA, THE MIDDLE EAST, AND INDIA (WHERE THEY ARE CALLED *KALONJI*). STORE THEM IN A COOL, DRY, DARK PLACE OR IN THE FREEZER.

BANANA NUT BREAD
MAKES 1 (9-INCH) LOAF
Active time: 15 min   Start to finish: 2¼ hr (includes cooling)

- ⅔ cup whole milk
- 1 tablespoon fresh lemon juice
- 2½ cups sifted cake flour (not self-rising; sift before measuring)
- 1 teaspoon baking powder
- ¾ teaspoon salt
- ½ teaspoon baking soda
- 1 stick (½ cup) unsalted butter, softened
- ⅔ cup sugar
- 2 large eggs
- 2 very ripe medium bananas
- 3 oz walnuts, chopped (1 cup)

▶ Put oven rack in middle position and preheat oven to 350°F. Grease a 9- by 5-inch loaf pan and line bottom of pan with wax paper or parchment, then grease paper.
▶ Stir together milk and lemon juice and let stand until milk curdles, about 1 minute.
▶ Whisk together flour, baking powder, salt, and baking soda in a bowl.
▶ Beat together butter and sugar in a large bowl with an electric mixer at high speed until pale and fluffy, about 2 minutes. Add eggs 1 at a time, beating until combined, then beat in bananas until combined (mixture will look curdled).
▶ Add flour mixture to banana mixture alternately with milk, mixing at low speed just until batter is smooth. Stir in walnuts. Pour into loaf pan and bake until a wooden pick or skewer inserted in center of bread comes out clean, about 1 hour.
▶ Cool bread in pan on a rack 20 minutes, then invert bread onto rack. Remove paper and turn bread right side up on rack to cool completely.

Cooks' note:
• Bread keeps, wrapped in plastic wrap, at room temperature 4 days or frozen 1 month.

PARSLEY CUMIN PARATHAS
MAKES 16 FLATBREADS
Active time: 1½ hr   Start to finish: 2½ hr

- 1½ teaspoons cumin seeds, toasted and cooled
- 1 teaspoon salt
- 1 cup all-purpose flour plus additional for dusting
- ¾ cup whole-wheat flour
- ⅓ cup coarsely chopped fresh flat-leaf parsley
- ½ cup water
- ¼ cup vegetable oil plus additional for griddle
- ⅓ cup ghee (Indian clarified butter; recipe follows)

Special equipment: **an electric coffee/spice grinder; a well-seasoned cast-iron griddle or large skillet**
Accompaniment: **sweet tamarind chutney**

▶ Grind cumin seeds with salt to a powder in grinder. Transfer to a large bowl and stir in flours, parsley, water, and oil and continue to stir until a dough forms.
▶ Turn out dough onto a work surface and knead until smooth and elastic, about 5 minutes. Several times during kneading, pick up dough and slap it against the work surface 8 to 10 times to relax dough. Cover dough with plastic wrap and let stand at room temperature 1 hour.
▶ Lightly oil griddle, then heat over moderately low heat until hot, 10 to 15 minutes.
▶ While griddle heats, divide dough into 4 portions, then roll out 1 portion on a lightly floured surface into an 11-inch round. Lightly brush round with some ghee and cut into quarters, then, starting with rounded edge nearest you, fold each quarter in thirds to form a slimmer triangle (bottom edge will still be rounded). Repeat with remaining dough to form a total of 16 slim triangles.
▶ Roll out 1 triangle on lightly floured surface first to widen it, then to lengthen it into a 9- by- 4-inch triangle, sprinkling with flour as necessary to prevent sticking. Transfer to a baking sheet and cover with a sheet of wax paper, then roll out remaining triangles in same manner, layering them between sheets of wax paper.
▶ Cook *parathas*, 3 or 4 at a time, on griddle until undersides are browned in spots, 2 to 3 minutes (*parathas* will puff, then deflate). Turn *parathas* over and lightly brush with ghee, then cook until other sides are golden brown in spots, 1 to 2 minutes. Turn over and brush once more, then cook until *parathas* are cooked through, 1 to 2 minutes.

▶ Transfer each batch of *parathas* to a sheet of foil as browned and wrap loosely to keep warm while cooking remaining *parathas*.

Cooks' note:
• *Parathas* are best when freshly made, but leftovers can be wrapped in foil and kept at room temperature, then reheated in a 350°F oven.

GHEE
(Indian Clarified Butter)
MAKES ABOUT ¾ CUP
Active time: 25 min   Start to finish: 30 min

  2 sticks unsalted butter, cut into 1-inch pieces

Special equipment: **cheesecloth**

▶ Bring butter to a boil in a 1- to 1½-quart heavy saucepan over moderate heat. Once foam completely covers butter, reduce heat to very low. Continue to cook butter, stirring occasionally, until a thin crust begins to form on surface and milky white solids fall to bottom of pan, about 8 minutes. Continue to cook butter, watching constantly and stirring occasionally to prevent burning, until solids turn light brown and butter deepens to golden and turns translucent and fragrant, 16 to 18 minutes.
▶ Remove ghee from heat and pour through a sieve lined with a triple layer of cheesecloth into a jar.

Cooks' note:
• Ghee keeps, covered and chilled, 2 months.

KITCHEN NOTE
CLARIFIED BUTTER IS MADE BY SLOWLY MELTING BUTTER UNTIL THE WATER EVAPORATES AND THE MILK SOLIDS SINK TO THE BOTTOM OF THE PAN. THE FROTH IS THEN SKIMMED AND THE CLEAR BUTTER IS POURED OUT, LEAVING THE SOLIDS BEHIND. FOR GHEE, THE BUTTER IS COOKED, UNSKIMMED, UNTIL THE MILK SOLIDS TURN LIGHT BROWN AND THE LIQUID BECOMES GOLDEN AND NUTTY IN FLAVOR.

SKILLET CORN BREAD
SERVES 8
Active time: 10 min   Start to finish: 25 min

  1 stick (½ cup) cold unsalted butter, cut into
      ½-inch cubes
1¼ cups cornmeal (preferably stone-ground; not coarse)
  ¼ cup all-purpose flour
  1 tablespoon sugar
  1 teaspoon baking soda
  ½ teaspoon salt
1½ cups well-shaken buttermilk
  2 large eggs

Special equipment: **a 9½- to 10-inch well-seasoned cast-iron skillet**

▶ Put oven rack in middle position and preheat oven to 450°F. Add butter to skillet and heat in oven until melted, about 5 minutes, then carefully pour into a bowl.
▶ Whisk together cornmeal, flour, sugar, baking soda, and salt in a large bowl.
▶ Whisk buttermilk and eggs into melted butter, then stir into cornmeal mixture until just combined. Pour batter into hot skillet and bake until a wooden pick or skewer inserted in center comes out clean, 15 to 20 minutes. Cool in skillet on a rack 5 minutes, then invert onto a platter and serve warm or at room temperature.

TOASTED BAGUETTE CRUMBS
MAKES ABOUT 3 CUPS
Active time: 10 min   Start to finish: 1¼ hr (includes cooling)

As a crisp topping for pasta or steamed vegetables, these are worlds apart from store-bought bread crumbs.

  1 (12-inch) piece day-old baguette, cut into ½-inch
      cubes (6 cups)

▶ Put oven rack in middle position and preheat oven to 375°F.
▶ Grind baguette cubes to coarse crumbs in 3 batches in a food processor. Spread evenly in a large shallow baking pan and bake, stirring once, until golden and crisp, 15 to 18 minutes. Cool completely.

NEW YORK PRETZELS

MAKES 8 LARGE PRETZELS

Active time: 45 min   Start to finish: 2½ hr

- 1 tablespoon sugar
- 1 (¼-oz) package active dry yeast (2½ teaspoons)
- 1½ cups lukewarm water (105–110°F)
- 3¾ to 4 cups all-purpose flour
- 1 tablespoon table salt
- 1 large egg, lightly beaten
- 2 teaspoons pretzel salt (see Sources)

Special equipment: **parchment paper**

▶ Stir together sugar, yeast, and lukewarm water in a glass measuring cup, then let stand until foamy, about 5 minutes. (If mixture doesn't foam, discard and start over with new yeast.)

▶ Whisk together 3½ cups flour and table salt in a large bowl. Add yeast mixture and stir with a wooden spoon until it forms a dough. Dust work surface with 1 tablespoon flour, then turn out dough and knead, gradually dusting with just enough additional flour to make a smooth sticky dough, about 8 minutes. (Dough needs to be somewhat sticky to facilitate rolling and forming into pretzels).

▶ Return dough to bowl and cover bowl tightly with plastic wrap, then let dough rise in a draft-free place at warm room temperature until doubled in bulk, about 45 minutes.

▶ Turn out dough onto a clean work surface and cut into 8 equal pieces. Using your palms, roll 1 piece back and forth on a clean dry work surface into a rope about 24 inches long.

If dough sticks to your hands, lightly dust them with flour. Twist dough into a pretzel shape. Dough will retract as you form the pretzel: pick up both ends and cross one over the other, making a loop about 2 to 3 inches in diameter, then twist the ends one full rotation. Now pull the ends toward you and attach them to the bottom of the pretzel (1 to 1½ inches apart), pressing gently to adhere.

▶ Transfer pretzel to an oiled baking sheet and form 7 more pretzels in same manner with remaining dough, spacing them about 1½ inches apart. Let pretzels stand, uncovered, about 20 minutes.

▶ Meanwhile, put oven rack in upper third of oven and preheat oven to 425°F. Bring a wide 6-quart pot of water to a boil.

▶ Using both hands, carefully add 3 pretzels, 1 at a time, to boiling water and cook, turning over once with tongs, until pretzels are puffed and shape is set, about 3 minutes. Transfer parboiled pretzels to a rack to cool. Repeat with remaining 5 pretzels in 2 batches.

▶ Line baking sheet with parchment paper and oil paper, then arrange pretzels on sheet. Brush pretzels lightly with some of egg and sprinkle with pretzel salt. Bake until golden brown and lightly crusted, about 35 minutes. Cool 15 minutes, then serve warm.

Cooks' notes:
• Dough can also be mixed and kneaded in a standing electric mixer fitted with dough hook.
• Pretzels are best the day they are made. (If kept overnight, salt may dissolve.)

SOUPS

MEXICAN CHILE AND MUSHROOM SOUP

SERVES 4 (FIRST COURSE)

Active time: 30 min   Start to finish: 35 min

- 3 large garlic cloves, left unpeeled
- 1 (½-inch-thick) slice large white onion
- 1 (3-inch-long) small dried ancho chile (¼ oz; see Sources)
- ½ cup water
- ¾ teaspoon salt
- ½ teaspoon dried oregano (preferably Mexican), crumbled
- 2 tablespoons vegetable oil
- 10 oz mushrooms, trimmed and thinly sliced
- 1 tablespoon tomato paste
- 3½ cups reduced-sodium chicken broth (28 fl oz)

▸Heat a dry 12-inch heavy skillet over moderate heat until hot, 3 to 5 minutes. Lightly smash garlic in skins with side of a large knife, then add to skillet along with onion slice and cook, turning over once or twice with tongs, until onion is well browned and garlic is slightly softened, about 8 minutes.

▸Meanwhile, discard stem, seeds, and veins from chile and tear chile into 4 pieces. Add chile to onion and garlic in skillet and toast, pressing flat with tongs and turning over occasionally, until chile turns a brighter red, about 1 minute.

▸Discard garlic skins and coarsely chop onion, then purée garlic, onion, and chile in a blender with water, salt, and oregano until smooth.

▸Heat oil in skillet over high heat until hot but not smoking, then sauté mushrooms, stirring occasionally, until golden and any liquid is evaporated, about 6 minutes. Reduce heat to moderate, then add tomato paste and cook, stirring, 1 minute. Add purée and cook, stirring, 3 minutes. Stir in broth and simmer 5 minutes.

WATERCRESS VICHYSSOISE

SERVES 4 (FIRST COURSE)

Active time: 30 min   Start to finish: 2¾ hr (includes chilling)

- 1 small boiling potato (¼ lb), peeled and cut into ½-inch pieces
- 1 small onion, finely chopped
- 2 cups reduced-sodium chicken broth (16 fl oz)
- 1 cup heavy cream
- 4 cups coarsely chopped watercress (1 large bunch)

▸Simmer potato, onion, broth, and cream, uncovered, in a 3- to 4-quart heavy saucepan until vegetables are softened, about 10 minutes. Stir in watercress and cook, uncovered, over moderately low heat 3 minutes.

▸Purée soup in 2 batches in a blender until very smooth, about 45 seconds per batch (use caution when blending hot liquids). Force soup through a fine-mesh sieve into a bowl, pressing hard on solids and then discarding them. Season with salt and pepper and let soup stand, uncovered, until cool, 45 minutes, then chill, covered, at least 1½ hours.

Cooks' notes:
• Soup can be chilled quickly in a metal bowl set in a larger bowl of ice and cold water. Stir occasionally for 15 minutes, then remove from cold water and refrigerate, covered, until cold, about 30 minutes.
• Soup can be chilled up to 2 days.

KITCHEN NOTE

ALTHOUGH WE ALWAYS PREFER HOMEMADE STOCK TO CANNED, MANY OF OUR QUICK SOUPS CALL FOR STORE-BOUGHT CHICKEN OR BEEF BROTH. WE RECOMMEND **REDUCED-SODIUM BROTHS** BECAUSE REGULAR BROTHS CAN BE QUITE SALTY.

TUSCAN BEAN AND SWISS CHARD SOUP

SERVES 4 TO 6 (MAIN COURSE)
Active time: 1 hr   Start to finish: 14 hr (includes making
stock and soaking beans)

- 1 lb dried white beans such as Great Northern, cannellini, or navy (2 cups), picked over and rinsed
- ¼ lb sliced pancetta, chopped
- 2 tablespoons olive oil
- 1 large onion, chopped
- 1 fennel bulb (sometimes called anise), stalks discarded and bulb chopped
- 4 garlic cloves, finely chopped
- 4 cups chicken stock (recipe follows) or reduced-sodium chicken broth (32 fl oz)
- 4 cups water
- 1 (3- by 2-inch) piece Parmigiano-Reggiano rind
- 1 Turkish or ½ California bay leaf
- ¼ teaspoon black pepper
- ½ lb Swiss chard (preferably red or rainbow), stems discarded and leaves halved lengthwise, then thinly sliced crosswise
- 1 teaspoon salt

▶ Soak beans in cold water to cover by 2 inches in a bowl at room temperature at least 8 hours, or quick-soak (see cooks' note, below). Drain in a colander.
▶ Cook pancetta in oil in a wide 6- to 8-quart heavy pot over moderate heat, stirring occasionally, until browned, about 5 minutes. Transfer pancetta with a slotted spoon to paper towels to drain.
▶ Cook onion and fennel in oil remaining in pot over moderate heat, stirring occasionally, until softened, 6 to 8 minutes. Add garlic and cook, stirring, 1 minute. Add beans, stock, water, cheese rind, bay leaf, and pepper and simmer, uncovered, until beans are tender, 45 minutes to 1 hour. Discard cheese rind and bay leaf.
▶ Stir in Swiss chard and salt and simmer, uncovered, stirring occasionally, until chard is tender, 8 to 10 minutes. Season soup with salt and pepper.

Cooks' notes:
• Beans can be soaked up to 12 hours.
• To quick-soak beans: Cover beans with cold water by 2 inches in a 5- to 6-quart pot and bring to a boil, uncovered.

Boil beans, uncovered, 2 minutes, then remove from heat and let stand, uncovered, 1 hour.
• Soup is best when made 1 day ahead (to give flavors time to develop). Cool completely, uncovered, then chill, covered. Reheat and, if necessary, thin with water.
• We removed the stems from the Swiss chard, but if you don't want to waste them, feel free to put them in the soup as well: Once the leaves are sliced, chop the stems and add them to the soup along with the leaves.

CHICKEN STOCK

MAKES ABOUT 14 CUPS
Active time: 30 min   Start to finish: 4½ hr

16½ cups cold water
- 1 (3½- to 4-lb) chicken, cut into 8 pieces, plus neck and giblets (except liver)
- 2 onions, left unpeeled, halved
- 2 whole cloves
- 4 garlic cloves, left unpeeled
- 1 celery rib, halved
- 2 carrots, halved
- 1 teaspoon salt
- 6 long fresh flat-leaf parsley sprigs
- 8 whole black peppercorns
- ½ teaspoon dried thyme, crumbled
- 1 Turkish or ½ California bay leaf

▶ Bring 16 cups cold water to a boil with chicken pieces (including neck and giblets) in an 8-quart pot, skimming froth. Add remaining ½ cup cold water and bring to a simmer, continuing to skim froth. Add remaining ingredients and simmer stock, uncovered, skimming froth occasionally, 3 hours.
▶ Pour stock through a fine-mesh sieve into a large bowl, discarding solids. If using stock right away, skim off and discard any fat. If not, cool completely, uncovered, before skimming fat (it will be easier to remove when cool), then chill, covered.

Cooks' note:
• Stock keeps, covered and chilled, 1 week, or frozen 3 months.

218

THAI-STYLE CHICKEN AND RICE SOUP

SERVES 8 (MAIN COURSE)

Active time: 50 min   Start to finish: 5½ hr (includes making stock)

Using shrimp instead of chicken in this recipe makes for an equally delicious soup.

- 8 cups chicken stock (recipe precedes) or reduced-sodium chicken broth (64 fl oz)
- 4 cups water
- 1 tablespoon Thai green curry paste (see Sources)
- 4 garlic cloves, coarsely chopped
- 1 (2-inch) piece peeled fresh ginger, coarsely chopped
- 1 teaspoon coriander seeds, crushed
- 2 cups loosely packed whole fresh cilantro leaves plus ½ cup chopped (from 2 large bunches)
- 1 cup jasmine rice
- ¾ lb boneless skinless chicken breast, thinly sliced crosswise, then slices cut lengthwise into thin strips, or ¾ lb medium shrimp in shell (31 to 35 per lb), peeled and deveined
- 1 (13- to 14-oz) can unsweetened coconut milk, stirred well
- ¼ lb snow peas, trimmed and cut diagonally into ¼-inch strips
- 2 tablespoons Asian fish sauce
- 2 tablespoons fresh lime juice
- 1½ teaspoons salt, or to taste

Accompaniment: **lime wedges**

▶ Simmer stock, water, curry paste, garlic, ginger, coriander seeds, and whole cilantro leaves in a 3- to 4-quart saucepan, uncovered, until ginger is softened, about 15 minutes. Pour through a paper-towel-lined sieve into a 5- to 6-quart heavy pot and discard solids. Stir rice into soup and simmer, uncovered, stirring occasionally, until tender, about 15 minutes.

▶ Add chicken or shrimp and poach at a bare simmer, uncovered, until just cooked through, about 3 minutes. Stir in coconut milk, snow peas, and fish sauce and simmer, uncovered, until peas are crisp-tender, about 2 minutes. Remove from heat and stir in lime juice, salt, and chopped cilantro.

SPICY TOMATO SOUP

SERVES 4 (FIRST COURSE)

Active time: 20 min   Start to finish: 40 min

- 2 (28- to 32-oz) cans whole tomatoes in juice (preferably organic)
- 1 large onion, coarsely chopped
- 2 teaspoons finely chopped garlic
- 1 teaspoon finely chopped fresh jalapeño chile, including seeds
- 2 teaspoons finely chopped peeled fresh ginger
- 3 tablespoons olive oil
- ½ teaspoon ground cumin
- 2¼ cups reduced-sodium chicken broth (18 fl oz)
- 1 tablespoon sugar, or to taste
- 2 teaspoons salt, or to taste

▶ Drain 1 can tomatoes, discarding juice, then purée with remaining can tomatoes (including juice) in a blender.

▶ Cook onion, garlic, chile, and ginger in oil in a 4- to 5-quart heavy nonreactive pot over moderate heat, stirring frequently, until onion is softened, about 8 minutes. Add cumin and cook, stirring, 1 minute. Stir in puréed tomatoes, broth, 1 tablespoon sugar, and 2 teaspoons salt and simmer, uncovered, stirring occasionally, 20 minutes. Working in 3 or 4 batches, blend soup in blender until smooth (use caution when blending hot liquids). Transfer soup as blended to a sieve set over a large bowl and force through sieve, discarding seeds.

▶ Stir in sugar and salt to taste. Reheat in cleaned saucepan if necessary.

Cooks' note:
• We prefer the taste of organic canned tomatoes in this particular recipe, as they tend to be sweeter. If using other canned tomatoes, you might want to add a bit more sugar to balance their acidity.

ZUPPA DI PESCE
(Italian Fish Soup)
SERVES 6 TO 8 (MAIN COURSE)
Active time: 1 hr   Start to finish: 2¾ hr (includes making stock)

For soup

- 1 lb cleaned squid, bodies and tentacles separated but kept intact
- ½ lb large shrimp in shell (21 to 25 per lb), peeled, leaving tail and first segment of shell intact, and deveined
- ⅛ teaspoon black pepper
- ¾ teaspoon salt
- ¼ cup olive oil
- 3 garlic cloves, finely chopped
- ½ teaspoon dried hot red pepper flakes
- ¼ teaspoon dried oregano, crumbled
- 1 cup dry white wine
- 4½ cups water
- 12 small hard-shelled clams such as littlenecks (less than 2 inches in diameter), scrubbed
- 12 mussels (preferably cultivated), scrubbed and beards removed
- 4 cups fish stock (recipe follows) or bottled clam juice (32 fl oz)
- 2 (14-oz) cans diced tomatoes in juice
- 1 teaspoon sugar
- 1 lb skinless halibut fillet, cut into 1-inch pieces
- ¼ cup chopped fresh basil
- ¼ cup chopped fresh flat-leaf parsley

For garlic toasts

- 1 (12-inch) Italian loaf, cut into ½-inch-thick slices
- 2 tablespoons olive oil
- 1 garlic clove, halved crosswise
- 2 tablespoons finely chopped fresh flat-leaf parsley

Accompaniment: **extra-virgin olive oil for drizzling**

Make soup:

▶ Rinse squid under cold water and pat dry. If squid are large, halve ring of tentacles, then cut longer tentacles crosswise into 2-inch pieces. Pull off flaps from squid bodies and cut into ¼-inch-thick slices. Cut bodies crosswise into ¼-inch-thick rings.

▶ Pat shrimp dry and sprinkle with pepper and ¼ teaspoon salt. Heat oil in a wide 6- to 8-quart heavy pot over moderately high heat until hot but not smoking, then sear shrimp in 2 batches, turning over once, until golden but not

cooked through, about 2 minutes per batch. Transfer shrimp with a slotted spoon to a bowl.

▶ Add garlic, red pepper flakes, and oregano to pot and sauté, stirring, until golden, about 30 seconds. Add wine and ½ cup water and bring to a boil. Stir in clams and cook, covered, over moderately high heat until shells open wide, checking frequently after 6 minutes and transferring as opened with a slotted spoon to bowl with shrimp. (Discard any unopened clams after 8 minutes.) Stir in mussels and cook, covered, over moderately high heat until shells open wide, checking frequently after 3 minutes and transferring as opened with a slotted spoon to bowl with shrimp. (Discard any unopened mussels after 6 minutes.)

▶ Put oven rack in middle position and preheat oven to 425°F.

▶ Add stock to pot along with remaining 4 cups water, tomatoes (with juice), sugar, and remaining ½ teaspoon salt and simmer, uncovered, 15 minutes.

Make toasts while stock simmers:

▶ Arrange bread slices in 1 layer on a baking sheet, then drizzle with oil and season with salt. Bake, turning over once, until golden, about 10 minutes total. Transfer toasts to a rack to cool slightly, then rub lightly with cut sides of garlic and sprinkle with parsley.

Finish soup:

▶ Add halibut to stock and cook at a bare simmer, covered, until just cooked through, about 2 minutes. Stir in squid and reserved shellfish, then remove from heat and let stand, covered, 1 minute. Stir in basil and parsley and serve immediately, with toasts alongside for dipping.

FISH STOCK
MAKES ABOUT 5 CUPS
Active time: 20 min   Start to finish: 1 hr

- 2 tablespoons olive oil
- 1 large onion, chopped
- 2 carrots, chopped
- 2 celery ribs, chopped
- 2 lb bones and trimmings of white fish such as sole, flounder, and whiting, chopped
- 8 cups water
- 2 tablespoons white-wine vinegar
- 4 whole black peppercorns
- 2 teaspoons salt

▸ Heat oil in a 5-quart heavy pot over moderately high heat until hot but not smoking, then sauté onion, carrots, and celery, stirring occasionally, until golden, 6 to 8 minutes.
▸ Add fish bones and trimmings, water, vinegar, peppercorns, and salt and bring to a boil, skimming froth. Reduce heat and simmer, uncovered, 30 minutes.
▸ Pour stock through a fine-mesh sieve into a large bowl, discarding solids. If using stock right away, skim off and discard any fat. If not, cool stock completely, uncovered, before skimming fat (it will be easier to remove when cool), then chill, covered.

Cooks' note:
• Stock keeps, covered and chilled, 1 week, or frozen 3 months.

SALMON AND DILL CHOWDER

SERVES 4 (MAIN COURSE)

Active time: 25 min   Start to finish: 45 min

4	bacon slices, cut crosswise into 1-inch pieces
1	medium onion, cut into ½-inch cubes
2	celery ribs, cut into ½-inch cubes
1	lb boiling potatoes, peeled and cut into 1-inch cubes
1	teaspoon salt
¼	teaspoon black pepper
1	cup water
2	cups whole milk
1	lb skinless salmon fillet, dark flesh removed and salmon cut into 1-inch pieces
2	tablespoons chopped fresh dill
1	tablespoon unsalted butter

▸ Cook bacon in a 3-quart heavy saucepan over moderate heat, stirring frequently, until crisp, then transfer with a slotted spoon to paper towels to drain. Pour off all but 2 tablespoons fat from saucepan, then add onion, celery, potatoes, salt, and pepper and cook, stirring occasionally, until onion is softened, 5 to 7 minutes. Stir in water and bring to a boil, then reduce heat and simmer, covered, until potatoes are almost tender, about 10 minutes.
▸ Add milk and simmer, uncovered, until potatoes are tender, 4 to 5 minutes. Stir in salmon, dill, and butter and simmer gently until salmon is just cooked through, 3 to 4 minutes. Serve sprinkled with bacon.

SPLIT PEA SOUP WITH PUMPERNICKEL CROUTONS

SERVES 6 TO 8 (MAIN COURSE; MAKES ABOUT 12 CUPS)

Active time: 35 min   Start to finish: 4 hr

2	meaty ham hocks (1¾ lb total)
16	cups water
4	large carrots
1	large onion, chopped
2	celery ribs, chopped
5	tablespoons olive oil
1	lb dried split peas (2¼ cups), picked over and rinsed
1	teaspoon table salt
¼	teaspoon black pepper
5	cups ½-inch cubes pumpernickel bread (from a 1¼-lb loaf)
1	teaspoon kosher salt
1	cup frozen peas (not thawed)

▸ Simmer ham hocks in 16 cups water in a deep 6-quart pot, uncovered, until meat is tender, 1½ to 2 hours.
▸ Transfer ham hocks to a cutting board and measure broth: If it measures more than 12 cups, continue boiling until reduced; if less, add enough water to total 12 cups. When hocks are cool enough to handle, discard skin and cut meat into ¼-inch pieces (reserve bones).
▸ Chop 2 carrots and cook along with onion and celery in 2 tablespoons oil in a 6- to 8-quart heavy pot over moderate heat, stirring, until softened, 6 to 8 minutes. Add split peas, table salt, pepper, ham hock broth, and reserved bones and simmer, uncovered, stirring occasionally, until peas are falling apart and soup is slightly thickened, about 1½ hours.
▸ Put oven rack in middle position and preheat oven to 400°F.
▸ While soup simmers, toss bread with remaining 3 tablespoons oil and kosher salt in a large bowl, then spread in 1 layer in a large shallow baking pan and bake until crisp, about 10 minutes. Cool croutons in pan on a rack.
▸ Halve remaining 2 carrots lengthwise, then cut crosswise into ¼-inch-thick slices. Remove bones from soup with a slotted spoon and discard. Add carrots and ham pieces to soup and simmer, uncovered, until carrots are tender, 10 to 15 minutes. Add frozen peas and simmer, uncovered, stirring, until just heated through, about 3 minutes. Season with salt.
▸ Serve soup with croutons.

221

FISH AND SHELLFISH

FISH

SAUTÉED COD WITH LENTILS
SERVES 4
Active time: 45 min   Start to finish: 45 min

For lentils

- 1 cup dried lentils (preferably French green lentils; 7 oz)
- 2 tablespoons unsalted butter
- 1 cup finely chopped onion
- 2 large garlic cloves, chopped
- ¾ teaspoon salt
- 3 tablespoons chopped fresh flat-leaf parsley
- 1 tablespoon fresh lemon juice
- ¼ teaspoon black pepper
- 1 tablespoon extra-virgin olive oil plus additional (optional) for drizzling

For fish

- 4 (5- to 6-oz) pieces cod fillet (¾ to 1 inch thick)
- ½ teaspoon salt
- ⅛ teaspoon black pepper
- 1 tablespoon unsalted butter
- 1 tablespoon olive oil

Garnish: **lemon wedges; chopped fresh flat-leaf parsley**

Prepare lentils:

▶ Cover lentils with cold water by 1½ inches in a 2-quart saucepan and bring to a boil. Simmer, uncovered, until lentils are just tender, 12 to 25 minutes. Drain in a sieve set over a bowl and reserve ½ cup cooking liquid.

▶ While lentils simmer, melt butter in a 2- to 3-quart heavy saucepan over moderately low heat, then cook onion, garlic, and salt, covered, stirring occasionally, until onion is pale golden, about 10 minutes. Remove lid and cook, uncovered, stirring occasionally, until golden, 5 to 10 minutes more.

▶ Stir in lentils and enough reserved cooking liquid to moisten (¼ to ½ cup) and cook until heated through.

▶ Just before serving, stir in parsley, lemon juice, pepper, and 1 tablespoon oil.

Cook fish while onion finishes cooking:

▶ Pat fish dry and sprinkle with salt and pepper.

▶ Heat butter and oil in a 10- to 12-inch nonstick skillet over moderately high heat until foam subsides, then sauté fish, turning over once, until browned and just cooked through, 6 to 8 minutes total.

▶ Serve fish with lentils and drizzle with additional extra-virgin olive oil if desired.

CURRIED SEA BASS
SERVES 4
Active time: 15 min   Start to finish: 30 min

- 1 shallot, finely chopped
- 2 tablespoons unsalted butter
- 1 teaspoon all-purpose flour
- 1 teaspoon curry powder (preferably Madras)
- ¾ cup heavy cream
- ¾ teaspoon salt
- 4 (6- to 7-oz) pieces black sea bass fillet, skinned
- ⅛ teaspoon black pepper

Accompaniment: **fresh lime wedges**

▶ Put oven rack in middle position and preheat oven to 450°F. Butter a 3-quart shallow baking dish.

▶ Cook shallot in butter in a small heavy skillet over moderate heat, stirring occasionally, until softened, 3 to 4 minutes. Sprinkle with flour and curry powder and cook, stirring, 1 minute. Add cream and bring to a boil, whisking constantly, then remove from heat and whisk in ¼ teaspoon salt.

▶ Fold each piece of fish in half, skinned side in, and arrange pieces in 1 layer in baking dish. Sprinkle fish with pepper and remaining ½ teaspoon salt. Pour sauce over fish and bake until fish is just cooked through, 10 to 12 minutes.

STEAMED STRIPED BASS WITH GINGER AND SCALLIONS

SERVES 6

Active time: 10 min   Start to finish: 30 min

 6 (¼-lb) pieces striped bass fillet with skin (1 inch thick)
 1 (½-inch) piece peeled fresh ginger, cut into very thin
    matchsticks
 1 bunch scallions (white and pale green parts only), cut
    lengthwise into very thin matchsticks (½ cup)
 3 tablespoons soy sauce
 1 teaspoon canola oil

Accompaniment: **steamed white rice**
Garnish: **fresh cilantro leaves**

▶ Arrange a steamer rack or an inverted pie plate in a deep
12-inch skillet and add 3 cups water to skillet. Cover skillet
and bring water to a boil.
▶ Pat fillets dry and arrange on a heatproof plate that will fit
into skillet with 1 inch clearance around plate. Sprinkle
ginger and ¼ cup scallions evenly on top of fish. Stir
together soy sauce and oil in a small bowl and drizzle evenly
over fillets. Carefully transfer plate with fish to rack in skillet
and cover tightly, then steam over moderately high heat until
fish is just cooked through, 15 to 20 minutes. Carefully
remove plate from skillet and sprinkle with remaining
¼ cup scallions.

EACH SERVING ABOUT 135 CALORIES AND 4 GRAMS FAT

KITCHEN NOTE

TO CUT LONG VEGETABLES INTO **MATCHSTICKS**:
CUT THE VEGETABLE CROSSWISE INTO PIECES OF
DESIRED LENGTH, THEN MAKE A FLAT SURFACE ON
A LONG SIDE BY CUTTING OFF A THIN STRIP FROM
ONE SIDE OF EACH PIECE. WITH THE FLAT SIDE
DOWN, CUT EACH PIECE INTO ⅛-INCH-THICK SLICES.
STACK TWO OR THREE SLICES AND CUT THEM INTO
⅛-INCH-THICK STRIPS.

CORNMEAL-CRUSTED FLOUNDER WITH TARTAR SAUCE

SERVES 4

Active time: 30 min   Start to finish: 30 min

For tartar sauce
 1 cup mayonnaise
 2 tablespoons chopped fresh flat-leaf parsley
 1 tablespoon finely chopped shallot
 1 tablespoon sweet relish
 2 teaspoons fresh lemon juice
 1 teaspoon whole-grain or coarse-grain mustard
 ¼ teaspoon salt
 ¼ teaspoon black pepper
For fish
 1 cup yellow cornmeal (not coarse)
 ¾ teaspoon salt
 ½ teaspoon black pepper
 ½ teaspoon cayenne
 ¾ cup all-purpose flour
 2 large eggs
 ¼ cup milk
 4 (5-oz) flounder fillets
 ¾ cup vegetable oil

Make tartar sauce:
▶ Pulse all sauce ingredients in a blender until parsley is
finely chopped.
Prepare fish:
▶ Stir together cornmeal, ¼ teaspoon salt, ¼ teaspoon black
pepper, and ¼ teaspoon cayenne in a shallow bowl. Stir
together flour, ¼ teaspoon salt, remaining ¼ teaspoon black
pepper, and remaining ¼ teaspoon cayenne in another
shallow bowl. Lightly beat together eggs, milk, and remaining ¼ teaspoon salt in a third shallow bowl.
▶ Pat fish dry and dip fillets 1 at a time in flour, shaking off
excess, then dip in egg mixture, letting excess drip off, and
dredge in cornmeal until evenly coated. Arrange fish in
1 layer on a sheet of wax paper.
▶ Heat oil in a 12-inch nonstick skillet over moderately high
heat until hot but not smoking, then fry fillets 2 at a time,
turning over once, until golden and just cooked through,
3 to 4 minutes per batch. Transfer with a slotted spatula to
a paper-towel-lined plate to drain.
▶ Serve fish with tartar sauce.

GRILLED HALIBUT WITH LEMONGRASS TOMATO SAUCE
SERVES 6
Active time: 30 min   Start to finish: 1 hr

  2 small shallots, finely chopped
  1 large garlic clove, finely chopped
  3 tablespoons olive oil
2½ lb plum tomatoes, chopped
  6 stalks fresh lemongrass, tough outer layers removed
      and lower 6 inches coarsely chopped
  ¾ teaspoon salt
  ½ teaspoon black pepper
  6 (1-inch-thick) pieces halibut steak with skin
      (6 oz each)

▶ Cook shallots and garlic in 1 tablespoon oil in a 3- to 4-quart heavy saucepan over moderately low heat, stirring occasionally, until softened, about 3 minutes. Add tomatoes, lemongrass, salt, and pepper and bring to a boil, stirring. Reduce heat and cook at a bare simmer, stirring occasionally, until tomatoes fall apart and form a chunky sauce, about 20 minutes.
▶ Force sauce through a medium-mesh sieve into a bowl, pressing hard on solids and then discarding them. Season with salt and pepper.
▶ Prepare grill for cooking. If using a charcoal grill, open vents on bottom of grill, then light charcoal. Charcoal fire is medium-hot when you can hold your hand 5 inches above rack for 3 to 4 seconds. If using a gas grill, preheat burners on high, covered, 10 minutes, then reduce heat to moderate.
▶ Brush fish on both sides with remaining 2 tablespoons oil, then season with salt and pepper. Grill fish, covered only if using gas grill, on lightly oiled grill rack, turning over once, until just cooked through, 7 to 8 minutes total.
▶ Serve fish with sauce.

Cooks' notes:
• If you aren't able to grill outdoors, fish can be grilled in a well-seasoned large ridged grill pan (without crowding) over moderately high heat, turning over once, until just cooked through, 8 to 9 minutes total.
• Sauce can be made 2 days ahead and chilled, covered. Bring to room temperature or reheat to warm before serving.

KITCHEN NOTE

FRESH LEMONGRASS DRIES OUT QUICKLY, SO BUY STALKS THAT ARE FAT AND FIRM. WRAPPED WELL IN PLASTIC, IT WILL KEEP FOR UP TO TWO WEEKS IN THE REFRIGERATOR. IT ALSO FREEZES WELL.

SALMON STEAKS WITH RED-WINE BUTTER
SERVES 4
Active time: 35 min   Start to finish: 35 min

  1 cup full-bodied dry red wine such as Côtes du Rhône
  ⅓ cup finely chopped shallots
  ½ cup fresh orange juice
  ¼ cup balsamic vinegar
  1 teaspoon tomato paste
  1 Turkish or ½ California bay leaf
  1 teaspoon finely grated fresh orange zest
  1 stick (½ cup) unsalted butter, softened
  1 teaspoon salt
  ¼ teaspoon black pepper
  4 (1-inch-thick) salmon steaks (½ lb each),
      bones removed
  2 tablespoons olive oil

▶ Boil wine, shallots, juice, vinegar, tomato paste, and bay leaf in a 1- to 2-quart heavy saucepan over moderately high heat until mixture is thick and jamlike and reduced to about ⅓ cup, about 20 minutes. Discard bay leaf. Transfer mixture to a small bowl set in a bowl of ice and cold water and stir until cold to the touch, about 5 minutes.
▶ Remove from ice water and stir in zest, butter, ¼ teaspoon salt, and remaining ⅛ teaspoon pepper with a rubber spatula until incorporated.
▶ Preheat broiler. Line rack of a broiler pan with foil.
▶ Pat fish dry, then brush both sides with oil (2 tablespoons total) and sprinkle with remaining ¾ teaspoon salt and remaining ⅛ teaspoon pepper. Broil fish about 5 inches from heat, turning over once, until just cooked through, 8 to 10 minutes total.
▶ Top each steak with 1 to 2 tablespoons red-wine butter.

Cooks' note:
• Leftover red-wine butter can be chilled, covered, up to 3 days or frozen 2 weeks.

TUNA IN TOMATO SAUCE

SERVES 4

Active time: 20 min   Start to finish: 35 min

- 2 tablespoons minced garlic
- ⅓ cup extra-virgin olive oil
- ½ teaspoon paprika
- ⅛ teaspoon cayenne
- 2 (14- to 15-oz) cans diced tomatoes in juice
- ½ teaspoon salt
  Pinch of sugar
- 1 (1½-lb) piece tuna, cut crosswise into
  ½-inch-thick pieces

▶ Cook garlic in oil in a 12-inch heavy skillet over moderate heat, stirring, until golden, about 1 minute. Add paprika and cayenne and cook, stirring, until fragrant, about 30 seconds. Stir in tomatoes (with juice), salt, and sugar and simmer, uncovered, stirring occasionally, until broken down, 20 to 25 minutes.

▶ Season tuna with salt and pepper and arrange in 1 layer on top of sauce. Cook, covered, 2 minutes, then remove from heat and let stand, covered, until top of fish is no longer red, 1 to 3 minutes.

▶ Transfer to a platter and spoon sauce on top.

TILAPIA WITH PROSCIUTTO AND SAGE

SERVES 4

Active time: 20 min   Start to finish: 20 min

Separating the two sides of the fillet helps to keep the thinner part from overcooking.

- 4 pieces skinless tilapia fillet (2 lb total)
- 8 thin slices prosciutto (not paper-thin; 6 oz total)
- 12 fresh sage leaves, stems discarded
- 4 teaspoons olive oil

▶ Cut fillets lengthwise to separate smaller and larger portions, then pat dry and season with pepper. Wrap each piece of fillet crosswise in a slice of prosciutto, leaving ends of fillet exposed if necessary and tucking 1 or 2 sage leaves between prosciutto and fillet (use 1 leaf for smaller pieces of fish).

▶ Heat 2 teaspoons oil in a 12-inch heavy nonstick skillet over moderately high heat until hot but not smoking, then sauté the 4 larger pieces of fish 4 minutes. Turn over and sauté until just cooked through, about 3 minutes more. Transfer to a platter and keep warm, loosely covered with foil. Wipe skillet clean and heat remaining 2 teaspoons oil, then sauté the 4 smaller pieces of fish, turning over once, until just cooked through, about 4 minutes total.

RED SNAPPER WITH CILANTRO, GARLIC, AND LIME

SERVES 6

Active time: 15 min   Start to finish: 20 min

- 6 (6- to 8-oz) red snapper fillets (½ inch thick) with skin
- 6 tablespoons extra-virgin olive oil
- 1 teaspoon salt
- ¾ teaspoon black pepper
- ½ cup finely chopped fresh cilantro
- 1½ tablespoons minced garlic
- 1½ tablespoons finely grated fresh lime zest

Accompaniment: **lime wedges**

▶ Preheat broiler and lightly oil a shallow baking pan (1 inch deep).

▶ Pat fish dry, then arrange, skin sides up, in 1 layer in baking pan. Brush both sides of fish with 3 tablespoons oil total and sprinkle with salt and pepper. Toss together cilantro, garlic, and zest in a small bowl.

▶ Broil fish 6 inches from heat, without turning over, until just cooked through, 8 to 10 minutes. Transfer, skin sides up, with a metal spatula to a platter, then sprinkle with cilantro mixture and drizzle with remaining 3 tablespoons oil.

KITCHEN NOTE

TO SKIN A FILLET OF FISH, USE A SHARP FILLET KNIFE OR CHEF'S KNIFE. ARRANGE THE FILLET SKIN SIDE DOWN AND, STARTING AT THE CORNER CLOSEST TO YOU, CUT A FLAP OF SKIN LOOSE FROM THE FLESH. HOLDING THE FLAP OF SKIN FIRMLY WITH A PAPER TOWEL, SCRAPE THE FLESH OFF THE SKIN BY HOLDING YOUR BLADE EDGE STEADY AGAINST THE SKIN AND PULLING THE FISH SKIN TOWARD YOU.

ROASTED SNAPPER WITH ARTICHOKES AND LEMON

SERVES 4

Active time: 25 min   Start to finish: 1 hr

5 tablespoons fresh lemon juice (from about 2 lemons),
     reserving juiced lemons
4 large artichokes with stems attached (10 to
     12 oz each)
6 tablespoons extra-virgin olive oil
1 teaspoon salt
⅜ teaspoon black pepper
4 (½-inch-thick) red snapper fillets with skin (6 oz each)
1 tablespoon chopped fresh tarragon

▸ Put oven rack in middle position and preheat oven to 425°F.

▸ Stir 2 tablespoons lemon juice into a large bowl half filled with cool water, then drop in juiced lemons. Cut 1 inch off top of 1 artichoke with a knife. Bend back outer leaves until they snap off close to base, then discard several more layers of leaves in same manner until you reach pale yellow leaves with pale green tips. (Dip artichoke in lemon water occasionally to limit discoloration.)

▸ Cut remaining leaves flush with top of artichoke bottom using a sharp knife, then remove choke by pulling out purple leaves and scraping out fuzzy layer with a spoon or melon-ball cutter. Trim ¼ inch from end of stem, then trim base and side of stem with a vegetable peeler or sharp knife. Drop artichoke into lemon water. Trim remaining 3 artichokes in same manner.

▸ Drain artichokes, pat dry, and cut each into 6 wedges. Arrange artichokes in 1 layer in a 13- by 9-inch glass or ceramic baking dish. Stir together 3 tablespoons oil, 2 tablespoons lemon juice, ¼ teaspoon salt, and ⅛ teaspoon pepper in a small bowl and pour over artichokes, turning to coat. Cover dish with foil and roast, turning artichokes over once or twice, until just tender, 20 to 25 minutes. (Leave oven on.)

▸ While artichokes roast, rub fish with 1 tablespoon oil and sprinkle all over with remaining ¾ teaspoon salt and remaining ¼ teaspoon pepper. Remove foil from baking dish and arrange fillets, skin sides up, in 1 layer on top of artichokes. Roast, uncovered, until fillets are just cooked through, about 9 minutes.

▸ Divide fish and artichokes among 4 plates using a spatula,

reserving pan juices. Stir together remaining 2 tablespoons oil, remaining tablespoon lemon juice, tarragon, and reserved pan juices and drizzle over fish.

Cooks' note:
• Artichokes can be trimmed 1 day ahead and chilled in lemon water, covered.

KITCHEN NOTE

WHEN **GRILLING FISH**, YOU WANT A HOT FIRE, BUT NOT SO HOT THAT IT COOKS THE OUTSIDE OF THE FISH BEFORE THE INTERIOR IS DONE. (GRILLING A WHOLE FISH CALLS FOR A LOWER HEAT THAN A THINNER FILLET.) TO AVOID OVERCOOKING FISH, REMOVE THE FISH FROM HEAT WHEN THE FLESH IS OPAQUE BUT STILL MOIST. CHECK FOR DONENESS BY PRODDING IT LIGHTLY WITH THE TIP OF A KNIFE: THE FLESH SHOULD JUST BEGIN TO SEPARATE INTO FLAKES (FISH THAT FLAKES EASILY IS OVERCOOKED).

INDIAN-SPICED STURGEON WITH MINT YOGURT SAUCE

SERVES 6

Active time: 40 min   Start to finish: 1¾ hr (includes marinating fish)

1 teaspoon fennel seeds, toasted (see Tips, page 8)
2 cups plain yogurt (16 oz)
1 garlic clove, minced
1 teaspoon minced peeled fresh ginger
½ teaspoon ground cumin
½ teaspoon ground coriander
¼ teaspoon black pepper
¼ teaspoon turmeric
⅛ teaspoon cayenne, or to taste
1 teaspoon salt
6 (1-inch-thick) pieces skinless sturgeon fillet or halibut
     fillet with skin (6 oz each)
3 tablespoons finely chopped fresh mint
½ teaspoon finely grated fresh lemon zest

Special equipment: **an electric coffee/spice grinder**

▸ Finely grind fennel seeds in grinder. Whisk together fennel and 1 cup yogurt with garlic, ginger, cumin, coriander, black pepper, turmeric, cayenne, and ½ teaspoon salt. Coat fish with yogurt mixture and marinate in a shallow baking dish, covered and chilled, 1 hour.

▸ While fish marinates, whisk together remaining cup yogurt, mint, zest, and remaining ½ teaspoon salt to make sauce.

▸ Prepare grill for cooking. If using a charcoal grill, open vents on bottom of grill, then light charcoal. Charcoal is medium-hot when you can hold your hand 5 inches above rack for 3 to 4 seconds. If using a gas grill, preheat burners on high, covered, 10 minutes, then reduce heat to moderate.

▸ Lift fish out of marinade, letting excess drip off (discard marinade), and grill fish, covered only if using a gas grill, on lightly oiled grill rack, turning over once, until just cooked through, about 12 minutes total. (If using halibut, grill skin sides down first and grill, turning once, 8 to 9 minutes total.)

▸ Serve fish with sauce.

Cooks' note:

• If you aren't able to grill outdoors, sturgeon can be grilled in a well-seasoned large ridged grill pan (without crowding) over moderately high heat, turning once, until just cooked through, about 12 minutes total. (Halibut will take 8 to 9 minutes total.)

FISH AND CHIPS

SERVES 4
Active time: 1½ hr   Start to finish: 2½ hr

4	large boiling potatoes (2¼ lb)
3	qt vegetable oil (96 fl oz)
2	cups all-purpose flour
1	(12-oz) bottle cold beer (preferably ale)
1	teaspoon salt
1½	lb haddock or cod fillets, skinned, pin bones removed, and fish cut diagonally into 1-inch-wide strips (5 to 6 inches long)
¼	teaspoon black pepper

Special equipment: **a deep-fat thermometer**
Accompaniment: **malt vinegar**

▸ Peel potatoes and halve lengthwise, then cut lengthwise into ½-inch-thick wedges, transferring as cut to a large bowl of ice and cold water. Chill 30 minutes.

▸ Heat oil in a deep 6-quart heavy pot over moderately high heat until it registers 325°F on thermometer. While oil heats, drain potatoes and dry thoroughly with paper towels. Fry one third of potatoes, stirring gently, until edges are just golden, about 4 minutes. Transfer with a slotted spoon to fresh paper towels to drain. Fry remaining potatoes in 2 batches (return oil to 325°F between batches). Remove oil from heat and reserve. Cool potatoes, about 25 minutes.

▸ Heat oil over moderately high heat until it registers 350°F. Put oven racks in upper and lower thirds of oven and preheat oven to 250°F.

▸ Fry potatoes again, in 3 batches, until deep golden brown and crisp, about 5 minutes per batch (return oil to 350°F between batches). Transfer with slotted spoon to fresh paper towels as fried and drain briefly, then arrange in 1 layer in a shallow baking pan and keep warm in upper third of oven.

▸ Increase oil temperature to 375°F. Sift 1½ cups flour into a bowl, then gently whisk in beer until just combined and stir in ¼ teaspoon salt.

▸ Pat fish dry. Sprinkle fish on both sides with remaining ¾ teaspoon salt and pepper, then dredge in remaining ½ cup flour, shaking off excess. Coat 4 pieces of fish in batter, 1 at a time, and slide into oil as coated. Fry fish, turning over frequently, until deep golden and cooked through, 4 to 5 minutes. Transfer to a paper-towel-lined baking sheet and keep warm in lower third of oven, then fry remaining fish in batches of 4 (return oil to 375°F between batches).

▸ Season fish and chips with salt.

Cooks' note:

• Chips can be fried for the first time 3 hours ahead and kept, uncovered, at room temperature until refrying.

SHELLFISH

CRAB CAKES WITH SPICY AVOCADO SAUCE

SERVES 4

Active time: 45 min   Start to finish: 1 hr

For sauce
- ½ ripe medium California avocado, pitted and peeled
- 1 tablespoon low-fat mayonnaise
- 1 tablespoon fresh lime juice
- ¼ teaspoon salt
- ¼ teaspoon sugar
- 1 fresh jalapeño or serrano chile, stemmed and quartered lengthwise (including seeds)
- ¼ cup fat-free (skim) milk

For crab cakes
- 1 lb jumbo lump crabmeat, picked over and coarsely shredded
- 3 tablespoons low-fat mayonnaise
- ¼ cup minced fresh chives
- 1 tablespoon fresh lemon juice
- 1 teaspoon Dijon mustard
- ¼ teaspoon black pepper
- ½ cup *panko* (Japanese bread crumbs; see Sources)
- 1 tablespoon unsalted butter
- 2 garlic cloves, smashed
- ½ teaspoon *herbes de Provence* or ¼ teaspoon dried thyme
- ¼ teaspoon salt

▶ Put oven rack in middle position and preheat oven to 400°F. Line a baking sheet with foil.

Make sauce:

▶ Pulse avocado with mayonnaise, lime juice, salt, sugar, and one fourth of chile in a food processor until chile is finely chopped. Add milk and purée until smooth. Add more chile if desired, processing until smooth. Transfer sauce to a bowl and chill, covered.

Make crab cakes:

▶ Stir together crabmeat, mayonnaise, chives, lemon juice, mustard, pepper, and 1 tablespoon *panko* in a large bowl until blended well, then chill, covered.

▶ Melt butter in a nonstick skillet over moderate heat, then cook garlic, stirring, until golden and fragrant, about

2 minutes. Add *herbes de Provence*, salt, and remaining 7 tablespoons *panko* and cook, stirring, until crumbs are golden brown, about 6 minutes. Transfer crumbs to a plate to cool and discard garlic.

▶ Divide crabmeat mixture into 4 mounds on a sheet of wax paper. Form 1 mound into a patty, then carefully turn patty in crumb mixture to coat top and bottom. Transfer to a baking sheet and repeat with remaining 3 mounds, then sprinkle remaining crumbs on top of crab cakes. Bake until heated through, about 15 minutes.

▶ Serve crab cakes with sauce.

EACH SERVING ABOUT 247 CALORIES AND 12 GRAMS FAT

Cooks' note:
• If *panko* is unavailable, plain dry bread crumbs are an acceptable substitute.

MUSSELS WITH BASIL CREAM

SERVES 2 (MAIN COURSE) OR 4 (FIRST COURSE)

Active time: 20 min   Start to finish: 25 min

- 1 small onion, finely chopped
- 2 garlic cloves, finely chopped
- 2 tablespoons unsalted butter
- ⅓ cup dry white wine
- 2 lb mussels (preferably cultivated), scrubbed and beards removed
- ½ cup heavy cream
- ¾ cup loosely packed fresh basil leaves
- ¼ teaspoon black pepper

▶ Cook onion and garlic in butter in a 5- to 6-quart heavy pot over moderately low heat, stirring, until softened, 3 to 5 minutes. Add wine and mussels and cook, covered, over moderately high heat until mussels just open wide, 6 to 8 minutes. (Discard any unopened mussels after 8 minutes.)

▶ Transfer mussels with a slotted spoon to a serving bowl, then transfer cooking liquid to a blender along with cream, basil, and pepper and blend until smooth (use caution when blending hot liquids). Season sauce with salt and pour over mussels.

SQUID IN VINEGAR SAUCE

SERVES 4

Active time: 25 min   Start to finish: 40 min

1   lb medium squid, cleaned
⅓   cup coconut vinegar, palm vinegar, sugarcane
      vinegar, or cider vinegar
¼   cup thinly sliced garlic (8 cloves)
¼   cup soy sauce
½   cup water
½   teaspoon black pepper
2   tablespoons vegetable oil
1   medium onion, halved lengthwise, then thinly
      sliced lengthwise
1   (14- to 15-oz) can diced tomatoes in juice

Accompaniment: **steamed white rice**

▶ Rinse squid under cold water and pat dry. Cut squid bodies into 1-inch-wide rings and leave tentacles whole.

▶ Bring vinegar, garlic, soy sauce, water, and pepper to a boil in a 2-quart heavy saucepan, then add squid (liquid will not cover squid) and cook over moderately high heat, stirring constantly, until opaque, 1 to 2 minutes. Remove from heat and immediately drain squid in a colander set over a bowl, reserving liquid.

▶ Heat oil in a 12-inch heavy skillet over high heat until hot but not smoking, then sauté onion, stirring, until lightly browned, about 3 minutes. Add tomatoes (with juice) and boil, stirring occasionally, until most of liquid is evaporated, about 3 minutes. Add squid cooking liquid and boil, stirring occasionally, until reduced by about half, about 8 minutes. Stir in squid and simmer until cooked through, about 2 minutes.

SHRIMP WITH NAPA CABBAGE AND GINGER

SERVES 4

Active time: 45 min   Start to finish: 45 min

1   bunch scallions, trimmed
1   lb large shrimp in shell (16 to 20 per lb), peeled
      and deveined
2   tablespoons medium-dry Sherry
1   teaspoon cornstarch
¼   teaspoon white pepper
1   teaspoon salt
1   (2-lb) head Napa cabbage, quartered lengthwise, cored,
      and cut crosswise into 1½-inch pieces (10 cups)
3   tablespoons vegetable oil
1   teaspoon minced peeled fresh ginger
1   red bell pepper, cut into ¼-inch-wide strips (1 cup)
1   tablespoon soy sauce

Accompaniment: **cooked rice**

▶ Cut white and pale green parts of scallions into 2-inch pieces and thinly slice dark green parts.

▶ Stir together shrimp, 1 tablespoon Sherry, cornstarch, white pepper, and ½ teaspoon salt in a bowl.

▶ Rinse cabbage in a colander. Tap colander lightly, then transfer cabbage to a large bowl with excess water still clinging to leaves.

▶ Heat a 14-inch wok or 12-inch heavy skillet over high heat until beginning to smoke, then add 2 tablespoons oil. When oil begins to smoke, add shrimp and stir-fry until golden and almost cooked through, about 4 minutes. Transfer to a clean bowl.

▶ Add remaining tablespoon oil to wok and heat until just smoking, then stir-fry ginger and white and pale green parts of scallions until slightly softened, about 2 minutes. Add bell pepper and stir-fry until softened, about 2 minutes. Stir in remaining tablespoon Sherry and cook until most of liquid is evaporated. Add cabbage with water from bowl, soy sauce, and remaining ½ teaspoon salt and cook, covered, until cabbage is tender, about 5 minutes.

▶ Stir in shrimp along with any juices accumulated in bowl and simmer, uncovered, until shrimp are just cooked through, about 1 minute. Add scallion greens and toss to combine well.

MEATS

BEEF

FILETS MIGNONS
WITH CREAMY PAPRIKA SAUCE

SERVES 4

Active time: 25 min   Start to finish: 30 min

 4 (1½-inch-thick) filets mignons (beef tenderloin
     steaks; 6 oz each)
 1 teaspoon salt
 ¾ teaspoon black pepper
 1 tablespoon vegetable oil
 1 tablespoon unsalted butter
 1 cup thinly sliced onion (1 large)
 ½ teaspoon finely chopped garlic
10 oz mushrooms, sliced
 1 tablespoon paprika (not hot)
 ⅔ cup sour cream
 1 tablespoon Dijon mustard
 2 teaspoons Worcestershire sauce

Accompaniment: buttered egg noodles

▶ Pat beef dry and sprinkle with ¾ teaspoon salt and
½ teaspoon pepper. Heat oil in a 10- to 12-inch heavy skillet
over moderately high heat until hot but not smoking, then
sauté beef, turning over once, about 10 minutes total for
medium-rare. Transfer beef to a plate and let stand, loosely
covered with foil, 10 minutes.
▶ While steaks stand, heat butter in skillet over moderate
heat until foam subsides, then cook onion, stirring
occasionally, until softened, 3 to 5 minutes. Add garlic,
mushrooms, remaining ¼ teaspoon salt, and remaining
¼ teaspoon pepper and cook, stirring constantly, until liquid
mushrooms give off is evaporated, 3 to 5 minutes. Add
paprika and cook, stirring constantly, 1 minute. Stir in sour
cream, mustard, and Worcestershire sauce and bring just to
a simmer (do not boil). Stir in any beef juices accumulated
on plate and thin sauce with up to ¼ cup water if necessary.
▶ Spoon sauce over steaks and noodles.

STEAK WITH ROASTED-PEPPER
AND ARTICHOKE RELISH

SERVES 4

Active time: 25 min   Start to finish: 25 min

 1 garlic clove
1½ teaspoons balsamic vinegar
 ¼ teaspoon Dijon mustard
 ¾ teaspoon salt
 ½ teaspoon black pepper
 ¼ teaspoon sugar
 3 tablespoons olive oil
 1 (12-oz) jar roasted red peppers, rinsed, patted dry,
     and cut crosswise into thin strips
 1 (6-oz) jar marinated artichoke hearts, rinsed, patted
     dry, and coarsely chopped
 2 tablespoons chopped fresh basil
 4 (½-inch-thick) boneless top loin (strip) steaks
     (6 oz each)

▶ Mince garlic and mash to a paste with a pinch of salt, then
transfer to a bowl. Whisk in vinegar, mustard, ¼ teaspoon
salt, ¼ teaspoon pepper, and sugar. Add 2 tablespoons oil in
a slow stream, whisking until emulsified. Stir in peppers,
artichokes, and basil, then add salt and pepper to taste.
▶ Pat steaks dry and sprinkle with remaining ½ teaspoon salt
and remaining ¼ teaspoon pepper. Heat remaining

tablespoon oil in a 12-inch heavy skillet over moderately high heat until hot but not smoking, then sauté steaks 2 at a time, turning over once, about 5 minutes per batch for medium-rare. Transfer steaks to plates as cooked.
▶ Serve steaks topped with relish.

BULGOGI
(Korean Marinated Beef)
SERVES 4 (MAIN COURSE)
Active time: 20 min   Start to finish: 40 min

This popular dish can be found on the menu at virtually every Korean restaurant in Manhattan. The beef is topped with various accompaniments such as a few raw garlic slices, kimchi (assorted spicy pickles), and steamed white rice, then wrapped in lettuce and eaten with your hands.

¼ cup soy sauce
1 tablespoon sugar
2 teaspoons Asian sesame oil
1 bunch scallions (white and pale green parts separated from greens), minced (½ cup)
1 tablespoon minced garlic
1 tablespoon minced peeled fresh ginger
3 tablespoons sesame seeds, toasted (see Tips, page 8)
1 lb flank steak, cut across the grain into very thin slices (no more than ⅛ inch thick)
1 tablespoon vegetable oil

Accompaniments: **butter lettuce or other soft-leaf lettuce; thinly sliced garlic; packaged kimchi (see Sources); steamed white rice**

▶ Stir together soy sauce, sugar, sesame oil, white and pale green scallions, garlic, ginger, and 2 tablespoons sesame seeds in a bowl until sugar is dissolved. Add steak and toss to coat, then marinate 15 minutes.
▶ Heat vegetable oil in a 12-inch heavy skillet over high heat until just smoking, then add steak in 1 layer and sauté, turning over occasionally, until browned and just cooked through, about 5 minutes total. Transfer to a platter and sprinkle with scallion greens and remaining tablespoon sesame seeds.
▶ Serve with accompaniments.

SKIRT STEAK WITH CILANTRO GARLIC SAUCE
SERVES 6
Active time: 20 min   Start to finish: 20 min

For sauce
1 medium garlic clove
½ teaspoon salt
1 cup coarsely chopped fresh cilantro
¼ cup olive oil
2 tablespoons fresh lemon juice
⅛ teaspoon cayenne
For steak
1 teaspoon ground cumin
½ teaspoon salt
½ teaspoon black pepper
2 lb skirt steak, cut crosswise into 3- to 4-inch pieces

Make sauce:
▶ Mince garlic and mash to a paste with salt. Transfer to a blender and add remaining sauce ingredients, then blend until smooth.
Grill steak:
▶ Stir together cumin, salt, and pepper in a small bowl. Pat steak dry, then rub both sides of pieces with cumin mixture.
▶ Heat an oiled well-seasoned ridged grill pan over high heat until hot but not smoking, then grill steak in 2 batches, turning over occasionally, about 2 minutes per batch for thin pieces or 6 to 8 minutes per batch for thicker pieces (medium-rare).
▶ Serve steak drizzled with sauce.

KITCHEN NOTE

FLANK STEAK, AVAILABLE IN ANY SUPERMARKET, IS RECOGNIZABLE BY ITS LONGITUDINAL GRAIN. IT HAS GREAT FLAVOR, AND IS BEST COOKED ONLY TO RARE OR MEDIUM-RARE. SKIRT STEAK, WHICH HAS A CROSSWISE GRAIN, IS OFTEN AVAILABLE IN SUPERMARKETS. IT HAS MORE FAT THAN FLANK STEAK, MAKING IT JUICIER AND RICHER. WHEN SLICING, BE SURE TO CUT BOTH STEAKS ACROSS THE GRAIN FOR MAXIMUM TENDERNESS.

INDIVIDUAL MEATLOAVES WITH BACON CRISPS

SERVES 4

Active time: 35 min   Start to finish: 45 min

  1   medium onion, finely chopped
  2   garlic cloves, finely chopped
  1   tablespoon olive oil
  1   cup fresh bread crumbs
  ¾   cup whole milk
  2   large eggs, lightly beaten
  3   tablespoons finely chopped fresh flat-leaf parsley
1½   tablespoons Worcestershire sauce
  ½   teaspoon Tabasco
1½   teaspoons salt
  ½   teaspoon black pepper
1½   lb meatloaf mix or equal parts ground beef chuck, pork, and veal
  ¼   cup ketchup
  2   tablespoons distilled white or cider vinegar
  4   bacon slices, cut into 1½-inch pieces

Special equipment: **an instant-read thermometer**

▶ Put oven rack in middle position and preheat oven to 400°F. Line a shallow baking pan with foil.
▶ Cook onion and garlic in oil in a 10-inch skillet over moderate heat, stirring frequently, until just softened, about 4 minutes.
▶ Stir together bread crumbs, milk, eggs, parsley, Worcestershire sauce, Tabasco, salt, and pepper in a large bowl. Gently combine meat if necessary, then add to bread-crumb mixture along with onion mixture and gently knead with your hands until just combined (mixture will be moist). Wipe out skillet and reserve.
▶ Using a 1-cup measure, drop slightly rounded cups of meat mixture into baking pan and lightly pat to form 4 domes.
▶ Stir together ketchup and vinegar and spoon over mounds. Bake meatloaves until center of each loaf registers 155°F on thermometer, about 25 minutes.
▶ While meatloaves bake, cook bacon in skillet over moderate heat, stirring occasionally, until crisp, about 7 minutes. Transfer with a slotted spoon to paper towels to drain.
▶ Turn on broiler and broil meatloaves 2 to 3 inches from heat until glaze is slightly caramelized, 1 to 2 minutes.
▶ Serve meatloaves topped with bacon.

VEAL CHOP WITH RADICCHIO, WHITE BEANS, AND ROSEMARY

SERVES 1

Active time: 30 min   Start to finish: 30 min

  2   garlic cloves
  ⅜   teaspoon salt
  2   tablespoons olive oil
  ½   teaspoon chopped fresh rosemary
  ½   teaspoon black pepper
  1   (½-inch-thick) loin veal chop (7 oz)
  5   oz radicchio, leaves torn into 2- to 3-inch pieces (3 cups)
  ⅓   cup canned small white beans, rinsed and drained
  2   teaspoons red-wine vinegar
  ½   cup reduced-sodium chicken broth
  ½   teaspoon cornstarch

▶ Mince 1 garlic clove and mash to a paste with ¼ teaspoon salt, then transfer to a shallow bowl. Stir in 1 tablespoon oil, ¼ teaspoon rosemary, and ¼ teaspoon pepper. Add veal and turn once or twice to coat.
▶ Heat remaining tablespoon oil in a 12-inch heavy skillet over moderate heat until hot but not smoking, then cook veal, turning over once, until golden and just cooked through, 6 to 7 minutes total. Transfer veal to a plate.
▶ Finely chop remaining garlic clove and add to skillet, then cook over moderate heat, stirring, until golden, about 30 seconds. Add radicchio and beans and cook, stirring, until radicchio begins to wilt, about 2 minutes. Add vinegar and cook until most of vinegar is evaporated. Whisk together broth and cornstarch, then add to bean mixture and boil, stirring and scraping up brown bits, until sauce is thickened slightly and about two thirds of liquid is evaporated, about 4 minutes. Remove from heat and stir in remaining ¼ teaspoon rosemary, remaining ⅛ teaspoon salt, and remaining ¼ teaspoon pepper. Serve veal with radicchio and beans.

KITCHEN NOTE

CANNED WHITE BEANS ARE ONE OF OUR FAVORITE PANTRY ITEMS. BE SURE TO RINSE AND DRAIN THEM THOROUGHLY BEFORE USING TO REMOVE THE COATING ON THE BEANS.

VEAL CUTLETS WITH ARUGULA AND TOMATO SALAD

SERVES 4

Active time: 30 min   Start to finish: 35 min

You can substitute skinless boneless chicken breasts for the veal cutlets.

   3   cups fine fresh bread crumbs (from 6 slices firm white
        sandwich bread)
   6   tablespoons olive oil
   3   tablespoons fresh lemon juice
   1   teaspoon black pepper
   1   teaspoon salt
   2   medium tomatoes (¾ lb total), cut into
        ½-inch-thick wedges
   1   small red onion, halved lengthwise, then thinly
        sliced crosswise (½ cup)
   4   veal cutlets (1¼ lb total)
   2   oz finely grated Parmigiano-Reggiano (1 cup; see
        Tips, page 8)
   2   large eggs
   6   tablespoons vegetable oil
  10   oz arugula (5 cups), leaves torn if large
   1   cup loosely packed fresh basil leaves, torn into
        bite-size pieces

▸ Put oven rack in middle position and preheat oven to 350°F.

▸ Spread bread crumbs in a shallow baking pan and toast until pale golden, 8 to 10 minutes. Reduce oven temperature to 200°F.

▸ Whisk together olive oil, juice, pepper, and ½ teaspoon salt in a large bowl until combined, then stir in tomatoes and onion.

▸ Gently pound cutlets to ⅛-inch thickness between 2 sheets of plastic wrap with flat side of a meat pounder or with a rolling pin. Sprinkle veal all over with remaining ½ teaspoon salt and season with pepper.

▸ Stir together bread crumbs and cheese in a large shallow bowl. Lightly beat eggs in another large shallow bowl. Dip veal 1 piece at a time in egg, letting excess drip off, then dredge in bread crumbs, coating completely, and arrange in 1 layer on a sheet of wax paper.

▸ Heat 3 tablespoons vegetable oil in a 12-inch heavy skillet over moderately high heat until hot but not smoking, then fry 2 cutlets, turning over once, until golden brown and just cooked through, about 6 minutes total. Transfer to paper towels to drain briefly, then transfer to baking pan and keep warm in oven. Add remaining 3 tablespoons oil to skillet and fry remaining cutlets in same manner.

▸ Add arugula and basil to tomato mixture and toss, then season with salt and pepper.

▸ Serve veal topped with salad.

PORK

HOISIN AND HONEY GLAZED PORK CHOPS

SERVES 4

Active time: 15 min   Start to finish: 45 min

   ¼   cup Asian oyster sauce
   2   tablespoons Dijon mustard
   2   tablespoons hoisin sauce
   1   teaspoon finely grated peeled fresh ginger
   2   tablespoons honey
   1   tablespoon soy sauce
   1   bunch scallions, trimmed and cut diagonally into
        2-inch pieces
   4   (1-inch-thick) pork chops (2 lb total)

Accompaniment: **steamed rice**

▸ Put oven rack in middle position and preheat oven to 400°F.

▸ Whisk together oyster sauce, mustard, hoisin sauce, ginger, and soy sauce in a large bowl. Add scallions and pork, turning pork to coat generously with sauce.

▸ Arrange pork in 1 layer in a 15- by 10-inch shallow baking pan (1 inch deep). Spoon remaining sauce with scallions over pork and roast until just cooked through, 15 to 20 minutes.

▸ Turn on broiler and broil pork 5 to 6 inches from heat until top is slightly caramelized, 2 to 5 minutes. Let stand, uncovered, 5 minutes.

▸ Serve pork topped with any pan juices.

PORK DUMPLINGS

SERVES 4 (MAIN COURSE; MAKES 32)
Active time: 1¼ hr   Start to finish: 1¼ hr

1¾ cups all-purpose flour plus additional for dusting
½ cup lukewarm water
1 (2-inch) piece peeled fresh ginger
½ cup light soy sauce
1 bunch scallions, thinly sliced
¾ lb ground pork (from shoulder; not lean)

Special equipment: **a 3¼-inch round cookie cutter**

▶ Stir together flour and lukewarm water in a bowl until a dough forms. Turn out dough onto a lightly floured surface and knead until just smooth, 1 to 2 minutes. Wrap dough tightly in plastic wrap and let stand at room temperature at least 10 minutes.
▶ While dough stands, halve ginger, then finely chop 1 half and cut remaining half into very thin matchsticks (less than ⅛ inch thick).
▶ Combine 5 tablespoons soy sauce with ginger matchsticks in a small bowl.
▶ Reserve 2 tablespoons scallions for garnish, then finely chop remainder and put in a bowl along with pork, finely chopped ginger, and remaining 3 tablespoons soy sauce. Gently knead with your hands in bowl until just combined, then chill, covered, 10 minutes.
▶ While pork mixture chills, line a large baking sheet with paper towels and dust lightly with flour, then lightly dust work surface with flour. Halve dough and pat 1 half into a flat square (keep remaining half wrapped in plastic wrap). Roll out dough into a 13-inch square (less than ⅛ inch thick) with a lightly floured rolling pin, dusting work surface with additional flour as needed, then cut out 12 rounds (very close together) using cookie cutter. (If dough is sticking to cutter, lightly dip cutter in flour and shake off excess before cutting out each round.) Reserve scraps.
▶ Transfer rounds to lined baking sheet and cover loosely with another layer of paper towels lightly dusted (on top) with flour. Roll out remaining half of dough and cut out 12 more rounds in same manner, then transfer rounds to lined baking sheet. Combine scraps of dough and wrap in plastic wrap, then let stand at least 10 minutes.
▶ While scraps stand, begin forming dumplings. Line another large baking sheet with paper towels and dust lightly with

flour. Put 1 dough round on fingers of 1 hand near palm and put 2 slightly rounded teaspoons pork mixture in center of round. Fold round in half, enclosing filling, and pinch edges together to seal. Put dumpling on lined baking sheet and form 23 more dumplings in same manner (you may have some filling left over). Cover dumplings loosely with more paper towels. Roll out scraps into a 10-inch square (less than ⅛ inch thick) and cut out 8 more rounds. Form 8 more dumplings for a total of 32. Discard remaining scraps.
▶ Gently drop all dumplings into a 6- to 8-quart pot of boiling water, gently stirring once to prevent sticking, and cook 6 minutes. (Dumplings will float to top while cooking.)
▶ Transfer dumplings with a slotted spoon to a serving dish and sprinkle with reserved scallions. Serve with ginger dipping sauce.

Cooks' note:
• Dumplings can be formed 1 day ahead. Chill in 1 layer, not touching, on lined baking sheet, loosely but completely covered with plastic wrap.

RICE-STUDDED MEATBALLS

SERVES 6 (MAIN COURSE) OR 10 (FIRST COURSE)
Active time: 20 min   Start to finish: 45 min

These rice-coated meatballs are traditionally made with sticky rice, but we've used long-grain rice, which is easier to find.

1 cup long-grain white rice
2 to 4 outer leaves of iceberg or romaine lettuce
1 lb ground pork or veal or meatloaf mix
1 tablespoon Chinese rice wine (preferably Shaoxing) or medium-dry Sherry
1 bunch scallions (white and pale green parts only), minced (⅓ cup)
½ cup diced (¼ inch) rinsed and drained canned water chestnuts
1 tablespoon cornstarch
1 tablespoon egg white, lightly beaten
1 teaspoon sugar
½ teaspoon Asian sesame oil
1 teaspoon salt
¼ teaspoon white pepper

Special equipment: **a large collapsible metal steamer rack**

▶ Soak rice in hot tap water in a large bowl while preparing meat mixture.

▶ While rice soaks, put a metal steamer rack in a deep 12-inch skillet or a wide 6-quart pot and add enough water to reach ½ inch below bottom of steamer rack. Remove steamer rack from skillet and line rack with lettuce.

▶ Stir together remaining ingredients (except rice) until combined well.

▶ Drain rice in a sieve and transfer to a shallow dish.

▶ Roll about 1 tablespoon meat mixture into a ball and roll in rice to coat, then transfer to steamer rack. Make about 30 more coated balls in same manner (use all of meat mixture; there will be leftover rice) and arrange in 1 layer on steamer rack.

▶ Bring water to a boil and set steamer rack in skillet. Cover tightly and steam over high heat until cooked through, about 25 minutes. Check water occasionally, adding more as necessary.

GRILLED PORK TENDERLOIN AND BELGIAN ENDIVE WITH TOMATO CHILE JAM

SERVES 4

Active time: 40 min   Start to finish: 45 min

1	large garlic clove
1½	teaspoons salt
2	teaspoons minced fresh rosemary
¼	teaspoon black pepper
2½	tablespoons olive oil
2	(¾-lb) pork tenderloins
2	lb plum tomatoes, halved lengthwise
⅓	cup sugar
1	teaspoon dried hot red pepper flakes
4	Belgian endives, halved lengthwise

Special equipment: **an instant-read thermometer**

▶ Mince garlic and mash to a paste with 1 teaspoon salt using a large heavy knife, then stir together garlic paste, rosemary, pepper, and 1 tablespoon oil in a small bowl. Pat pork dry and rub all over with paste. Marinate, uncovered, at room temperature 20 minutes.

▶ While pork marinates, prepare grill for cooking. If using a charcoal grill, open vents on bottom of grill, then light

charcoal. Charcoal fire is medium-hot when you can hold your hand 5 inches above rack for 3 to 4 seconds. If using a gas grill, preheat burners on high, covered, 10 minutes, then reduce heat to moderate.

▶ While grill heats, set a box grater into a shallow dish, then rub cut sides of tomatoes against large teardrop-shaped holes to remove as much tomato pulp as possible (discard skins). Boil tomato pulp, sugar, red pepper flakes, and remaining ½ teaspoon salt in a 4-quart heavy saucepan, uncovered, stirring occasionally, until reduced to about 1½ cups, 15 to 20 minutes. Transfer tomato jam to a bowl set in a larger bowl of ice and cold water and cool to room temperature, stirring.

▶ Brush both sides of endive halves with remaining 1½ tablespoons oil and season with salt. Grill pork and endives on lightly oiled grill rack, turning over occasionally, until thermometer inserted diagonally into center of pork registers 150°F and endives are tender, 8 to 10 minutes. Transfer pork to a cutting board and let stand 5 minutes. (Internal temperature will rise to about 155°F while standing.)

▶ Serve pork with endives and tomato chile jam.

Cooks' notes:
• If you aren't able to grill outdoors, you can use a hot lightly oiled well-seasoned large ridged grill pan. Grill the pork first, then the endives, both over moderately high heat.
• You can substitute 1 (28- to 32-ounce) can whole tomatoes in juice (not drained) for plum tomatoes. Break up canned tomatoes with a spoon while boiling.

KITCHEN NOTE

DON'T OVERCOOK YOUR PORK BECAUSE YOU'RE WORRIED ABOUT TRICHINOSIS. COOKING PORK TO MEDIUM—THE FINAL INTERNAL TEMPERATURE AFTER STANDING FIVE TO TEN MINUTES SHOULD BE 150°-155°F—IS WELL BEYOND THE TEMPERATURE NEEDED TO KILL THE TRICHINELLA PARASITE (WHICH TODAY INFECTS 1 PERCENT OR LESS OF AMERICAN HOGS). THE MEAT WILL STILL BE JUICY AND TENDER, WITH A PALE PINK BLUSH.

SAUTÉED PORK CHOP WITH SAGE-CIDER CREAM SAUCE

SERVES 1

Active time: 15 min   Start to finish: 25 min

  1 (1-inch-thick) rib pork chop
  1 tablespoon extra-virgin olive oil
⅓ cup finely chopped onion
  2 tablespoons cider vinegar
½ cup water
¼ cup heavy cream
  1 teaspoon finely chopped fresh sage
1½ teaspoons finely chopped fresh flat-leaf parsley

Special equipment: **an instant-read thermometer**

▶ Pat chop dry and season with salt and pepper. Heat oil in an 8- to 10-inch heavy skillet over moderately high heat until hot but not smoking, then brown chop, turning over once, 5 to 6 minutes total. Transfer with tongs to a plate.

▶ Pour off all but 1 teaspoon fat from skillet and reduce heat to moderate, then cook onion, stirring occasionally, until softened and golden brown, 2 to 4 minutes. Add vinegar and boil until liquid is evaporated, about 3 seconds.

▶ Return chop to skillet along with any juices accumulated on plate, then add water, cream, and sage and simmer, covered, without turning, until thermometer inserted horizontally into center of chop (do not touch bone) registers 150°F, 5 to 6 minutes. Transfer chop to a clean plate, then simmer sauce, uncovered, stirring, until liquid is reduced to about 3 tablespoons, 1 to 2 minutes. Stir in parsley and salt and pepper to taste. Spoon sauce over chop.

CHEESE-STUFFED SMOKED PORK CHOPS ON WARM CABBAGE CARAWAY SLAW

SERVES 4

Active time: 25 min   Start to finish: 35 min

½ small head of cabbage, cored and thinly sliced (6 cups)
  1 carrot, coarsely grated
¼ cup cider vinegar
  1 teaspoon sugar
½ teaspoon caraway seeds, lightly crushed
½ teaspoon salt

  4 (¾-inch-thick) smoked bone-in pork chops (2 lb total)
¼ lb Gouda or Gruyère, coarsely grated (1 cup)
  2 tablespoons vegetable oil

▶ Toss together cabbage, carrot, vinegar, sugar, caraway seeds, and salt in a bowl and let stand, tossing occasionally, 15 minutes.

▶ Holding a sharp small knife parallel to a work surface, cut a wide pocket in each chop, beginning at rounded edge and cutting horizontally through to bone. Divide cheese among pockets, packing it and pressing chops flat. Pat chops dry and season with pepper.

▶ Heat 1 tablespoon oil in a wide 3- to 4-quart heavy pot over moderate heat until hot but not smoking, then cook slaw, tossing frequently, until cabbage is crisp-tender, 5 to 7 minutes.

▶ Heat remaining tablespoon oil in a 12-inch heavy skillet over moderately high heat until hot but not smoking, then sauté chops, turning over once, until browned, 2 to 4 minutes total. Cover skillet and cook chops until just heated through and cheese is melted, about 3 minutes more.

▶ Divide slaw among 4 plates and top with chops.

LAMB

MIDDLE EASTERN SPICED LAMB STEAKS WITH POACHED QUINCE

SERVES 4

Active time: 25 min   Start to finish: 45 min

If you aren't familiar with quinces, you might mistake them for hard, yellow apples. They are too tart to eat raw, but become fragrantly delicious (and a lovely shade of pink) when cooked with sugar.

For quince and sauce

2½ cups water
¾ cup sugar
  1 teaspoon fresh lemon juice
  1 quince (about 10 oz), peeled, quartered, cored, and cut into ½-inch pieces

For lamb

  2 (¾-inch-thick) bone-in lamb steaks from leg (1½ lb total), trimmed of excess fat

¾ teaspoon salt
¼ teaspoon black pepper
¼ teaspoon ground cumin
¼ teaspoon ground coriander
⅛ teaspoon ground cinnamon
1 tablespoon olive oil
1 teaspoon fresh lemon juice, or to taste

Poach quince:

▶ Bring water, sugar, and lemon juice to a simmer in a 2- to 2½-quart saucepan, stirring until sugar is dissolved, then add quince. Cut out a round of parchment or wax paper to fit just inside saucepan and cover quince directly with parchment or wax paper. Simmer, gently stirring once or twice, until quince is tender, about 35 minutes. Drain quince in a sieve set over a bowl and reserve ½ cup syrup for sauce.

Cook lamb (10 minutes before quince is done simmering):

▶ Pat lamb dry. Stir together salt, pepper, cumin, coriander, and cinnamon in a small bowl, then sprinkle spice mixture all over lamb. Heat oil in a 12-inch heavy skillet over moderately high heat until hot but not smoking, then cook lamb 4 minutes. Turn over and cook 3 minutes more for medium-rare. Transfer lamb to a cutting board and let stand 5 minutes.

Make sauce while lamb stands:

▶ Reduce heat to moderate and add reserved quince syrup to skillet, then boil, stirring and scraping up any brown bits, until liquid is reduced by about half, about 2 minutes. Transfer sauce to a gravy boat or small bowl and stir in lemon juice and salt to taste.

▶ Thinly slice lamb and serve with quince and sauce.

KITCHEN NOTE

LAMB LOIN CHOPS ARE SMALLER AND MORE EXPENSIVE THAN CHOPS FROM THE RACK, BUT THEY ARE A BIT MORE TENDER. WE PREFER HIGH-HEAT METHODS FOR COOKING EITHER KIND OF CHOP—GRILLING, BROILING, AND SAUTÉING ALL WORK WELL.

GRILLED CHARMOULA LAMB CHOPS
SERVES 1
Active time: 30 min   Start to finish: 1 hr (includes marinating)

This recipe makes more charmoula—*a Moroccan herb and spice paste—than you'll need. You can use the leftover to rub on chicken or salmon before grilling.*

1 small onion, chopped
½ cup loosely packed fresh cilantro sprigs
½ cup loosely packed fresh flat-leaf parsley leaves
2 small garlic cloves, finely chopped
¼ cup olive oil
2 teaspoons fresh lemon juice
¾ teaspoon salt
¾ teaspoon ground cumin
½ teaspoon sweet paprika
⅛ teaspoon cayenne
2 (1¼-inch-thick) loin lamb chops (10 oz total), trimmed

▶ Blend all ingredients except lamb chops in a blender until smooth, about 1 minute. Pat chops dry and transfer to a plate, then rub chops all over with 2 tablespoons *charmoula* and marinate, covered, at room temperature 30 minutes.

▶ While chops marinate, prepare grill for cooking. If using a charcoal grill, open vents on bottom of grill, then light charcoal. Charcoal fire is medium-hot when you can hold your hand 5 inches above rack for 3 to 4 seconds. If using a gas grill, preheat burners on high, covered, 10 minutes, then reduce heat to moderate.

▶ Grill chops, covered only if using a gas grill, on lightly oiled grill rack, turning over once, until medium-rare, about 8 minutes total. Transfer to a plate and let stand, loosely covered, 10 minutes.

Cooks' notes:
• If you aren't able to grill outdoors, chops can be cooked in a hot lightly oiled well-seasoned ridged grill pan over moderate heat.
• *Charmoula* keeps, its surface covered with plastic wrap, 1 week. It will lose its bright green color after a couple of days.

MOROCCAN LAMB AND EGGPLANT MATZO PIE WITH SPICY TOMATO SAUCE

SERVES 8 (MAIN COURSE)

Active time: 1¼ hr   Start to finish: 1¾ hr

  8   tablespoons olive oil plus additional for brushing
       on matzo
  1   medium onion, finely chopped
1½   lb ground lamb
  3   garlic cloves, finely chopped
2½   teaspoons salt
1½   teaspoons *ras-el-hanout* (Moroccan spice blend;
       recipe follows, or see Sources)
  1   teaspoon dried oregano, crumbled
  1   teaspoon dried mint, crumbled
  ½   teaspoon black pepper
  ¼   teaspoon cinnamon
  2   (28- to 32-oz) cans whole tomatoes in juice,
       chopped (6 cups), reserving juice
  2   lb eggplant, peeled and cut crosswise into
       ⅓-inch slices
  6   matzos (6 inches square)
  ¼   teaspoon cayenne
  ¾   teaspoon sugar

Make lamb filling:

▶ Heat 3 tablespoons oil in a 12-inch heavy skillet (2 inches deep) over moderately high heat until hot but not smoking, then sauté onion, stirring occasionally, until golden, about 5 minutes. Add lamb and sauté, stirring and breaking up lumps, until no longer pink, about 5 minutes. Add two thirds of garlic, 1½ teaspoons salt, and 1 teaspoon *ras-el-hanout* with oregano, mint, pepper, and cinnamon, then sauté, stirring, 1 minute.

▶ Stir in 4 cups tomatoes with some of juice (reserving remaining tomatoes and juice for sauce) and simmer, uncovered, stirring occasionally, until slightly thickened, 10 to 12 minutes.

Roast eggplant and assemble pie:

▶ Preheat broiler.

▶ Toss eggplant slices with 4 tablespoons oil and ½ teaspoon salt in a bowl. Brush a large shallow baking pan (½ to 1 inch deep) generously with oil and arrange as many slices as possible in 1 layer. Broil, in batches if necessary, 5 to 7 inches from heat, turning slices over as they brown (about halfway through broiling), until tender, 12 to 15 minutes total.

▶ Put oven rack in middle position and preheat oven to 350°F.

▶ Soak matzos, 1 or 2 at a time, in a pan of warm water until matzos are slightly softened but still hold their shape, 1 to 1½ minutes. Let excess water drip off and transfer matzos to paper towels or kitchen towels to drain.

▶ Arrange 2 matzos side by side in a generously oiled 13- by 9- by 2-inch (3-quart) baking dish to nearly cover bottom. Spread 3 cups lamb filling over matzos in pan. Arrange 2 matzos side by side on top, then spread remaining filling over them. Arrange eggplant slices in 1 layer over filling (overlapping slices slightly if necessary), then arrange remaining 2 matzos on top and brush with oil. Bake, covered with foil, 20 minutes, then remove foil and continue to bake until filling is hot, about 10 minutes more.

Make tomato sauce while pie bakes:

▶ Purée remaining 2 cups chopped tomatoes with juice in a blender. Heat remaining tablespoon oil in cleaned skillet over moderate heat, then cook cayenne, remaining garlic, and remaining ½ teaspoon each salt and *ras-el-hanout*, stirring, until garlic is golden, about 1 minute. Add tomato purée and sugar and simmer, uncovered, stirring occasionally, until slightly thickened, 4 to 6 minutes.

Cooks' note:

• Lamb filling and tomato sauce can be made 1 day ahead and cooled completely, then chilled separately, covered. Bring to room temperature before using.

KITCHEN NOTE

MORE EXOTIC VERSIONS OF **RAS-EL-HANOUT** MAY BE FOUND IN MOROCCO AND OTHER PARTS OF NORTH AFRICA, BUT OUR MIX OF SUPERMARKET SPICES WORKS JUST FINE. THIS VIBRANT SPICE BLEND MAKES AN EXCELLENT ADDITION TO LAMB BURGERS OR ROASTED CHICKEN. STORE IN AN AIR-TIGHT CONTAINER IN A COOL, DARK, DRY PLACE.

RAS-EL-HANOUT
(Moroccan Spice Blend)

MAKES 2 TABLESPOONS

Active time: 5 min   Start to finish: 5 min

- 1 teaspoon ground cumin
- 1 teaspoon ground ginger
- 1 teaspoon salt
- ¾ teaspoon black pepper
- ½ teaspoon ground cinnamon
- ½ teaspoon ground coriander
- ½ teaspoon cayenne
- ½ teaspoon ground allspice
- ¼ teaspoon ground cloves

▶ Whisk together all ingredients in a small bowl until combined well.

LAMB AND ORZO STUFFED PEPPER WITH CHUNKY TOMATO SAUCE

SERVES 1

Active time: 25 min   Start to finish: 55 min

- 1 tablespoon plus 1 teaspoon extra-virgin olive oil
- 1 small orange bell pepper with stem (6 to 8 oz)
- 1 medium onion, coarsely chopped
- ¼ teaspoon salt
- 3 tablespoons orzo (1¼ oz)
- ¼ lb ground lamb
- 1½ tablespoons chopped fresh dill
- 2 medium tomatoes, coarsely chopped (1 cup)

▶ Put oven rack in middle position and preheat oven to 425°F. Oil a 9-inch glass or ceramic pie plate with 1 teaspoon oil.

▶ Halve bell pepper lengthwise through stem, then discard ribs and seeds.

▶ Cook onion with salt in remaining tablespoon oil in a 10-inch heavy skillet over moderate heat, stirring occasionally, until softened and beginning to brown, 7 to 9 minutes.

▶ While onion is cooking, cook orzo in a 2-quart pot of boiling salted water (see Tips, page 8) until al dente. Reserve ¼ cup cooking water, then drain orzo in a sieve.

▶ Spread half of onion in pie plate. Add lamb to remaining onion in skillet and cook, breaking up large clumps with a fork, until meat is no longer pink, about 3 minutes. Remove from heat and stir in orzo, reserved cooking water, 1 tablespoon dill, and salt and pepper to taste.

▶ Stir tomatoes into onion in pie plate and season with salt and pepper. Nestle bell pepper halves, cut sides up, in tomato and onion mixture and season with salt and pepper. Divide lamb mixture between bell pepper halves, then cover pie plate with a sheet of oiled foil (oiled side down) and bake until pepper is tender when pierced with a fork, 25 to 30 minutes. Sprinkle with remaining ½ tablespoon dill.

Cooks' note:
• If you have to buy more than the amount of ground lamb needed for this recipe, use the leftover meat to make a juicy lamb burger a day or two later.

POULTRY

CHICKEN

BRAISED CHICKEN WITH CELERY ROOT AND GARLIC

SERVES 4
Active time: 20 min   Start to finish: 45 min

Cooking the garlic inside the skin not only saves time but also mellows the harshness of its flavor and results in tender cloves that can be peeled easily. Squeeze the cloves out of their skins and eat them with the chicken and the bread.

- 3 lb chicken parts such as breasts and thighs (with skin and bone) and drumsticks
- 1¼ teaspoons salt
- ½ teaspoon black pepper
- 1 tablespoon olive oil
- 1 tablespoon unsalted butter
- 1 celery root (sometimes called celeriac; 1¼ lb), peeled with a sharp knife and cut into ¾-inch cubes
- 1 head garlic, cloves separated and left unpeeled
- 1¼ cups reduced-sodium chicken broth (10 fl oz)
- 2 fresh thyme sprigs

Accompaniment: **crusty bread**
Garnish: **fresh thyme**

▶ Pat chicken dry and sprinkle all over with salt and pepper. Heat oil in a 12-inch heavy skillet over moderately high heat until hot but not smoking, then brown chicken, starting skin sides down, turning over once, 8 to 10 minutes total. Transfer to a plate and pour off all but 1 tablespoon fat from skillet.
▶ Add butter to skillet and heat over moderately high heat until foam subsides, then sauté celery root and garlic, stirring frequently, until celery root is browned, about 5 minutes.
▶ Add broth and thyme and deglaze skillet by boiling, stirring and scraping up any brown bits, 1 minute. Return chicken, skin sides up, to skillet along with any juices accumulated on plate, then reduce heat and simmer, covered, until chicken is cooked through, 15 to 20 minutes for white meat, about 25 minutes for dark meat. Transfer chicken to a serving bowl as cooked and keep warm, loosely covered with foil.
▶ When all chicken pieces are done cooking, transfer sauce and vegetables to bowl with chicken, discarding thyme.

ROASTED CHICKEN WITH GARLIC CONFIT

SERVES 4
Active time: 15 min   Start to finish: 40 min

- 12 garlic cloves (about 1 head), lightly smashed and peeled
- 3 fresh thyme sprigs
- ¾ cup plus 1 tablespoon olive oil
- 1 (3-lb) chicken, quartered
- 1 tablespoon unsalted butter, softened
- 2 teaspoons salt
- ½ teaspoon black pepper

▶ Put oven rack in upper third of oven and preheat oven to 500°F.
▶ Cook garlic and thyme in ¾ cup oil in a 1- to 1½-quart heavy saucepan over low heat, uncovered, until garlic is very tender but not golden, about 25 minutes.
▶ While garlic cooks, pat chicken pieces dry and rub all over with butter and remaining tablespoon oil. Sprinkle all over with salt and pepper. Arrange chicken, skin sides up, in a shallow baking pan and roast 20 minutes.
▶ Transfer garlic to a small bowl along with 1 tablespoon garlic oil and mash with a fork. Spread mashed garlic over skin of roasted chicken, then return chicken to oven and roast until just cooked through and skin is crisp, about 5 minutes more.

Cooks' notes:
• Garlic cloves can be cooked 1 week ahead and kept in oil, covered and chilled.
• Leftover garlic oil keeps, covered and chilled, 1 week. It can be used for sautéing greens or tossing with pasta.

CHICKEN IN ALMOND SAUCE

SERVES 4
Active time: 45 min   Start to finish: 45 min

- ¾ cup sliced almonds
- 6 skinless boneless chicken breast halves (2 lb total)
- 1 teaspoon salt
- 1 (3-inch) cinnamon stick
- 1 teaspoon dried oregano (preferably Mexican), crumbled
- 2 Turkish bay leaves or 1 California
- 2 tablespoons vegetable oil
- 3 bacon slices, chopped
- 1 cup chopped onion
- 1 tablespoon chopped garlic
- 1 cup reduced-sodium chicken broth or water
- ½ teaspoon black pepper
- 1 tablespoon chopped fresh flat-leaf parsley

▸ Put oven rack in middle position and preheat oven to 375°F.

▸ Spread ¼ cup almonds on a baking sheet and toast in oven until golden, 8 to 10 minutes.

▸ Meanwhile, finely grind remaining ½ cup almonds in a food processor, about 1 minute (don't grind to a paste).

▸ Pat chicken dry and sprinkle with ½ teaspoon salt.

▸ Heat a dry 12-inch heavy skillet over moderate heat, then toast ground almonds, cinnamon stick, oregano, and bay leaves, stirring constantly, until almonds are pale golden, about 2 minutes. Transfer to a bowl and wipe skillet clean.

▸ Heat oil in skillet over high heat until hot but not smoking, then sauté chicken, turning over once, until golden, about 5 minutes total. Transfer chicken to a plate.

▸ Add bacon to skillet and cook over moderate heat, stirring, until bacon begins to render fat and turn golden, about 1 minute. Add onion and garlic and cook, stirring occasionally, until golden, about 3 minutes. Stir in ground almond mixture and chicken broth and boil, stirring and scraping up brown bits, 1 minute. Stir in pepper and remaining ½ teaspoon salt. Add chicken, turning to coat, then reduce heat to moderate and simmer, covered, until chicken is just cooked through, about 5 minutes. Stir in parsley and sliced almonds and discard cinnamon stick and bay leaves.

▸ Serve chicken with sauce spooned on top.

CAJUN CHICKEN STEW

SERVES 6
Active time: 1¼ hr   Start to finish: 1¾ hr

- 3 to 6 tablespoons vegetable oil
- 1 (3- to 3½-lb) chicken, cut into serving pieces
- 2½ teaspoons salt
- ½ cup all-purpose flour
- 1 medium onion, chopped
- 1 medium green bell pepper, chopped
- 1 celery rib, chopped
- 3 cups water
- ¼ teaspoon cayenne, or to taste
- ¾ cup thinly sliced scallion greens

Accompaniment: **cooked white rice**

▸ Heat 3 tablespoons oil in a 4- to 5-quart heavy pot (preferably cast-iron) over moderately high heat until hot but not smoking. Pat chicken dry and sprinkle with salt. Brown chicken in 4 batches, turning, about 5 minutes per batch, transferring as browned to a large bowl.

▸ Add enough of remaining oil to pot to total ¼ cup fat, then stir in flour with a flat metal or wooden spatula and cook over moderately low heat, scraping back and forth constantly (not stirring), until roux is the color of milk chocolate, 10 to 20 minutes. Add onion, bell pepper, and celery and cook, scraping back and forth occasionally, until onion is softened, about 8 minutes.

▸ Add water to roux mixture and bring to a boil, stirring occasionally until roux is incorporated. (Roux will appear curdled initially, but will come together as it reaches a boil.) Add chicken and any juices accumulated in bowl, then simmer, partially covered, until chicken is cooked through, 30 to 35 minutes. Stir in cayenne, scallion greens, and salt to taste.

Cooks' note:

• Stew improves in flavor when made 1 day ahead (without scallion greens) and cooled completely, uncovered, then chilled, covered. Reheat, then stir in scallion greens.

GRILLED CHICKEN BREASTS IN SPICED YOGURT

SERVES 6
Active time: 15 min   Start to finish: 35 min

- 2¼ cups plain yogurt (18 oz; preferably whole-milk)
- 3 tablespoons olive oil
- 2½ tablespoons fresh lemon juice
- 2 teaspoons salt
- 1 tablespoon chili powder
- ¾ teaspoon ground cumin
- ¾ teaspoon ground coriander
- ¾ teaspoon black pepper
- ¼ teaspoon cinnamon
- 6 skinless boneless chicken breast halves (2¼ to 2½ lb total)
- 1 cup loosely packed small fresh mint leaves
- 2 tablespoons minced shallot

▸ Whisk together 1 cup yogurt, 2 tablespoons olive oil, 1 tablespoon lemon juice, salt, and spices, then add chicken and turn until coated well. Marinate at room temperature 20 minutes.

▸ While chicken marinates, prepare grill for cooking. If using a charcoal grill, open vents on bottom of grill, then light charcoal. Charcoal fire is medium-hot when you can hold your hand 5 inches above rack for 3 to 4 seconds. If using a gas grill, preheat burners on high, covered, 10 minutes, then reduce heat to moderate.

▸ While grill heats, whisk together remaining 1¼ cups yogurt, remaining 1½ tablespoons lemon juice, and salt to taste.

▸ Grill chicken (discard marinade), covered only if using gas grill, on lightly oiled grill rack, turning over occasionally, until just cooked through, 10 to 12 minutes total. Transfer chicken to a platter.

▸ Toss together mint, shallot, and remaining tablespoon oil in a small bowl. Drizzle chicken with yogurt sauce and top with mint salad.

Cooks' note:

• If you aren't able to grill outdoors, chicken can be cooked in a hot lightly oiled well-seasoned large ridged grill pan over moderate heat.

CHICKEN SCHNITZEL WITH CAPERS AND PARSLEY

SERVES 4
Active time: 25 min   Start to finish: 40 min

- 4 (¼-inch-thick) chicken cutlets (1¼ to 1½ lb total)
- ½ cup all-purpose flour
- 1 teaspoon salt
- ¼ teaspoon black pepper
- 2 large eggs
- 1 cup plain fine dry bread crumbs
- 4 to 6 tablespoons vegetable oil
- 2½ tablespoons unsalted butter
- 2 tablespoons drained bottled capers, rinsed and patted dry
- 2 tablespoons chopped fresh flat-leaf parsley

Accompaniment: **lemon wedges**

▸ Preheat oven to 200°F. Put an ovenproof platter in oven to warm.

▸ Gently pound each cutlet between 2 sheets of plastic wrap to ⅛-inch thickness with flat side of a meat pounder or with a rolling pin.

▸ Stir together flour, salt, and pepper in a shallow bowl or a pie plate. Whisk together eggs and a pinch of salt in another shallow bowl, then put bread crumbs in a third shallow bowl.

▸ Pat chicken dry and dredge in seasoned flour, shaking off excess. Dip in eggs, letting excess drip off, then dredge in bread crumbs, coating completely. Transfer to a wax-paper-lined tray and chill 10 minutes.

▸ Heat 2 tablespoons oil in a 12-inch heavy nonstick skillet over moderately high heat until hot but not smoking, then fry cutlets in 2 or 3 batches (without crowding), turning over once, until golden brown and just cooked through, about 3 minutes per batch. (Add 2 tablespoons oil to skillet between batches.) Drain cutlets on paper towels, then transfer to platter in oven to keep warm.

▸ Add butter and capers to skillet and heat over moderate heat, swirling skillet, until butter is melted. Stir in parsley and pour sauce over cutlets.

TO CUT A CHICKEN INTO EIGHT PIECES
(ONE PAIR EACH OF DRUMSTICKS, THIGHS, BREASTS, AND WINGS), START BY REMOVING THE BACKBONE. SEPARATE THE LEGS FROM THE BREAST SECTION BY PULLING A DRUMSTICK TOWARD YOU AND CUTTING OFF THE WHOLE LEG (THIGH AND DRUMSTICK), THEN CUT DRUMSTICK FROM THIGH AT THE JOINT. HALVE THE BREAST SECTION BY PUTTING IT SKIN SIDE DOWN AND CUTTING STRAIGHT THROUGH THE BREASTBONE. EITHER CUT EACH BREAST HALF DIAGONALLY (FOR A MEATIER WING) OR SIMPLY CUT OFF THE WING AT THE JOINT.

BAKED CHICKEN WITH WHITE BEANS AND TOMATOES

SERVES 4

Active time: 35 min   Start to finish: 1 hr

6	bacon slices (¼ lb total), cut into 1-inch pieces
4	large chicken thighs with skin and bone (1½ lb total)
¼	teaspoon black pepper
¾	teaspoon salt
2	medium onions, chopped (1½ cups)
1	(14- to 16-oz) can stewed tomatoes including juice
2	(15- to 16-oz) cans small white beans, rinsed and drained

▶ Put oven rack in middle position and preheat oven to 350°F.

▶ Cook bacon in a 10-inch heavy ovenproof skillet over moderate heat, stirring occasionally, until browned and crisp, about 8 minutes. Transfer bacon with a slotted spoon to paper towels to drain, reserving fat in skillet.

▶ While bacon browns, pat chicken dry and season with pepper and ½ teaspoon salt. Brown chicken in fat in skillet over moderately high heat, turning over once, about 8 minutes total, then transfer chicken with tongs to paper towels to drain.

▶ Pour off all but 3 tablespoons fat from skillet and reduce heat to moderate. Cook onions in skillet with remaining ¼ teaspoon salt, stirring and scraping up any brown bits, until golden brown, about 10 minutes. Stir in tomatoes (with

juice) and boil, uncovered, 3 minutes, to concentrate juices slightly. Stir in bacon and beans and bring to a simmer. Nestle chicken, skin side up, in beans and bake, uncovered, until chicken is cooked through, 20 to 25 minutes.

Cooks' note:
• If you don't have an ovenproof skillet, after simmering bean mixture transfer it to a shallow 2- to 3-quart baking dish, then add chicken and bake as directed above.

CHICKEN IN DILL MUSTARD SAUCE

SERVES 4

Active time: 20 min   Start to finish: 45 min

¼	cup all-purpose flour
½	teaspoon salt
½	teaspoon black pepper
4	whole chicken legs (2 lb total)
3	tablespoons vegetable oil
¾	cup chopped shallots
½	cup dry white wine
1	cup reduced-sodium chicken broth
2	teaspoons whole-grain or coarse-grain mustard
¼	cup chopped fresh dill

▶ Whisk together flour, ¼ teaspoon salt, and ¼ teaspoon pepper in a pie plate or shallow bowl. Pat chicken dry, then dredge legs, 1 at a time, in flour, shaking off excess. Transfer to a sheet of wax paper, arranging chicken in 1 layer.

▶ Heat oil in a 12-inch heavy skillet over moderately high heat until hot but not smoking, then brown chicken, skin sides down first, turning over once, 6 to 8 minutes total. Transfer chicken to a plate, then pour off all but 1 tablespoon fat from skillet.

▶ Add shallots to skillet and sauté, stirring occasionally, until golden brown, 2 to 3 minutes. Add wine and deglaze skillet by boiling, stirring and scraping up brown bits. Add broth, mustard, remaining ¼ teaspoon salt, and remaining ¼ teaspoon pepper. Bring to a simmer, then return chicken to skillet, skin sides up, along with any juices from plate, and cook over moderate heat, covered, until chicken is cooked through, about 25 minutes. Transfer chicken to a platter and boil sauce until reduced to about 1 cup and slightly thickened, 3 to 5 minutes. Remove from heat and stir in dill, then pour sauce over chicken.

FIVE-SPICE CHICKEN WINGS

SERVES 4 (MAIN COURSE)

Active time: 15 min   Start to finish: 35 min

1½   teaspoons minced garlic
1½   teaspoons Chinese five-spice powder
1¼   teaspoons salt
1½   teaspoons soy sauce
3   lb chicken wings (about 16)

▸ Preheat broiler and oil rack of a broiler pan.
▸ Stir together garlic, five-spice powder, salt, and soy sauce in a large bowl.
▸ Cut off and discard tips from chicken wings with kitchen shears or a large heavy knife, then halve wings at joint. Pat dry and add to spice mixture, tossing to coat.
▸ Arrange wings in 1 layer on broiler pan and broil 6 to 7 inches from heat, turning over once, until browned and cooked through, 16 to 20 minutes total.

ASSORTED FOWL

CORNISH HENS WITH SWEET VERMOUTH GARLIC GLAZE

SERVES 4

Active time: 20 min   Start to finish: 45 min

2   (1½-lb) Cornish hens, halved lengthwise through breast
½   teaspoon salt
¼   teaspoon black pepper
1   cup sweet (red) vermouth
6   large garlic cloves, quartered lengthwise
4   fresh or dried thyme sprigs
1   cup water

▸ Put oven rack in middle position and preheat oven to 450°F.
▸ Pat hens dry and sprinkle with salt and pepper. Roast, cut sides down, in a large shallow baking pan (1 inch deep) until just cooked through, about 30 minutes.
▸ While hens roast, simmer vermouth, garlic, thyme, and ½ cup water, uncovered, in a 2-quart heavy saucepan until garlic is soft, about 15 minutes. Discard thyme. Mash garlic

into sauce with a fork and simmer until reduced to a glaze (about 3 tablespoons).
▸ Brush glaze onto hens and roast 5 minutes more. Pour remaining ½ cup water into saucepan, swirling to dissolve any remaining glaze, and reserve.
▸ Transfer hens to a serving dish and let stand, loosely covered with foil, 5 minutes. Straddle baking pan across 2 burners, then add reserved liquid from saucepan and deglaze baking pan by boiling over moderate heat, stirring and scraping up brown bits, until reduced slightly, 2 to 3 minutes. Season pan juices with salt and pepper and pour over hens.

PAN-GRILLED PAILLARDS OF DUCK

SERVES 4

Active time: 40 min   Start to finish: 40 min

1   whole boneless Moulard duck breast with skin (2 lb total; see Sources and cooks' note, below), halved
2   tablespoons water
2   teaspoons salt
2   teaspoons ground ginger
1   teaspoon black pepper
1   teaspoon curry powder
1   teaspoon cinnamon
2   navel oranges, cut into ¼-inch-thick slices

Special equipment: a well-seasoned ridged grill pan

▸ Pull skin off duck and thinly slice skin, then cook skin with water in a 10- to 12-inch heavy skillet over moderately low heat, stirring occasionally, until fat is rendered and cracklings are browned and crisp, about 15 minutes. Drain in a sieve set over a bowl and reserve rendered fat. Spread cracklings on paper towels to drain.
▸ Remove tender from underside of each breast half if attached and reserve for another use, then trim silver membrane from each breast half. Halve each breast half horizontally to make a total of 4 thin pieces. Gently pound each piece between 2 sheets of plastic wrap to an even ¼-inch thickness with flat side of a meat pounder or with a rolling pin.
▸ Heat grill pan over moderately high heat until hot but not smoking.
▸ While pan heats, stir together salt, ginger, pepper, curry,

and cinnamon in a small bowl. Sprinkle each duck paillard with ½ teaspoon spice mixture per side and lightly brush with some rendered duck fat. Grill duck, turning over once, 3 to 4 minutes total for medium-rare, then transfer to a cutting board and let stand, loosely covered with foil.
▶ While paillards stand, lightly brush orange slices with some rendered duck fat, then sprinkle with remaining spice mixture. Grill orange slices, turning over once, until just warmed through and grill marks appear, about 1 minute total, then transfer with duck to a platter.
▶ Season cracklings with salt and pepper and sprinkle over duck and oranges.

Cooks' note:
• You can substitute 2 whole boneless Long Island duck breasts. Remove skin from duck breasts but do not halve or pound. Cook breasts 2 minutes per side.

TURKEY CHEDDAR BURGERS
SERVES 4
Active time: 20 min   Start to finish: 35 min

For burgers
  1 large shallot, finely chopped
  2 tablespoons olive oil
  ½ teaspoon salt
  ¼ teaspoon black pepper
1½ lb ground turkey (not labeled "all breast meat")
  5 oz extra-sharp Cheddar, cut into 4 (½-inch-thick) slices
  4 hamburger or kaiser rolls
For sun-dried tomato mayonnaise
  ¼ cup oil-packed sun-dried tomatoes, drained
  1 tablespoon water
  2 teaspoons cider vinegar
  ¼ teaspoon salt
  ¼ cup mayonnaise

Accompaniment: **lettuce leaves**

Make burgers:
▶ Put oven rack in middle position and preheat oven to 350°F.
▶ Cook shallot in oil with salt and pepper in an 8-inch heavy skillet over moderate heat, stirring occasionally, until golden, 2 to 3 minutes, then transfer to a bowl. Add turkey and mix gently but thoroughly.
▶ Turn out turkey mixture onto a sheet of wax paper and divide into 8 equal mounds. Pat 1 mound into a 4-inch patty and top with 1 piece of cheese, then put a second mound on top, patting it onto other patty to enclose cheese. Pinch edges together to seal and shape into a single patty. Make 3 more burgers in same manner.
▶ Heat an oiled well-seasoned ridged grill pan over moderately high heat until hot but not smoking, then grill burgers, turning over once, until just cooked through (no longer pink), 8 to 9 minutes total.
▶ While burgers cook, heat rolls on a baking sheet in oven until crusty, about 5 minutes. Transfer rolls to a rack to cool slightly.
Make mayonnaise and assemble burgers:
▶ Purée tomatoes with water, vinegar, and salt in a blender or mini food processor, scraping down sides as necessary, then blend in mayonnaise.
▶ Cut rolls in half horizontally (if necessary) and spread cut sides with tomato mayonnaise. Serve burgers on rolls with lettuce.

KITCHEN NOTE
WHEN MAKING TURKEY BURGERS, LOOK FOR **GROUND TURKEY** THAT IS NOT LABELED "ALL BREAST MEAT." A BURGER THAT IS MADE FROM ALL WHITE MEAT WILL DRY OUT FASTER THAN ONE MADE WITH A MIX OF BOTH WHITE AND DARK MEATS. HOWEVER, WE THINK THE BEST TURKEY BURGERS ARE MADE WITH ALL DARK MEAT.

BRUNCH AND SANDWICHES

BRUNCH DISHES

CHEESE MATZO BLINTZES WITH ASPARAGUS AND DILL

SERVES 4 TO 6

Active time: 1¼ hr   Start to finish: 2½ hr

For crêpes

2½ cups whole milk

1⅓ cups matzo meal

4 large eggs

¼ cup vegetable oil plus additional for
    brushing skillet

½ teaspoon salt

For filling

1 lb medium asparagus, trimmed

3 cups small-curd cottage cheese
   (4% milkfat; 24 oz)

¼ cup finely chopped fresh dill

1 large egg, lightly beaten

½ teaspoon black pepper

¼ teaspoon salt

For topping

½ stick (¼ cup) unsalted butter

2 bunches scallions, trimmed and cut into
   1-inch pieces

¼ teaspoon salt

¼ teaspoon black pepper

2 tablespoons chopped fresh dill

Make crêpes:

▶Blend milk, matzo meal, eggs, oil, and salt in a blender until smooth. Let batter stand 30 minutes.

▶Stir batter before using. Lightly brush a 10-inch nonstick skillet with oil and heat over moderately high heat until hot but not smoking. Holding skillet off heat, pour in ⅓ cup batter, immediately tilting and rotating skillet to coat bottom. (If batter sets before skillet is coated, reduce heat slightly for next crêpe.) Return skillet to heat and cook crêpe until top is set and edge and bottom are golden, about 1 minute.

Remove skillet from heat and loosen edge of crêpe with a flexible heatproof spatula. Quickly invert skillet over a plate to release crêpe. Make 11 more crêpes in same manner, brushing skillet lightly with oil for each and stacking crêpes on plate as cooked.

▶Put oven rack in middle position and preheat oven to 350°F.

Make filling:

▶Cook asparagus in a wide 4- to 5-quart pot of boiling salted water (see Tips, page 8), uncovered, until just tender, about 5 minutes. Transfer asparagus with a slotted spoon to a cutting board to cool. Cut off and reserve tips, then finely chop stalks.

▶Stir together cottage cheese, chopped stalks, dill, egg, pepper, and salt.

Assemble blintzes:

▶Put 1 crêpe, paler side up, on a work surface and spread a scant ⅓ cup of filling in a horizontal line just below center of crêpe, leaving a ¾-inch border at each end. Fold in sides of crêpe over ends of filling, then, beginning at bottom, roll up to enclose filling. Transfer, seam side down, to a lightly buttered 15- by 10-inch shallow baking pan. Fill and transfer remaining 11 crêpes in same manner.

▶Bake blintzes, covered with foil, until filling is hot, 30 to 35 minutes.

Make topping just before blintzes are ready to serve:

▶Heat butter in a 10- to 12-inch skillet over moderate heat until foam subsides. Add scallions and cook, stirring, until tender, about 5 minutes. Stir in asparagus tips, salt, and pepper and cook, stirring, until asparagus is heated through, 1 to 2 minutes. Remove from heat and stir in dill. Spoon topping over blintzes.

Cooks' notes:

• If you are new to making crêpes, you may want to make an extra half batch of batter to allow for a few imperfect crêpes.

• Crêpes can be made 1 day ahead and cooled completely, then wrapped tightly in plastic wrap and chilled.

• Asparagus can be cooked (but not chopped) 1 day ahead and chilled, covered.

POACHED EGGS WITH ROASTED TOMATOES AND PORTABELLAS

SERVES 4

Active time: 20 min Start to finish: 20 min

  4 (3-inch-wide) portabella mushroom caps,
      stems discarded
  2 plum tomatoes, halved lengthwise
  3 tablespoons olive oil
  ½ teaspoon salt
  ¼ teaspoon black pepper
  1 teaspoon distilled white vinegar
  4 large eggs
  ½ teaspoon balsamic vinegar
  4 thin slices Fontina cheese
  1 tablespoon finely chopped fresh chives

▸Preheat broiler.

▸Brush mushrooms and tomatoes with oil and sprinkle with salt and pepper. Arrange mushrooms, stemmed sides down, and tomato halves, cut sides up, on a broiler pan.

▸Broil vegetables about 6 inches from heat, turning over mushrooms halfway through cooking, until tender and tomatoes are slightly charred, about 7 minutes total. (Leave broiler on.)

▸While vegetables broil, fill a deep 10-inch skillet with 1¼ inches cold water. Add white vinegar and bring to a simmer.

▸Break 1 egg into a cup, then slide egg into simmering water. Repeat with remaining eggs, spacing them in skillet, and poach at a bare simmer until whites are firm but yolks are still runny, 2 to 3 minutes.

▸Gently transfer eggs with a slotted spoon to paper towels to drain and season with salt and pepper.

▸Sprinkle stemmed sides of mushrooms with balsamic vinegar, then put 1 tomato half, cut side up, on each mushroom and top with an egg. Cover eggs with cheese slices and broil until cheese is just melted, about 1 minute. Sprinkle with chives and serve immediately.

Cooks' note:

• The eggs in this recipe are not fully cooked, which may be of concern if salmonella is a problem in your area. You can substitute pasteurized eggs (in the shell) or cook eggs until yolks are set.

KITCHEN NOTE

USING THE FRESHEST EGGS POSSIBLE IS THE KEY TO **GREAT POACHED EGGS**. FRESHER EGGS HAVE THICKER WHITES AND STRONGER YOLK MEMBRANES, WHICH KEEP THE YOLK TOGETHER; THE THICKER THE WHITE, THE BETTER IT CLINGS TO THE YOLK. ADDING A LITTLE VINEGAR TO THE POACHING WATER HELPS THE WHITE SET FASTER.

PASTA FRITTATA WITH BROCCOLI RABE AND SUN-DRIED TOMATOES

SERVES 4 TO 6

Active time: 20 min Start to finish: 45 min

  ½ lb dried linguine
  ½ lb broccoli rabe, coarsely chopped (4 cups)
  2 tablespoons olive oil
  2 oil-packed sun-dried tomatoes, drained and
      thinly sliced (1 tablespoon)
  6 large eggs
1½ oz finely grated Parmigiano-Reggiano (¾ cup;
      see Tips, page 8)
  ¼ cup whole milk
  1 teaspoon salt
  ½ teaspoon black pepper

▸Put oven rack in upper third of oven and preheat oven to 400°F.

▸Cook pasta in a 6- to 8-quart pot of boiling salted water (see Tips, page 8) according to package instructions; 2 minutes before pasta is done cooking, add broccoli rabe and cook 2 minutes. Drain pasta and broccoli rabe and pat dry.

▸Heat oil in a 10-inch heavy ovenproof nonstick skillet over high heat until hot but not smoking, then sauté pasta, broccoli rabe, and tomatoes, stirring frequently, 2 minutes. Whisk together eggs, cheese, milk, salt, and pepper and pour over pasta mixture. Transfer skillet to oven and bake until frittata is set (eggs should be just firm), 20 to 25 minutes. Transfer frittata to a cutting board and cut into wedges.

PASTRAMI SPINACH OMELETS

SERVES 4

Active time: 30 min   Start to finish: 30 min

    5 tablespoons olive oil
    2 (5-oz) bags baby spinach
    ¼ lb thinly sliced pastrami, coarsely chopped (¾ cup)
    1 oz finely grated parmesan (½ cup)
   12 large eggs
    1 teaspoon salt

▶ Heat 1 tablespoon oil in a 12-inch heavy skillet over moderate heat until hot but not smoking. Add spinach all at once and cook, stirring, until wilted, about 3 minutes. Transfer to a colander and drain, pressing lightly. Toss spinach with pastrami, ¼ cup cheese, and salt and pepper to taste in a bowl.

▶ Whisk together 3 eggs and ¼ teaspoon salt in a bowl until blended. Heat 1 tablespoon oil in an 8-inch nonstick skillet over moderate heat until hot but not smoking. Add whisked eggs and cook, lifting up cooked egg around edge occasionally to let raw egg flow underneath, until omelet is set but top is still slightly moist, 1 to 2 minutes. Spoon one fourth of spinach mixture over half of omelet and sprinkle with 1 tablespoon cheese. Fold other half of omelet over filling using a heatproof rubber spatula and transfer to a plate. Keep warm, covered with foil.

▶ Make 3 more omelets in same manner with remaining eggs, salt, oil, spinach mixture, and cheese.

BAKED FRENCH TOAST

SERVES 6

Active time: 10 min   Start to finish: 1¼ hr

       Butter for greasing baking dish
    3 cups half-and-half or whole milk
    3 large eggs
    1 teaspoon vanilla
    ⅛ teaspoon salt
    3 tablespoons sugar
   12 (¾-inch-thick) diagonally cut baguette slices
       from a day-old baguette

Accompaniment: **maple syrup, confectioners sugar, or jam**

▶ Put oven rack in middle position and preheat oven to 425°F. Generously butter a 13- by 9-inch baking dish.

▶ Whisk together half-and-half, eggs, vanilla, salt, and 2 tablespoons sugar. Arrange baguette slices in 1 layer in dish and pour custard over bread. Turn bread slices over once or twice to coat and let stand at room temperature 30 minutes.

▶ Sprinkle top evenly with remaining tablespoon sugar and bake until custard is set and top is golden brown, 30 to 35 minutes.

BIG APPLE PANCAKE

SERVES 2

Active time: 15 min   Start to finish: 30 min

    ½ stick (¼ cup) unsalted butter
    1 large sweet apple such as Gala or Golden Delicious,
       peeled, cored, and cut into ¼-inch-wide wedges
    ½ cup whole milk
    ½ cup all-purpose flour
    4 large eggs
    3 tablespoons granulated sugar
    ½ teaspoon vanilla
    ¼ teaspoon salt
       Confectioners sugar for dusting

Special equipment: **a well-seasoned 10- to 11-inch heavy cast-iron skillet or other ovenproof skillet**

▶ Put oven rack in middle position and preheat oven to 450°F.

▶ Melt butter in skillet over moderate heat, then transfer 2 tablespoons to a blender. Add apple wedges to skillet and cook, turning over once, until beginning to soften, 3 to 5 minutes.

▶ While apple cooks, add milk, flour, eggs, granulated sugar, vanilla, and salt to butter in blender and blend until smooth.

▶ Pour batter over apple and transfer skillet to oven. Bake until pancake is puffed and golden, about 15 minutes. Dust with confectioners sugar and serve immediately.

SWEET-POTATO HASH

SERVES 6

Active time: 40 min   Start to finish: 40 min

 5 tablespoons extra-virgin olive oil
 2 lb sweet potatoes, peeled and cut into ½-inch cubes
 ¾ lb hot Italian sausages, casings discarded and sausage
      coarsely crumbled
 1 cup chopped onion
 1 lb sweet Italian frying peppers, seeded and cut into
      ½-inch pieces
 ½ cup chopped fresh cilantro
 ½ teaspoon salt
 ¼ teaspoon black pepper
 6 large eggs

▶ Put oven rack in middle position and preheat oven to
200°F.
▶ Heat 2 tablespoons oil in a 12-inch nonstick heavy skillet
over moderately low heat until hot but not smoking, then
cook sweet potatoes, stirring occasionally, until tender and
browned, about 15 minutes.
▶ Meanwhile, heat 1 tablespoon oil in a 9- to 10-inch heavy
skillet over moderate heat until hot but not smoking, then
cook sausage, stirring occasionally and breaking up large
lumps, until browned, about 8 minutes. Add onion and cook,
stirring occasionally, until softened, 8 to 10 minutes, then
add frying peppers and cook, stirring occasionally, until
tender, about 5 minutes.
▶ Add sausage mixture, cilantro, salt, and pepper to potatoes
in skillet and toss to combine, then transfer to a large
shallow serving dish and keep warm in oven while preparing
eggs. (Wipe out nonstick skillet with a paper towel.)
▶ Carefully break eggs into a bowl without breaking yolks.
▶ Heat remaining 2 tablespoons oil in 12-inch nonstick
skillet over moderate heat until hot but not smoking, then
pour eggs into skillet and season with salt and pepper. Cook
eggs, covered, until edges of whites are crisp and browned
but yolks are still soft, 2 to 2½ minutes. Slide eggs onto
hash and serve immediately.

Cooks' note:
• The egg yolks in this recipe are not fully cooked. If
salmonella is a problem in your area, bake until yolks are
completely set.

SANDWICHES

GRILLED CHEDDAR AND FENNEL SANDWICHES WITH CURRY MAYO

SERVES 4

Active time: 25 min   Start to finish: 25 min

 2 tablespoons finely chopped shallot
 2 teaspoons curry powder (preferably Madras)
 1 teaspoon vegetable oil
 ½ cup mayonnaise
 1 tablespoon fresh lemon juice
 1 baguette
 1½ tablespoons unsalted butter, softened
 ½ lb extra-sharp Cheddar
 ¼ cup very thinly sliced fennel bulb (sometimes called
      anise; quartered lengthwise and cored before slicing)

▶ Cook shallot and curry powder in oil in a 12-inch heavy
nonstick skillet over moderate heat, stirring, 2 minutes, then
transfer to a small bowl and stir in mayonnaise and lemon
juice. Wipe skillet clean and set aside.
▶ Cut 16 (¼-inch-thick) diagonal slices (about 6 inches long)
from baguette. Spread 1 side of each slice with butter, then
turn over and spread opposite side with curry mayonnaise.
Cut cheese into thin slices no wider than bread slices. Divide
cheese among 8 slices of bread, then top with fennel and
remaining slices of bread, buttered sides up.
▶ Heat skillet over moderate heat until hot, then cook
sandwiches in 2 batches, turning over once and pressing
occasionally, until browned and cheese is melted, about
7 minutes per batch.

BACON AND AVOCADO SANDWICHES

SERVES 2

Active time: 20 min   Start to finish: 20 min

  6 bacon slices
  5 tablespoons mayonnaise
  3 tablespoons chopped fresh chives
  2 tablespoons chopped fresh dill
  1 firm-ripe California avocado (8 to 10 oz)
  1 teaspoon fresh lemon juice
  4 slices whole-grain bread, toasted
½ cup radish sprouts

▸Cook bacon in a 12-inch heavy skillet over moderate heat, turning occasionally, until crisp, then transfer with tongs to paper towels to drain.

▸Stir together mayonnaise, chives, dill, and salt and pepper to taste in a small bowl.

▸Halve, pit, and peel avocado, then slice lengthwise. Gently toss slices with lemon juice.

▸Make sandwiches with toast, herb mayonnaise, avocado, bacon, and sprouts, seasoning with salt and pepper.

SHRIMP AND MANGO WRAPS

SERVES 4

Active time: 30 min   Start to finish: 30 min

⅓ cup sour cream
⅓ cup mayonnaise
¼ cup chopped fresh basil
  2 tablespoons chopped fresh chives
2¼ teaspoons salt
¼ teaspoon black pepper
  1 tablespoon fresh lemon juice
1½ lb large shrimp in shell (16 to 20 per lb), peeled
     and deveined
  1 (1-lb) firm-ripe mango, peeled and cut into
     ⅓-inch cubes
  4 (10-inch) flour tortillas
  1 (6-oz) bunch watercress, tough stems discarded

▸Pulse sour cream, mayonnaise, basil, chives, ¼ teaspoon salt, and pepper in a blender until herbs are finely chopped and mixture is pale green.

▸Bring 2 quarts water with lemon juice and remaining 2 teaspoons salt to a boil in a 3-quart saucepan, then poach shrimp, uncovered, at a bare simmer until just cooked through, about 3 minutes. Transfer shrimp with a slotted spoon to a bowl of ice and cold water to stop cooking. Let shrimp chill in water 2 minutes, then drain and pat dry. Coarsely chop shrimp, then add to dressing along with mango and stir to combine.

▸Toast tortillas 1 at a time directly on burner (gas or electric) at moderately high heat, turning over and rotating with tongs, until puffed slightly and browned in spots but still flexible, 30 to 40 seconds. Transfer to a clean kitchen towel as toasted and stack, loosely wrapped in towel.

▸Divide watercress among tortillas, arranging it across middle, then top with 1¼ cups shrimp salad. Tuck in ends of wraps, then roll up tightly to enclose filling. Cut wraps in half diagonally.

CHEESESTEAK SANDWICHES

SERVES 4

Active time: 25 min   Start to finish: 30 min

  3 medium onions, thinly sliced (3 cups)
½ stick (¼ cup) unsalted butter
10 oz mushrooms, trimmed and thinly sliced (4 cups)
1½ lb sliced rare roast beef, cut into 1-inch pieces and
     pieces separated
¼ cup water
  4 (6-inch-long) sections soft Italian bread
½ lb sliced provolone or mild Cheddar

▸Preheat broiler.

▸Cook onions in butter in a 12-inch heavy skillet over moderately high heat, stirring occasionally, until pale golden, 5 to 7 minutes. Add mushrooms and cook, stirring occasionally, until mushrooms are golden, 5 to 7 minutes. Stir in beef, water, and salt and pepper to taste and cook, stirring, until heated through, about 1 minute.

▸Halve bread horizontally without cutting all the way through and open cut sides, then put bread in a shallow baking pan. Divide beef mixture evenly among bread and top with cheese. Broil about 6 inches from heat until cheese is melted, 1 to 2 minutes.

PASTA AND GRAINS

PASTA

MANICOTTI

SERVES 6
Active time: 1¼ hr Start to finish: 2 hr

For sauce
- 3 tablespoons olive oil
- 1 medium onion, chopped
- 3 garlic cloves, minced
- 2 (28- to 32-oz) cans Italian tomatoes in juice, drained, reserving juice, and finely chopped
- ½ cup water
- 1 teaspoon sugar
- 1 teaspoon salt
- ¼ cup chopped fresh basil

For crêpes
- 3 large eggs
- 1½ cups water
- 1¼ cups all-purpose flour
- ½ teaspoon salt
- 1 tablespoon unsalted butter, melted

For filling
- 2 lb fresh ricotta (3 cups)
- 2 large eggs
- 1 oz finely grated Parmigiano-Reggiano (½ cup; see Tips, page 8)
- ⅓ cup chopped fresh flat-leaf parsley
- ½ teaspoon salt
- ½ teaspoon black pepper
- ½ lb fresh mozzarella

Special equipment: **2 glass or ceramic baking dishes, one 13 by 9 inches and one 8 inches square**

Make sauce:
▶ Heat oil in a 5- to 6-quart heavy pot over moderately high heat until hot but not smoking, then sauté onion, stirring occasionally, until golden, about 6 minutes. Add garlic and sauté, stirring, until golden, about 1 minute. Add tomatoes (with juice), water, sugar, and salt and simmer, uncovered, stirring occasionally, until thickened, about 30 minutes. Stir in basil and remove from heat.

Make crêpes:
▶ Break up eggs with a wooden spoon in a bowl and stir in water until combined (don't beat). Sift in flour and salt, then stir batter until just combined. Force through a medium-mesh sieve into another bowl.
▶ Lightly brush an 8-inch nonstick skillet with melted butter and heat over moderate heat until hot. Ladle about ¼ cup batter into skillet, tilting and rotating skillet to coat bottom, then pour excess batter back into bowl. (If batter sets before skillet is coated, reduce heat slightly for next crêpe.) Cook until underside is just set and lightly browned, about 30 seconds, then invert crêpe onto a clean kitchen towel to cool completely. Make at least 11 more crêpes in same manner, brushing skillet with butter as needed and stacking crêpes in 3 piles.

Make filling and assemble manicotti:
▶ Stir together ricotta, eggs, Parmigiano-Reggiano, parsley, salt, and pepper.
▶ Put oven rack in middle position and preheat oven to 425°F.
▶ Cut mozzarella lengthwise into ¼-inch-thick sticks.
▶ Spread 2 cups sauce in larger baking dish and 1 cup in smaller one. Arrange 1 crêpe, browned side up, on a work surface, then spread about ¼ cup filling in a line across center and top with a mozzarella strip. Fold in sides to enclose filling, leaving ends open, and transfer, seam side down, to either baking dish. Fill 11 more crêpes in same manner, arranging snugly in 1 layer in both dishes (8 in larger dish and 4 in smaller). Spread 1 cup sauce over manicotti in larger dish and ½ cup in smaller dish. Tightly cover dishes with foil and bake until sauce is bubbling and filling is hot, 15 to 20 minutes.
▶ Serve remaining sauce on the side.

Cooks' note:
• Manicotti can be assembled (but not baked) 1 day ahead and chilled, covered with foil. Chill remaining sauce, covered, separately. Let manicotti stand at room temperature 15 minutes before baking, covered with foil. Reheat sauce, thinning slightly with water.

CASTELLANE WITH MASCARPONE AND ROASTED GRAPE TOMATOES

SERVES 6

Active time: 25 min   Start to finish: 45 min

  2 pt grape tomatoes or cherry tomatoes, halved lengthwise
1¼ teaspoons salt
 ¾ teaspoon black pepper
  1 lb *castellane* pasta or medium (regular) shells
1¼ cups mascarpone cheese (from a 1-lb container)
  2 oz finely grated Parmigiano-Reggiano (1 cup; see Tips, page 8)
 ¼ cup minced fresh chives

▸ Put oven rack in upper third of oven and preheat oven to 400°F. Line a large shallow baking pan (1 inch deep) with foil and butter foil.

▸ Arrange tomatoes, cut sides up, in pan and sprinkle with ½ teaspoon salt and ¼ teaspoon pepper. Roast until slightly plumped, 15 to 20 minutes.

▸ Cook pasta in a 6- to 8-quart pot of boiling salted water (see Tips, page 8), stirring occasionally, until al dente. Reserve 1½ cups pasta cooking water, then drain pasta well and transfer to a large bowl. Add mascarpone and stir until melted. Add reserved cooking water, tomatoes, half of parmesan, 3 tablespoons chives, remaining ¾ teaspoon salt, and remaining ½ teaspoon pepper and toss well, then cool to warm.

▸ Butter a 3-quart (13- by 9-inch) gratin or other shallow baking dish. Toss pasta mixture again, then spoon into gratin dish. Sprinkle remaining parmesan over top. Bake pasta until golden and bubbly, 18 to 20 minutes. Sprinkle with remaining tablespoon chives.

Cooks' notes:

• Pasta can be prepared (but not baked) 3 hours ahead and kept, uncovered, at room temperature.

• You can serve the freshly tossed pasta without baking it. Sprinkle with remaining parmesan and chives.

CAVATAPPI WITH WHITE BEANS AND GOLDEN ONIONS

SERVES 6

Active time: 20 min   Start to finish: 35 min

   3 tablespoons olive oil
   2 medium onions, halved lengthwise and cut lengthwise into thin slices (2½ cups)
   1 large garlic clove, finely chopped
   2 large red bell peppers, cut lengthwise into ⅛-inch-wide strips (4 cups)
   2 teaspoons finely chopped fresh jalapeño chile, including seeds, or to taste
   1 teaspoon salt
  ¼ teaspoon black pepper
  ¾ cup water
1 lb *cavatappi* (ridged corkscrew pasta)
   1 (16- to 19-oz) can white beans such as Great Northern or cannellini, rinsed and drained
   2 oz finely grated Parmigiano-Reggiano (1 cup; see Tips, page 8)
  ½ cup finely chopped fresh flat-leaf parsley

▸ Heat 2 tablespoons oil in a 12-inch heavy skillet over moderately high heat until hot but not smoking, then sauté onions, stirring occasionally, until golden, about 10 minutes. Add garlic and sauté, stirring, 1 minute, then transfer onions to a bowl.

▸ Add remaining tablespoon oil to skillet and sauté bell peppers, chile, salt, and pepper, stirring occasionally, until bell peppers are tender, about 8 minutes. Add onions and water and bring to a boil, stirring and scraping up brown bits from bottom of skillet, then remove from heat.

▸ While peppers sauté, cook pasta in a 6- to 8-quart pot of boiling salted water (see Tips, page 8), stirring occasionally, until al dente. Reserve ¾ cup cooking water, then drain pasta well in a colander and return to pot. Add onion mixture, reserved cooking water, beans, half of cheese, and half of parsley and toss well.

▸ Serve sprinkled with remaining cheese and parsley.

KITCHEN NOTE

MASCARPONE ("MAS-CAR-*POE*-NAY") IS A SPREADABLE DOUBLE-CREAM COW'S-MILK CHEESE. IT IS SNOWY WHITE IN COLOR WITH A SLIGHTLY SWEET, BUTTERY FLAVOR. ITALIANS EAT IT OVER FRUIT WITH SUGAR, OR BY ITSELF, SIMPLY SPRINKLED WITH COCOA POWDER OR DRIZZLED WITH HONEY. IF UNOPENED, MASCARPONE WILL KEEP, REFRIGERATED, FOR THREE WEEKS; ONCE OPENED IT SHOULD BE USED WITHIN ONE WEEK.

ORZO WITH HAM AND GOAT CHEESE

SERVES 6

Active time: 10 min   Start to finish: 25 min

 1 lb orzo (rice-shaped pasta)
 ½ lb sliced ham, coarsely chopped (2 cups)
 ½ lb mild soft goat cheese, crumbled
 5 scallions, thinly sliced

▸ Preheat broiler and lightly oil a flameproof 3-quart shallow baking dish (2 inches deep).

▸ Cook orzo in a 6-quart pot of boiling salted water (see Tips, page 8) until al dente. Reserve ¾ cup pasta cooking water, then drain orzo in a colander. Toss hot orzo with remaining ingredients, reserved cooking water, and salt and pepper to taste in a large bowl until cheese is melted.

▸ Transfer orzo mixture to baking dish and broil about 2 inches from heat until lightly browned, about 4 minutes.

PENNE WITH SMOKED TROUT AND SUGAR SNAP PEAS

SERVES 4

Active time: 30 min   Start to finish: 40 min

 1 lb penne rigate
 ¾ lb sugar snap peas, trimmed and halved diagonally
 ⅔ cup heavy cream
 1 (½-lb) whole smoked trout, head, skin, bones, and tail discarded and flesh coarsely flaked
 1 tablespoon finely grated fresh lemon zest
 ¼ cup chopped fresh dill
 ½ teaspoon salt
 ½ teaspoon black pepper

▸ Cook pasta in a large pot of boiling salted water (see Tips, page 8) 2 minutes less than package instructions indicate, then add sugar snaps and cook until sugar snaps are tender, about 2 minutes more. Reserve ¼ cup cooking water, then drain pasta and sugar snaps in a colander and return to pot.

▸ Boil cream in a 1- to 1½-quart heavy saucepan, uncovered, 2 minutes, then add to pasta along with trout, zest, reserved cooking water, dill, salt, and pepper and toss until combined.

KITCHEN NOTE

ADDING A SUBSTANTIAL AMOUNT OF **SALT** TO THE WATER IN WHICH YOU BOIL YOUR PASTA BOOSTS THE FLAVOR OF THE COMPLETED DISH. WE RECOMMEND USING AT LEAST 1 TABLESPOON SALT FOR EVERY 4 QUARTS OF WATER.

LINGUINE WITH EGGPLANT

SERVES 6

Active time: 45 min   Start to finish: 45 min

 6 tablespoons extra-virgin olive oil
 1 lb eggplant, cut into ½-inch cubes
 2 cups chopped onion (2 medium)
 1 tablespoon finely chopped garlic
 2 (14-oz) cans diced tomatoes in juice
 2 teaspoons finely chopped fresh oregano
 ½ teaspoon salt
 ¼ teaspoon dried hot red pepper flakes
 1 lb dried linguine
 1 tablespoon finely chopped fresh flat-leaf parsley
 2 oz finely grated Pecorino Romano (1 cup)

▸ Heat ¼ cup oil in a 12-inch nonstick skillet over moderately high heat until beginning to smoke, then cook eggplant, stirring occasionally, until browned and tender, about 10 minutes. Transfer to paper towels to drain.

▸ Add onion, garlic, and remaining 2 tablespoons oil to skillet and cook over moderate heat, stirring occasionally, until onion is golden, 8 to 10 minutes. Add tomatoes (with juice), oregano, salt, and red pepper flakes and simmer, uncovered, until sauce is thickened and most of liquid is evaporated, about 10 minutes.

▸ While sauce simmers, cook linguine in a 6- to 8-quart pot of boiling salted water (see Tips, page 8) until al dente. Reserve 1 cup cooking water, then drain pasta in a colander and return to pot. Add tomato sauce and toss to coat, then add eggplant, parsley, and some reserved cooking water if necessary (to thin sauce) and gently toss. Season with salt and pepper and transfer to a bowl. Sprinkle with some cheese and serve remainder on the side.

TUNA NOODLE CASSEROLE

SERVES 4 TO 6

Active time: 1 hr   Start to finish: 1½ hr

1	medium onion, finely chopped
4½	tablespoons unsalted butter
10	oz mushrooms, trimmed and sliced ¼ inch thick (4 cups)
2	teaspoons soy sauce
¼	cup Sherry
¼	cup all-purpose flour
2	cups reduced-sodium chicken broth
1	cup whole milk
2	teaspoons fresh lemon juice
¼	teaspoon salt
1	(6-oz) can tuna in olive oil, drained
6	oz dried curly egg noodles (3¼ cups)
1½	cups coarse fresh bread crumbs
¼	lb coarsely grated Cheddar (1 cup)
1	tablespoon vegetable oil

▸ Put oven rack in middle position and preheat oven to 375°F. Butter a shallow 2-quart baking dish.

▸ Cook onion in 1½ tablespoons butter with a pinch of salt in a 12-inch heavy skillet over moderately low heat, covered, stirring occasionally, until softened, about 5 minutes. Increase heat to moderately high and add mushrooms, then sauté, stirring occasionally, until mushrooms begin to give off liquid, about 2 minutes. Add soy sauce and continue to sauté mushrooms, stirring, until liquid mushrooms give off is evaporated. Add Sherry and boil, stirring occasionally, until evaporated. Remove from heat.

▸ Melt remaining 3 tablespoons butter in a 2- to 3-quart heavy saucepan over moderately low heat and whisk in flour, then cook roux, whisking, 3 minutes. Add broth in a stream, whisking, and bring to a boil, whisking. Whisk in milk and simmer sauce, whisking occasionally, 5 minutes. Stir in mushroom mixture, lemon juice, and salt. Flake tuna into sauce and stir gently. Season sauce with salt and pepper.

▸ Cook noodles in a 5- to 6-quart pot of boiling salted water (see Tips, page 8) until al dente. Drain noodles in a colander and return to pot. Add sauce and stir gently to combine. Transfer mixture to baking dish, spreading evenly.

▸ Toss together bread crumbs and cheese in a bowl. Drizzle with oil and toss again, then sprinkle evenly over casserole. Bake until topping is crisp and sauce is bubbling, 20 to 30 minutes.

HERBED SPAETZLE

SERVES 8 (SIDE DISH)

Active time: 40 min   Start to finish: 40 min

Spaetzle, tender little morsels that are like a cross between a noodle and a dumpling, are common to Austrian, German, and Swiss cuisines.

3	cups all-purpose flour
1¾	teaspoons salt
1¼	cups whole milk
3	large eggs
½	cup crème fraîche
2	tablespoons olive oil
1½	sticks (¾ cup) unsalted butter
1	tablespoon coarsely chopped fresh flat-leaf parsley
1	tablespoon coarsely chopped fresh chives
2	teaspoons coarsely chopped fresh thyme
2	teaspoons coarsely chopped fresh sage
½	teaspoon freshly grated nutmeg
½	teaspoon black pepper

Special equipment: **a spaetzlemaker (see Sources), a food mill fitted with a medium disk, or a colander with ¼-inch holes**

▸ Bring a 4- to 6-quart heavy pot of salted water (see Tips, page 8) to a boil and keep at a bare simmer. Fill a large bowl with very cold water and set aside.

▸ Whisk together flour and 1 teaspoon salt in a bowl. Whisk together milk, eggs, and crème fraîche in another bowl, then whisk into flour until batter is smooth.

▸ Working over barely simmering water, force half of batter through spaetzlemaker, food mill, or colander into water. As spaetzle float to surface (after about 1 minute), transfer to bowl of cold water with a mesh skimmer or sieve, then into a large sieve to drain. Repeat with remaining batter. Toss drained spaetzle with oil.

▸ Cut 1 stick butter into tablespoon pieces, then heat in a deep 12-inch heavy nonstick skillet over moderately high heat until foam subsides and add spaetzle. (Skillet will be full.) Sauté, stirring occasionally, until golden on the edges, 10 to 15 minutes. Cut remaining ½ stick butter into tablespoon pieces and add to spaetzle along with parsley, chives, thyme, sage, nutmeg, pepper, and remaining ¾ teaspoon salt. Gently stir to coat.

SPAGHETTI WITH CREMINI MUSHROOMS, LEMON, AND THYME

SERVES 4

Active time: 45 min   Start to finish: 45 min

1	lb spaghetti
1	cup coarse fresh bread crumbs (from 2 slices firm white sandwich bread)
3	tablespoons olive oil
1	teaspoon salt
½	stick (¼ cup) unsalted butter
1½	lb cremini mushrooms, trimmed and cut into ¼-inch-thick slices (6 cups)
1	teaspoon finely grated fresh lemon zest
3	garlic cloves, chopped
1	teaspoon Worcestershire sauce
2	tablespoons fresh lemon juice
1	teaspoon minced fresh thyme
½	teaspoon black pepper
2	tablespoons minced fresh flat-leaf parsley
1	oz finely grated Parmigiano-Reggiano (½ cup; see Tips, page 8) plus additional for serving

Garnish: lemon wedges

▶ Cook pasta in a large pot of boiling salted water (see Tips, page 8) until barely al dente.

▶ While pasta cooks, stir together bread crumbs, 1 tablespoon oil, and ¼ teaspoon salt in a bowl until combined well. Transfer to a 12-inch heavy skillet and cook over moderate heat, stirring, until golden, 3 to 5 minutes, then return to bowl.

▶ Heat 2 tablespoons butter and remaining 2 tablespoons oil in skillet over moderately high heat until foam subsides, then sauté mushrooms, stirring, until golden, about 4 minutes. Add zest and garlic and sauté, stirring, until mushrooms

exude liquid, about 3 minutes. Add Worcestershire sauce and lemon juice and cook, stirring, until most of liquid is evaporated, about 2 minutes. Stir in thyme, pepper, and remaining ¾ teaspoon salt.

▶ Reserve 1 cup pasta cooking water, then drain pasta in a colander.

▶ Transfer mushroom mixture to pasta pot, then add ½ cup reserved cooking water and bring to a boil. Stir in parsley and remaining 2 tablespoons butter. Return pasta to pot along with cheese, tossing to combine. If pasta seems dry, moisten with more cooking water.

▶ Serve pasta sprinkled with bread crumbs and additional cheese.

GRAINS

BULGUR WITH APRICOTS AND ALMONDS

SERVES 4 (SIDE DISH)

Active time: 20 min   Start to finish: 30 min

⅓	cup sliced almonds (1 oz)
1	small onion, finely chopped
1½	tablespoons olive oil
1¼	cups medium bulgur
1⅓	cups water
¾	teaspoon salt
¼	teaspoon black pepper
¼	cup chopped dried apricots (2 oz)
½	tablespoon unsalted butter, cut into pieces
3	tablespoons coarsely chopped fresh flat-leaf parsley

▶ Toast almonds in a dry small heavy skillet over moderate heat, stirring, until fragrant and pale golden, about 2 minutes.

▶ Cook onion in oil in a 3-quart heavy saucepan over moderate heat, stirring frequently, until softened and beginning to brown, about 8 minutes. Add bulgur and cook, stirring, 2 minutes.

▶ Stir in water, salt, and pepper and simmer, covered, 5 minutes. Remove from heat, then add apricots and butter and stir until butter is melted. Let stand, covered, 5 minutes. Stir in parsley and almonds.

PARMESAN AND BLACK PEPPER POLENTA

SERVES 4 TO 6 (SIDE DISH)
Active time: 5 min   Start to finish: 15 min

4½   cups water
1¼   teaspoons salt
2   tablespoons unsalted butter
1   cup instant polenta
1   oz finely grated Parmigiano-Reggiano (½ cup; see Tips, page 8)
¼   teaspoon black pepper

▶ Bring water to a boil with salt and butter in a 4-quart heavy saucepan, then add polenta in a thin stream, whisking. Cook polenta at a bare simmer, whisking and turning down heat as needed to prevent spattering, 5 minutes. Remove from heat and stir in cheese.
▶ Serve sprinkled with black pepper.

VEGETARIAN BROWN RICE SUSHI ROLLS

SERVES 1
Active time: 25 min   Start to finish: 1¼ hr

Brown rice is not traditionally used for sushi, but since it's such a healthy grain, we've bent the rules. You'll have leftover vegetables, which are great for salads. For sources for the Asian ingredients and the sushi mat, see Sources.

Scant ⅔ cup short-grain brown rice
1   cup plus 1 teaspoon water
2   teaspoons soy sauce
2   tablespoons seasoned rice vinegar
1   teaspoon wasabi powder
2   (8¼- by 7¼-inch) sheets roasted nori (dried laver)
½   Kirby cucumber, peeled, seeded, and cut into
      ¹⁄₁₆-inch-thick matchsticks
½   carrot, cut into ¹⁄₁₆-inch-thick matchsticks
½   firm-ripe small California avocado
¾   oz radish sprouts, roots trimmed

Special equipment: **a bamboo sushi mat**
Accompaniments: **soy sauce for dipping; sliced *gari* (pickled ginger)**

▶ Rinse rice well and bring to a boil with 1 cup water and 1 teaspoon soy sauce in a 1- to 1½-quart heavy saucepan. Reduce heat to very low and simmer, tightly covered, until water is absorbed, about 40 minutes. Remove from heat and let rice stand, covered, 10 minutes.
▶ While rice stands, stir together vinegar and remaining teaspoon soy sauce.
▶ Transfer rice to a wide nonmetal bowl (preferably wood, ceramic, or glass) and sprinkle with vinegar mixture, tossing gently with a large spoon to combine. Cool rice, tossing occasionally, about 15 minutes.
▶ Stir together wasabi and remaining teaspoon water to form a stiff paste. Let stand at least 15 minutes (to allow flavors to develop).
▶ Place sushi mat on a work surface with slats running crosswise. Arrange 1 sheet nori, shiny side down, on mat, lining up a long edge of sheet with edge of mat nearest you. Using damp fingers, gently press half of rice (about ¾ cup) onto nori in 1 layer, leaving a 1¾-inch border on side farthest from you.
▶ Arrange half of cucumber in an even strip horizontally across rice, starting 1 inch from side nearest you. (You may need to cut pieces to fit from side to side.) Arrange half of carrot just above cucumber in same manner. Peel avocado half and cut lengthwise into thin slices, then arrange half of slices just above carrot in same manner. Repeat with radish sprouts, letting some sprout tops extend beyond edge.
▶ Beginning with edge nearest you, lift mat up with your thumbs, holding filling in place with your fingers, and fold mat over filling so that upper and lower edges of rice meet, then squeeze gently but firmly along length of roll, tugging edge of mat farthest from you to tighten. (Nori border will still be flat on mat.) Open mat and roll log forward to seal with nori border. (Moisture from rice will seal roll.) Transfer roll, seam side down, to a cutting board. Make second log in same manner, then cut each log crosswise into 6 pieces with a wet thin-bladed knife.
▶ Serve rolls with wasabi paste, soy sauce, and ginger.

Cooks' notes:
• If you prefer to use white sushi rice, cook the same amount of rice with 1 cup water 15 minutes. Omit all soy sauce from rice and replace with ¼ teaspoon salt dissolved in 2 tablespoons rice vinegar.
• If you aren't able to find seasoned rice vinegar, dissolve 2 teaspoons sugar in 2 tablespoons unseasoned rice vinegar.

SPINACH AND RICE WITH LEMON

SERVES 4 TO 6 (SIDE DISH)
Active time: 45 min   Start to finish: 45 min

2   tablespoons unsalted butter
¼   cup finely chopped shallots
1   cup long-grain white rice
1⅔   cups reduced-sodium chicken broth (13 fl oz)
2   tablespoons extra-virgin olive oil
1   tablespoon chopped garlic
3   (10-oz) bags spinach, tough stems discarded
1   teaspoon salt
¼   teaspoon black pepper
2   to 3 teaspoons fresh lemon juice

▸ Heat butter in a 1- to 2-quart heavy saucepan over moderately low heat until foam subsides, then cook shallots, stirring occasionally, until beginning to turn golden, about 2 minutes. Add rice and cook, stirring constantly, until grains turn opaque, about 2 minutes. Reduce heat to low, then stir in broth and cook, covered, until liquid is absorbed and rice is just tender, about 15 minutes. Remove from heat and let stand, covered, until ready to use.
▸ While rice cooks, heat oil in a 6- to 8-quart heavy pot over moderate heat until hot but not smoking, then cook garlic, stirring constantly, until beginning to turn golden, about 1 minute. Add all of spinach, salt, and pepper and cook, turning and stirring with tongs, until wilted and tender, about 3 minutes, then stir in 2 teaspoons lemon juice.
▸ Add rice and stir until just combined. Season with salt and pepper, then add remaining teaspoon lemon juice if desired.

RADICCHIO AND RED-WINE RISOTTO

SERVES 4
Active time: 45 min   Start to finish: 45 min

3½   cups reduced-sodium chicken broth (28 fl oz)
3½   cups water
1   cup finely chopped onion
3   tablespoons unsalted butter
1   Turkish or ½ California bay leaf
½   teaspoon salt
½   lb radicchio, quartered, cored, and cut crosswise into ½-inch slices
1½   cups Arborio rice (10 oz)
1½   cups dry red wine
1½   oz finely grated Parmigiano-Reggiano (¾ cup)

▸ Bring broth and water to a simmer in a 2½- to 3-quart saucepan and keep at a bare simmer.
▸ Cook onion in butter with bay leaf and salt in a wide 4-quart heavy pot over moderate heat, stirring, until onion is pale golden, about 10 minutes.
▸ While onion cooks, cook radicchio in boiling salted water (see Tips, page 8) in a 4- to 6-quart pot until just tender, about 3 minutes. Drain in a colander and transfer to a bowl of ice and cold water to stop cooking. Drain and squeeze dry.
▸ Add rice to onion and cook, stirring, 2 minutes. Add wine and boil, stirring, until most of wine is absorbed, about 5 minutes. Stir in ½ cup simmering broth mixture and cook, stirring constantly and keeping at a strong simmer, until most of broth is absorbed. Continue cooking risotto and adding broth, about ½ cup at a time, stirring constantly and letting each addition be absorbed before adding next, until rice is tender and creamy-looking but still al dente, about 18 minutes total (you may have some broth left over). Discard bay leaf, then add radicchio and cheese and cook, stirring, until heated through, about 1 minute. Add salt and pepper to taste and serve immediately.

KITCHEN NOTE

THE KEY TO **CREATING A PERFECT RISOTTO** IS PATIENCE: STIR CONSTANTLY, ADD THE BROTH SLOWLY, AND TASTE OFTEN AS YOU APPROACH THE END OF THE COOKING TIME. COOK THE RICE UNTIL CREAMY YET AL DENTE, AND SERVE THE RISOTTO IMMEDIATELY IN WARMED SHALLOW BOWLS.

SHRIMP AND PEA RISOTTO
SERVES 4 (MAIN COURSE)
Active time: 40 min   Start to finish: 40 min

- ¾ lb medium shrimp in shell (31 to 35 per lb), peeled, deveined, and shells reserved
- 7 cups water
- 1¼ teaspoons salt
- 1 cup thawed frozen baby peas (5 oz)
- ¼ cup chopped fresh chives
- 1 teaspoon finely grated fresh lemon zest
- ½ teaspoon black pepper
- 1 medium onion, finely chopped
- 3 tablespoons unsalted butter
- 1⅓ cups Arborio rice (9 oz)
- ¾ cup dry white wine

▶ Bring shrimp shells and 7 cups water to a simmer and keep at a bare simmer, covered.

▶ Toss shrimp with ½ teaspoon salt, then chill, covered.

▶ Toss together peas, chives, zest, and pepper in a bowl.

▶ Cook onion in butter with remaining ¾ teaspoon salt in a wide 4- to 5-quart heavy pot over moderately low heat, stirring, until softened, 3 to 5 minutes.

▶ Add rice and cook, stirring, 2 minutes. Increase heat to moderate, then add wine and cook, stirring, 1 minute. Stir in ½ cup simmering shrimp broth (pour through a sieve, then discard shells) and cook, stirring constantly and keeping at a strong simmer, until most of broth is absorbed. Continue cooking and adding broth, about ½ cup at a time, stirring constantly and letting each addition be absorbed before adding next, until rice is tender and creamy-looking but still al dente, about 18 minutes total. Add shrimp and pea mixture and continue to cook, stirring and adding more broth as necessary, until shrimp are just cooked through, 3 to 5 minutes. (You may have some broth left over.) Season with salt and serve risotto immediately.

Cooks' note
• If you can get fresh shelled peas, cook them in a pan of boiling water until they are just tender, 3 to 5 minutes, then drain and toss them with the chives, zest, and pepper.

COCONUT RICE
SERVES 8 (SIDE DISH)
Active time: 10 min   Start to finish: 35 min

- 2 cups long-grain rice
- 1 tablespoon unsalted butter
- 1 (13- to 14-oz) can unsweetened coconut milk
- 1 cup water
- 1 (3-inch) cinnamon stick
- ¼ teaspoon salt

▶ Rinse rice in a sieve under cold running water 2 to 3 minutes, then drain well.

▶ Melt butter in a 2- to 3-quart heavy saucepan over moderately high heat. Add rice and cook, stirring constantly, until it becomes opaque, about 3 minutes.

▶ Stir in coconut milk, water, cinnamon, and salt and bring to a boil. Reduce heat to low and simmer, covered, 20 minutes, then remove from heat and let stand, covered, 5 minutes. Discard cinnamon stick and fluff rice with a fork.

VEGETABLES

ROASTED ASPARAGUS WITH FETA

SERVES 6
Active time: 10 min   Start to finish: 25 min

2½ lb medium asparagus, trimmed
2 tablespoons extra-virgin olive oil
½ teaspoon salt
¼ teaspoon black pepper
2 oz feta (preferably French), crumbled (½ cup)

▶ Put oven rack in lower third of oven and preheat oven to 500°F.
▶ Toss asparagus with oil, salt, and pepper in a large shallow baking pan and arrange in 1 layer. Roast, shaking pan once about halfway through roasting, until asparagus is just tender when pierced with a fork, 8 to 14 minutes total.
▶ Serve asparagus sprinkled with cheese.

GREEN BEANS WITH HAZELNUT BUTTER

SERVES 4
Active time: 15 min   Start to finish: 30 min

3 tablespoons unsalted butter, softened
2 tablespoons finely chopped shallot
½ teaspoon finely grated fresh lemon zest
2 teaspoons fresh lemon juice
½ teaspoon salt
½ teaspoon coarsely ground black pepper
⅓ cup hazelnuts (1½ oz), toasted (see Tips, page 8), any loose skins rubbed off, and nuts finely chopped
1½ lb green beans, trimmed

▶ Stir together butter, shallot, zest, lemon juice, salt, and pepper in a small bowl until combined. Add hazelnuts and stir until combined well.
▶ Cook beans in a 4- to 5-quart pot of boiling salted water (see Tips, page 8), uncovered, until just tender, 5 to 8 minutes. Drain beans in a colander, then return hot beans to pot and toss with hazelnut butter.

BROCCOLI SPEARS IN GARLIC SAUCE

SERVES 6
Active time: 25 min   Start to finish: 25 min

1½ lb broccoli (1 head)
1 tablespoon canola oil
4 garlic cloves, lightly smashed
3 tablespoons Asian oyster sauce
½ cup chicken stock (page 218) or reduced-sodium broth
1 teaspoon Asian sesame oil

▶ Peel off tough outer skin of broccoli stem, then halve broccoli crosswise (top half with florets should equal length of bottom half). Cut bottom half (stem) lengthwise into ½-inch-wide wedges, then cut top half (stem with florets) into long spears with ½-inch-wide wedges.
▶ Heat a wok over high heat until beginning to smoke, then add canola oil and swirl to coat sides. Stir-fry garlic until golden, about 30 seconds, then add broccoli and stir-fry 5 minutes. Stir in oyster sauce and stock and cook, covered, until broccoli is crisp-tender, about 3 minutes. Remove from heat and toss with sesame oil.

EACH SERVING ABOUT 66 CALORIES AND 4 GRAMS FAT

CARROTS WITH GREMOLATA

SERVES 4 TO 6
Active time: 20 min   Start to finish: 20 min

2 lb carrots, cut into ¼-inch slices
¼ cup finely chopped fresh flat-leaf parsley
2 teaspoons minced garlic
2 teaspoons finely grated fresh lemon zest
½ teaspoon salt
⅛ teaspoon black pepper
2 tablespoons olive oil

▶ Steam carrots in a steamer set over boiling water, covered, until tender, about 5 to 7 minutes.
▶ While carrots steam, toss together parsley, garlic, zest, salt, and pepper in a large bowl to make *gremolata*.
▶ Add hot carrots and oil to bowl and toss.

BRAISED CELERY HEARTS

SERVES 4
Active time: 10 min   Start to finish: 30 min

  1 (1-lb) bag celery hearts (about 2)
  2 tablespoons unsalted butter
  1 cup reduced-sodium chicken broth
 ⅛ teaspoon salt
 ⅛ teaspoon black pepper

▶ Keeping celery ribs attached at base, peel outer ribs of celery hearts with a vegetable peeler, then trim ends and halve hearts lengthwise.
▶ Melt butter in a 12-inch heavy skillet over moderate heat, then cook celery, turning with tongs occasionally, until pale golden on all sides, about 8 minutes. Add remaining ingredients and cook, covered, until liquid is evaporated and celery is tender and golden, about 20 minutes. Serve warm.

CAULIFLOWER WITH BACON, CAPERS, PEPPERS, AND RAISINS

SERVES 4 TO 6
Active time: 20 min   Start to finish: 30 min

  3 oz bacon (3 or 4 slices), cut crosswise into ¼-inch strips
  2 lb cauliflower, cut into 2- to 2½-inch-wide florets
  1 red bell pepper, seeded and cut into ½-inch pieces
 ¾ cup heavy cream
 ½ cup golden raisins
  1 tablespoon drained bottled capers
  1 teaspoon finely chopped garlic
  1 Turkish or ½ California bay leaf
  1 tablespoon fresh lemon juice

▶ Cook bacon in a 10- to 12-inch heavy skillet over moderate heat, stirring occasionally, until lightly browned but not crisp, about 4 minutes. Add cauliflower and cook, stirring occasionally, until lightly browned, about 5 minutes. Add bell pepper, cream, raisins, capers, garlic, and bay leaf and cook over moderately low heat, covered, stirring occasionally, until cauliflower is tender, about 12 minutes. Add lemon juice and salt and pepper to taste, then discard bay leaf.

CELERY-ROOT PURÉE WITH TRUFFLE BUTTER

SERVES 8 TO 10
Active time: 20 min   Start to finish: 35 min

Truffles add a flavorful woodsy note, but if you make this French-influenced celery-root purée without them, it will still be delicious.

  3 lb celery root (sometimes called celeriac; 2 large), peeled with a knife and cut into ½-inch pieces
1¾ lb boiling potatoes (3 large), peeled and cut into ½-inch pieces
  1 cup heavy cream
  4 oz black truffle butter (see Sources) or 1 stick (½ cup) unsalted butter
  1 teaspoon salt
 ¼ teaspoon black pepper

▶ Cover celery root and potatoes with cold salted water (see Tips, page 8) by 2 inches in a 4- to 6-quart heavy pot, then simmer, covered, until celery root is very tender, about 15 minutes.
▶ While vegetables simmer, bring cream, butter, salt, and pepper just to a simmer, stirring until butter is melted.
▶ Drain vegetables in a colander and transfer to a food processor. Add hot cream mixture in a steady stream, pulsing until smooth. (Alternatively, mash vegetables with hot cream mixture using a potato masher.)

Cooks' note:
• Purée can be made 1 day ahead and cooled, uncovered, then chilled, covered. Reheat in an ovenproof dish, covered, in the oven or microwave until hot.

CORN AND ZUCCHINI SAUTÉ

SERVES 4 TO 6

Active time: 20 min   Start to finish: 25 min

- 2 tablespoons extra-virgin olive oil
- ½ cup chopped scallions
- ½ teaspoon finely chopped garlic
- 2 cups corn (from about 4 ears)
- 2 medium zucchini (1 lb total), quartered lengthwise, then cut crosswise into ¼-inch-thick pieces
- ¼ teaspoon ground cumin
- ¼ teaspoon salt
- ⅛ teaspoon black pepper
- ½ cup chopped fresh cilantro

▶ Heat oil in a 12-inch heavy skillet over moderate heat until hot but not smoking, then cook scallions, stirring occasionally, until softened, about 3 minutes. Add garlic and cook, stirring, 1 minute. Add corn, zucchini, cumin, salt, and pepper and cook, stirring occasionally, until zucchini is tender, 4 to 6 minutes. Stir in cilantro and season with salt and pepper.

EGGPLANT PARMESAN

SERVES 8 (MAIN COURSE)

Active time: 1 hr   Start to finish: 2½ hr

- 2½ lb medium eggplants (3), cut crosswise into ⅓-inch-thick rounds
- 3¼ teaspoons salt
- 5 lb plum tomatoes
- 1½ cups plus 3 tablespoons olive oil
- 2 large garlic cloves, finely chopped
- 20 fresh basil leaves, torn in half
- ¾ teaspoon black pepper
- ¼ teaspoon dried hot red pepper flakes
- 1 cup all-purpose flour
- 5 large eggs
- 3½ cups *panko* (Japanese bread crumbs; see Sources)
- 2 oz finely grated Parmigiano-Reggiano (⅔ cup; see Tips, page 8)
- 1 lb chilled fresh mozzarella (not unsalted), thinly sliced

▶ Toss eggplant with 2 teaspoons salt in a colander set over a bowl, then drain 30 minutes.

▶ While eggplant drains, cut an X in bottom of each tomato with a sharp paring knife and blanch tomatoes in a 5-quart pot of boiling water 1 minute. Transfer tomatoes with a slotted spoon to a cutting board and, when cool enough to handle, peel off skin, beginning from scored end, with paring knife.

▶ Coarsely chop tomatoes, then coarsely purée in batches in a blender. Heat 3 tablespoons oil in a 5-quart heavy pot over moderately high heat until hot but not smoking, then sauté garlic, stirring, until golden, about 30 seconds. Add tomato purée, basil, 1 teaspoon salt, ½ teaspoon black pepper, and red pepper flakes and simmer, uncovered, stirring occasionally, until slightly thickened, 25 to 30 minutes.

▶ Put oven rack in middle position and preheat oven to 375°F.

▶ Stir together flour, remaining ¼ teaspoon salt, and remaining ¼ teaspoon pepper in a shallow bowl. Lightly beat eggs in a second shallow bowl, then stir together *panko* and ⅓ cup Parmigiano-Reggiano in a third shallow bowl.

▶ Working with 1 slice at a time, dredge eggplant in flour, shaking off excess, then dip in egg, letting excess drip off, and dredge in *panko* until evenly coated. Transfer eggplant to sheets of wax paper, arranging slices in 1 layer.

▶ Heat remaining 1½ cups oil in a deep 12-inch nonstick skillet over moderately high heat until hot but not smoking, then fry eggplant 4 slices at a time, turning over once, until golden brown, 5 to 6 minutes per batch. Transfer with tongs to paper towels to drain.

▶ Spread 1 cup tomato sauce in bottom of a rectangular 3½-quart (13- by 11- by 2-inch) baking dish. Arrange about one third of eggplant slices in 1 layer over sauce, overlapping slightly if necessary. Cover eggplant with about one third of remaining sauce (about 1¼ cups) and one third of mozzarella. Continue layering with remaining eggplant, sauce, and mozzarella. Sprinkle top with remaining ⅓ cup Parmigiano-Reggiano.

▶ Bake, uncovered, until cheese is melted and golden and sauce is bubbling, 35 to 40 minutes.

Cooks' note:
• Tomato sauce can be made 1 day ahead and chilled, covered.

CURRIED EGGPLANT

SERVES 6 (SIDE DISH) OR 4 (MAIN COURSE)
Active time: 40 min   Start to finish: 1¼ hr

You can use either Chinese or Japanese eggplants for this recipe; both varieties have purple skin, a long, slender shape, and small seeds.

>   3 lb Asian eggplants (6), cut crosswise into
>   ⅓-inch-thick rounds
> 1¾ teaspoons salt
>   1 large garlic clove, chopped
>   1 tablespoon finely chopped peeled fresh ginger
>   2 teaspoons chopped fresh jalapeño chile,
>   including seeds
>   1 teaspoon yellow or brown mustard seeds
>   1 teaspoon cumin seeds
> ½ teaspoon turmeric
>   3 tablespoons vegetable oil
>   1 large onion, halved lengthwise and thinly sliced
>   lengthwise
>   1 (3-inch) cinnamon stick
> ¾ cup water
>   1 tablespoon packed brown sugar
>   3 tablespoons chopped fresh cilantro
> ¼ cup roasted cashews (1¼ oz), chopped

Accompaniment: steamed basmati or jasmine rice

▶ Toss eggplant with 1 teaspoon salt in a colander set over a bowl, then drain 30 minutes. Rinse eggplant, then drain, pressing gently on eggplant to extract any excess liquid.
▶ While eggplant drains, mash garlic, ginger, and jalapeño to a paste with ½ teaspoon salt using a mortar and pestle (or mince and mash with a large heavy knife and transfer to a cup), then stir in mustard and cumin seeds and turmeric.
▶ Heat oil in a 5-quart heavy pot over moderately high heat until hot but not smoking, then sauté onion, stirring occasionally, until softened and golden, 8 to 10 minutes. Add spice paste and cinnamon stick, then reduce heat to moderate and cook, stirring, 1 minute.
▶ Add eggplant and cook, stirring, until it begins to soften, about 3 minutes. Stir in water, brown sugar, and remaining ¼ teaspoon salt and simmer, covered, stirring occasionally, until eggplant is tender but not falling apart, 20 to 25 minutes. Season eggplant with additional salt.
▶ Discard cinnamon stick and serve eggplant sprinkled with cilantro and cashews.

BRAISED FENNEL

SERVES 4
Active time: 15 min   Start to finish: 25 min

>   2 fennel bulbs (sometimes called anise; 10 to 12 oz each)
>   with fronds
> 1½ tablespoons extra-virgin olive oil
> ¼ teaspoon salt
> ⅛ teaspoon black pepper
> ½ cup reduced-sodium chicken broth
> ¼ cup water

▶ Cut off and discard stalks from fennel bulbs, reserving fronds. Chop 1 tablespoon fronds and discard remainder. Cut bulbs lengthwise into ½-inch-thick slices, leaving core intact.
▶ Heat oil in a 12-inch heavy skillet over moderately high heat until hot but not smoking, then brown fennel slices well, turning over once, 3 to 4 minutes total.
▶ Reduce heat to low. Sprinkle fennel with salt and pepper, then add broth and water. Cook, covered, until fennel is tender, 10 to 12 minutes.
▶ Serve sprinkled with fennel fronds.

KITCHEN NOTE

WHEN SHOPPING FOR **EGGPLANTS**, CHOOSE FIRM, SMOOTH-SKINNED EGGPLANTS THAT ARE HEAVY FOR THEIR SIZE, AND AVOID ANY WITH SOFT OR BROWN SPOTS. MANY RECIPES CALL FOR SALTING EGGPLANT BEFORE IT IS COOKED TO GET RID OF ANY BITTER TASTE IT MAY HAVE. SMALL, YOUNG EGGPLANTS GENERALLY DON'T NEED SALTING.

MUSHROOMS WITH GARLIC BUTTER

SERVES 4 (FIRST COURSE OR SIDE DISH)

Active time: 10 min   Start to finish: 35 min

 3 slices firm white sandwich bread, crust discarded
     and bread cut into ¼-inch cubes (1¼ cups)
 3 tablespoons unsalted butter
 1 tablespoon finely chopped garlic
 ½ teaspoon salt
 ¼ teaspoon black pepper
 ¾ lb small white mushrooms, trimmed
 2 tablespoons finely chopped fresh flat-leaf parsley

▶ Put oven rack in middle position and preheat oven to 375°F.

▶ Toast bread cubes in a shallow baking pan (1 inch deep), stirring once, until golden and crisp, 6 to 8 minutes.

▶ Meanwhile, melt butter with garlic, salt, and pepper (on the stove or in a microwave).

▶ Put mushrooms in an 8-inch square baking dish and toss with garlic butter. Bake, stirring occasionally, until mushrooms are soft and juicy, 15 to 20 minutes.

▶ Just before serving, toss mushrooms with parsley and croutons.

BRAISED MUSTARD GREENS WITH GARLIC

SERVES 1

Active time: 10 min   Start to finish: 20 min

 ½ lb mustard greens, stems and center ribs discarded
     and leaves coarsely chopped (4 cups packed)
 1 garlic clove, finely chopped
 1 tablespoon extra-virgin olive oil
 ⅓ cup water

▶ Blanch mustard greens in a 4-quart heavy pot of boiling salted water (see Tips, page 8) 1 minute. Drain greens in a colander and wipe pot dry.

▶ Cook garlic in oil in pot over moderate heat, stirring, until pale golden, about 30 seconds. Add greens and water and simmer, partially covered, stirring occasionally, until tender, 5 to 6 minutes. Season with salt and pepper.

SPICY OKRA

SERVES 4

Active time: 15 min   Start to finish: 15 min

 2 (10-oz) packages frozen cut okra
 1 tablespoon vegetable oil
 1 medium onion, coarsely chopped
 1 (14-oz) can diced tomatoes in juice
 1 fresh habanero chile, pierced 3 times with a fork
 ½ teaspoon salt
 ¼ teaspoon black pepper

▶ Rinse okra under hot water in a colander.

▶ Heat oil in a 10-inch heavy skillet over moderately high heat until hot but not smoking, then sauté onion, stirring, until golden, about 3 minutes. Add tomatoes (with juice) and chile and boil, stirring, until tomatoes are softened and liquid is reduced by about half, 5 to 10 minutes. Add okra and cook, gently stirring, until okra is tender, about 5 minutes. Stir in salt and pepper and discard chile.

Cooks' note:
• For a less spicy dish, substitute a serrano or jalapeño chile for the habanero chile.

CREAMED ONIONS

SERVES 6
Active time: 40 min Start to finish: 1½ hr

 2 lb white pearl onions, left unpeeled
1¼ teaspoons salt
 3 tablespoons unsalted butter
 1 tablespoon all-purpose flour
 1 cup heavy cream or half-and-half
 ¼ teaspoon black pepper
 ¼ teaspoon freshly grated nutmeg
1½ cups coarse fresh white bread crumbs (from ¼ lb
      bread with crusts removed)

▸ Blanch onions in a 3-quart pot of boiling water 1 minute, then drain in a colander and transfer to a bowl of cold water to stop cooking. Drain and peel onions.

▸ Butter a 2-quart baking dish. Put onions and 1 teaspoon salt in same pot and add fresh water to cover by 1 inch. Bring to a boil, then reduce heat and simmer, covered, until onions are tender, about 20 minutes. Drain well in colander and transfer to baking dish.

▸ Put oven rack in middle position and preheat oven to 350°F.

▸ Melt 1 tablespoon butter in a 1- to 2-quart heavy saucepan over moderately low heat, then add flour and cook roux, stirring, 1 minute. Add cream in a stream, whisking, and bring to a simmer, whisking. Simmer sauce, stirring occasionally, 2 minutes. Stir in pepper, nutmeg, and remaining ¼ teaspoon salt and pour sauce over onions.

▸ Melt remaining 2 tablespoons butter in a 10-inch nonstick skillet over moderately low heat, then cook bread crumbs, stirring, until golden, 3 to 5 minutes.

▸ Sprinkle toasted crumbs evenly over onions and bake until sauce is bubbling, about 30 minutes.

Cooks' note:

• Creamed onions (without bread crumbs) can be assembled 1 day ahead and chilled, covered. Bring to room temperature before proceeding.

FRIED ONION RINGS

MAKES ABOUT 40 ONION RINGS (SERVES 4 TO 6)
Active time: 1 hr Start to finish: 1½ hr

 2 large Spanish onions (2 lb total)
 2 cups well-shaken buttermilk
 4 teaspoons salt
 2 teaspoons black pepper
 2 cups all-purpose flour
 4 to 6 cups vegetable shortening (preferably trans-fat-free)
      or vegetable oil (32 to 48 fl oz)

Special equipment: a deep-fat thermometer

▸ Cut onions crosswise into ½-inch-thick slices and separate slices into rings, reserving small inner rings for another use if desired.

▸ Line 1 or 2 trays with wax paper. Stir together buttermilk, 2 teaspoons salt, and 1 teaspoon pepper in a large bowl, then gently stir in onion rings. Let stand, turning occasionally, 10 minutes. Drain in a colander.

▸ Whisk together flour, remaining 2 teaspoons salt, and remaining teaspoon pepper in a wide shallow bowl. Dredge onion rings a few at a time in flour, shaking off excess, and arrange in 1 layer on trays. Let onions stand 15 minutes (for batter to set).

▸ Preheat oven to 200°F.

▸ Melt enough shortening in a deep 10- to 12-inch heavy skillet to measure about 1 inch and heat over moderately high heat until it registers 360°F on thermometer. Fry onion rings in batches of 4 to 6, without crowding, turning over once or twice, until golden, about 3 minutes per batch. Transfer as cooked to paper towels to drain, then transfer to 1 or 2 large baking sheets (overlap rings slightly if necessary) and keep warm in oven while frying remaining batches. (Return oil to 360°F between batches.) Serve immediately.

KITCHEN NOTE

WE TESTED OUR **ONION RINGS** WITH BOTH VEGETABLE OIL AND WITH SHORTENING. EACH YIELDS A CRISP, CRUNCHY COATING, BUT WE PREFERRED THE FULLER FLAVOR THAT THE SHORTENING IMPARTS.

TWICE-BAKED POTATOES WITH CORNED BEEF AND CABBAGE

SERVES 4 (MAIN COURSE)

Active time: 20 min   Start to finish: 2 hr

4	russet (baking) potatoes (2 lb)
2	cups coarsely chopped cabbage (½ lb)
½	cup whole milk
6	oz sliced cooked corned beef, coarsely chopped (1¼ cups)
¾	stick (6 tablespoons) unsalted butter, melted

▸ Put oven rack in middle position and preheat oven to 400°F.

▸ Prick potatoes several times with a fork and bake on a baking sheet until tender, about 1 hour.

▸ While potatoes bake, cook cabbage in a 3-quart saucepan of boiling salted water (see Tips, page 8) until tender, 6 to 8 minutes, then drain well in a colander.

▸ Cool potatoes 20 minutes. Increase oven temperature to 450°F. Cut off top quarter lengthwise from cooled potatoes. Scoop flesh from tops into a bowl, then discard tops. Scoop flesh from potato bottoms into bowl, leaving ¼-inch-thick shells, and mash flesh with a potato masher. Stir in milk, cabbage, beef, 5 tablespoons butter, and salt and pepper to taste.

▸ Spoon potato filling into shells, mounding it, then drizzle with remaining tablespoon butter and bake on baking sheet until heated through, 15 to 20 minutes.

PANFRIED POTATOES WITH LEMON

SERVES 4

Active time: 35 min   Start to finish: 35 min

2	tablespoons extra-virgin olive oil
1½	lb boiling potatoes, cut into ½-inch cubes
6	scallions, white and green parts chopped separately
1	teaspoon finely grated fresh lemon zest

▸ Heat oil in a 12-inch nonstick skillet over moderately high heat until hot but not smoking, then sauté potatoes and white parts of scallions, stirring frequently, until potatoes are browned and tender, 15 to 20 minutes. Stir in scallion greens and zest and sauté, stirring, 2 minutes. Season with salt and pepper.

MASHED POTATOES WITH CARROTS AND LEEKS

SERVES 4

Active time: 25 min   Start to finish: 30 min

1	leek (white and pale green parts only), coarsely chopped
2	lb potatoes, preferably Yukon Gold or russet (baking) potatoes
2	carrots, cut into ½-inch chunks
½	stick (¼ cup) unsalted butter
¾	cup whole milk
¾	teaspoon salt
¼	teaspoon black pepper

▸ Wash chopped leek well in a bowl of cold water, then lift out and drain well.

▸ Peel potatoes and cut into 2-inch pieces, then cover with cold water in a 3- to 4-quart saucepan. Bring to a boil, then reduce heat and simmer, uncovered, until potatoes are tender, about 18 minutes. Drain in a colander and return to saucepan.

▸ While potatoes simmer, cook carrots in a 1- to 1½-quart saucepan of boiling salted water (see Tips, page 8) until just tender, 5 to 6 minutes, then drain in colander. Cook leek in butter in a 10-inch skillet over moderately low heat, stirring occasionally, until very tender, about 6 minutes. Add milk, salt, and pepper and simmer, stirring, 2 minutes.

▸ Add leek mixture to potatoes and coarsely mash with a potato masher, then stir in carrots.

KALE, BUTTERNUT SQUASH, AND PANCETTA PIE
SERVES 6 (MAIN COURSE)
Active time: 1 hr   Start to finish: 1½ hr

- 3 tablespoons olive oil
- 1 (1-lb) piece butternut squash, peeled, seeded, and cut into ½-inch pieces (3½ cups)
- ¾ teaspoon salt
- ½ teaspoon black pepper
- 1 medium onion, finely chopped
- 4 (⅛-inch-thick) slices pancetta (Italian unsmoked cured bacon; 3½ oz; see Sources), finely chopped
- 3 garlic cloves, finely chopped
- 2 teaspoons finely chopped fresh sage
- 1½ lb kale, stems and center ribs discarded and leaves coarsely chopped (16 cups)
- ¼ cup water
- 7 tablespoons unsalted butter, melted
- 8 (17- by 12-inch) phyllo sheets, thawed if frozen
- 1 oz finely grated Parmigiano-Reggiano (½ cup; see Tips, page 8)

Special equipment: a 9-inch round heavy nonstick springform pan

▶Put oven rack in middle position and preheat oven to 425°F.

▶Heat 2 tablespoons oil in a 12-inch heavy skillet over moderately high heat until hot but not smoking, then sauté squash with ¼ teaspoon salt and ¼ teaspoon pepper, stirring frequently, until browned and just beginning to soften, about 5 minutes. Transfer to a plate and spread in 1 layer to cool.

▶Add remaining tablespoon oil to skillet and reduce heat to moderate, then cook onion, pancetta, garlic, sage, remaining ½ teaspoon salt, and remaining ¼ teaspoon pepper, stirring frequently, until onion is softened, about 7 minutes. Stir in kale and water and cook, covered, stirring occasionally, until kale is just tender, about 6 minutes. (Skillet will be full, but volume will reduce as vegetables steam.) Cool, uncovered, to room temperature.

▶Brush springform pan with some of butter. Unroll phyllo and cover stack with plastic wrap and a dampened kitchen towel. Keeping remaining phyllo covered and working quickly, gently fit 1 sheet into pan with ends overhanging and brush with butter (including overhang). Rotate pan

slightly and top with another sheet (sheets should not align) and brush in same manner. Repeat with 5 more sheets, rotating pan each time so sheets cover entire rim.

▶Spread half of kale mixture in phyllo shell. Gently stir together squash and cheese in a bowl and spread evenly over kale. Top with remaining kale.

▶Put remaining sheet of phyllo on a work surface and brush with butter. Fold in half crosswise and butter again. Fold again (to quarter) and brush with butter, then lay over center of filling. Bring overhang edges of phyllo up over filling (over quartered sheet of phyllo) to enclose. Brush top with butter and bake until deep golden brown, 20 to 25 minutes.

▶Cool pie in pan on a rack 5 minutes. Remove side of pan and transfer to a platter. Cut into wedges (leave bottom of pan under pie).

Cooks' note:
• Pie can be baked 2 hours ahead and left in pan, uncovered. Reheat in a preheated 350°F oven.

SAUTÉED WATERCRESS WITH YELLOW SQUASH AND SESAME SEEDS
SERVES 1
Active time: 15 min   Start to finish: 15 min

- 1 tablespoon soy sauce
- 2 teaspoons fresh lemon juice
- 1 teaspoon sugar
- 1 medium yellow summer squash (6 oz)
- ½ tablespoon vegetable oil
- 1 bunch watercress (6 oz), coarse stems discarded
- ½ teaspoon sesame seeds, toasted (see Tips, page 8)

▶Stir together soy sauce, lemon juice, sugar, and a pinch of salt in a small bowl.

▶Cut a ¼-inch-thick slice lengthwise from each of the 4 sides of squash. Discard squash core, then cut slices lengthwise into ⅛-inch-thick strips.

▶Heat oil in a 10-inch skillet over moderately high heat until hot but not smoking, then sauté squash, stirring, 1 minute. Add watercress and half of soy mixture, then cook, stirring, until watercress is just wilted, about 1 minute. Transfer vegetables with tongs to a small bowl, discarding any excess liquid. Drizzle with remaining soy mixture and sprinkle with sesame seeds. Serve immediately.

SMOTHERED YELLOW SQUASH WITH BASIL

SERVES 4

Active time: 15 min   Start to finish: 30 min

Smothering is a Cajun cooking term that refers to browning anything from meat to vegetables in oil, then braising it in a small amount of liquid, tightly covered, until tender.

  2 **tablespoons olive oil**
1½ **lb medium yellow squash, halved lengthwise and cut crosswise into ⅛-inch-thick slices**
  2 **garlic cloves, finely chopped**
  ½ **cup water**
  ¼ **teaspoon salt**
  ⅛ **teaspoon black pepper**
  ¼ **cup finely chopped fresh basil**

▶ Heat 1 tablespoon oil in a 12-inch heavy skillet over moderately high heat until hot but not smoking, then sauté half of squash, stirring occasionally, until browned, about 5 minutes. Transfer browned squash to a bowl, then heat remaining tablespoon oil and sauté remaining squash in same manner. Return squash in bowl to skillet. Add garlic and sauté, stirring occasionally, 1 minute. Add water, salt, and pepper and simmer briskly, covered, until squash is tender and most of liquid is evaporated, 6 to 7 minutes. Stir in basil.

SPAGHETTI SQUASH WITH PARSLEY WALNUT PESTO

SERVES 4

Active time: 25 min   Start to finish: 30 min

  1 **(3½- to 4-lb) spaghetti squash**
  ¼ **cup walnuts (¾ oz)**
  ½ **garlic clove**
1⅓ **cups packed fresh flat-leaf parsley**
  3 **tablespoons extra-virgin olive oil**
2½ **tablespoons finely grated Pecorino**
  1 **tablespoon water**
  1 **teaspoon salt**
  ¼ **teaspoon black pepper**
  ¼ **teaspoon finely grated fresh lemon zest**

▶ Pierce squash all over with a sharp small knife. Cook in a microwave oven (see cooks' note, below) at high power (100 percent) 8 minutes, then turn over and microwave until squash gives when pressed gently, 8 to 10 minutes more. Cool squash 5 minutes.
▶ While squash cooks, toast nuts in a dry small heavy skillet over moderate heat, stirring frequently, until fragrant and a shade darker, about 6 minutes, then cool completely.
▶ Pulse nuts and garlic in a food processor until finely ground. Add parsley, oil, cheese, water, salt, pepper, and zest and pulse until parsley is coarsely chopped.
▶ While squash is still hot, cut off stem from squash and discard, then carefully halve squash lengthwise (it will emit steam) and discard seeds. Working over a bowl, scrape out squash flesh with a fork, loosening and separating strands. Toss with pesto in a bowl.

Cooks' note:
• We tested this recipe in an 800-watt microwave oven. If yours is less powerful (or more), adjust the cooking times accordingly.

BAKED SWEET POTATOES WITH SCALLIONS AND CILANTRO

SERVES 4

Active time: 5 min   Start to finish: 40 min

  4 **small slender sweet potatoes (2 lb total)**
  3 **tablespoons unsalted butter, softened**
  2 **scallions, finely chopped**
  2 **tablespoons finely chopped fresh cilantro**
  ½ **teaspoon salt**
  ¼ **teaspoon black pepper**

▶ Prick potatoes several times with a fork and put directly on oven rack in middle position. Put a sheet of foil on lower rack (to catch any drips) and heat oven to 450°F. Bake potatoes until soft when squeezed, 30 to 35 minutes.
▶ Mash together butter, scallions, cilantro, salt, and pepper. Slit potatoes lengthwise and put some butter mixture in center of each.

KITCHEN NOTE

GNARLED **CELERY ROOT** (SOMETIMES CALLED CELERIAC) YIELDS AN INCOMPARABLE VELVETY TEXTURE WHEN COOKED. YOU'LL NEED TO SCRUB IT WELL BEFOREHAND, SINCE IT IS USUALLY SANDY. A SMALL SHARP KNIFE IS BEST FOR PEELING. FIRST GIVE THE SPHERE SOLID FOOTING ON THE CUTTING BOARD BY LOPPING OFF THE TOP AND BOTTOM, THEN GUIDE THE KNIFE BLADE IN A SINGLE SWEEP FROM TOP TO BOTTOM, HUGGING THE CURVES AND REMOVING THE PEEL ONE SLICE AT A TIME, WORKING AROUND THE SPHERE.

ROOT VEGETABLE GRATIN

SERVES 4 TO 6

Active time: 20 min   Start to finish: 45 min

    Butter for greasing baking pan
 1 cup heavy cream
 ½ cup whole milk
 1 teaspoon finely chopped fresh thyme
 1 teaspoon salt
 ½ teaspoon black pepper
 1 lb celery root (sometimes called celeriac)
 1 lb carrots (4 large)
 2 tablespoons all-purpose flour
 2 oz Gruyère, coarsely grated (½ cup)

▶ Put oven rack in middle position and preheat oven to 400°F. Butter an 8-inch flameproof ceramic dish or metal baking pan.

▶ Simmer cream, milk, thyme, salt, and pepper, uncovered, in a 4-quart heavy saucepan over moderate heat until reduced to about ¾ cup, 10 to 13 minutes.

▶ While mixture simmers, peel celery root with a sharp knife, then cut into large wedges. Coarsely grate carrots and celery root in a food processor. Toss with flour in a large bowl until coated well, then add to cream mixture and simmer, uncovered, stirring frequently, 5 minutes.

▶ Transfer to baking dish and smooth top. Sprinkle evenly with Gruyère and bake until bubbling, about 10 minutes.

▶ Turn on broiler and broil gratin 5 to 6 inches from heat until top is golden brown, 3 to 5 minutes. Let stand 10 minutes before serving.

ZUCCHINI AND TOMATOES WITH MINT

SERVES 6

Active time: 20 min   Start to finish: 40 min

 3 tablespoons olive oil
 1 medium onion, quartered, then thinly sliced crosswise
 2 garlic cloves, thinly sliced
 1 (14- to 15-oz) can diced tomatoes in juice
 2 tablespoons drained bottled capers, rinsed
 ¼ teaspoon salt
 ¼ teaspoon black pepper
 3 medium zucchini, halved lengthwise, then cut crosswise into ⅓-inch-thick slices
 ¼ cup finely chopped fresh mint

▶ Heat oil in a 12-inch heavy skillet over moderately high heat until hot but not smoking, then sauté onion, stirring occasionally, until golden and softened, 8 to 10 minutes. Add garlic and cook, stirring, 1 minute.

▶ Stir in tomatoes (with juice), capers, salt, and pepper and bring to a boil. Add zucchini and cook, covered, over moderate heat, stirring occasionally, until zucchini is just tender, about 15 minutes. Remove lid, then boil, stirring occasionally, until most of liquid is evaporated, about 5 minutes. Remove from heat and stir in mint.

SALADS

MAIN COURSE SALADS

SMOKED-CHICKEN AND CRANBERRY SALAD

SERVES 4
Active time: 20 min   Start to finish: 25 min

½ cup dried cranberries (2¾ oz)
3 tablespoons olive oil
1 tablespoon fresh lime juice
¾ lb sliced smoked chicken breast, cut into ½-inch pieces (3 cups)
⅓ cup sliced almonds with skins, toasted (see Tips, page 8) and cooled (1¼ oz)
3 celery ribs, thinly sliced
¼ cup chopped fresh cilantro

▸Soak cranberries in a bowl of warm water to cover 15 minutes, then drain well in a sieve and chop. Whisk together oil and lime juice in a bowl, then add cranberries, remaining ingredients, and salt and pepper to taste, tossing to coat.

KITCHEN NOTE

IT'S VERY IMPORTANT TO **WASH SALAD GREENS**, EVEN IF THEY'RE ORGANIC OR LABELED "PRE-WASHED." WE LIKE TO WASH OUR GREENS IN A JUST-CLEANED SINK OF COLD WATER. GENTLY AGITATE THE LEAVES UNDERWATER, LETTING ANY SAND OR LITTLE BUGS DRIFT TO THE BOTTOM OF THE SINK, THEN LIFT THE GREENS OUT OF THE WATER INTO A COLANDER. FOR PARTICULARLY SANDY GREENS, YOU MAY NEED TO REPEAT THIS STEP UNTIL THERE IS NOT A TRACE OF GRIT ON THE BOTTOM OF THE SINK. DRY THE GREENS IN BATCHES IN A SALAD SPINNER, THEN TRANSFER TO BAGS LINED WITH PAPER TOWELS. DO NOT WASH GREENS MORE THAN A DAY OR TWO BEFORE USING.

SERRANO HAM SALAD WITH ALMOND GARLIC SAUCE

SERVES 4
Active time: 30 min   Start to finish: 30 min

For help in finding the Spanish ingredients in this recipe, see Sources.

1 garlic clove
½ teaspoon salt
½ cup plus 2 tablespoons slivered blanched almonds (3 oz), toasted (see Tips, page 8) and cooled
½ cup water
3 tablespoons extra-virgin olive oil
1 tablespoon Sherry vinegar
¼ teaspoon Tabasco
⅛ teaspoon black pepper
1 (7- to 8-oz) bottle Spanish *piquillo* peppers, rinsed, drained, and patted dry
1 head romaine (1 lb), outer leaves discarded and head cut crosswise into ¼-inch slices (8 cups)
¼ lb thinly sliced Serrano ham

▸Mince garlic and mash to a paste with salt using a heavy knife or a mortar and pestle. Transfer to a blender along with ½ cup almonds, water, oil, vinegar, Tabasco, and black pepper, then blend until dressing is very smooth, about 1 minute. Coarsely chop remaining 2 tablespoons almonds.
▸Cut a lengthwise slit in peppers and discard any seeds, then cut peppers into ¼-inch-wide strips.
▸Divide romaine and peppers among 4 plates, then arrange ham on top. Drizzle each serving with some dressing and sprinkle with chopped almonds. Serve remaining dressing on the side.

SOBA SALAD WITH CARROT AND ZUCCHINI

SERVES 4

Active time: 30 min   Start to finish: 30 min

- 3 to 4 tablespoons fresh lime juice
- 6 tablespoons soy sauce
- 1½ tablespoons finely minced peeled fresh ginger
- 1½ teaspoons sugar
- ¼ cup vegetable oil
- ½ lb soba noodles, freshly cooked to tender, rinsed under cold water, and drained
- 3 carrots, cut into ⅛-inch matchsticks
- 2 medium zucchini, cut into ⅛-inch matchsticks
- 1 bunch scallions, thinly sliced crosswise

▶ Whisk together lime juice (to taste), soy sauce, ginger, sugar, and oil in a large bowl. Add remaining ingredients and toss to combine. Season with salt and pepper. Serve at room temperature.

HERBED TOMATO PASTA SALAD

SERVES 4

Active time: 20 min   Start to finish: 30 min

- 2½ lb cherry tomatoes, quartered
- 1 teaspoon sugar
- 1¼ cups mixed chopped fresh herbs
- 1 lb *campanelle* (bell-shaped pasta)
- 5 garlic cloves, chopped
- ¾ cup extra-virgin olive oil

Accompaniment: **grated ricotta salata**

▶ Stir together tomatoes, sugar, and herbs in a large bowl until combined well. Cook pasta in boiling salted water (see Tips, page 8) until al dente, then drain well. Add hot pasta to tomato mixture.
▶ Cook garlic in oil in a 1-quart saucepan over moderately high heat, stirring, 1 minute. Add garlic with oil to pasta and toss to combine. Season with salt and pepper.

TUNA PASTA SALAD

SERVES 6

Active time: 15 min   Start to finish: 30 min

- ¾ cup mayonnaise
- 2 tablespoons fresh lemon juice
- 1 lb penne rigate, freshly cooked to tender, rinsed under cold water, and drained
- 1 tablespoon finely grated fresh lemon zest (see Tips, page 8)
- 1 (6-oz) can tuna packed in olive oil, drained
- 1 (15-oz) can white beans, rinsed and drained
- ½ cup thinly sliced fresh basil

▶ Whisk together mayonnaise and lemon juice in a large bowl. Add remaining ingredients and toss to combine. Season with salt and pepper. Serve at room temperature.

CREAMY TOFU SALAD

SERVES 4

Active time: 15 min   Start to finish: 20 min

This looks and tastes like egg salad, even though it's made with tofu.

- 1 (14-oz) package firm tofu, rinsed and drained
- ½ cup mayonnaise
- 1 teaspoon fresh lemon juice
- 1 teaspoon turmeric
- ½ teaspoon dry mustard
- 2 celery ribs, finely chopped
- ¼ cup chopped fresh chives
- ½ teaspoon salt, or to taste
- ¼ teaspoon black pepper, or to taste

Accompaniments: **sandwich bread; lettuce leaves; sliced tomato**

▶ Finely mash tofu with a fork in a bowl, then drain in a sieve set over another bowl, about 15 minutes (discard liquid).
▶ While tofu drains, whisk together mayonnaise, lemon juice, turmeric, and mustard in bowl, then stir in tofu, celery, chives, salt, and pepper.

SALADS WITH GREENS

ROASTED SQUASH, CHESTNUT, AND CHICORY SALAD WITH CRANBERRY VINAIGRETTE

SERVES 6

Active time: 45 min   Start to finish: 45 min

- 2 tablespoons extra-virgin olive oil plus additional for greasing
- 1 (2-lb) acorn squash
- 1 teaspoon salt
- ½ teaspoon black pepper
- 1 cup peeled cooked whole chestnuts (from a 7- to 8-oz jar), cut into thirds
- 4 (¼-inch-thick) slices pancetta (6 oz total), cut into ¼-inch dice
- ¼ cup fresh cranberries, finely chopped
- 1 tablespoon packed dark brown sugar
- ¼ cup water
- 2 tablespoons whole-grain mustard
- ¾ lb chicory (curly endive), trimmed and torn into 2-inch pieces (10 cups)

▶ Put oven rack in middle position and preheat oven to 450°F. Line a large shallow baking pan with foil and oil generously with olive oil.

▶ Cut off stem end of squash, then put cut side down and halve lengthwise. Discard seeds, then cut squash into ½-inch-thick slices. Peel if desired with a paring knife and transfer slices to a bowl. Add 1 tablespoon olive oil, ½ teaspoon salt, and ¼ teaspoon pepper and gently toss to coat. Arrange in 1 layer in baking pan and roast until golden, about 15 minutes. Remove from oven and turn squash over with a spatula. Add chestnuts to pan in an even layer, then continue to roast until squash is golden and tender, 10 to 15 minutes. Keep warm, covered with foil.

▶ While squash roasts, cook pancetta in a dry 10-inch heavy skillet over high heat until browned, about 4 minutes. Transfer pancetta with a slotted spoon to paper towels to drain, reserving fat in skillet.

▶ Reheat pancetta fat over moderately high heat until hot but not smoking, then add cranberries and brown sugar and stir once to combine. Remove from heat and add water, stirring and scraping up brown bits from bottom of skillet.

▶ Transfer cranberry mixture to a bowl and whisk in mustard, remaining tablespoon olive oil, remaining ½ teaspoon salt, and remaining ¼ teaspoon pepper.

▶ Toss together chicory, roasted acorn squash, and chestnuts. Just before serving, toss with dressing and sprinkle with pancetta.

Cooks' note:
• Squash and chestnuts can be roasted 4 hours ahead and kept at room temperature. Reheat before tossing with chicory.

KITCHEN NOTE

HEAT, LIGHT, AND AGE ARE ALL DETRIMENTAL TO **OLIVE AND NUT OILS**, SO KEEP THEM IN A COOL, DARK PLACE AND USE WITHIN A YEAR. NUT OILS (AND ASIAN SESAME OIL), WHICH ARE ESPECIALLY PERISHABLE, SHOULD BE STORED IN THE REFRIGERATOR AND BROUGHT TO ROOM TEMPERATURE BEFORE USING.

WATERMELON, ARUGULA, AND PINE NUT SALAD

SERVES 4

Active time: 15 min   Start to finish: 15 min

- 1 tablespoon fresh lemon juice
- 1 tablespoon red-wine vinegar
- ½ teaspoon table salt, or to taste
- 2 tablespoons extra-virgin olive oil
- 3 cups cubed (½ to ¾ inch) seeded watermelon, drained (from a 2½-lb piece, rind discarded)
- 6 cups baby arugula (6 oz)
- ¼ cup pine nuts (1 oz)
- ⅓ cup crumbled feta or ricotta salata (1½ oz)
  Coarsely ground black pepper to taste
  Fleur de sel to taste (optional)

▶ Whisk together lemon juice, vinegar, and table salt in a large bowl, then add oil in a slow stream, whisking until emulsified.

▶ Add watermelon, arugula, and pine nuts and toss to coat, then sprinkle with cheese, pepper, and *fleur de sel* (if using).

FRISÉE SALAD WITH CUCUMBER AND RADISHES

SERVES 4

Active time: 25 min   Start to finish: 25 min

½ seedless cucumber (usually plastic-wrapped), peeled, halved lengthwise, cored, and thinly sliced diagonally (2 cups)
2 teaspoons rice vinegar (not seasoned)
2 teaspoons extra-virgin olive oil
½ teaspoon salt
¼ teaspoon black pepper
2 oz frisée, trimmed (3 cups loosely packed)
1 bunch watercress, trimmed and tough stems discarded (3 cups loosely packed)
2 oz baby spinach (2 cups loosely packed)
6 radishes, sliced and cut into matchsticks

▶ Toss cucumber with vinegar, oil, salt, and pepper in a large bowl and let stand 10 minutes.
▶ Add frisée, watercress, spinach, and radishes and toss well.

Cooks' note:
• To save time, you can use 6 oz mesclun (premixed baby greens) total instead of the frisée, watercress, and spinach.
EACH SERVING ABOUT 45 CALORIES AND 3 GRAMS FAT

ENDIVE AND RADICCHIO SALAD

SERVES 4 TO 6

Active time: 20 min   Start to finish: 20 min

3 Belgian endives
¼ lb radicchio
1 tablespoon Dijon mustard
1 tablespoon Sherry vinegar
½ teaspoon sugar
½ teaspoon salt
½ teaspoon black pepper
3 tablespoons grapeseed or canola oil
1 teaspoon Asian sesame oil
2 scallions, finely chopped (¼ cup)
1 tablespoon sesame seeds, toasted (see Tips, page 8)
1 teaspoon black sesame seeds (optional)

▶ Trim endives and halve lengthwise. Cut pieces in half crosswise, then cut lengthwise into ¼-inch-wide strips.
▶ Cut radicchio in half and discard core, then cut lengthwise into ¼-inch-wide strips. Soak radicchio and endives in a large bowl of very cold water to crisp, 10 minutes, then drain and dry.
▶ Whisk together mustard, vinegar, sugar, salt, pepper, grapeseed oil, and sesame oil in another large bowl until emulsified.
▶ Add endives, radicchio, scallions, and sesame seeds and toss until coated well.

VEGETABLE SALADS AND SLAWS

WATERMELON, CUCUMBER, AND JICAMA SALAD

SERVES 6

Active time: 30 min   Start to finish: 30 min

4 cups cubed (½ inch) seeded watermelon (from a 3-lb piece, rind discarded)
2 cups cubed (½ inch) peeled jicama (1 lb)
2 cups cubed (½ inch) peeled and seeded cucumber (1½ lb)
½ cup fresh lime juice
¼ cup chopped fresh mint
¼ cup chopped fresh cilantro
¼ cup chopped fresh basil
1 teaspoon salt

▶ Toss together all ingredients in a serving bowl. Serve immediately.

Cooks' notes:
• Watermelon and vegetables can be cubed and combined 6 hours ahead and chilled, covered. Add lime juice, herbs, and salt just before serving.
• Herbs can be chopped and combined 6 hours ahead and chilled, covered.

BEET AND FETA SALAD

SERVES 1

Active time: 10 min Start to finish: 25 min

    4 small canned whole beets (1 to 1½ inches in
          diameter), drained
    1 teaspoon fresh lemon juice
    ⅛ teaspoon salt
    1 tablespoon plus 1 teaspoon extra-virgin olive oil
    1 tablespoon crumbled feta
    ¾ cup microgreens or mesclun (mixed baby
          salad greens)

▶ Quarter beets and put on a plate. Whisk together lemon juice and salt in a small bowl, then add oil in a slow stream, whisking until combined well. Season dressing with pepper and spoon 1 tablespoon over beets. Marinate 15 minutes.
▶ Sprinkle feta over beets. Just before serving, toss greens with remaining dressing and mound alongside beets.

WARM BROCCOLI SALAD WITH SHERRY VINAIGRETTE

SERVES 4

Active time: 30 min Start to finish: 30 min

    1 large egg
  1½ lb broccoli, heads cut into 2-inch-long florets
          (1 inch wide) and stems peeled and cut crosswise
          into ¼-inch slices
  1½ tablespoons Sherry vinegar
    2 teaspoons Dijon mustard
    ½ teaspoon salt
    ¼ teaspoon black pepper
    1 garlic clove, smashed
    ½ cup olive oil
    3 slices rye or firm white sandwich bread, crusts
          removed and bread cut into ½-inch cubes

▶ Cover egg with cold water by 1 inch in a 1- to 2-quart heavy saucepan and bring to a rolling boil, partially covered. Reduce heat to low and cook, covered, 30 seconds. Remove from heat and let stand, covered, 15 minutes. Transfer egg with a slotted spoon to a bowl of ice and cold water and let stand 5 minutes.
▶ While egg cooks, steam broccoli in a steamer set over

boiling water, covered, until just tender, 2 to 4 minutes, then transfer to a large bowl.
▶ Whisk together vinegar, mustard, salt, and pepper in a small bowl.
▶ Cook garlic in oil in a 10-inch heavy skillet over moderate heat until golden, 1 to 2 minutes, then discard garlic, reserving oil. Add bread to oil and cook, turning, until golden. Transfer croutons with a slotted spoon to paper towels to drain, reserving oil. Peel egg and force through a medium-mesh sieve using back of a spoon, then add to broccoli.
▶ Add 3 tablespoons hot oil to vinegar mixture, whisking until emulsified, then add to broccoli along with croutons and toss to combine.

KITCHEN NOTE

THE PROPORTIONS FOR A **CLASSIC VINAIGRETTE** ARE GENERALLY TWO OR THREE PARTS OIL TO ONE PART ACID. YOU'LL NEED LESS OIL IF YOU ARE USING A LOW-ACID VINEGAR, MORE OIL IF USING A HIGH-ACID VINEGAR. DEEP-FLAVORED GREENS CAN HANDLE A MORE ACIDIC DRESSING, WHICH MIGHT OVERWHELM MORE TENDER GREENS.

CELERY, RADISH, AND OLIVE SALAD

SERVES 2

Active time: 15 min Start to finish: 15 min

    1 bunch celery
    4 radishes, trimmed and cut into ⅛-inch-thick slices
   10 pitted Kalamata or other brine-cured black
          olives, chopped
  1½ tablespoons extra-virgin olive oil
    1 tablespoon finely chopped fresh chives
    2 teaspoons fresh lemon juice
    ⅛ teaspoon salt
    ⅛ teaspoon black pepper

▶ Remove outer dark green ribs of celery and reserve for another use. Remove leaves and reserve in a bowl. Cut off and discard base of celery heart, then cut ribs crosswise into ¼-inch-thick slices and add to celery leaves along with remaining ingredients. Toss to coat.

CREAMY CUCUMBERS

SERVES 4

Active time: 20 min   Start to finish: 20 min

- 1 large seedless cucumber (usually plastic-wrapped), thinly sliced crosswise
- 1 tablespoon salt
- ½ cup sour cream
- 2 tablespoons cider vinegar
- 1 teaspoon sugar
- ⅛ teaspoon black pepper
- 1 small red onion, halved lengthwise and thinly sliced crosswise (1 cup)

▶ Toss cucumber with salt in a colander and drain 15 minutes.

▶ Whisk together sour cream, vinegar, sugar, and pepper in a bowl until just combined.

▶ Rinse cucumber under cold water, then wrap in a kitchen towel and squeeze out excess moisture. Add cucumber and onion to sour cream mixture and toss to coat.

POTATO SALAD WITH MINT AND PEAS

SERVES 6

Active time: 15 min   Start to finish: 25 min

- 2 lb small red potatoes
- 2 tablespoons white-wine vinegar
- 1 tablespoon minced shallot
- 1 teaspoon salt
- ½ teaspoon black pepper
- 3 tablespoons extra-virgin olive oil
- 1 cup thawed frozen or cooked fresh baby peas (5 oz)
- ⅓ cup chopped or torn fresh mint leaves

▶ Cover potatoes with cold salted water (see Tips, page 8) in a 3-quart saucepan, then simmer, covered, until tender, 10 to 15 minutes.

▶ While potatoes cook, whisk together vinegar, shallot, salt, and pepper in a large serving bowl.

▶ Drain potatoes and halve or quarter if desired. Add to vinegar mixture while warm and toss to coat. Add oil, peas, and mint and toss to combine. Season with salt and pepper and serve warm or at room temperature.

KITCHEN NOTE

IT'S BEST TO **DRESS A POTATO SALAD WHILE IT'S STILL WARM**; WARM POTATOES ABSORB THE DRESSING BETTER THAN COLD ONES.

HOT-AND-SOUR COLESLAW

SERVES 4 TO 6

Active time: 20 min   Start to finish: 20 min

- 1 small head cabbage (2 lb), quartered, cored, and thinly sliced
- ½ lb carrots (3 medium), shredded
- ⅓ cup finely chopped scallions
- 1¾ teaspoons salt
- ¼ cup cider vinegar
- ¼ cup sugar
- 2 tablespoons finely chopped peeled fresh ginger
- ½ teaspoon dried hot red pepper flakes

▶ Toss together cabbage, carrots, scallions, and salt in a large bowl and let stand until cabbage is slightly wilted, about 5 minutes.

▶ Bring vinegar, sugar, ginger, and red pepper flakes to a boil in a very small saucepan, stirring until sugar is dissolved, then pour over cabbage mixture and toss to coat.

CONDIMENTS

SUN-DRIED TOMATO BUTTER

MAKES ABOUT ⅔ CUP
Active time: 15 min   Start to finish: 45 min

Put a slice of this butter on any grilled or panfried meat or fish, or slather it on warm corn bread.

- 1 stick (½ cup) unsalted butter, softened
- 2 tablespoons finely chopped drained oil-packed sun-dried tomatoes
- ½ teaspoon anchovy paste
- ¼ teaspoon finely grated fresh orange zest
- ¼ teaspoon finely chopped fresh rosemary
- ⅛ teaspoon salt
- ⅛ teaspoon black pepper

▶ Pulse together all ingredients in a food processor until tomato is finely chopped and butter is pale pink. Transfer to a sheet of wax paper or parchment paper and roll into a log about 1½ inches thick. Twist ends of paper to enclose butter and chill until firm, about 30 minutes.

KITCHEN NOTE

WE PREFER TO BUY **SUN-DRIED TOMATOES** PACKED IN OIL (RATHER THAN THOSE PACKAGED DRY IN POUCHES). PLUMP AND PLIABLE, THEY'RE READY TO USE IN PASTAS OR SALADS.

SKILLET BLACKBERRY JAM

MAKES ABOUT 1½ CUPS
Active time: 10 min   Start to finish: 45 min (includes chilling)

Be sure to use powdered fruit pectin in this recipe—don't substitute liquid pectin or a low-sugar variety.

- 1 lb blackberries (4 cups)
- ¾ cup sugar
- 2 tablespoons powdered fruit pectin
- 1 tablespoon fresh lemon juice

▶ Mash blackberries with a potato masher or a fork in a large bowl.
▶ Stir together berries, sugar, pectin, and lemon juice in a 12-inch nonstick skillet, then boil, stirring occasionally, until slightly thickened, about 7 minutes. Transfer jam to a large shallow bowl and chill, its surface covered with wax paper, until softly set, at least 30 minutes. (Jam will set further if chilled longer.)

Cooks' note:
• Jam keeps, chilled in an airtight container, 2 weeks.

FRESH MINT CHUTNEY

MAKES ABOUT ⅔ CUP
Active time: 15 min   Start to finish: 15 min

This chutney is great with sautéed scallops, grilled shrimp, or grilled lamb.

- 1 cup loosely packed fresh mint leaves
- 4 scallions, coarsely chopped
- 1 small fresh green serrano chile, coarsely chopped (1 to 1½ teaspoons), including seeds
- 1 large garlic clove, chopped
- ¼ cup fresh lime juice
- 2 tablespoons water
- 2 teaspoons sugar
- ¾ teaspoon ground cumin
- ¾ teaspoon salt

▶ Coarsely purée all ingredients in a food processor.

Cooks' note:
• Chutney is best eaten the day it is made (the color will turn overnight). Keep chilled, covered.

DESSERTS

CAKES

ALMOND CAKE WITH BERRIES

SERVES 6 TO 8
Active time: 20 min   Start to finish: 45 min

For cake

Butter for greasing pan
½ cup all-purpose flour plus additional for dusting pan
1 cup sliced almonds (preferably with skins; 3½ oz)
⅔ cup sugar
4 large egg yolks
3 tablespoons whole milk
¾ teaspoon vanilla
¼ teaspoon salt
2 large egg whites

For berry syrup

⅓ cup water
¼ cup sugar
1 tablespoon fresh lemon juice
⅛ teaspoon almond extract
2 cups blackberries (9 oz)
1 cup raspberries (4½ oz)

Garnish: confectioners sugar

Make cake:

▶ Put oven rack in middle position and preheat oven to 400°F. Generously butter a 9- by 2-inch round cake pan and dust with flour, knocking out excess.

▶ Pulse almonds with ⅓ cup sugar in a food processor until finely ground. Transfer almond sugar to a large bowl and add yolks, flour (½ cup), milk, vanilla, and salt, whisking until combined (batter will be thick).

▶ Beat whites with a pinch of salt in a bowl using an electric mixer at medium-high speed until they just hold soft peaks. Add remaining ⅓ cup sugar a little at a time, beating at medium speed, then beat at high speed until whites hold stiff, glossy peaks.

▶ Fold about one third of whites into batter to lighten, then fold in remaining whites gently but thoroughly.

▶ Pour batter into cake pan and bake until cake is springy to the touch and a wooden pick or skewer inserted in center comes out clean, 18 to 20 minutes. Cool cake in pan on a rack 5 minutes, then invert onto rack and cool 10 minutes.

Make berry syrup while cake bakes:

▶ Bring water and sugar to a boil in a 1-quart heavy saucepan, stirring until sugar is dissolved. Cool syrup 20 minutes, then stir in lemon juice and extract. Gently stir in berries.

▶ Arrange cake, right side up, on a plate and spoon berries over top, then slowly pour fruit syrup evenly over cake. Dust with confectioners sugar if desired.

CHOCOLATE LAYER CAKE WITH MILK CHOCOLATE FROSTING

SERVES 8 TO 10
Active time: 1 hr   Start to finish: 2½ hr (includes cooling)

For cake

2 cups all-purpose flour
⅔ cup unsweetened cocoa powder (not Dutch-process)
1½ teaspoons baking soda
½ teaspoon salt
2 sticks (1 cup) unsalted butter, softened
1 cup packed dark brown sugar
¾ cup granulated sugar
4 large eggs at room temperature for 30 minutes
2 oz unsweetened chocolate, melted and cooled
1½ teaspoons vanilla
1½ cups well-shaken buttermilk

For frosting

⅔ cup whole milk
3 large egg yolks
1 tablespoon plus 1 teaspoon all-purpose flour
1⅓ cups confectioners sugar
1 teaspoon vanilla
3 sticks (1½ cups) unsalted butter, cut into tablespoon pieces and softened
8 oz milk chocolate, melted and cooled
2 oz unsweetened chocolate, melted and cooled

Make cake:

▶ Put oven rack in middle position and preheat oven to 350°F. Butter 2 (9- by 2-inch) round cake pans and line bottom of each with a round of parchment or wax paper. Butter paper and dust pans with flour, knocking out excess.

▶ Sift together flour, cocoa, baking soda, and salt into a small bowl. Beat together butter and sugars in a large bowl using an electric mixer at medium-high speed until light and fluffy, 3 to 4 minutes in a stand mixer or 4 to 5 minutes with a handheld. Add eggs 1 at a time, beating well after each addition. Add chocolate and vanilla and beat until just combined. Reduce speed to low and add flour mixture and buttermilk alternately in 3 batches, beginning with flour mixture and mixing until just combined.

▶ Divide batter between cake pans, spreading evenly, and bake until a wooden pick or skewer inserted in center of each cake layer comes out clean, 25 to 35 minutes.

▶ Cool cake layers in pans on racks 10 minutes. Run a thin knife around edge of each layer, then invert onto racks. Peel off paper and cool layers completely.

Make frosting:

▶ Heat milk in a 1- to 1½-quart heavy saucepan over moderate heat until hot. Whisk together yolks, flour, ⅓ cup confectioners sugar, and a pinch of salt in a bowl, then add hot milk in a stream, whisking. Transfer custard to saucepan and bring to a boil over moderate heat, whisking. Reduce heat and simmer, whisking, 2 minutes (mixture will be very thick), then transfer to a large bowl. Cover surface of custard with a buttered round of wax paper and cool completely, about 45 minutes.

▶ Add vanilla and remaining cup confectioners sugar to custard and beat with cleaned beaters at moderate speed until combined well, then increase speed to medium-high and beat in butter, 2 tablespoons at a time, until smooth. Add chocolates and beat until combined well.

Frost cake:

▶ Halve each cake layer horizontally using a long serrated knife. Layer cake, using a heaping ½ cup frosting between each layer, then frost top and sides with remaining frosting.

Cooks' notes:

• Cake layers can be made (but not halved) 1 day ahead and kept, wrapped well in plastic wrap, at room temperature.

• Frosting can be made 1 day ahead and chilled, covered. Bring to room temperature (do not use a microwave) and beat with an electric mixer before using.

ESPRESSO AND MASCARPONE ICEBOX CAKE
SERVES 10 TO 12

Active time: 30 min   Start to finish: 9½ hr (includes chilling)

  3 cups chilled heavy cream
 ½ cup plus 1 tablespoon sugar
  1 cup mascarpone cheese (9 oz) at room temperature
  1 (9-oz) box chocolate wafers such as Nabisco Famous
  1 tablespoon instant-espresso powder (see Sources)

Special equipment: **a 9½- to 10-inch springform pan; an offset metal spatula**

▶ Beat 2 cups cream with 6 tablespoons sugar in a bowl with an electric mixer at medium speed until it just holds soft peaks, 2 to 4 minutes. Reduce speed to low, then add mascarpone and mix until combined.

▶ Spread 1¼ cups mascarpone mixture evenly in bottom of springform pan and cover with 14 wafers, overlapping slightly if necessary. Spread with another 1¼ cups mascarpone mixture, followed by 14 more wafers arranged in same manner. Spread remaining mascarpone mixture on top. Smooth top with offset spatula, then cover pan with foil and freeze until firm, about 1 hour.

▶ Transfer from freezer to refrigerator and chill, covered, until a sharp knife inserted into center cuts through softened wafers easily, about 8 hours.

▶ Pulse remaining chocolate wafers in a food processor until finely ground.

▶ Beat remaining cup cream with espresso powder and remaining 3 tablespoons sugar using cleaned beaters at medium speed until it just holds stiff peaks, about 3 minutes.

▶ Remove foil and side of pan and frost cake all over with espresso cream. Sprinkle edge of top lightly with wafer crumbs. Serve cold.

Cooks' notes:

• Cake (without espresso cream) can be chilled 2 days.

• Cake can be frosted with espresso cream 4 hours ahead and chilled, loosely covered with foil.

COOKIES AND BARS

CARDAMOM BUTTER SQUARES
MAKES ABOUT 6 DOZEN
Active time: 35 min   Start to finish: 5½ hr (includes chilling and letting icing set)

Yvonne M. Parnes of Batavia, Ohio, got the recipe for these rich, buttery cookies in an e-mail from the McCormick spice company. We like them plain, but drizzled with espresso icing and bittersweet chocolate, they are truly out of this world.

For cookies

 3 cups all-purpose flour
 1 teaspoon baking powder
 ¾ teaspoon salt
1½ teaspoons ground cardamom
 ½ teaspoon ground cinnamon
 ¼ teaspoon ground allspice
 2 sticks (1 cup) unsalted butter, softened
1¼ cups granulated sugar
 2 large eggs
 1 teaspoon vanilla

For espresso and chocolate icings

 1 teaspoon instant-espresso powder (see Sources)
 1 teaspoon vanilla
1½ to 2 tablespoons milk
 1 cup confectioners sugar
 3 oz fine-quality bittersweet chocolate
    (not unsweetened), melted

Special equipment: **2 small heavy-duty sealable plastic bags (for icing; not pleated)**

Make cookies:
▶ Whisk together flour, baking powder, salt, cardamom, cinnamon, and allspice in a bowl.
▶ Beat together butter and sugar in a large bowl with an electric mixer at medium-high speed until pale and fluffy, about 2 minutes in a stand mixer (preferably fitted with paddle attachment) or 4 minutes with a handheld. Beat in eggs and vanilla. Reduce speed to low, then mix in flour mixture until just combined.
▶ Form dough into 2 (12-inch) logs (1½ inches in diameter), each on its own sheet of plastic wrap. Use plastic wrap and

your hands to roll, press, and square off sides of logs. Chill logs on a baking sheet until slightly firm, about 1 hour, then smooth logs with plastic wrap and flat side of a ruler to achieve straight sides. Chill logs on baking sheet until firm, about 1 hour.
▶ Put oven racks in upper and lower thirds of oven and preheat oven to 350°F.
▶ Cut enough scant ¼-inch-thick slices from a log with a knife to fill 2 large ungreased baking sheets, arranging slices about 1 inch apart (chill remaining dough, wrapped in plastic wrap).
▶ Bake cookies, switching position of sheets halfway through baking, until edges are golden, 10 to 12 minutes total. Cool cookies on sheets 3 minutes, then transfer to racks to cool completely. Make more cookies with remaining dough on cooled baking sheets.

Ice cookies:
▶ Whisk together espresso powder, vanilla, and 1½ tablespoons milk until espresso powder is dissolved, then add confectioners sugar and enough additional milk to make a thick but pourable icing. Spoon into a sealable bag and snip ⅛ inch off a bottom corner.
▶ Spoon melted chocolate into another sealable bag and snip ⅛ inch off a bottom corner.
▶ Pipe some espresso icing and chocolate over each cookie and let cookies stand on racks until icing sets, about 2 hours.

Cooks' notes:
• Dough logs can be chilled 5 days or frozen, wrapped in a double layer of plastic wrap, 1 month (thaw in refrigerator just until they can be sliced).
• Cookies keep, layered between sheets of wax paper, in an airtight container at room temperature 1 week.

KITCHEN NOTE

CARDAMOM IS THE DRIED FRUIT OF A GINGER FAMILY PLANT. THE OVAL PODS CONTAIN LOTS OF BROWN AROMATIC SEEDS. IF POSSIBLE, USE ONLY WHOLE PODS AND SEED THEM BY HAND AS NEEDED. GROUND CARDAMOM LABELED "DECORTICATED," WHICH MEANS THAT ONLY THE INNER SEED IS GROUND AND NOT THE OUTER HULL, IS INCREASINGLY AVAILABLE IN SUPERMARKETS AND IS MORE POTENT THAN REGULAR GROUND CARDAMOM.

RUGELACH

MAKES ABOUT 44 COOKIES
Active time: 40 min   Start to finish: 9¾ hr (includes chilling dough)

- 2   cups all-purpose flour
- ½   teaspoon salt
- 2   sticks (1 cup) unsalted butter, softened
- 8   oz cream cheese, softened
- ½   cup plus 4 teaspoons sugar
- 1   teaspoon cinnamon
- 1   cup apricot preserves or raspberry jam
- 1   cup loosely packed golden raisins, chopped
- 1¼   cups walnuts (¼ lb), finely chopped
      Milk for brushing cookies

Special equipment: **parchment paper; a small offset metal spatula**

▸ Whisk together flour and salt in a bowl. Beat together butter and cream cheese in a large bowl with an electric mixer at medium-high speed until combined well. Add flour mixture and stir with a wooden spoon until a soft dough forms. Gather dough into a ball and wrap in plastic wrap, then flatten (in wrap) into a roughly 7- by 5-inch rectangle. Chill until firm, 8 to 24 hours.

▸ Put oven rack in middle position and preheat oven to 350°F. Line bottom of a 1- to 1½-inch-deep large shallow baking pan with parchment paper.

▸ Cut dough into 4 pieces. Chill 3 pieces, wrapped in plastic wrap, and roll out remaining piece into a 12- by 8-inch rectangle on a well-floured surface with a floured rolling pin. Transfer dough to a sheet of parchment, then transfer to a tray and chill while rolling out remaining dough in same manner, transferring each to another sheet of parchment and stacking on tray.

▸ Whisk together ½ cup sugar and cinnamon. Arrange 1 dough rectangle on work surface with a long side nearest you. Spread ¼ cup preserves evenly over dough with offset spatula. Sprinkle ¼ cup raisins and a rounded ¼ cup walnuts over jam, then sprinkle with 2 tablespoons cinnamon sugar.

▸ Using parchment as an aid, roll up dough tightly into a log. Place, seam side down, in lined baking pan, then pinch ends closed and tuck underneath. Make 3 more logs in same manner and arrange 1 inch apart in pan. Brush logs with milk and sprinkle each with 1 teaspoon of remaining

granulated sugar. With a sharp large knife, make ¾-inch-deep cuts crosswise in dough (not all the way through) at 1-inch intervals. (If dough is too soft to cut, chill until firmer, 20 to 30 minutes.)

▸ Bake until golden, 45 to 50 minutes. Cool to warm in pan on a rack, about 30 minutes, then transfer logs to a cutting board and slice cookies all the way through.

INSIDE-OUT CARROT CAKE COOKIES

MAKES ABOUT 13 COOKIES
Active time: 20 min   Start to finish: 45 min

- 1⅛   cups all-purpose flour
- 1   teaspoon cinnamon
- ½   teaspoon baking soda
- ½   teaspoon salt
- 1   stick (½ cup) unsalted butter, softened
- ⅓   cup plus 2 tablespoons packed light brown sugar
- ⅓   cup plus 2 tablespoons granulated sugar
- 1   large egg
- ½   teaspoon vanilla
- 1   cup coarsely grated carrots (2 medium)
- 1   scant cup walnuts (3 oz), chopped
- ½   cup raisins (2½ oz)
- 8   oz cream cheese, softened
- ¼   cup honey

▸ Put oven racks in upper and lower thirds of oven and preheat oven to 375°F. Butter 2 baking sheets.

▸ Whisk together flour, cinnamon, baking soda, and salt in a bowl.

▸ Beat together butter, sugars, egg, and vanilla in a bowl with an electric mixer at medium speed until pale and fluffy, about 2 minutes. Mix in carrots, nuts, and raisins at low speed, then add flour mixture and mix until just combined.

▸ Drop 1½ tablespoons batter per cookie 2 inches apart on baking sheets and bake, switching position of sheets halfway through baking, until cookies are lightly browned and springy to the touch, 12 to 16 minutes total. Cool cookies on sheets on racks 1 minute, then transfer cookies to racks to cool completely.

▸ While cookies bake, blend cream cheese and honey in a food processor until smooth.

▸ Sandwich flat sides of cookies together with a generous tablespoon of cream cheese filling in between.

POLISH APRICOT-FILLED COOKIES

MAKES ABOUT 5 DOZEN
Active time: 1½ hr   Start to finish: 4 hr (includes chilling)

Fredricka Schwanka of Terryville, Connecticut, re-created her grandmother's recipe for these pastrylike cookies.

For pastry dough
2¼ cups all-purpose flour
½ teaspoon salt
8 oz cream cheese, softened
2 sticks (1 cup) unsalted butter, softened
1 large egg, lightly beaten with 2 teaspoons water
    for egg wash

For apricot filling
1¾ cups coarsely chopped dried apricots (10 oz)
½ cup golden raisins
⅔ cup mild honey
¼ cup sweet orange marmalade
½ teaspoon cinnamon
1 cup water

Special equipment: **parchment paper**
Garnish: **confectioners sugar**

Make dough:
▶ Whisk together flour and salt in a bowl until combined.
▶ Beat cream cheese and butter in a large bowl with an electric mixer at medium-high speed until pale and creamy, about 3 minutes in a stand mixer (preferably fitted with a paddle attachment) or 6 minutes with a handheld. Reduce mixer speed to low, then add flour mixture and mix just until combined.
▶ Divide dough into 4 equal pieces and wrap each in plastic wrap. Chill until firm, about 1½ hours.

Make filling while pastry chills:
▶ Bring apricots, raisins, honey, marmalade, cinnamon and water to a boil in a 2- to 3-quart heavy saucepan over moderate heat, stirring. Reduce heat and simmer, stirring, until dried fruit is softened and mixture is thick, about 10 minutes. Transfer to a small bowl and cool until warm, about 20 minutes. Transfer to a food processor and pulse until finely chopped. Chill until cold, about 2 hours.

Assemble and bake cookies:
▶ Put oven rack in middle position and preheat oven to 375°F. Line a large baking sheet with parchment.

▶ Roll out 1 piece of dough (keep remaining pieces chilled) between 2 (12-inch) sheets of well-floured wax paper with a rolling pin into a roughly 11-inch square. (If dough gets too soft, transfer dough in wax paper to a baking sheet and chill until firm.) Discard top sheet of wax paper and trim dough with a pastry wheel or sharp knife into a 10-inch square. Cut square into 4 equal strips, then cut crosswise in fourths again to form a total of 16 (2½-inch) squares.
▶ Working quickly, put 1 heaping teaspoon filling in center of each square. Brush 2 opposite corners with egg wash, then bring corners together and pinch firmly to adhere. (If dough becomes too soft, freeze it on a baking sheet for a few minutes.)
▶ Arrange cookies 2 inches apart on baking sheet. Bake until golden, 17 to 20 minutes, then transfer with a metal spatula to racks to cool completely. Make more cookies with remaining dough and filling on a lined cooled baking sheet.

Cooks' notes:
• Cookies keep, layered between sheets of wax paper or parchment, in an airtight container at room temperature 4 days.
• You will have leftover filling, which is wonderful spread on toast or an English muffin.

MINI CHOCOLATE SANDWICH COOKIES
MAKES ABOUT 200 SANDWICHES
Active time: 1½ hr   Start to finish: 3 hr

When Abby Cohen of Oakland, California, was in college, her friend Michael Gevelber would receive these cookies in care packages sent by his Czechoslovakian mother. They taste best when made and filled 1 day ahead.

For cookies
2 cups all-purpose flour
½ teaspoon salt
1½ sticks (¾ cup) unsalted butter, softened
⅔ cup sugar
2 whole large eggs
2 large egg yolks
3 oz fine-quality semisweet chocolate, finely chopped,
    melted, and cooled
2 oz fine-quality bittersweet chocolate (not unsweetened),
    finely chopped, melted, and cooled

For filling

- **2** large eggs
- **1** cup confectioners sugar
- **1½** sticks (¾ cup) unsalted butter, cut into ¼ -inch cubes
- **4** oz fine-quality bittersweet chocolate (not unsweetened), finely chopped

Special equipment: **an instant-read thermometer**

Make cookies:

▶ Whisk together flour and salt in a bowl until combined.

▶ Beat together butter and sugar in a large bowl with an electric mixer at medium-high speed until pale and fluffy, about 2 minutes in a stand mixer (preferably fitted with paddle attachment) or 4 minutes with a handheld. Add whole eggs, yolks, and chocolates, beating until combined. Reduce speed to low, then add flour mixture and mix until combined well.

▶ Put oven racks in upper and lower thirds of oven and preheat oven to 350°F.

▶ Drop ½ teaspoons of batter 1 inch apart on 2 ungreased baking sheets. Bake, switching position of sheets halfway through baking, until cookies are puffed up, 7 to 8 minutes total, then transfer with a metal spatula to racks to cool completely. Cool baking sheets and make more cookies with remaining dough on cooled sheets.

Make filling:

▶ Whisk together eggs, confectioners sugar, butter, and chocolate in top of a double boiler or a large metal bowl set over a pot of barely simmering water and cook, whisking, until a thermometer registers 170°F. Remove top of double boiler (or bowl) from pot and set in a larger bowl of ice and cold water, then stir occasionally until cold. Remove from ice water and beat with cleaned beaters at medium-high speed until pale and fluffy, about 3 minutes.

Fill cookies:

▶ Spread ½ teaspoon filling on flat side of 1 cookie, then form a sandwich with another cookie. Fill remaining cookies in same manner.

Cooks' note:

• Filled cookies keep, layered between sheets of wax paper or parchment, in an airtight container at room temperature 4 days.

CONFECTIONS

FLEUR DE SEL CARAMELS

MAKES ABOUT 40 CANDIES
Active time: 45 min   Start to finish: 2¾ hr (includes cooling)

- **1** cup heavy cream
- **5** tablespoons unsalted butter, cut into pieces
- **1** teaspoon *fleur de sel* (see Sources)
- **1½** cups sugar
- **¼** cup light corn syrup
- **¼** cup water

Special equipment: **parchment paper; a deep-fat thermometer**

▶ Line bottom and sides of an 8-inch square baking pan with parchment, then lightly oil parchment.

▶ Bring cream, butter, and *fleur de sel* to a boil in a small saucepan, then remove from heat.

▶ Boil sugar, corn syrup, and water in a 3- to 4-quart heavy saucepan, stirring until sugar is dissolved. Boil, without stirring but gently swirling pan, until mixture is a light golden caramel.

▶ Carefully stir in cream mixture (mixture will bubble up) and simmer, stirring frequently, until caramel registers 248°F on thermometer, 10 to 15 minutes. Pour into baking pan and cool 2 hours. Cut into 1-inch pieces, then wrap each piece in a 4-inch square of wax paper, twisting 2 ends to close.

KITCHEN NOTE

FLEUR DE SEL, THE SEA SALT FROM FRANCE'S BRITTANY REGION, IS COVETED FOR ITS LIGHTWEIGHT, FLAVORFUL CRYSTALS THAT ARE HARVESTED FROM THE SURFACES OF SALT PONDS. BE AWARE THAT YOU CAN'T SUBSTITUTE IT MEASURE FOR MEASURE WITH REGULAR SALT; IT IS BETTER TO ERR ON THE CAUTIOUS SIDE.

CORNFLAKE ALMOND CRUNCH
MAKES ABOUT 6 CUPS

Active time: 15 min   Start to finish: 1 hr

- 1 cup sliced almonds (4 oz)
- 4 cups cornflakes (4 oz)
- 1 large egg white
- 3 tablespoons plus 2 teaspoons sugar
- ¼ teaspoon salt

▸ Put oven rack in middle position and preheat oven to 325°F.

▸ Toast almonds in a large shallow baking pan until pale golden, 8 to 10 minutes. Cool, then toss with cornflakes in a large bowl.

▸ Line bottom of cooled baking pan with foil, then lightly oil foil. Whisk together egg white, 3 tablespoons sugar, and salt in a small bowl, then add to cornflake mixture and toss gently to coat well. Spread mixture in pan in a thin, even layer and sprinkle with remaining 2 teaspoons sugar. Bake until nuts and coating are golden, 15 to 20 minutes. Cool completely in pan on a rack. Peel off foil and break into pieces.

CRISPY RICE AND FRUIT BARK
MAKES ABOUT 36 PIECES CANDY

Active time: 15 min   Start to finish: 2½ hr (includes chilling)

- 8 oz fine-quality milk chocolate, chopped
- 1½ cups crispy rice cereal
- ⅓ cup dried soft apricots (2 oz), chopped
- ⅓ cup soft raisins (2 oz)

▸ Melt chocolate in a large metal bowl set over a saucepan of barely simmering water, stirring occasionally. Meanwhile, line bottom and sides of a 13- by 9-inch baking pan with foil, leaving a 1-inch overhang, then lightly oil foil.

▸ When chocolate is smooth, remove bowl from pan and cool chocolate to warm, then add cereal and fruit, stirring gently until combined well. Spread evenly in baking pan and chill until firm, at least 2 and up to 24 hours. Lift candy in foil from pan and transfer to a cutting board. Peel off foil and break candy into 2-inch pieces.

PIES AND TARTS

CHOCOLATE CREAM PIE
SERVES 8 TO 10

Active time: 45 min   Start to finish: 8 hr (includes chilling)

For crust
- 1⅓ cups chocolate wafer crumbs (from about 26 cookies such as Nabisco Famous)
- 5 tablespoons unsalted butter, melted
- ¼ cup sugar

For filling
- ⅔ cup sugar
- ¼ cup cornstarch
- ½ teaspoon salt
- 4 large egg yolks
- 3 cups whole milk
- 5 oz fine-quality bittersweet chocolate (not unsweetened), melted
- 2 oz unsweetened chocolate, melted
- 2 tablespoons unsalted butter, softened
- 1 teaspoon vanilla

For topping
- ¾ cup chilled heavy cream
- 1 tablespoon sugar

Make crust:

▸ Put oven rack in middle position and preheat oven to 350°F.

▸ Stir together crumbs, butter, and sugar and press on bottom and up side of a 9-inch pie plate (1-quart capacity). Bake until crisp, about 15 minutes, and cool on a rack.

Make filling:

▸ Whisk together sugar, cornstarch, salt, and yolks in a 3-quart heavy saucepan until combined well, then add milk in a stream, whisking. Bring to a boil over moderate heat, whisking, then reduce heat and simmer, whisking, 1 minute (filling will be thick).

▸ Force filling through a fine-mesh sieve into a bowl, then whisk in chocolates, butter, and vanilla. Cover surface of filling with a buttered round of wax paper and cool completely, about 2 hours.

▸ Spoon filling into crust and chill pie, loosely covered, at least 6 hours.

Make topping:

▶ Just before serving, beat cream with sugar in a bowl until it just holds stiff peaks, then spoon on top of pie.

Cooks' note:

• Pie (without topping) can be chilled up to 1 day.

LATTICE-CRUST PEAR PIE

SERVES 6 TO 8
Active time: 1 hr   Start to finish: 5½ hr (includes making pastry and cooling pie)

  3 tablespoons all-purpose flour
 ¼ teaspoon freshly grated nutmeg
 ⅛ teaspoon salt
 ⅔ cup plus 1 tablespoon sugar
2½ lb firm-ripe Bartlett or Anjou pears, peeled, each cut into 8 wedges, and cored
  1 tablespoon fresh lemon juice
     Pastry dough (recipe follows)
  1 tablespoon milk

▶ Put oven rack in middle position and preheat oven to 425°F.
▶ Whisk together flour, nutmeg, salt, and ⅔ cup sugar, then gently toss with pears and lemon juice.
▶ Roll out 1 piece of dough (keep remaining piece chilled) on a lightly floured surface with a lightly floured rolling pin into a 13-inch round, then fit into a 9½-inch glass or metal pie plate. Trim edge, leaving a ½-inch overhang. Chill shell while rolling out dough for top crust.
▶ Roll out remaining piece of dough on lightly floured surface with lightly floured rolling pin into a roughly 16- by 11-inch rectangle. Cut crosswise into 12 (1-inch-wide) strips with a pastry wheel or a sharp knife. Spoon filling into shell. Weave a lattice pattern over pie with pastry strips. Trim edges of all strips close to edge of pie plate. Fold bottom crust up over edges of lattice and crimp edge. Brush lattice (not edge) with milk and sprinkle lattice with remaining tablespoon sugar.
▶ Bake pie on a baking sheet 20 minutes, then reduce oven temperature to 375°F and cover edge of pie with a pie shield or foil. Continue to bake until crust is golden brown and filling is bubbling, 50 to 60 minutes more. Cool pie on a rack to warm or room temperature, at least 2 hours.

PASTRY DOUGH

MAKES ENOUGH FOR 1 DOUBLE-CRUST 9- TO 9½-INCH PIE
Active time: 20 min   Start to finish: 1¼ hr

2½ cups all-purpose flour
1½ sticks (¾ cup) cold unsalted butter, cut into ½-inch pieces
 ¼ cup cold vegetable shortening
 ½ teaspoon salt
  5 to 7 tablespoons ice water

Special equipment: a pastry or bench scraper

▶ Blend together flour, butter, shortening, and salt in a bowl with your fingertips or a pastry blender (or pulse in a food processor) until most of mixture resembles coarse meal with some small (roughly pea-size) butter lumps. Drizzle evenly with 5 tablespoons ice water and gently stir with a fork (or pulse in food processor) until incorporated.
▶ Squeeze a small handful: If it doesn't hold together, add more ice water, 1 tablespoon at a time, stirring (or pulsing) until incorporated, then test again. (Do not overwork mixture, or pastry will be tough.)
▶ Turn mixture out onto a work surface and divide into 8 portions. With heel of your hand, smear each portion once or twice in a forward motion to help distribute fat. Gather dough together with scraper and press into 2 balls, then flatten each into a 5-inch disk. Wrap disks separately in plastic wrap and chill until firm, at least 1 hour.

Cooks' note:

• Dough can be chilled up to 1 day.

KITCHEN NOTE

FRAISAGE, A FRENCH TECHNIQUE, IS A FINAL ENERGETIC BLENDING OF PASTRY INGREDIENTS THAT HELPS DISTRIBUTE THE FAT EVENLY AND GIVES THE DOUGH JUST ENOUGH STRUCTURE TO PREVENT IT FROM TEARING.

CHOCOLATE HAZELNUT TART
SERVES 8 TO 10

Active time: 25 min   Start to finish: 45 min

1½   cups graham cracker crumbs
¾   stick (6 tablespoons) unsalted butter, melted
¼   teaspoon salt
1   cup hazelnuts (4¾ oz), coarsely chopped
1   cup heavy cream
10½   oz fine-quality bittersweet chocolate (not unsweetened), finely chopped
½   cup chocolate-hazelnut spread such as Nutella

Special equipment: a 9-inch (24-cm) springform pan

Make crust and toast nuts:

▶ Put oven racks in upper and lower thirds of oven and preheat oven to 350°F. Invert bottom of springform pan (so that turned-up edge is underneath for easier removal of tart) and close side of pan onto bottom.
▶ Stir together crumbs, butter, and ⅛ teaspoon salt in a bowl, then press onto bottom of springform pan. Bake crust in lower third of oven 7 minutes, then cool crust in pan on a rack.
▶ While crust bakes, toast hazelnuts in a shallow baking pan in upper third of oven, stirring once, until golden, about 7 minutes. Transfer to a plate and cool to room temperature.
Make filling while crust cools:
▶ Bring cream to a boil in a 1- to 2-quart saucepan, then pour over chocolate in a heatproof bowl, whisking until chocolate is melted and smooth. Whisk in chocolate-hazelnut spread until combined, then whisk in nuts and remaining ⅛ teaspoon salt.
▶ Pour filling onto cooled crust and put in freezer until just set, about 25 minutes. (Tart should not be frozen.) Remove side of pan before serving tart.

Cooks' notes:
• Tart can be made 4 days ahead and chilled in pan, covered.
• We used store-bought graham cracker crumbs to save time; if you prefer to make your own in a food processor, you'll need 13 crackers, each about 4¾ by 2¼ inches.
• Freezing the tart helps to chill it quickly. If you're not in a rush, simply chill the tart in the refrigerator until you're ready to serve it.

FROZEN DESSERTS

RHUBARB FROZEN YOGURT TORTE
SERVES 8

Active time: 20 min   Start to finish: 3¾ hr (includes freezing)

¾   cup water
2   teaspoons unflavored gelatin (from a ¼-oz envelope)
4   cups sliced fresh rhubarb stalks or thawed frozen rhubarb (1 lb)
½   cup plus 2 tablespoons sugar
3   cups vanilla low-fat yogurt
12   *amaretti* (crisp Italian macaroons; see Sources), finely chopped (¾ cup)
1   lb strawberries

Special equipment: an ice cream maker; an 8-inch springform pan

▶ Put ¼ cup water in a small cup, then sprinkle gelatin on top and let gelatin soften while cooking rhubarb.
▶ Cook rhubarb, ½ cup sugar, and remaining ½ cup water in a heavy saucepan over moderate heat, stirring occasionally, until very soft, about 7 minutes. Add gelatin mixture, stirring until dissolved, then cool 10 minutes. Purée in a food processor until smooth, then add yogurt and blend until combined. Freeze in ice cream maker.
▶ Spread cookie crumbs evenly over bottom of springform pan. Spoon frozen yogurt gently over crumbs and carefully smooth top. Wrap pan in plastic wrap and freeze until yogurt is firm, at least 2 hours.
▶ Soak a kitchen towel in hot water and wring it dry. Wrap hot towel around pan, then release side of pan and let torte stand at room temperature 20 minutes.
▶ Meanwhile, quarter strawberries, then toss with remaining 2 tablespoons sugar, and let stand 15 minutes.
▶ Cut torte into 8 wedges and serve with strawberries.

Cooks' note:
• Whole torte (or leftovers) can be frozen, wrapped well, up to 5 days.
EACH SERVING (1 WEDGE WITH BERRIES) ABOUT 193 CALORIES AND 1 GRAM FAT

WATERMELON SORBET WITH WINE BASIL GELÉE

SERVES 6 TO 8

Active time: 1 hr   Start to finish: 3¼ hr (includes chilling)

For sorbet

- ¾ cup sugar
- ¼ cup water
- 1 teaspoon finely grated fresh lemon zest
- 5 cups coarsely chopped seeded watermelon (from a 4-lb piece, rind discarded)
- 2 tablespoons fresh lemon juice, or to taste

For gelée

- ¼ cup loosely packed fresh basil leaves
- 1½ cups dry white wine
- ½ cup sugar
- 1 teaspoon finely grated fresh lemon zest
- ½ cup plus 2 tablespoons water
- 2 teaspoons unflavored gelatin (from a ¼-oz envelope)
- 2 tablespoons fresh lemon juice, or to taste

Special equipment: **an ice cream maker**

Make sorbet:

▶ Bring sugar, water, and zest to a boil in a 2-quart heavy saucepan, stirring until sugar is dissolved, then reduce heat and simmer, without stirring, washing down any sugar crystals on side of pan with a pastry brush dipped in cold water, 2 minutes.

▶ Put watermelon in a blender, then add syrup and lemon juice and blend until smooth. Pour through a fine-mesh sieve into a large bowl, pressing on pulp and discarding any solids.

▶ Freeze in ice cream maker, then transfer to an airtight container and freeze until firm.

Make gelée while sorbet freezes:

▶ Blanch basil in a 3-quart pot of boiling salted water 5 seconds, then drain and transfer to a bowl of ice and cold water to stop cooking. Drain basil and squeeze dry.

▶ Bring wine, sugar, zest, and ½ cup water to a boil in cleaned 2-quart heavy saucepan, stirring until sugar is dissolved, then simmer 2 minutes.

▶ While wine syrup simmers, sprinkle gelatin over remaining 2 tablespoons water in a large metal bowl and let soften 1 minute.

▶ Pour about ½ cup wine syrup through a medium-mesh sieve lined with a dampened paper towel into gelatin mixture (reserve lined sieve), then stir until gelatin is dissolved.

▶ Blend remaining syrup with basil and lemon juice in cleaned blender until smooth (use caution when blending hot liquids), then pour through lined sieve into gelatin mixture. Set bowl in a larger bowl of ice and cold water and let stand, stirring occasionally, until cold, about 15 minutes, then chill in refrigerator, uncovered, until set, at least 2 hours.

▶ Gently whisk gelée to break into small pieces and serve as a bed for scoops of sorbet.

Cooks' notes:

• Sorbet can be made 1 day ahead.

• Gelée (unbroken) can be refrigerated up to 8 hours. (Cover after 2 hours.)

KITCHEN NOTE

LEFTOVER SYRUP FROM **CANNED LYCHEES** MAKES A DELICIOUS SWEETENER FOR ICED TEA.

LYCHEE COCONUT SORBET WITH MANGO AND LIME

SERVES 4

Active time: 15 min   Start to finish: 30 min

- 1 (15- to 20-oz) can lychees in syrup
- ½ cup well-stirred sweetened cream of coconut (preferably Coco López brand; not coconut milk or coconut cream)
- 3 to 3½ tablespoons fresh lime juice
- 1 firm-ripe large mango (1 lb), peeled and sliced
- 1 teaspoon finely grated fresh lime zest

Special equipment: **an ice cream maker**

▶ Drain lychees, reserving syrup, then purée lychees, cream of coconut, ¼ cup syrup, and 2½ tablespoons lime juice in a blender until smooth. Freeze in ice cream maker.

▶ While sorbet freezes, toss together mango, zest, and remaining lime juice to taste (½ to 1 tablespoon).

▶ Serve scoops of sorbet over mango slices.

CARAMEL ESPRESSO FLOAT

SERVES 4

Active time: 20 min   Start to finish: 30 min

This float was inspired by the Italian dessert affogato al caffè, *which consists of ice cream that has been "drowned" in hot coffee. We added caramelized sugar to the coffee for extra depth.*

  6   tablespoons granulated sugar
  2   cups water
  ¼   cup instant-espresso powder (see Sources)
  2   cups ice cubes
  ½   cup chilled heavy cream
  3   tablespoons confectioners sugar
  4   generous scoops premium vanilla ice cream
  2   tablespoons chopped nuts, such as almonds or
       hazelnuts, toasted (see Tips, page 8)
  3   tablespoons bittersweet chocolate shavings (made
       with a vegetable peeler; from a 3-oz bar)

▶ Cook granulated sugar in a dry 2- to 3-quart heavy saucepan over moderate heat, undisturbed, until it begins to melt. Continue to cook, stirring occasionally with a fork, until sugar melts into a deep golden caramel. Remove from heat and carefully add 1 cup water (caramel will harden and steam vigorously). Cook over high heat, stirring, until caramel is dissolved, then remove pan from heat. Add espresso powder and stir until dissolved. Add remaining cup water and ice cubes and stir until espresso is cold. Discard any unmelted ice cubes.

▶ Beat cream with confectioners sugar in a bowl with an electric mixer until it just holds soft peaks. Divide ice cream among 4 (8-ounce) glasses, then pour ½ cup espresso over each serving and top with whipped cream, nuts, and chocolate.

FRUIT FINALES

SWEET CHERRY COBBLER

SERVES 4

Active time: 20 min   Start to finish: 1¼ hr

For filling
  3   cups frozen dark sweet cherries (14 oz; not thawed)
  ¼   cup sugar
  2   teaspoons cornstarch
       Scant ¼ teaspoon cinnamon
For topping
  ¾   cup all-purpose flour
  1   tablespoon sugar
  ¼   teaspoon baking soda
  ¼   teaspoon baking powder
  ⅛   teaspoon salt
  1½ tablespoons cold unsalted butter, cut into ½-inch cubes
  ⅓   cup well-shaken low-fat buttermilk

▶ Put oven rack in middle position and preheat oven to 425°F.

Make filling:

▶ Cook all filling ingredients with a pinch of salt in a 2-quart heavy saucepan over moderate heat, stirring occasionally, until sugar begins to dissolve, about 3 minutes. Spoon filling into a 9-inch ceramic or glass pie plate (1 inch deep).

Make topping and bake cobbler:

▶ Whisk together flour, 2 teaspoons sugar, baking soda, baking powder, and salt in a bowl. Blend in butter with your fingertips or a pastry blender until mixture resembles coarse meal. Stir in buttermilk with a fork until just combined (do not overmix). Drop dough in 4 mounds over filling, leaving space between mounds. Sprinkle topping with remaining teaspoon sugar.

▶ Bake until topping is golden brown and fruit is bubbling, about 25 minutes. Cool slightly and serve warm.

EACH SERVING ABOUT 241 CALORIES AND 4 GRAMS FAT

KITCHEN NOTE

CARAMEL IS MADE BY COOKING SUGAR JUST SHY OF ITS BURNING POINT. WHEN MAKING CARAMEL, DON'T WALK AWAY FROM THE STOVE: THE SUGAR CAN GO FROM A NUTTY, GOLDEN BROWN TO BURNT IN A FLASH.

APPLE PRUNE BROWN BETTY

SERVES 6

Active time: 35 min   Start to finish: 1¾ hr

¾ cup pitted prunes (dried plums; 6 oz)
1¼ lb Gala apples (3 medium), peeled, halved, cored,
        and cut into ⅓-inch-thick slices
2 tablespoons fresh lemon juice
2 cups toasted baguette crumbs (page 215)
¾ stick (6 tablespoons) unsalted butter, melted
¾ cup packed dark brown sugar
¾ teaspoon cinnamon
¼ teaspoon salt

Accompaniment: **heavy cream**

▶ Put oven rack in middle position and preheat oven to 350°F.

▶ Cover prunes with boiling-hot water in a bowl and let stand 15 minutes. Drain and quarter prunes, then toss with apples and lemon juice. Stir together crumbs and butter in another bowl. Stir together brown sugar, cinnamon, and salt in a separate bowl. Spread one third of crumbs in a 9-inch pie plate. Cover with half of apple mixture, then sprinkle with half of sugar mixture. Sprinkle with half of remaining crumbs and cover with remaining apples, then remaining sugar mixture. Top with remaining crumbs.

▶ Bake, covered with foil, until apples are tender, about 40 minutes. Increase oven temperature to 425°F, remove foil, and bake until top is golden brown, about 10 minutes more. Serve warm.

COCONUT RICE PUDDING

SERVES 4

Active time: 45 min   Start to finish: 1 hr

1½ cups cold unsalted cooked rice
3 cups whole milk
½ cup well-stirred canned unsweetened coconut milk
⅓ cup sugar
¼ teaspoon salt
½ teaspoon vanilla

Garnish: **sweetened flaked coconut, toasted**

▶ Simmer rice, milk, coconut milk, sugar, and salt, uncovered, in a 2½- to 3-quart heavy saucepan over moderate heat, stirring frequently, until thickened, about 40 minutes. Stir in vanilla. Serve warm.

WATERMELON PUDDING

SERVES 6

Active time: 30 min   Start to finish: 4 hr (includes chilling)

This is a variation on the Sicilian classic gelo di melone, *which is steeped with jasmine flowers. We substituted anise seeds but kept the traditional garnishes.*

6 cups coarsely chopped seeded watermelon (from a
        4½-lb piece, rind discarded)
¼ cup cornstarch
½ cup plus 1 teaspoon sugar
1 teaspoon anise seeds
2 teaspoons fresh lemon juice, or to taste
⅓ cup heavy cream

Garnish: **chopped shelled pistachios (not dyed red); white or dark chocolate shavings, removed with a vegetable peeler**

▶ Purée watermelon in a blender until smooth, then force through a fine-mesh sieve into a 2-quart saucepan, pressing on pulp and then discarding any remaining solids.

▶ Ladle about ¼ cup watermelon juice into a small bowl and stir in cornstarch until smooth.

▶ Bring remaining watermelon juice to a boil with ½ cup sugar and anise seeds, stirring until sugar is dissolved. Stir cornstarch mixture again, then whisk into boiling juice. Reduce heat and simmer, whisking occasionally, 3 minutes. Whisk in lemon juice.

▶ Pour pudding through cleaned sieve into a bowl, then transfer to a wide 1-quart serving dish or 6 (⅔-cup) ramekins and chill, uncovered, until cold, about 30 minutes. Cover loosely and chill until set, at least 3 hours.

▶ Just before serving, beat cream with remaining teaspoon sugar in another bowl with an electric mixer until it just holds stiff peaks.

▶ Serve pudding topped with whipped cream.

Cooks' note:
• Pudding can be chilled up to 1 day.

SOURCES

INGREDIENTS

Almond flour—New York Cake and Baking Distributors (212-675-2253).

Amaretti—Italian markets.

Ancho chiles (dried)—Latino markets and Chile Today–Hot Tamale (800-468-7377).

Bai grapao (holy basil leaves)—some Asian markets and Temple of Thai (877-811-8773).

Banana leaves—Southeast Asian markets and Temple of Thai (877-811-8773).

Beef or veal demi-glace concentrate—some specialty foods shops and cooking.com (stock requires a dilution ratio of 1:16; ¼ cup concentrate to 4 cups water). You can also buy Demi-Glace Gold (veal) and reconstitute according to package instructions—More Than Gourmet (800-860-9385).

Black truffle butter—specialty foods shops and D'Artagnan (800-327-8246).

Cane syrup—Steens (800-725-1654).

Champagne vinegar—specialty foods shops.

Chee fah **chiles** (fresh)—some Asian markets and Temple of Thai (877-811-8773).

Chinese long beans—Asian markets and Temple of Thai (877-811-8773).

Cipolline—specialty produce markets.

Confit duck gizzards—D'Artagnan (800-327-8246).

Creole mustard—many specialty foods shops, some supermarkets, and cajungrocer.com.

Diplii diplii (long peppers)—Adriana's Caravan (800-316-0820).

Whole boneless Moulard duck breast—D'Artagnan (800-327-8246).

Duck legs (fresh)—some specialty foods shops and D'Artagnan (800-327-8246).

Farmer cheese—many cheese shops and Murray's Cheese Shop (888-692-4339).

Fig balsamic vinegar—specialty foods shops and Adriana's Caravan (212-972-8804).

Fleur de sel—specialty foods shops and SaltWorks (800-353-7258).

Foie gras terrine—some specialty foods shops and D'Artagnan (800-327-8246; sold in ½-lb or 1½-lb portions).

Ga-pi (Thai shrimp paste)—Asian markets and Temple of Thai (877-811-8773).

Garam masala—Indian markets and Kalustyan's (800-352-3451).

Sliced *gari* (pickled ginger)—Asian markets and sushifoods.com.

Grachai (lesser galangal or wild ginger; fresh, frozen, or bottled)—Southeast Asian markets and Temple of Thai (877-811-8773).

Greater galangal (fresh or frozen)—Southeast Asian markets and Temple of Thai (877-811-8773).

Green peppercorns in brine—specialty foods shops and many supermarkets.

Grits (stone-ground)—John Martin Taylor (800-828-4412; www.hoppinjohns.com).

Hazelnut oil—specialty foods shops.

Hibiscus (dried)—Latino markets and Melissa Guerra (877-875-2665; ask for *flor de Jamaica*).

Instant espresso powder—some supermarkets, specialty foods shops, and The Baker's Catalogue (800-827-6836).

Kaffir lime leaves (fresh or frozen)—Southeast Asian markets and Temple of Thai (877-811-8773).

Kimchi (assorted spicy pickles)—Asian markets and many supermarkets.

Lavender flowers (dried edible)—Kalustyan's (800-352-3451).

Lavender flowers (fresh edible)—farmers markets and specialty produce markets.

Lemongrass (fresh)—Asian markets.

Lemon verbena or lemon balm—farmers markets and specialty produce markets.

Lingonberry sauce—specialty foods shops.

Mango nectar—Latino markets, specialty foods shops, and many supermarkets.

Mango purée (canned)—Kalustyan's (800-352-3451).

Marcona almonds—specialty foods shops and The Spanish Table (206-682-2827).

Mirin—Asian markets, some supermarkets, and Uwajimaya (800-889-1928).

Morels (fresh or dried)—specialty foods shops and Marché aux Delices (888-547-5471).

Nigella seeds—specialty foods shops and Kalustyan's (800-352-3451).

Roasted nori (dried laver)—Asian markets and sushifoods.com.

Pancetta (Italian unsmoked bacon)—specialty foods shops.

Panko—Asian markets and Uwajimaya (800-889-1928).

Pappadams—Indian markets, specialty foods shops, and Kalustyan's (800-352-3451).

Paprika (smoked hot or sweet Spanish)—The Spanish Table (206-682-2827) and La Tienda (888-472-1022).

Passion-fruit purée (frozen)—Latino markets.

Porcini mushrooms (sometimes called cèpes; fresh)—specialty foods shops and Marché aux Delices (888-547-5471).

Pretzel salt—King Arthur Flour (800-827-6836).

Prik haeng (dried red chiles)—Asian markets and Temple of Thai (877-811-8773).

Quail (semiboneless)—some specialty foods shops, D'Artagnan (800-327-8246), and Cavendish Game Birds (802-885-1183).

Quince paste—specialty foods shops and The Spanish Table (206-682-2827).

Radish sprouts—Asian markets, natural foods stores, and some supermarkets.

Ras-el-hanout—specialty foods shops and Kalustyan's (800-352-3451).

Red *prik kii noo* (fresh bird's eye chiles)— Southeast Asian markets and Temple of Thai (877-811-8773).

Short-grain brown rice—natural foods stores.

Sushi rice—Asian markets, specialty foods shops, and some supermarkets.

Rice vinegar (seasoned)—Asian markets and sushifoods.com.

Ricotta salata—Italian markets, cheese shops, and specialty foods shops.

Rye flour—natural foods stores.

Serrano ham—specialty foods shops and The Spanish Table (206-682-2827).

Sherry vinegar—specialty foods shops and The Spanish Table (206-682-2827).

Spanish *piquillo* peppers—The Spanish Table (206-682-2827).

Tamarind concentrate—Indian markets and Kalustyan's (800-352-3451).

Thai apple eggplant—Asian markets and Temple of Thai (877-811-8773).

Thai green curry paste—Asian markets and some specialty foods shops.

Thai pickled garlic—Southeast Asian markets and Temple of Thai (877-811-8773).

Thai yellow bean sauce—Asian markets and Temple of Thai (877-811-8773).

Veal (or duck and veal) demi-glace—specialty foods shops and D'Artagnan (800-327-8246). You can also buy Demi-Glace Gold (veal) and reconstitute according to package instructions—specialty foods shops and More Than Gourmet (800-860-9385).

Venison tenderloin—some specialty foods shops and D'Artagnan (800-327-8246).

Pure walnut oil—some specialty foods shops and Dean & DeLuca (800-221-7714).

Wasabi powder—Asian markets and sushifoods.com.

White *verjus*—some specialty foods shops and Dean & DeLuca (800-221-7714).

Wilton paste food coloring (in Teal, Sky Blue, Leaf Green, Lemon Yellow, and Pink)— wilton.com.

EQUIPMENT

Alphabet cookie cutters (2- to 3-inch)— Sweet Celebrations (800-328-6722).

Bamboo sushi mat—Asian markets and sushifoods.com.

Egg toppers—cookware shops, Sur La Table (800-243-0852), and Bridge Kitchenware (800-274-3435).

Japanese Benriner—Asian markets, cookware shops, and Uwajimaya (800-889-1928).

Madeleine pan with 12 (3- by 2-inch) molds—many cookware shops and Bridge Kitchenware (800-274-3435).

Mortar and pestle (2-cup)—Asian markets and Temple of Thai (877-811-8773).

Popsicle molds and sticks—cookware shops and Broadway Panhandler (866-266-5927).

Silpat nonstick bakeware liner—cookware shops and Bridge Kitchenware (800-274-3435).

Spaetzlemaker—cookware shops and Bridge Kitchenware (800-274-3435).

Timbale molds (metal)—cookware shops and Bridge Kitchenware (800-274-3435).

CREDITS

Sang An: Children's Birthday Party, pp. 12–21. Keep Your Cool, pp. 170–173. Celery-Root Purée with Truffle Butter, p. 203. All Photographs © 2004.

Andrea Fazzari: Grilled Shrimp Rémoulade, p. 6. Casual Vegetarian Thanksgiving, pp. 68–75. Born on the Bayou, pp. 164–169. All Photographs © 2004.

Matthew Hranek: Nordic Nights, pp. 94–101. All Photographs © 2004.

Richard Gerhard Jung: Dinner for a Dozen, pp. 102–107. All Photographs © 2004.

Alexander Lobrano: Artichoke, endpaper. Photograph © 2004.

John Midgley: Dinner and a Movie, pp. 174–177. All Photographs © 2004.

Victoria Pearson: All Weekend Long, pp. 144–163. All Photographs © 2004.

Petrina Tinslay: Garden Scene, p. 93. Here Comes the Sun, pp. 136–143. All Photographs © 2004.

Mikkel Vang: Engagement Party, pp. 42–49. A Bohemian Thanksgiving, pp. 11, 56–67. Hanukkah Dinner, pp. 76–81. New Orleans Christmas, pp. 82–91, back jacket. Toast of the Town, pp. 108–113. Reimagining Gigi, pp. 178–185. All Photographs © 2004.

George Whiteside: Father's Day Tuscan Dinner, pp. 50–55. Eat Art, pp. 114–123. Perfect Harmony, pp. 124–135. Bringing It All Back Home, pp. 2, 186–193. Chinese Long Beans, endpaper. All Photographs © 2004.

Anna Williams: Valentine's Day Dinner, pp. 22–29. Russian Easter Feast, pp. 30–41. All Photographs © 2004.

Romulo Yanes: Chocolate Layer Cake, front jacket. Flavors of Summer, pp. 194–197. An Autumnal Dinner, pp. 198–201. All Photographs © 2004.

INDEX

TABLE SETTING ACKNOWLEDGMENTS

All items shown in photographs but not listed below are from private collections.

Back Jacket
See table setting credits for New Orleans Christmas.

Frontispiece
Page 2: Dessert glass—Calvin Klein Home (877-256-7373).

Celebrations
Page 11: See table setting credits for Bohemian Thanksgiving.

Children's Birthday Party
Page 13: Girl's floral dress and boy's striped cotton shirt—Estella (212-255-3553).

Page 16: Girl's Fair Isle sweater—Garnet Hill (800-870-3513; garnethill.com).

Page 18: Boy's chocolate brown robot shirt—Estella.

Valentine's Day Dinner
Page 22: Gable decanter—Calvin Klein Home (800-294-7978). Thai Honeysuckle candles—Red Flower (redflowerworld.com).

Page 23: Silver-rimmed side plate—The Terence Conran Shop (212-755-9079). Etched glass jug and Champagne glasses—Takashimaya New York (800-753-2038).

Page 24: Platinum garland plate and "Ellipse" salad fork—Calvin Klein Home.

Page 27: Silver-rimmed dinner plate—The Terence Conran Shop. Grape-etched tumbler—Takashimaya New York.

Russian Easter Feast
Page 31: Claret silk tie-up top by Megan Park—Max (303-321-4949).

Page 37: "Coalport" platter—Clary & Co. Antiques Ltd. (212-229-1773).

Engagement Party
Pages 42–43: Ginori "Amadeus Green" dinner plate and Anna Weatherly "Thistle" salad plates—Michael C. Fina (800-289-3462). Wineglasses—Dean & DeLuca (800-221-7714).

Page 46, lower left: White pants—Ralph Lauren (888-475-7674). Pink skirt and green pants—Les Copains Boutique (212-327-3014).

Father's Day Tuscan Dinner
Page 50: Italian "Eugubina" vase—Ceramica (800-228-0858). "Daniela" flatware—Match (201-792-9444).

Page 52: "French Faience" plate—Treillage (212-535-2288).

Bohemian Thanksgiving
Pages 57 and 61: Ceramic pitcher, candlesticks, and bread plates—ABC Carpet & Home (212-473-3000). Soup plates and dinner plates—Joan Platt (212-876-9228). Wineglasses—juliska.com.

Page 66: Serving plate and dessert plates—Joan Platt.

Casual Vegetarian Thanksgiving
Page 69: Wineglasses and decanter—Nicole Farhi (212-223-8811). White "T" chairs—westelm.com. RSO Brights salad plates and dinner plates—Lindt Stymeist (973-783-7201). Wool felt fabric, glass vase, and napkins—The Conran Shop (866-755-9079).

Hanukkah Dinner
Page 76: Porcelain chargers—Michael Wainwright (413-644-0070). "Forget Me Not" blue plates—bisonhome.com.au. Bone-handled knives and forks and side plates—John Derian (212-677-3917). Napkins—Barneys New York (212-826-8900). Leather bracelets—Hermès (800-441-4488). "Matthias" 15-inch candleholder and "Table Romania" 23-inch candleholder—Distant Origin (212-941-0024). "Flutissimo Mille Nuits" Champagne flutes, "Harcourt" wineglasses, "Mille Nuits" 5-arm candelabra, "Medallion" 3-arm candelabra, and "Medallion" 1-arm candleholder—Baccarat (800-777-0100). "Florence" tumblers—juliska.com.

Page 77: Silver tray—Hermès. Bowl—Michael Wainwright. "Isabella" carafe—juliska.com.

Page 80, right: "Egala Tea" cups—Armani Casa (212-334-1271). Cocktail napkins—Barneys New York.

New Orleans Christmas
Page 83: Dinner plates and "Kilbarry" side plates—waterford.com. "Kawali" wineglasses and water glasses—Christofle (212-308-9390). "Cholet" chandelier by Canopy Designs and "Tea" silk with red "Posey" embroidery by The Silk Trading Co.—ABC Carpet & Home (212-473-3000). Sterling "Beaded" flatware—Georg Jensen (212-759-6457). Napkins—Barneys New York (212-826-8900). Vintage Christmas ornaments—Paula Rubenstein (212-966-8954).

Page 84, left: White napkin—Barneys New York.

Page 90: Porcelain bowl—Global Table (212-431-5839).

The Menu Collection
Page 93: "Century" serving bowl and glass carafes—Crate & Barrel (800-996-9960).

Nordic Nights
Page 95: "Ottagonale" liqueur glasses by Carlo Moretti—Moss (866-888-6677; mossonline.com).

Page 97: Table—ABC Carpet & Home (212-473-3000). "Simple" water glasses by Deborah Ehrlich—Moss. "DATA" flatware by Carl-Gustaf Jahnsson—ikea-usa.com. Votive candles—Global Table (212-431-5839; globaltable.com). Vase and "Elements" bowls—Crate & Barrel (800-967-6696; crateandbarrel.com). Women's light slim-fit shirt—Pink (212-838-1928). Men's light blue chambray button-down shirt—Prada (888-977-1900).

Page 101: White and blue coaster—Hable Construction (212-343-8555). "Simple" white wineglasses by Deborah Ehrlich—Moss.

Dinner for a Dozen
Page 102: "Eternite" dinner plate and charger—Rosenthal (800-804-8070). Purple silk napkin—ABH Design (212-249-2276).

TABLE SETTING ACKNOWLEDGMENTS

Page 103: Silver-rimmed white salad plates and "Arpa" salad fork—Armani Casa (212-334-1271).

Page 107: "Celebration" service plate—Rosenthal.

Eat Art
Page 115: "Queen" martini glass—Rosenthal (800-804-8070).

Page 117: "Verio Black Circle" soup bowl and "Epoque" plate—Rosenthal. Flatware—MoMA Design Store (800-447-6662). "T. Vac" chair—Vitra (888-278-2855).

Page 118: Ivory "Graffiti" dinner plates, black "Graffiti" plates, "Geometry" cake stand and "Parker" wine goblets—Calvin Klein (212-292-9000). "Panton" chairs—Vitra. "Arpa" silver-plate flatware—Armani Casa (212-334-1271). Napkins—La Cafetière (866-486-0667). Bowl—Rosenthal.

Page 123: "Bergendof" glass—Calvin Klein.

Here Comes the Sun
Page 137: "Crescent" glasses—Crate & Barrel (800-967-6696; crateandbarrel.com). Plate by Christiane Perrochon—Takashimaya New York (800-753-2038).

Page 138, left: Plum linen napkin—Takashimaya New York.

All Weekend Long
Page 145: Glass bowl—Aero (212-966-1500).

Page 146, left: "Fiume" square plate—Armani Casa (212-334-1271).

Page 150, right: "Platinum" dessert plate—Crate & Barrel (800-967-6696). "Milano" fork—The Conran Shop (866-755-9079).

Page 152 "Geisha" square plate—Armani Casa.

Page 153: "Geisha" rectangular platter—Armani Casa. "Chaleur" pitcher—Global Table (212-431-5839). Orange pillow—Aero.

Page 154, right: "Chaleur" bowl—Global Table. "Piano" wood-handled serving spoon—Moss (212-204-7100).

Page 158, left: "Windsor" fork—Bodum (bodum.com).

Page 158, right: "Flores" napkin—Armani Casa.

Page 163: "Desire DOF" crystal glass—Hoya Crystal (800-654-0016).

Keep Your Cool
Page 170: "Ambra" flatware and "Califfo" chargers—Armani Casa (212-334-1271). "Tints" goblets and "Random Cut" wine-glasses—Calvin Klein Home (800-294-7978).

Page 172, right: "Orion" bowl—Clio (212-966-8991).

Dinner and a Movie
Page 174: Navy sweater—Hermès (800-441-4488). Brioni wool burgundy polo—Guy LaFerrera (561-620-0011). Brown cotton pants—Prada (888-977-1900). Red shirt and jeans—GapKids (gapkids.com). Black cotton jacket—Les Copains Boutique (212-327-3014). T-shirt—Petit Bateau (petit-bateau.com). "Tempo" glasses—Crate & Barrel (800-967-6696). Bone china dinner plates—Rhubarb (201-460-1020).

Reimagining Gigi
Page 178: Webster silver cup—R&P Kassai (212-302-7070).

Page 179: "Flemish" flatware—R&P Kassai. "Califfo" dinner plates—Armani Casa (212-334-1271).

Page 180: "Bagatelle" silver tray and "Babylone" dessert plates—Christofle (212-308-9390). Gown—special order at Zac Posen (212-925-1263; zacposen.com). Earrings—VBH Gallery (212-717-9800). "Miss Protocole" watch—Piaget Boutiques (877-8-PIAGET).

Page 183: Napkin by Silk Trading Company—ABC Carpet & Home (212-473-3000).

Page 184: "Chantilly" cake knife—R&P Kassai. Duchess Blue Silk by Silk Trading Company—ABC Carpet & Home.

Bringing It All Back Home
Page 186: Burgundy napkins and dinner plates—Calvin Klein Home (877-256-7373). Flatware—Michael Wainwright Pottery (413-303-0131). Blue delft salad plates—Nieman Marcus (niemanmarcus.com). Glass candlesticks, wineglasses, and water glasses—Takashimaya New York (212-350-0100). Candles—The Candle Shop (212-989-0148; candleshop.com). Purple dress by Alberta Ferretti—Bergdorf Goodman (212-753-7300). Men's shirt—Giorgio Armani (giorgioarmani.com).

Page 187: Rounded square dish—Global Table (212-431-5839).

Page 192: Dessert glass—Calvin Klein Home.

Flavors of Summer
Page 194: Plate—Davistudio (davistudio.com). Small bowl—Rosenthal (800-804-8070). Linen napkin—Archipelago (212-334-9460).

Page 195: Plate by Christiane Perrochon—The Gardener (510-548-4545).

If you are not already a subscriber to *Gourmet* magazine and would be interested in subscribing, please call *Gourmet*'s toll-free number, (800) 365-2454 or e-mail subscriptions@gourmet.com.

If you are interested in purchasing additional copies of this book or other *Gourmet* cookbooks, please call (800) 245-2010.